A Hawaiian Reader Volume II
Edited by A. Grove Day and Carl Stroven

The magic islands of Hawaii are endowed with an exotic literary heritage, drawn from legends of ancient Polynesian voyagers and logs of early explorers to stories by some of the great writers of our own tie.

This rich collection, originally printed as *The Spell of Hawaii*, is a companion volume to *A Hawaiian Reader*. The twenty-four selections are representative of the best literature of Hawaii, bringing together pieces that have appeared since the earlier volume, as well as many fascinating older ones omitted because of space limitations.

The arrangement of the selections is chronological, according to the date of the event represented. Hence the reader, beginning with James A. Michener's evocation of the volcanic birth of these North Pacific islands, can obtain an exciting review of the unique history of Hawaii. Following legends from the earliest settlers come accounts of the first visit of foreigners to the warring small kingdoms.

Thereafter the selections reflect life during the ruling dynasties as well as Hawaii under the American flag, and offer stories by such masters as Mark Twain, Robert Louis Stevenson, Jack London, Eugene Burdick, and others not so well known. Each piece is preceded by a special introduction.

A Hawaiian Reader Volume II

Selected and Edited by
A. Grove Day and Carl Stroven

MUTUAL PUBLISHING

Acknowledgments

"From the Boundless Deep" from *Hawaii*, by James A. Michener. © Copyright 1959 by James A. Michener. Reprinted by permission of Random House, Inc.

"Two Ghost Stories of Old Hawaii" by Johannes C. Andersen from *Myths and Legends of the Polynesians*, George G. Harrap & Co., Ltd., London, 1929. Canadian reprint rights by permission of the publishers.

"The Floating Islands and the Return of Lono" by S. M. Kamakau, reprinted from *The Ruling Chiefs of Hawaii*, printed and published in 1961 by The Kamehameha Schools Press, Honolulu, by permission of James W. Bushong.

"Hawaiian Hospitality" by Blake Clark from the book, *Hawaii the 49th State*, copyright 1940, 1947 by Blake Clark. Reprinted by permission of Doubleday & Company, Inc.

"You Can't Do That" by John P. Marquand. Copyright 1935 by The Curtis Publishing Company. Copyright © renewed 1962 by John P. Marquand Jr. and Christina M. Welch. Reprinted by permission of Brandt & Brandt.

"Gibson, the King's Evil Angel" from *Rascals in Paradise* by James A. Michener and A. Grove Day. © Copyright 1957 by James A. Michener and A. Grove Day. Reprinted by permission of Random House, Inc.

"Claus Spreckels and the Hawaiian Revolution" by Jacob Adler, from *Journal of the West*, January 1966, reprinted by permission of *Journal of the West* and the author.

"Kauai and the 'Wettest Spot'" by Clifford Gessler, reprinted from *Hawaii: Isles of Enchantment*, © D. Appleton-Century, 1937, by permission of the author.

"Rest Camp on Maui" from *A Role in Manila* by Eugene Burdick. © Copyright 1966 by the Estate of Eugene Burdick. "Rest Camp on Maui" originally appeared in *Harper's*, July, 1946. Reprinted by arrangement with The New American Library, Inc., New York.

"I'll Crack Your Head *Kotsun*" by Milton Murayama, reprinted by permission of *Arizona Quarterly* and the author.

Copyright © 1968 by A. Grove Day and Carl Stroven
Published by Mutual Publishing

This book contains the complete text of the original hardbound edition of *Spell of Hawaii*.
No part of this book may be reproduced in any form or by any electronic or mechanical means, including information storage and retrieval devices or systems, without prior written permission from the publisher, except that brief passages may be quoted for reviews.

All rights reserved
First Printing June 1998
1 2 3 4 5 6 7 8 9
Library of Congress Card Catalogue Number 68-11908
ISBN 1-56647-207-5
Cover design by Tamara Moan, Bechlen/Gonzalez Inc.
Cover photo courtesy of the Hawai'i State Archives; backcover photos clockwise: Bishop Museum, A. Grove Day, Baker-Van Dyke Collection, Baker-Van Dyke Collection

Mutual Publishing
1215 Center Street, Suite 210
Honolulu, Hawaii 96816
Telephone (808) 732-1709 • Fax (808) 734-4094
e-mail: mutual@lava.net • Url: http://www.pete.com/mutual

Printed in Australia

Editor's Note

The first anthology of selections from the rich store of literature about Hawaii was compiled by the present editors in *A Hawaiian Reader*, published in 1959, when Hawaii became the Fiftieth State.

This new collection, *A Hawaiian Reader, Volume II*, brings together some of the best pieces of writing about the Islands that have appeared meanwhile, as well as many fascinating older ones that could not, because of limited space, be included in the first volume. The criteria on which the selections were chosen are similar to those for the first volume *A Hawaiian Reader*: Does this piece have literary quality? Is its content interesting? Is it, whether fact or fiction, authentic? Does it capture in some significant way the spirit of the place and time?

The arrangement of the twenty-four selections is chronological, according to the date of the event represented, beginning with Michener's evocation of the volcanic formation of the Islands and continuing with legends of the ancient Polynesian settlers. Then follow extracts from the logs of early voyagers, journals of the first missionaries, narratives of travelers and sojourners, and short stories and nonfiction by later writers that include Mark Twain, Robert Louis stevenson, Jack London, James A. Michener, Eugene Burdick, and others not so well known.

Each selection is preceded by a brief introduction concerning the author and the particular piece. The texts have not been changed except to modernize spellings and punctuation, and to use standard forms of some Hawaiian names. Ellipsis dots in certain nonfiction selections indicate that passages have been omitted for the purpose of condensation. A glossary of Hawaiian words in the book appears at the end.

University of Hawaii
A.G.D.
C.S.

He lahui oluolu ka lahui Hawaii, a me ke aloha. He hookipa ame ke aulike kekahi i kekahi. He lahui hoomanao i ka poe hana pono ia lakou. Pela ke ano o ka lahui Hawaii i ka wa kahiko.

The Hawaiian race is a kindly and an affectionate one, hospitable and helpful one to the other; a race grateful to those who have been good to them. Such were the ways of the Hawaiians of old days.

—KEPELINO KEAUOKALANI, *Traditions of Hawaii*

Contents

James A. Michener	From the Boundless Deep	3
Johannes C. Andersen	Two Ghost Stories of Old Hawaii	21
James King	Captain Cook at Kealakekua Bay	29
S. M. Kamakau	The Floating Islands and the Return of Lono	43
John Nicol	The Cooper and the Kings	54
John Bartlett	Attack on the *Gustavus III*	59
Blake Clark	Hawaiian Hospitality	63
J. P. Marquand	You Can't Do That	73
Archibald Campbell	A Scotsman in Honolulu, 1809	97
Otto von Kotzebue	The Russians Meet Kamehameha I	104
Lucy G. Thurston	The Missionaries Arrive	120
William Ellis	Missionaries Climb Kilauea	129
Samuel L. Clemens	Mark Twain on the Kona Coast	144
Isabella Bird	Impressions of Honolulu, 1873	155
C. W. Stoddard	On the Reef	165
James A. Michener and A. Grove Day	Gibson, the King's Evil Angel	180
R. L. Stevenson	The Bottle Imp	217
R. L. Stevenson	Open Letter to the Rev. Dr. Hyde of Honolulu	246
Jacob Adler	Claus Spreckels and the Hawaiian Revolution of 1893	260
Jack London	The Sheriff of Kona	272
Jack London	The House of the Sun	286
Clifford Gessler	Kauai and the "Wettest Spot"	298
Eugene Burdick	Rest Camp on Maui	309
Milton Murayama	I'll Crack Your Head *Kotsun*	323
	Glossary of Hawaiian Words	337

James A. Michener

From the Boundless Deep

James A. Michener, one of the most popular writers of our generation, was picked up on the streets of Doylestown, Pennsylvania, as a nameless waif and adopted by Mabel Michener, a kindly woman who brought him up along with her own son. Surviving dire poverty by various jobs, which included writing a sports column at the age of fifteen and acting as spotter of "short-change artists" at an amusement park, young Michener hitchhiked through all but three of the forty-eight states. A scholarship took him to Swarthmore College, and after travels in Europe he became a professor and editor. Although reared as a Quaker, Michener in 1942 volunteered for combat duty in the Navy. He visited about fifty Pacific islands as part of his aircraft maintenance work; from this experience came his first book, *Tales of the South Pacific* (1947), source of the Broadway musical show *South Pacific* and the subsequent motion picture. Later volumes about the Pacific include *Return to Paradise* (1951) and the giant novel *Hawaii* (1959), a portion of which was made into a film about the missionary era.

Hawaii, whatever faults it may have, is on the whole the best novel yet written about the coming of the various peoples to the future fiftieth state. One of its main themes is the idea that "paradise" is not a place which one may discover, but a stage that can serve as "a crucible of exploration and development." For this reason Michener opened his half-million-word book with a description of the unpeopled stage on which his drama of the building of a Pacific Eden would be enacted.

MILLIONS upon millions of years ago, when the continents were already formed and the principal features of the earth had been decided, there existed, then as now, one aspect of the world that dwarfed all others. It was a mighty ocean, resting uneasily to the east of the largest continent, a restless, ever-changing, gigantic body of water that would later be described as pacific.

Over its brooding surface immense winds swept back and forth, whipping the waters into towering waves that crashed down upon the world's seacoasts, tearing away rocks and eroding the land. In its dark bosom, strange life was beginning to form, minute at first, then gradually of a structure now lost even to memory. Upon its farthest reaches birds with enormous wings came to rest, and then flew on.

Agitated by a moon stronger then than now, immense tides ripped across this tremendous ocean, keeping it in a state of torment. Since no great amounts of sand had yet been built, the waters where they reached shore were universally dark, black as night and fearful.

Scores of millions of years before man had risen from the shores of the ocean to perceive its grandeur and to venture forth upon its turbulent waves, this eternal sea existed, larger than any other of the earth's features, vaster than the sister oceans combined, wild, terrifying in its immensity and imperative in its universal role.

How utterly vast it was! How its surges modified the very balance of the earth! How completely lonely it was, hidden in the darkness of night or burning in the dazzling power of a younger sun than ours.

At recurring intervals the ocean grew cold. Ice piled up along its extremities, and so pulled vast amounts of water from the sea, so that the wandering shoreline of the continents sometimes jutted miles farther out than before. Then, for a hundred thousand years, the ceaseless ocean would tear at the exposed shelf of the continents, grinding rocks into sand and incubating new life.

Later, the fantastic accumulations of ice would melt, setting cold waters free to join the heaving ocean, and the coasts of the continents would lie submerged. Now the restless energy of the sea deposited upon the ocean bed layers of silt and skeletons and salt. For a million years the ocean would build soil, and then the ice would return; the waters would draw away; and the land would lie exposed. Winds from the north and south would howl across the empty seas and lash stupendous waves upon the shattering shore. Thus the ocean continued its alternate building and tearing down.

Master of life, guardian of the shorelines, regulator of temperatures and heaving sculptor of mountains, the great ocean existed.

Millions upon millions of years before man had risen upon earth, the central areas of this tremendous ocean were empty, and where famous islands now exist, nothing rose above the rolling waves. Of course, crude forms of life sometimes moved through the deep, but for the most part the central ocean was marked only by enormous waves that arose at the command of moon and wind. Dark, dark, they swept the surface of the empty sea, falling only upon themselves, terrible and puissant and lonely.

Then one day, at the bottom of the deep ocean, along a line running two thousand miles from northwest to southeast, a rupture appeared in the basalt rock that formed the ocean's bed. Some great fracture of the earth's basic structure had occurred, and from it began to ooze a white-hot, liquid rock. As it escaped from its internal prison, it came into contact with the ocean's wet and heavy body. Instantly, the rock exploded, sending aloft through the nineteen thousand feet of ocean that pressed down upon it columns of released steam.

Upward, upward, for nearly four miles they climbed, those agitated bubbles of air, until at last upon the surface of the sea they broke loose and formed a cloud. In that instant, the ocean signaled that a new island was building. In time it might grow to become an infinitesimal speck of land that would mark the great central void. No human beings then existed to celebrate the event. Perhaps some weird and vanished flying thing spied the escaping steam and swooped down to inspect it; more likely the roots of this future island were born in darkness and great waves and brooding nothingness.

For nearly forty million years, an extent of time so vast that it is meaningless, only the ocean knew that an island was building in its bosom, for no land had yet appeared above the surface of the sea. For nearly forty million years, from that extensive rupture in the ocean floor, small amounts of liquid rock seeped out, each forcing its way up through what had escaped before, each contributing some small portion to the accumulation that was building on the floor of the sea. Sometimes a thousand years, or ten thousand, would silently pass before any new eruption of material would take place. At other times gigantic pressures would accumulate beneath the rupture and with unimaginable violence rush through the existing apertures, throwing clouds of steam miles above the surface of the ocean. Waves would be generated which would circle the globe and crash upon themselves as they collided twelve thousand miles away.

Such an explosion, indescribable in its fury, might in the end raise the height of the subocean island a foot.

But for the most part, the slow constant seepage of molten rock was not violently dramatic. Layer upon layer of the earth's vital core would creep out, hiss horribly at the cold sea water, and then slide down the sides of the little mountains that were forming. Building was most sure when the liquid rock did not explode into minute ashy fragments, but cascaded viscously down the sides of the mountains, for this bound together what had gone before, and established a base for what was to come.

How long ago this building took place, how infinitely long ago! For nearly forty million years the first island struggled in the bosom of the sea, endeavoring to be born as observable land. For nearly forty million submerged years its subterranean volcano hissed and coughed and belched and spewed forth rock, but it remained nevertheless hidden beneath the dark waters of the restless sea, to whom it was an insignificant irritation, a small climbing pretentious thing of no consequence.

And then one day, at the northwest end of the subocean rupture, an eruption of liquid rock occurred that was different from any others that had preceded. It threw forth the same kind of rock, with the same violence, and through the same vents in the earth's core. But this time what was thrown forth reached the surface of the sea. There was a tremendous explosion as the liquid rock struck water and air together. Clouds of steam rose miles into the air. Ash fell hissing upon the heaving waves. Detonations shattered the air for a moment and then echoed away in the immensity of the empty wastes.

But rock had at last been deposited above the surface of the sea. An island—visible were there but eyes to see, tangible were there fingers to feel—had risen from the deep.

The human mind, looking back upon this event—particularly if the owner of the mind has once stepped upon that island—is likely to accord it more significance than it merits. Land was finally born, yes. The forty million years of effort were finally crowned by the emergence of a pile of rocks no larger than a man's body, that is true. But the event was actually of no lasting significance, for in the long history of the ocean many such piles had momentarily broken the surface and then subsided, forbidden and forgotten. The only thing significant about the initial appearance of this first island along the slanting crack was the fact that it held on and grew. Stubbornly, inch by painful inch, it grew. In fact, it was the uncertainty and agony of its growth that were significant.

The chance emergence of the island was nothing. Remember this. Its emergence was nothing. But its persistence and patient accumulation of stature were everything. Only by relentless effort did it establish its right to exist. For the first ten thousand years after its tentative emergence, the little pile of rock in the dead, vast center of the sea fluctuated between life and death like a thing struck by evil. Sometimes molten lava would rise through the internal channels and erupt from a vent only a few inches above the waves. Tons upon tons of material would gush forth and hiss madly as it fell back into the ocean. Some, fortunately, would cling to the newborn island, building it sturdily many feet into the air, and in that time it might seem as if the island were indeed secure.

Then from the south, where storms breed in the senseless deep, a mighty wave would form and rush across the world. Its coming would be visible from afar, and in gigantic, tumbling, whistling, screaming power it would fall upon the little accumulation of rocks and pass madly on.

For the next ten thousand years there would be no visible island, yet under the waves, always ready to spring back to life, there would rest this huge mountain tip, rising nineteen thousand feet from the floor of the ocean, and when a new series of volcanic thrusts tore through the vents, the mountain would patiently build itself aloft for another try. Exploding, hissing, and spewing forth ash, the great mountain would writhe in convulsions. It would pierce the waves. Its island would be born again.

This was the restless surge of the universe, the violence of birth, the cold tearing away of death; and yet how promising was this interplay of forces as an island struggled to be born, vanishing in agony, then soaring aloft in triumph. You men who will come later to inhabit these islands, remember the agony of arrival, the rising and the fall, the nothingness of the sea when storms throw down the rock, the triumph of the mountain when new rocks are lifted aloft.

For a million years the island hung in this precarious balance, a child of violence; but finally, after incredibly patient accumulation, it was established. Now each new lava flow had a solid base upon which to build, and inch by inch the debris agglutinated until the island could be seen by birds from long distances. It was indeed land, habitable had there been existing men, with shelters for boats, had there been boats, and with rocks that could have been used for building homes and temples. It was now, in the real sense of the word, an island, taking its rightful place in the center of the great ocean.

But before life could prosper on this island, soil was needed, and as yet none existed. When molten lava burst upon the air it generally exploded into ash, but sometimes it ran as a viscous fluid down the sides of mountains, constructing extensive sheets of flat rock. In either case, the action of wind and rain and cooling nights began to pulverize the newly born lava, decomposing it into soil. When enough had accumulated, the island was ready.

The first living forms to arrive were inconspicuous, indeed almost invisible, lichens and low types of moss. They were borne by the sea and by winds that howled back and forth across the oceans. With a tenacity equal to that of the island itself these fragments of life established themselves, and as they grew they broke down more rocks and built more soil.

At this time there existed, on the distant continents visited by the ocean, a well-established plant and animal society composed of trees and lumbering animals and insects. Some of these forms were already well adapted for life on the new island, but were prevented from taking residence by two thousand miles of open ocean.

Consequently, there began an appalling struggle. Life, long before man's emergence, stood poised on distant shores, pressing to make new exploratory journeys like those that had already populated the existing earth with plants and animals. But against these urgent forms stood more than two thousand miles of turbulent ocean, storm-ridden, salty, and implacable.

The first sentient animals to reach the island were of course fish, for they permeated the ocean, coming and going as they wished. But they could not be said to be a part of the island. The first non-oceanic animal to visit was a bird. It came, probably from the north on an exploratory mission in search of food. It landed on the still-warm rocks, found nothing edible, and flew on, perhaps to perish in the southern seas.

A thousand years passed, and no other birds arrived. One day a coconut was swept ashore by a violent storm. It had been kept afloat on the bosom of the sea by its buoyant husk, traveling more than three thousand miles from the southwest, a marvel of persistence. But when it landed, it found no soil along the shore and only salt water, so it perished, but its husk and shell helped form soil for those that would come later.

The years passed. The sun swept through its majestic cycles. The moon waxed and waned, and tides rushed back and forth across the surface of the world. Ice crept down from the north, and for ten thousand years covered the islands, its weight and power breaking down rocks and forming earth.

The years passed, the empty, endless, significant years. And then one day another bird arrived on the island, also seeking food. This time it found a few dead fish along the shore. As if in gratitude, it emptied its bowels on the waiting earth and evacuated a tiny seed which it had eaten on some remote island. The seed germinated and grew. Thus, after the passage of eons of time, growing life had established itself on the rocky island.

Now the passage of time becomes incomprehensible. Between the arrival of the first, unproductive bird, and the second bearing in its bowels the vital seed, more than twenty thousand years had elapsed. In another twenty thousand years a second bit of life arrived, a female insect, fertilized on some distant island on the night before a tremendous storm. Caught up in the vast winds that howled from the south, she was borne aloft to the height of ten thousand feet and driven northward for more than two thousand miles, to be dropped at last upon this new and remote island, where she gave birth. Insects had arrived.

The years passed. Other birds arrived, but they bore no seeds. Other insects were blown ashore, but they were not females, or if they were, not pregnant. But once every twenty or thirty thousand years—a period longer than that of historic man—some one bit of life would reach the island, by accident; and by accident it would establish itself. In this hit-or-miss way, over a period of time that the mind can barely digest, life populated the island.

One of the most significant days in the history of the island came when a bird staggered in from some land far to the southwest, bearing in its tangled feathers the seed of a tree. Perched upon a rock, the bird pecked at the seed until it fell away, and in the course of time a tree grew. Thirty thousand years passed, and by some accident equally absurd, another tree arrived, and after a million years of chances, after five million years of storms and birds and drifting sea-soaked logs bearing snails and borers, the island had a forest with flowers and birds and insects.

Nothing, nothing that ever existed on this island reached it easily. The rocks themselves were forced up fiery chimneys through miles of ocean. They burst in horrible agony onto the surface of the earth. The lichens that arrived came borne by storms. The birds limped in on deadened wings. Insects came only when accompanied by hurricanes, and even trees arrived in the dark belly of some wandering bird, or precariously perched upon the feathers of a thigh.

Timelessly, relentlessly, in storm and hunger and hurricane the island was given life, and this life was sustained only by constant new volcanic eruptions that spewed forth new lava that could be broken down into life-sustaining soil. In violence the island lived, and in violence a great beauty was born.

The shores of the island, weathered by the sea, were stupendous cliffs that caught the evening sun and glowed like serrated pillars of gold. The mountains were tall and jagged, their lower levels clothed in dark-green trees, their upper pinnacles shod in ice, while the calm bays in which the grandeur of the mountains was reflected were deeply cut into the shore. Valleys and sweet plains, waterfalls and rivers, glades where lovers would have walked and confluences where towns could have been built, the lovely island had all these accouterments, these alluring invitations to civilization.

But no man ever saw them, and the tempting glades entertained no lovers, for the island had risen to its beauty long, long before the age of man; and at the moment of its greatest perfection it began to die. In violence it had been born; in violence it would die.

There was a sudden shudder of the earth, a slipping and a sliding, and when the readjustment was ended, covering a period of thousands of years, the island had sunk some twelve hundred feet lower into the ocean, and ice nevermore formed upon its crests. The volcanoes stopped, and no new lava poured forth to create new soil to replace that which had sunk into the sea. For a million years winds howled at the hills, the ocean gnawed away at the ramparts. Year by year the island withered and grew less. It began to shred away, to shatter and to fall back into the ocean from which it had sprung.

A million years passed, and then a million more, and the island which had grown so patiently at the northwest tip of the great crack in the ocean floor slowly, slowly vanished. The birds that had fed upon its hills went elsewhere, bearing in their bowels new seeds. From its shore fertilized insects were storm-blown to other islands, and life went on. Once every twenty or thirty thousand years some fragment of nature escaped from this island, and life went on.

But as the island subsided, a different form of life sprang into increased activity. In the warm, clear, nutritious waters that surrounded the shores, coral polyps began to flourish, and slowly they left behind them as they died their tiny calciferous skeletons, a few feet below the surface of the sea. In a thousand years they built a submerged ring around the island. In a thousand more they added to its form, and as the eons passed, these tiny coral animals built a reef.

Ice melted in the north, and the coral animals were drowned in vast weights of unexpected water. The seas changed temperature and the animals died. Torrents of rain poured down from island hills and silted up the shoreline, strangling the tiny coral. Or new ice caps formed far to the north and south, pulling water away from the dying island. Then the coral were exposed and died at once.

Always, like everything to do with this island, throughout its entire history, the coral lived precariously, poised between catastrophes. But in the breathing space available, the coral built. And so it was that this tiny animal, this child of cataclysm, built a new island to replace the old as it gradually wore itself away and sank into the sea.

How terrible this passage of life and death! How meaningless that an island that had been born of such force and violence, that had been so fair upon the bosom of the great ocean, so loved of birds, so rich in trees, so willing to entertain man, should he ever arrive . . . how wasteful it was that this island should have grown in agony and died in equal agony before ever a human eye had seen its majesty.

Across a million years, down more than ten million years, it existed silently in the unknown sea and then died, leaving only a fringe of coral where sea birds rest and where gigantic seals of the changing ocean play. Ceaseless life and death, endless expenditure of beauty and capacity, tireless ebb and flow and rising and subsidence of the ocean. Night comes and the burning day, and the island waits, and no man arrives. The days perish and the nights, and the aching beauty of lush valleys and waterfalls vanishes, and no man will ever see them. All that remains is a coral reef, a calcium wreath on the surface of the great sea that had given the island life, a memorial erected by the skeletons of a billion billion billion little animals.

While this first island was rising to prominence and dying back to nothingness, other would-be islands, stretching away to the southeast, were also struggling to attain brief existence followed by certain death. Some started their cycle within the same million years as did the first. Others lagged. The latest would not puncture the surface of the sea until the first was well into its death throes, so that at any moment from the time the first island began to die, man, had he then existed, could have witnessed in this two-thousand-mile chain of islands every sequential step in the process of life and death. Like an undulating wave of the sea itself, the rocky islands rose and fell; but whereas the cycle of an ocean wave is apt to be a few minutes at the most, the cycle of the rising and falling of these islands was of the nature of sixty million years.

Each island, at any given moment of time, existed certainly and securely within that cycle: it was either rising toward birth and significance, or it was perishing. I do not mean that man, had he been able to witness the cycle, could have identified which part of the cycle a given island was in; there must have been periods of millions of years when no one could have ascertained that condition. But the impersonal, molten center of the earth knew, for it was sending that island no new supplies of lava. The waiting sea knew, for it could feel the cliffs falling into its arms a little more easily. And the coral polyps knew, because they sensed that it was now time to start enacting a memorial to this island which would soon be dead ... that is, within twenty or thirty million years.

Endless cycle, endless birth and death, endless becoming and disappearing. Once the terrifying volcanic explosions cease, the island is already doomed. Peace and calm seas and the arrival of birds bearing seeds are pleasant to experience, but the residence of beauty is surely nominated for destruction. A song at night of insects, the gentle splash of surf against the sand, and a new ice age is beginning which will freeze out all life. Limitless cycle, endless change.

Toward the end of the master cycle, when the western islands were dying and the eastern were abuilding, a new volcano pushed its cone above the surface of the ocean, and in a series of titanic explosions erupted enough molten rock to establish securely a new island, which after eons of time would be designated by men as the capital island of the group. Its subsequent volcanic history was memorable in that its habitable land resulted from the wedding of two separate chains of volcanoes.

After the parent volcano had succeeded in establishing an island, its mighty flanks produced many subsidiary vents through which lava poured; whereupon a greater volcano, separated from the first by miles of ocean, sprang into being and erected its own majestic construction, marked by an equal chain of events.

For eons of time the two massive volcano systems stood in the sea in fiery competition, and then, inevitably, the first began to die back, its fires extinguished, while the second continued to pour millions of tons of lava down its own steep flanks. Hissing, exploding, crackling, the rocks fell into the sea in boundless accumulation, building the later volcano ever more solidly, ever more thickly at its base on the remote floor of the ocean.

In time, sinking lava from the second master builder began to creep across the feet of the first, and then to climb its sides and finally to throw itself across the exposed lava flows that had constituted the earlier island. Now the void in the sea that had separated the two was filled, and they became one. Locked in fiery arms, joined by intertwining ejaculations of molten rock, the two volcanoes stood in matrimony, their union a single fruitful and growing island.

Its soil was later made from dozens of smaller volcanoes that erupted for a few hundred thousand years, then passed into death and silence. One exploded in dazzling glory and left a crater looking like a punch bowl. Another, at the very edge of the island, from where it could control the sea approaches, left as its memory a gaunt headland shaped like a diamond.

When the island was well formed—and what a heavenly, sweet, enchanting island it was—some force of nature, almost as if by subtle plan, hid in its bowels a wealth of incalculable richness. It could not be diamonds, because the island was 250,000,000 years too young to have acquired the carboniferous plant growth that produced diamonds. It could not be either oil or coal, for the same reason. It wasn't gold, for neither the age nor the conditions required for the building of that metal were present on this island. It was none of these commonly accepted treasures, but it was a greater.

The volcanic basalt from which the island was built was porous, and when the tremendous storms which swept the ocean struck the island, the waters they disgorged ran partly out to sea in surface rivers, seeped partly into the heart of the island. Billions of tons of water thus crept down into the secret reservoirs of the island.

They did not stay there, of course, for since the rock was porous, there were avenues that led back out to sea, and in time the water was lost. But if any animal—a man perhaps—could penetrate the rocks, he could intercept the water and put it to his use, for the entire island was a catchment; the entire core of the island was permeated with life-giving water.

But that was not the special treasure of this particular island, for a man could bore into almost any porous rock on any island, and catch some water. Here, on this island, there was to be an extra treasure, and the way it was deposited was something of a miracle.

When the ice came and went, causing the great ocean to rise, when the island itself sank slowly and then rebuilt with new lava—when these titanic convulsions were in progress, the south shore of the island was alternately exposed to sunlight or buried fathoms deep in ocean. When the first condition prevailed, the exposed shore was cut by mountain streams which threw their debris across the plain, depositing there claylike soils and minute fragments of lava. Sometimes the sea would wash in bits of animal calcium, or a thundering storm would rip away a cliff face and throw its remnants over the shore. Bit by bit, over a hundred thousand years at a time, the shore accumulated its debris.

Then, when next the ocean rose, it would press down heavily upon this shelving land, which would lie for ages, submerged under tons of dark, green water. But while the great brutal ocean thus pressed down hydraulically, it at the same time acted as a life-giving agent, for through its shimmering waves filtered silt and dead bodies and water-logged fragments of trees and sand. All these things, the gifts both of land and sea, the immense weight of ocean would bind together until they united to form rock.

Cataclysmically the island would rise from the sea to collect new fragments washed down from the hills, then sink beneath the waves to accumulate new deposits of life-building slime. But whenever the monstrous ocean would beat down heavily upon the shore for ten thousand years at a time, new rock was formed, an impermeable shield that sloped down from the lower foothills and extended well out to sea. It was a cap rock, imprisoning in a gigantic underground reservoir all that lay beneath it.

What lay trapped below, of course, was water. Secretly, far beneath the visible surface of the island, imprisoned by this watertight cap of rock, lay the purest, sweetest, most copious water in all the lands that bordered upon or existed in the great ocean. It lay there under vast pressure, so that it was not only available, should a man deduce its secret hiding, but it was ready to leap forth twenty or thirty or forty feet into the air, and engulf with life-giving sweetness any man who could penetrate the imprisoning rock and set it free. It waited, an almost inexhaustible supply of water to sustain life. It waited, a universe of water hidden beneath the cap rock. It waited.

The adventurous plants and insects that had reached the earliest northwest island had plenty of time in which to make their way to the newer lands as the latter rose to life. It might take a million years for a given grass to complete its journey down the chain. But there was no hurry. Slowly, with a patience that is difficult to comprehend, trees and vines and crawling things crept down the islands, while in other parts of the world a new and more powerful animal was rising and preparing himself for his invasion of the islands.

Before the two-volcanoed island with its trapped treasure of water had finished growing, man had developed in distant areas. Before the last island had assumed its dominant shape, men had erected in Egypt both mighty monuments and a stable form of government. Men could already write and record their memories.

While volcanoes still played along the chain, China developed a sophisticated system of thought and Japan codified art principles that would later enrich the world. While the islands were taking their final form, Jesus spoke in Jerusalem and Mohammed came from the blazing deserts with a new vision of heaven, but no men knew the heaven that awaited them on these islands.

For these lands were the youngest part of the earth's vast visible surface. They were new. They were raw. They were empty. They were waiting. Books which we still read today were written before these islands were known to anyone except the birds of passage. Songs which we still sing were composed and recorded while these islands remained vacant. The Bible had been compiled, and the Koran.

Raw, empty, youthful islands, sleeping in the sun and whipped by rain, they waited.

Since, when they were finally discovered, they were destined to be widely hailed as paradises, it is proper to study them carefully in their last, waiting moments, those sad, sweet, overpowering days before the first canoes reached them.

They were beautiful, that is true. Their wooded mountains were a joy. Their cool waterfalls, existing in the thousands, were spectacular. Their cliffs, where the restless ocean had eroded away the edges of great mountains, dropped thousands of feet clear into the sea, and birds nested on the vertical stones. Rivers were fruitful. The shores of the islands were white and waves that washed them were crystal-blue. At night the stars were close, great brilliant dots of fire fixing forever the location of the islands and forming majestic pathways for the moon and sun.

How beautiful these islands were! How shot through with harmony and peace! How the mind lingers on their pristine grandeur, a grandeur that nothing so far devised could permanently destroy. If paradise consists solely of beauty, then these islands were the fairest paradise that man ever invaded, for the land and sea were beautiful, and the climate was congenial.

But if the concept of paradise includes also the ability to sustain life, then these islands, as they waited in the time of Jesus and Mohammed, were far from heavenly. They contained almost no food. Of all the things that grew on their magnificent hillsides, nothing could be relied upon to sustain life adequately. There were a few pandanus trees whose spare and bitter fruits could be chewed for minimum existence. There were a few tree ferns whose cores were just barely edible, a few roots. There were fish if they could be caught and birds if they could be trapped. But there was nothing else.

Few more inhospitable major islands have ever existed than this group. Here are the things they did not have: no chickens, or pigs, or cattle, or edible dogs; no bananas, no taro, no sweet potatoes, no breadfruit; no pineapple, or sugar, or guava, or gourds, or melons, or mangoes, no fruit of any kind; no palms for making sugar; no food. The islands did not even have that one essential, that miraculous sustainer of tropical life, the coconut. Some had drifted to the shores, but in salty soil along the beaches they could not grow.

Any man who came to the islands would, if he wanted to live, have to bring with him all food. If he were wise, he would also bring most of the materials required for building a civilized society, since the islands had no bamboo for decorating a home, no candlenuts for lamps, no mulberry bark for making tapa. Nor were there any conspicuous flowers: neither frangipani, nor hibiscus, nor bright croton, nor colorful orchids. Instead of these joy-giving, life-sustaining plants there was a hidden tree, useless except that its wood when dried yielded a persistent perfume, and this was the tree of death, the sandalwood tree. Of itself, it was neither poisonous nor cruel, but the uses to which it would be put on these islands would make it a permanent blight.

The soil of the islands was not particularly good. It was not rich and black like the soil which Russian peasants were already farming, nor loamy and productive like that known to the Dakota and Iowa tribes of Indians. It was red and of a sandlike consistency, apparently rich in iron because it had been formed of decomposed basalt, but lacking in other essentials. If a farmer could add to this soil the missing minerals and supply it with adequate water, it had the capacity to produce enormously. But of itself it was not much, for the minerals were absent, and so was the water.

Tremendous quantities of rain did fall on the islands, but it fell in an unproductive manner. From the northeast, trade winds blew constantly, pushing ahead of them low clouds pregnant with sweet water. But along the northeast shores of each island high cliffs rose, and mountains, and these reached up and knocked the water out of the clouds, so that it fell in cascades where it could not be used and never reached the southwest plains where the red soil was. Of the flat lands that could be tilled, fully three fourths were in effect deserts. If one could capture the wasted water that ran useless down the steep mountainsides and back out to sea, bringing it through the mountains and onto the flat lands, then crops could be grown. Or if one could discover the secret reservoirs waiting in the kidneys of the islands, one would have ample water and more than ample food. But until this was accomplished, men who lived on these islands would never have enough water or enough food.

And so these beautiful, inhospitable islands waited for some breed of men to invade them with food and courage and determination. The best that could be said of the islands, as they waited, was that they held no poisonous snakes, no fevers, no mosquitoes, no disfiguring diseases, and no plagues.

There was one additional aspect that must be remembered. Of all the growing things that existed in these islands at the time of Jesus, ninety-five out of every hundred grew nowhere else in the world. These islands were unique, alone, apart, off the main stream of life, a secluded backwater of nature . . . or, if you prefer, an authentic natural paradise where each growing thing had its opportunity to develop in its own unique way, according to the dictates and limitations of its own abilities.

I spoke of that adventurous bird that brought the first seed in its bowels. It was a grass seed, perhaps, one whose brothers and sisters, if the term may be used of grasses, stayed behind on their original islands, where they developed as the family had always done for millions of generations. On those original islands the grass maintained its standard characteristics and threw forth no venturesome modifications; or, if such mutations were offered, the stronger normal stock quickly submerged them, and the dead average was preserved.

But on the new islands the grass, left alone in beauty and sun and rain, became a different grass, unique and adapted to these islands. When men looked at such grass, millions of years later, they would be able to discern that it was a grass, and that it had come from the original stock still existing elsewhere; but they would also see that it was nevertheless a new grass, with new qualities, new vitality, and new promise.

Did an insect from one of the huge continents reach these islands? If so, here he became a different insect, his legs longer or his nose more adapted to boring. Birds, flowers, worms, trees, and snails ... all developed unique forms and qualities in these islands.

There was then, as there is now, no place known on earth that even began to compete with these islands in their capacity to encourage natural life to develop freely and radically up to its own best potential. More than nine out of ten things that grew here, grew nowhere else on earth.

Why this should have been so remains a mystery. Perhaps a fortunate combination of rainfall, climate, sunlight, and soil accounted for this miracle. Perhaps eons of time in which diverse growing things were left alone to work out their own best destinies was the explanation. Perhaps the fact that when a grass reached here it had to stand upon its own capacities and could not be refertilized by grasses of the same kind from the parent stock, perhaps that is the explanation. But whatever the reason, the fact remains: in these islands new breeds developed, and they prospered, and they grew strong, and they multiplied. For these islands were a crucible of exploration and development.

And so, with these capacities, the islands waited. Jesus died on a cross, and they waited. England was settled by mixed and powerful races, and the islands waited for their own settlers. Mighty kings ruled in India, and in China and in Japan, while the islands waited.

Inhospitable in fact, a paradise in potential, with almost no food available, but with enormous riches waiting to be developed, the islands waited. Volcanoes, still building the ramparts with fresh flows of lava, hung lanterns in the sky so that if a man and his canoe were lost on the great dark bosom of the sea, wandering fitfully this

...hat, he might spot the incandescent glow of the underside ...t cloud, and thus find a fiery star to steer by.

Large gannets and smaller terns skimmed across the waters leading to land, while frigate birds drew sharp and sure navigation lines from the turbulent ocean wastes right to the heart of the islands, where they nested. If a man in a canoe could spot a frigate bird, its cleft tail cutting the wind, he could be sure that land lay in the direction toward which the bird had flown at dusk.

These beautiful islands, waiting in the sun and storm, how much they seemed like beautiful women waiting for their men to come home at dusk, waiting with open arms and warm bodies and consolation. All that would be accomplished in these islands, as in these women, would be generated solely by the will and puissance of some man. I think the islands always knew this.

Therefore, men of Polynesia and Boston and China and Mount Fuji and the barrios of the Philippines, do not come to these islands empty-handed, or craven in spirit, or afraid to starve. There is no food here. In these islands there is no certainty. Bring your own food, your own gods, your own flowers and fruits and concepts. For if you come without resources to these islands you will perish.

But if you come with growing things, and good foods and better ideas, if you come with gods that will sustain you, and if you are willing to work until the swimming head and the aching arms can stand no more, then you can gain entrance to this miraculous crucible where the units of nature are free to develop according to their own capacities and desires.

On these harsh terms the islands waited.

Johannes C. Andersen

Two Ghost Stories of Old Hawaii

One of the most prominent students of Polynesian lore was Johannes Carl Andersen (1873–1962), born in Denmark. He was librarian for many years of the Alexander Turnbull Library in Wellington, New Zealand, and edited the *Journal of the Polynesian Society* from 1925 to 1947. He was honored by the award of the Royal Society Medal for Ethnology in 1944. During his long life Andersen published a number of articles and several books, such as *Polynesian Literature: Maori Poetry* (1946) and *Myths and Legends of the Polynesians* (1928), from which the following two tales are taken. Based upon the Alexander Fornander Collection of Hawaiian legends, both these lucid retellings deal with the eerie belief in "kapuku," or restoration of a corpse to life.

The Feather Cloak of Hawaii

THE Hawaiians have a story of the feather cloak that served as the first known pattern. Eleio was a kukini, or trained runner, in the service of Kakaalaneo, chief of Maui. He was not only a swift and tireless runner, but was also a kahuna, initiated into the observances that enabled him to see spirits, that made him skilled in medicine, and able to return a wandering spirit to its dead body if the work of dissolution had not begun.

Eleio had been sent to Hana to fetch awa root for the chief, and was expected to be back so that the chief might have his prepared drink for supper. Soon after leaving Olowalu, Eleio saw a beautiful young woman ahead of him. He hastened his steps but, exert himself as he would, she kept the same distance between them. Being the fleetest kukini of his time, it piqued him that a woman should be able to prevent his overtaking her, so he determined to capture her, and devoted all his energies to that object. She led him a long chase over rocks, hills, mountains, deep ravines, precipices, and gloomy streams, till they came to the cape of Hana-manu-loa at Kahiki-nui, beyond Kaupo, where he caught her just at the entrance to a puoa—a kind of tower made of bamboo, with a platform halfway up, where the dead bodies of persons of distinction were exposed to the elements.

When he caught her she turned to him and said, "Let me live! I am not human, but a spirit, and in this enclosure is my dwelling." He answered, "I have thought for some time that you were a spirit; no human being could have so outrun me."

She then said, "Let us be friends. In yonder house live my parents and relatives. Go to them and ask for a hog, rolls of kapa, some fine mats, and a feather cloak. Describe me to them, and tell them that I give all those things to you. The feather cloak is not finished; it is now only a fathom and a half square, and was intended to be two fathoms. There are in the house enough feathers and netting to finish it. Tell them to finish it for you." The spirit then disappeared.

Eleio entered the puoa, climbed onto the platform, and saw the dead body of the girl. She was in every way as beautiful as the spirit, and had apparently been dead but a short time. He left the puoa and hurried to the house pointed out as the home of her parents, and he saw a woman wailing, whom he recognized, from her resemblance, as the mother of the girl.

He saluted her with an aloha. "I am a stranger here," said he, "but I had a traveling companion who guided me to yonder puoa and then disappeared." At these words the woman ceased her wailing and called to her husband, to whom she repeated what the stranger had said.

"Does this house belong to you?" asked Eleio.

"It does," they answered.

"Then," said Eleio, "my message is to you." He repeated to them the message of the young girl, and they willingly agreed to give up all the things which their loved daughter had herself thus given away. But when they spoke of killing the hog and making a feast for him, he said, "Wait a little, and let me ask if all these people round about me are your friends?"

They answered, "They are our relatives—the uncles, aunts, and cousins of the spirit who seems to have chosen you either as husband or as brother."

"Will they do your bidding in everything?" he asked.

The parents answered that they could be relied on. He directed them to build a large arbor, to be entirely covered with ferns, ginger, maile, ieie—sweet and odorous foliage of the islands. An altar was to be erected at one end of the arbor and appropriately decorated. The order was willingly carried out, men, women, and children working with a will, so that in a couple of hours the whole structure was finished. He then directed the hog to be cooked, also red and white fish, red, white, and black cocks, and varieties of banana called lele and maoli to be placed on the altar. He directed all women and children to enter their houses and assist with their prayers, all pigs, chickens, and dogs to be hidden in dark houses to keep them quiet, and that strict silence be kept. The men at work were asked to remember the gods, and to invoke their assistance for Eleio.

He then started for Hana, pulled up a couple of bushes of awa of Kaeleku, famous for its medicinal virtue, and was back again before the hog was cooked. The awa was prepared, and when everything was ready for the feast he offered all to the gods and prayed for their assistance in what he was about to perform.

The spirit of the girl had been lingering near him all the time, seeming to be attracted to him, but of course invisible to everyone else. When he had finished his invocation he turned and caught the spirit, and holding his breath and invoking the gods he hurried to the puoa, followed by the parents, who now began to understand that he was about to attempt the kapuku, or restoration of the dead to life. Arrived at the puoa, he placed the spirit against the insteps of the girl and pressed it firmly in, meanwhile continuing his invocation. The spirit entered its former body kindly enough until it came to the knees, when it refused to go farther, fearing pollution, but Eleio by the strength of his prayers induced it to go farther, and farther, the father, mother, and male relatives assisting with their prayers, and at length the spirit was persuaded to take entire possession of the body, and the girl came to life again.

She was submitted to the usual ceremonies of purification by the priest, after which she was led to the prepared arbor, where there was a happy reunion. They feasted on the food prepared for the gods, whose guests they were, enjoying the material essence of the food after its spiritual essence had been accepted by the gods.

After the feast the feather cloak, the rolls of fine kapa, and the beautiful mats were brought and displayed to Eleio; and the father said to him, "Take as wife the woman you have restored, and remain here with us; you shall be our son, sharing equally in the love we have for her."

But Eleio, thinking of his chief, said, "No, I accept her as a charge; but, for wife, she is worthy to be one for a higher in rank. If you will trust her to my care, I will take her to my master; for her beauty and her charms make her worthy to be his wife and our queen."

"She is yours to do with as you will," said the father. "It is as if you had created her; for without you where would she be now? We ask only this, that you will always remember that you have parents and relatives here, and a home whenever you may wish it."

Eleio then requested that the feather cloak be finished for him before he returned to the chief. All who could work feathers set about it at once, including the girl herself, whose name, Eleio now learned, was Kanikani-aula. When it was finished he set out on his return, accompanied by the girl and taking the feather cloak and the awa that remained after a portion had been used during his incantations. They traveled slowly, according to the strength of Kanikani-aula, who now, in the body, could not equal the speed she had possessed as a spirit.

Arriving at Launi-upoko, Eleio turned to her and said, "You wait here, hidden in the bushes, while I go on alone. If by sundown I do not return, I shall be dead. You know the road by which we came; return then to your people. But if all goes well I shall be back in a little while."

He then went on, and when he reached Makila, on the confines of Lahaina, he saw a number of people heating an imu, or ground oven. On perceiving him they seized and started to bind him, saying it was the order of the chief that he should be roasted alive; but he ordered them away with the request, "Let me die at the feet of my master," and went on.

When at last he stood before Kakaalaneo, the chief said to him, "How is this? Why are you not cooked alive as I ordered? How came you to pass my guards?"

The runner answered, "It was the wish of the slave to die, if die he must, at the feet of his master; but if so, it would be an irreparable loss to you, my master; for I have that with me which will add to your fame, now, and to posterity."

"And what is that?" asked the king.

Eleio unrolled his bundle, and displayed to the astonished chief the glories of the feather cloak, a garment unknown till then. Needless to say, he was pardoned and restored to favor, the awa he had brought from Hana being reserved for the chief's special use in his offerings to the gods that evening.

When the chief heard the whole story of the reason for the absence of Eleio he ordered the girl to be brought, that he might see her, and express gratitude for the wonderful garment. When she arrived he was so charmed with her appearance, with her manner and conversation, that he asked her to become his queen.

Hiku and Kawelu

NOT far from the summit of Hualalai, on the island of Hawaii, in a cave on the southern side of the ridge, lived Hina and her son Hiku, a kupua, or demigod. During the whole of his childhood and youth Hiku had lived alone with his mother on the summit of the mountain, and had never once been permitted to descend to the plains below to see the abodes of men or to learn their ways. From time to time his ear had caught the sound of the distant hula and the voices of the merrymakers, and he had often wished to see those who danced and sang in those far-off coconut groves. But his mother, experienced in the ways of the world, had always refused her consent. Now at length he felt that he was a man; and as the sounds of mirth arose to his ears again, he asked his mother that he might go and mingle with the people on the shore. His mother, seeing that his mind was made up, reluctantly gave her consent, warning him not to linger, but to return in good time. So, taking in his hand his faithful arrow, Pua-ne, which he always carried, off he started.

This arrow was possessed of supernatural powers, being able to answer his call, and by its flight to direct his steps.

He descended over the rough lava and through the groves of koa that cover the southwestern slopes of the mountain, until, nearing its base, he stood on a distant hill; and, consulting his arrow by shooting it far into the air, he watched its flight until it struck on a distant hill above Kailua. To this hill he directed his steps and picked up his arrow in due time, again shooting it into the air. The second flight landed the arrow near the coast of Holualoa, six or eight miles south of Kailua. It struck on a barren waste of lava beside the water hole of Wai-kalai, known also as the Wai-a-Hiku (Water of Hiku), used by the people to this day.

Here he quenched his thirst; and nearing the village of Holualoa he again shot the arrow, which entered the courtyard of the alii (chief) of Kona, and from the women it singled out the chiefess Kawelu, and landed at her feet. Seeing the noble air of Hiku as he approached to claim his arrow, she stealthily hid it, and challenged him to find it. Then Hiku called to the arrow, "Pua-ne! Pua-ne!" and the arrow answered, "Ne," thus revealing its hiding place.

This incident of the arrow, and the grace and manliness of Hiku, won the heart of the young chiefess, and she was soon possessed by a strong passion for him, and determined to make him her husband. With her arts she detained him for several days at her home, and when he at last was determined to set out for the mountains she shut him up in the house and detained him by force. But the words of his mother came to his mind, and he sought means of breaking away from his prison. He climbed to the roof, and, removing a portion of the thatch, made his escape.

When his flight was discovered by Kawelu, she was distracted with grief; she refused to be comforted, refused all food, and before many days had passed, she died. Messengers were dispatched, who brought back the unhappy Hiku, the cause of all the sorrow. He had loved her though he had fled, and now, when it was too late, he wept over her. The spirit had departed to the netherworld of Milu, but, stung by the reproaches of her kindred and friends, and urged by his real love for Kawelu, Hiku resolved to attempt the perilous descent into the netherworld, and if possible bring back her spirit to the world it had left.

Two Ghost Stories of Old Hawaii

With the assistance of his friends he collected from the mountains great lengths of kowali (convolvulus vine). He also prepared a coconut shell, splitting it into two closely fitting parts. Then, anointing himself with a mixture of rancid coconut oil and kukui (candlenut) oil, which gave him a strong, corpselike odor, he started with his companions in canoes for the point on the sea where the sky hangs down to meet the water.

Arrived at the spot, he directed his comrades to lower him into the abyss called the Lua-o-Milu (Cave of Milu). Taking with him his coconut shell, and seating himself on the cross-stick of the swing, he was quickly lowered down by the long rope of vines held by his friends in the canoe above.

Soon he entered the great cavern where the spirits of the dead were gathered together. As he came among them, their curiosity was aroused to learn who he was; and he heard many remarks such as, "Whew! what an odor this corpse has!" and "He must have been dead a long time!" Even Milu himself, as he sat on the bank watching the spirits, was deceived, or he would never have permitted the entry of the living man into the regions ruled by him.

Hiku and his swing, which was like the one with one rope only used in Hawaii, attracted considerable attention. One spirit in particular watched him most intently—the spirit of Kawelu. There was mutual recognition, and with the permission of Milu she darted up to him, and swung with him on the kowali. As they were enjoying together this favorite Hawaiian pastime, the friends above were informed of the success of the ruse by means of a preconcerted signal, and rapidly drew them upward. At first Kawelu was too much absorbed in the sport to notice this; but when at length her attention was aroused by seeing the great distance of those beneath her she was about to flit away like a butterfly. Hiku, however, quickly clapped the coconut shells together, imprisoning her within them, and both were soon drawn up to the canoes above.

They returned to the shores of Holualoa, where Hiku landed at once and hastened to the house where the body of Kawelu still lay. Kneeling by its side, he made an incision in the great toe of the left foot, and into this with great difficulty he forced the reluctant spirit, binding up the wound so that it could not escape from the cold and clammy flesh in which it was now imprisoned. Then he began to rub and chafe the foot, working the spirit farther and farther up the limb. Gradually, as the heart was reached, the blood began to flow through the body; the breast began gently to heave, and soon the eyes opened, and the spirit gazed out from them as if just awakened from sleep. Kawelu was restored to consciousness, and seeing the beloved Hiku bending tenderly over her, she said, "How could you be so cruel as to leave me?"

All remembrance of the Lua-o-Milu and what had taken place there had disappeared, and she took up the thread of consciousness just where she had left it a few days before. Great joy filled the hearts of the people of Holualoa as they welcomed back to their midst the loved Kawelu and the hero Hiku, who from that day was not separated from her.

In this myth the entrance to the Lua-o-Milu is placed out to sea; but the more usual accounts place it at the mouth of the great valley of Waipio, in a place called Keoni, where the sands have long since covered up and concealed this passage to the netherworld.

Every year, it is told, the procession of ghosts marches silently down the Mahiki road, and at this point enters the Lua-o-Milu. This company of the dead is said to have been seen in quite recent times. A man, walking in the evening, saw the company appear in the distance; and, knowing that should they encounter him his death was certain, he hid himself behind a tree, and, trembling with fear, gazed at the dread sight. There was Kamehameha the conqueror, with all his chiefs and warriors in battle array, thousands of heroes who had won renown in the olden time. They kept perfect step as they marched along in utter silence, and, passing through the woods down to Waipio, disappeared from his view.

James King

Captain Cook at Kealakekua Bay

James King (1750–84) entered the British Navy at the age of twelve, and by 1771 he had risen to the rank of lieutenant. After a period of scientific study at Paris and Oxford he was recommended as a competent astronomer to accompany James Cook on his third and last Pacific voyage; he had previously served under Cook as second lieutenant on the flagship *Resolution*.

Captain Cook and his men, on the *Discovery* and *Resolution*, discovered the northwestern islands of Kauai, Niihau, and Oahu in January, 1778. After some months in Alaskan and Siberian waters, they returned to the Sandwich Islands, as Cook named them, and discovered the southeastern group, slowly sailing around the southern side of the island of Hawaii and at last finding an anchorage at Kealakekua Bay on the western side.

At the time of Cook's death ashore on February 14, 1779, King and his party were at a native temple on the other side of the bay. They were attacked by Hawaiian warriors but defended themselves until reinforcements under William Bligh came from the ships. King succeeded to the command of the *Discovery* when Captain Charles Clerke died on the way back to England.

Writing almost as well as his leader, King was the author with Cook of *A Voyage to the Pacific Ocean ... 1776–80* (London, 1784), from which the following selection is drawn. He was a likable young man as well as a competent officer and scientist. It is no wonder that the Hawaiians, who thought he was Cook's son, urged him to hide ashore and remain with them when the two ships left the islands on the return to England.

KEALAKEKUA BAY is situated on the west side of the island of Hawaii, in a district called Kona. It is about a mile in depth, and bounded by two low points of land at the distance of half a league and bearing south-southeast and north-northwest from each other.

On the north point, which is flat and barren, stands the village of Kaawaloa, and in the bottom of the bay, near a grove of tall coconut trees, there is another village of a more considerable size called Kakooa: between them runs a high rocky cliff, inaccessible from the seashore. On the south side the coast, for about a mile inland, has a rugged appearance, beyond which the country rises with a gradual ascent, and is overspread with cultivated enclosures and groves of coconut trees, where the habitations of the natives are scattered in great numbers. The shore, all around the bay, is covered with a black coral rock, which makes the landing very dangerous in rough weather, except at the village of Kakooa, where there is a fine sandy beach, with a morai, or burying place, at one extremity, and a small well of fresh water at the other.

This bay appearing to Captain Cook a proper place to refit the ships and lay in an additional supply of water and provisions, we moored on the north side, about a quarter of a mile from the shore, Kaawaloa bearing northwest. As soon as the inhabitants perceived our intention of anchoring in the bay, they came off from the shore in astonishing numbers, and expressed their joy by singing and shouting, and exhibiting a variety of wild and extravagant gestures. The sides, the decks, and rigging of both ships were soon completely covered with them; and a multitude of women and boys who had not been able to get canoes came swimming round us in shoals; many of whom, not finding room on board, remained the whole day playing in the water.

Among the chiefs who came on board the *Resolution* was a young man called Palea, whom we soon perceived to be a person of great authority. On presenting himself to Captain Cook he told him that he was Jakanee to the king of the island, who was at that time engaged on a military expedition at Maui, and was expected to return within three or four days. A few presents from Captain Cook attached him entirely to our interests, and he became exceedingly useful to us in the management of his countrymen, as we had soon occasion to experience. For we had not been long at anchor when it was observed that the *Discovery* had such a number of people hanging on one side as occasioned her to heel considerably, and that the men were unable to keep off the crowds which continued pressing into her. Captain Cook, being apprehensive that she might suffer some injury, pointed out the danger to Palea, who immediately went to their assistance, cleared the ship of its incumbrances, and drove away the canoes that surrounded her.

The authority of the chiefs over the inferior people appeared, from this incident, to be of the most despotic kind. A similar instance of it happened the same day on board the *Resolution*, where, the crowd being so great as to impede the necessary business of the ship, we were obliged to have recourse to the assistance of Kanaina, another of their chiefs, who had likewise attached himself to Captain Cook. The inconvenience we labored under being made known, he immediately ordered his countrymen to quit the vessel, and we were not a little surprised to see them jump overboard, without a moment's hesitation—all except one man, who, loitering behind and showing some unwillingness to obey, Kanaina took him up in his arms and threw him into the sea.

Both these chiefs were men of strong and well-proportioned bodies, and of countenances remarkably pleasing. Kanaina especially, whose portrait was drawn by Mr. Webber, was one of the finest men I ever saw. He was about six feet high, had regular and expressive features, with lively, dark eyes; his carriage was easy, firm, and graceful.

It has been already mentioned that during our long cruise off this island, the inhabitants had always behaved with great fairness and honesty in their dealings, and had not shown the slightest propensity to theft; which appeared to us the more extraordinary because those with whom we had hitherto held any intercourse were of the lowest rank, either servants or fishermen. We now found the case exceedingly altered. The immense crowd of islanders, which blocked up every part of the ships, not only afforded frequent opportunity of pilfering without risk of discovery, but our inferiority in number held forth a prospect of escaping with impunity in case of detection. Another circumstance to which we attributed this alteration in their behavior was the presence and encouragement of their chiefs; for generally tracing the booty into the possession of some men of consequence, we had the strongest reason to suspect that these depredations were committed at their instigation.

Soon after the *Resolution* had got into her station, our two friends Palea and Kanaina brought on board a third chief named Koa, who, we were told, was a priest, and had been in his youth a distinguished warrior. He was a little old man of emaciated figure, his eyes exceedingly sore and red and his body covered with a white leprous scurf, the effects of an immoderate use of awa. Being led into the cabin, he approached Captain Cook with great veneration, and threw over his shoulders a piece of red cloth, which he had brought along with him. Then, stepping a few paces back, he made an offering of a small pig, which he held in his hand while he pronounced a discourse that lasted for a considerable time.

This ceremony was frequently repeated during our stay at Hawaii, and appeared to us from many circumstances to be a sort of religious adoration. Their idols we found always arrayed with red cloth, in the same manner as was done to Captain Cook, and a small pig was their usual offering to the akuas. Their speeches, or prayers, were uttered too with a readiness and volubility that indicated them to be according to some formulary.

When this ceremony was over, Koa dined with Captain Cook, eating plentifully of what was set before him, but, like the rest of the inhabitants of the islands in these seas, could scarcely be prevailed on to taste a second time our wine or spirits. In the evening, Captain Cook, attended by Mr. Bayly and myself, accompanied him on shore. We landed at the beach and were received by four men, who carried wands tipped with dogs' hair and marched before us, pronouncing with a loud voice a short sentence, in which we could only distinguish the word "Lono." The crowd which had been collected on the shore retired at our approach, and not a person was to be seen except a few lying prostrate on the ground, near the huts of the adjoining village.

Before I proceed to relate the adoration that was paid to Captain Cook and the peculiar ceremonies with which he was received on this fatal island, it will be necessary to describe the morai, situated, as I have already mentioned, at the south side of the beach at Kakooa. It was a square, solid pile of stones, about forty yards long, twenty broad, and fourteen in height. The top was flat and well paved, and surrounded by a wooden rail, on which were fixed the skulls of the captives, sacrificed on the death of their chiefs. In the center of the area stood a ruinous old building of wood, connected with the rail on each side by a stone wall, which divided the whole space into two parts. On the side next the country were five poles, upward of twenty feet high, supporting an irregular kind of scaffold; on the opposite side, toward the sea, stood two small houses, with a covered communication.

We were conducted by Koa to the top of this pile by an easy ascent, leading from the beach to the northwest corner of the area. At the entrance we saw two large wooden images, with features violently distorted, and a long piece of carved wood, of a conical form inverted, rising from the top of their heads; the rest was without form, and wrapped around with red cloth. We were here met by a tall young man with a long beard, who presented Captain Cook to the images; and after chanting a kind of hymn, in which he was joined by Koa, they led us to that end of the morai where the five poles were fixed. At the foot of them were twelve images ranged in a semicircular form, and before the middle figure stood a high stand or table exactly resembling the whatta of Tahiti, on which lay a putrid hog, and under it pieces of sugar cane, coconuts, breadfruits, plantains, and sweet potatoes. Koa, having placed the captain under this stand, took down the hog and held it toward him, and after having a second time addressed him in a long speech, pronounced with much vehemence and rapidity, he let it fall on the ground, and led him to the scaffolding, which they began to climb together, not without great risk of falling.

At this time we saw, coming in solemn procession, at the entrance of the top of the morai, ten men carrying a live hog and a large piece of red cloth. Being advanced a few paces, they stopped and prostrated themselves, and Kaireekeea, the young man above mentioned, went to them, and receiving the cloth, carried it to Koa, who wrapped it round the captain, and afterward offered him the hog, which was brought by Kaireekeea with the same ceremony.

Whilst Captain Cook was aloft, in this awkward situation, swathed round with red cloth and with difficulty keeping his hold amongst the pieces of rotten scaffolding, Kaireekeea and Koa began their office, chanting sometimes in concert, and sometimes alternately. This lasted a considerable time; at length Koa let the hog drop, when he and the captain descended together. He then led him to the images before mentioned, and having said something to each in a sneering tone, snapping his fingers at them as he passed, he brought him to that in the center, which, from its being covered with red cloth, appeared to be in greater estimation than the rest. Before this figure he prostrated himself and kissed it, desiring Captain Cook to do the same—who suffered himself to be directed by Koa throughout the whole of this ceremony.

We were now led back into the other division of the morai, where there was a space, ten or twelve feet square, sunk about three feet below the level of the area. Into this we descended, and Captain Cook was seated between two wooden idols, Koa supporting one of his arms, whilst I was desired to support the other. At this time arrived a second procession of natives, carrying a baked hog and a pudding, some breadfruit, coconuts, and other vegetables. When they approached us, Kaireekeea put himself at their head, and presenting the pig to Captain Cook in the usual manner, began the same kind of chant as before, his companions making regular responses. We observed that after every response their parts became gradually shorter, till, toward the close, Kaireekeea's consisted of only two or three words, which the rest answered by the word "Lono."

When this offering was concluded, which lasted a quarter of an hour, the natives sat down, fronting us, and began to cut up the baked hog, to peel the vegetables, and break the coconuts, whilst others employed themselves in brewing the awa, which is done by chewing it in the same manner as at the Friendly Islands. Kaireekeea then took part of the kernel of a coconut, which he chewed, and wrapping it in a piece of cloth, rubbed with it the captain's face, head, hands, arms, and shoulders.

The awa was then handed round, and after we had tasted it, Koa and Palea began to pull the flesh of the hog in pieces and to put it into our mouths. I had no great objection to being fed by Palea, who was very cleanly in his person; but Captain Cook, who was served by Koa, recollecting the putrid hog, could not swallow a morsel; and his reluctance, as may be supposed, was not diminished when the old man, according to his own mode of civility, had chewed it for him.

When this last ceremony was finished, which Captain Cook put an end to as soon as he decently could, we quitted the morai, after distributing amongst the people some pieces of iron and other trifles, with which they seemed highly gratified. The men with wands conducted us to the boats, repeating the same words as before. The people again retired and the few that remained prostrated themselves as we passed along the shore. We immediately went on board, our minds full of what we had seen and extremely well satisfied with the good dispositions of our new friends. The meaning of the various ceremonies with which we had been received and which, on account of their novelty and singularity, have been related at length, can only be the subject of conjectures, and those uncertain and partial; they were, however, without doubt expressive of high respect on the part of the natives and, as far as related to the person of Captain Cook, they seemed approaching to adoration.

The next morning I went on shore with a guard of eight marines, including the corporal and lieutenant, having orders to erect the observatory in such a situation as might best enable me to superintend and protect the waterers and the other working parties that were to be on shore. As we were viewing a spot conveniently situated for this purpose in the middle of the village, Palea, who was always ready to show both his power and his good will, offered to pull down some houses that would have obstructed our observations. However, we thought it proper to decline this offer and fixed on a field of sweet potatoes adjoining to the morai, which was readily granted us; and the priests, to prevent the intrusion of the natives, immediately consecrated the place by fixing their wands round the wall by which it was enclosed.

This sort of religious interdiction they call tabu, a word we heard often repeated during our stay amongst these islanders, and found to be of very powerful and extensive operation. . . .

No canoes ever presumed to land near us; the natives sat on the wall, but none offered to come within the tabu'd space till he had obtained our permission. But though the men at our request would come across the field with provisions, yet not all our endeavors could prevail on the women to approach us. Presents were tried, but without effect; Palea and Koa were tempted to bring them, but in vain; we were invariably answered that the akua and Kalaniopuu (which was the name of their king) would kill them. This circumstance afforded no small matter of amusement to our friends on board, where the crowds of people, and particularly of women, that continued to flock thither obliged them almost every hour to clear the vessel, in order to have room to do the necessary duties of the ship. On these occasions two or three hundred women were frequently made to jump into the water at once, where they continued swimming and playing about till they could again procure admittance. . . .

I shall now return to our transactions on shore at the observatory, where we had not been long settled before we discovered in our neighborhood the habitations of a society of priests, whose regular attendance at the morai had excited our curiosity. Their huts stood round a pond of water and were surrounded by a grove of coconut trees which separated them from the beach and the rest of the village, and gave the place an air of religious retirement. On my acquainting Captain Cook with these circumstances, he resolved to pay them a visit; and as he expected to be received in the same manner as before, he brought Mr. Webber with him to make a drawing of the ceremony. On his arrival at the beach, he was conducted to a sacred building called Hale no Lono, or the House of Lono, and seated before the entrance, at the foot of a wooden idol of the same kind as those on the morai.

I was here again made to support one of his arms, and after wrapping him in red cloth, Kaireekeea, accompanied by twelve priests, made an offering of a pig with the usual solemnities. The pig was then strangled, and a fire being kindled, it was thrown into the embers, and after the hair was singed off it was again presented, with a repetition of the chanting, in the manner before described. The dead pig was then held for a short time under the captain's nose; after which it was laid, with a coconut, at his feet, and the performers sat down. The awa was then brewed and handed round; a fat hog, ready dressed, was brought in; and we were fed as before.

During the rest of the time we remained in the bay, whenever Captain Cook came on shore, he was attended by one of these priests, who went before him, giving notice that the Lono had landed, and ordering the people to prostrate themselves. The same person also constantly accompanied him on the water, standing in the bow of the boat, with a wand in his hand, and giving notice of his approach to the natives who were in canoes, on which they immediately left off paddling and lay down on their faces till he had passed. Whenever he stopped at the observatory, Kaireekeea and his brethren immediately made their appearance with hogs, coconuts, breadfruit, etc., and presented them with the usual solemnities. It was on these occasions that some of the inferior chiefs frequently requested to be permitted to make an offering to the Lono. When this was granted, they presented the hog themselves, generally with evident marks of fear in their countenances, whilst Kaireekeea and the priests chanted their accustomed hymns.

The civilities of this society were not, however, confined to mere ceremony and parade. Our party on shore received from them every day a constant supply of hogs and vegetables, more than sufficient for our subsistence; and several canoes loaded with provisions were sent to the ships with the same punctuality. No return was ever demanded or even hinted at in the most distant manner. Their presents were made with a regularity more like the discharge of a religious duty than the effect of mere liberality, and when we inquired at whose charge all this munificence was displayed, we were told it was at the expense of a great man called Kaoo, the chief of all the priests, and grandfather to Kaireekeea, who was at that time absent attending the king of the island. . . .

In the afternoon [January 24] Kalaniopuu arrived and visited the ships in a private manner, attended only by one canoe in which were his wife and children. He stayed on board till near ten o'clock, when he returned to the village of Kowrowa.

The next day, about noon, the king, in a large canoe attended by two others, set out from the village and paddled toward the ships in great state. Their appearance was grand and magnificent. In the first canoe were Kalaniopuu and his chiefs, dressed in their rich feathered cloaks and helmets, and armed with long spears and daggers; in the second came the venerable Kaoo, the chief of the priests, and his brethren, with their idols displayed on red cloth. These idols were busts of a gigantic size, made of wickerwork, and curiously covered with small feathers of various colors, wrought in the same manner with their cloaks. Their eyes were made of large pearl oysters, with a black nut fixed in the center; their mouths were set with a double row of the fangs of dogs, and, together with the rest of their features, were strangely distorted. The third canoe was filled with hogs and various sorts of vegetables. As they went along, the priests in the center canoe sung their hymns with great solemnity; and after paddling round the ships, instead of going on board as was expected, they made toward the shore at the beach where we were stationed.

As soon as I saw them approaching, I ordered out our little guard to receive the king; and Captain Cook, perceiving that he was going on shore, followed him and arrived nearly at the same time. We conducted them into the tent, where they had scarcely been seated when the king rose up and in a very graceful manner threw over the captain's shoulders the cloak he himself wore, put a feathered helmet on his head, and a curious fan into his hand. He also spread at his feet five or six other cloaks, all exceedingly beautiful, and of the greatest value. His attendants then brought four very large hogs, with sugar canes, coconuts, and breadfruit; and this part of the ceremony was concluded by the king's exchanging names with Captain Cook, which amongst all the islanders of the Pacific Ocean is esteemed the strongest pledge of friendship.

A procession of priests, with a venerable old personage at their head, now appeared, followed by a long train of men leading large hogs, and others carrying plantains, sweet potatoes, etc. By the looks and gestures of Kaireekeea, I immediately knew the old man to be the chief of the priests before mentioned, on whose bounty we had so long subsisted. He had a piece of red cloth in his hands, which he wrapped around Captain Cook's shoulders, and afterward presented him with a small pig in the usual form. A seat was then made for him, next to the king; after which Kaireekeea and his followers began their ceremonies, Kaoo and the chiefs joining in the responses.

I was surprised to see in the person of this king the same infirm and emaciated old man that came on board the *Resolution* when we were off the northeast side of the island of Maui; and we soon discovered amongst his attendants most of the persons who at that time had remained with us all night. Of this number were the two younger sons of the king, the eldest of whom was sixteen years of age, and his nephew Kamehameha [future king of the united islands], whom at first we had some difficulty recollecting, his hair being plastered over with a dirty brown paste and powder, which was no mean heightening to the most savage face I ever beheld.

Captain Cook at Kealakekua Bay

As soon as the formalities of the meeting were over, Captain Cook carried Kalaniopuu, and as many chiefs as the pinnace could hold, on board the *Resolution*. They were received with every mark of respect that could be shown them; and Captain Cook, in return for the feathered cloak, put a linen shirt on the king and girt his own hanger round him. The ancient Kaoo, and about half a dozen more old chiefs, remained on shore and took up their abode at the priests' houses.

During all this time, not a canoe was seen in the bay, and the natives either kept within their huts or lay prostrate on the ground. Before the king left the *Resolution*, Captain Cook obtained leave for the natives to come and trade with the ships as usual; but the women, for what reason we could not learn, still continued under the effects of the tabu—that is, were forbidden to stir from home, or to have any communication with us.

The quiet and inoffensive behavior of the natives having taken away every apprehension of danger, we did not hesitate to trust ourselves amongst them at all times, and in all situations. The officers of both ships went daily up the country in small parties, or even singly, and frequently remained out the whole night. It would be endless to recount all the instances of kindness and civility which we received upon those occasions. Wherever we went, the people flocked about us, eager to offer every assistance in their power, and highly gratified if their services were accepted. Various little arts were practiced to attract our notice or to delay our departure. The boys and girls ran before, as we walked through their villages, and stopped us at every opening where there was room to form a group for dancing. At one time, we were invited to accept a draft of coconut milk, or some other refreshment, under the shade of their huts; at another, we were seated within a circle of young women, who exerted all their skill and agility to amuse us with songs and dances.

The satisfaction we derived from their gentleness and hospitality was, however, frequently interrupted by that propensity to stealing which they have in common with all the other islanders of these seas. This circumstance was the more distressing as it sometimes obliged us to have recourse to acts of severity which we should willingly have avoided if the necessity of the case had not absolutely called for them. Some of their most expert swimmers were one day discovered under the ships, drawing out the filling nails of the sheathing, which they performed very dexterously by means of a short stick with a flint stone fixed in the end of it. To put a stop to this practice, which endangered the very existence of the vessels, we at first fired small-shot at the offenders; but they easily got out of our reach by diving under the ship's bottom. It was therefore found necessary to make an example, by flogging one of them on board the *Discovery*. . . .

This day [February 1] died William Watman, a seaman of the gunner's crew—an event which I mention the more particularly as death had hitherto been very rare amongst us. He was an old man, and much respected on account of his attachment to Captain Cook. . . .

At the request of the king of the island, he was buried on the morai, and the ceremony was performed with as much solemnity as our situation permitted. Old Kaoo and his brethren were spectators, and preserved the most profound silence and attention whilst the service was reading. When we began to fill up the grave, they approached it with great reverence, threw in a dead pig, some coconuts, and plantains, and for three nights afterward they surrounded it, sacrificing hogs and performing their usual ceremonies of hymns and prayers, which continued till daybreak. At the head of the grave we erected a post and nailed upon it a square piece of board, on which was inscribed the name of the deceased, his age, and the day of his death. This they promised not to remove, and we have no doubt but that it will be suffered to remain as long as the frail materials of which it is made will permit.

The ships being in great want of fuel, the captain desired me, on February 2, to treat with the priests for the purchase of the rail that surrounded the top of the morai. I must confess I had, at first, some doubt about the decency of this proposal and was apprehensive that even the bare mention of it might be considered by them as a piece of shocking impiety. In this, however, I found myself mistaken. Not the smallest surprise was expressed at the application, and the wood was readily given, even without stipulating for anything in return.

Whilst the sailors were taking it away, I observed one of them carrying off a carved image and, on further inquiry, I found that they had conveyed to the boats the whole semicircle. Though this was done in the presence of the natives, who had not shown any mark of resentment at it, but had even assisted them in the removal, I thought it proper to speak to Kaoo on the subject; who appeared very indifferent about the matter and only desired that we would restore the center image I have mentioned before, which he carried into one of the priest's houses.

Kalaniopuu and his chiefs had for some days past been very inquisitive about the time of our departure. This circumstance had excited in me a great curiosity to know what opinion this people had formed of us and what were their ideas respecting the cause and objects of our voyage. I took some pains to satisfy myself on these points, but could never learn anything further than that they imagined we came from some country where provisions had failed, and that our visit to them was merely for the purpose of filling our bellies.

Indeed, the meager appearance of some of our crew, the hearty appetites with which we sat down to their fresh provisions, and our great anxiety to purchase and carry off as much as we were able led them, naturally enough, to such a conclusion. To these may be added a circumstance which puzzled them exceedingly, our having no women with us, together with our quiet conduct and unwarlike appearance. It was ridiculous enough to see them stroking the sides and patting the bellies of the sailors (who were certainly much improved in the sleekness of their looks during our short stay in the island) and telling them, partly by signs and partly by words, that it was time for them to go, but if they would come again the next breadfruit season, they should be better able to supply their wants.

We had now been sixteen days in the bay, and if our enormous consumption of hogs and vegetables be considered, it need not be wondered that they should wish to see us take our leave. It is very probable, however, that Kalaniopuu had no other view in his inquiries at present than a desire of making sufficient preparation for dismissing us with presents suitable to the respect and kindness with which he had received us. For, on our telling him we should leave the island on the next day but one, we observed that a sort of proclamation was immediately made through the villages to require the people to bring in their hogs and vegetables for the king to present to the Lono on his departure....

As I happened to remain the last on shore, and waited for the return of the boat, several came crowding about me and, having made me sit down by them, began to lament our separation. It was, indeed, not without difficulty I was able to quit them. And here I hope I may be permitted to relate a trifling occurrence, in which I was principally concerned. Having had the command of the party on shore, during the whole time we were in the bay, I had an opportunity of becoming better acquainted with the natives, and of being better known to them, than those whose duty required them to be generally on board. As I had every reason to be satisfied with their kindness in general, so I cannot too often, nor too particularly, mention the unbounded and constant friendship of their priests. On my part, I spared no endeavors to conciliate their affection and gain their esteem; and I had the good fortune to succeed so far that, when the time of our departure was made known, I was strongly solicited to remain behind, not without offers of the most flattering kind. When I excused myself by saying that Captain Cook would not give his consent, they proposed that I should retire into the mountains, where, they said, they would conceal me till the departure of the ships. And, on my further assuring them that the captain would not leave the bay without me, Kalaniopuu and Kaoo waited upon Captain Cook, whose son they supposed I was, with a formal request that I might be left behind. The captain, to avoid giving a positive refusal to an offer so kindly intended, told them that he could not part with me at that time, but that he should return to the island next year and would then endeavor to settle the matter to their satisfaction.

S. M. Kamakau

The Floating Islands and the Return of Lono

Many accounts are available from English sources dealing with the discovery of the Hawaiian Islands, the reception of the sailors by the natives, and the misunderstanding that led to the death of Captain Cook. The native side of this story, however, is virtually unknown.

The first accounts based on native sources of Cook's adventures in the archipelago began appearing in the Hawaiian language newspaper *Kuokoa* in 1865. They were the work of Samuel Manaiakalani Kamakau, who was born at Waialua, Oahu, in October, 1815. As a promising student he was a member of the second class to enter Lahainaluna Seminary on the island of Maui, set up to train young Hawaiians to become Congregationalist ministers. Remaining at this mission school for seven years, both as pupil and as teacher's assistant, he carried on research in Hawaiian lore for the seminar of the Reverend Sheldon Dibble and later became a charter member of the Royal Hawaiian Historical Society, founded in 1841. Kamakau married and began teaching on Maui, and at one time held the post of district judge at Wailuku, but after slightly more than a year on the bench was removed for malfeasance. From 1851 until the year of his death in 1876 he served many times in the legislature of the kingdom.

Kamakau wrote more than two hundred newspaper articles. From these two volumes have been published: *Ka Po'e Kahiko: The People of Old* (1964) and *The Ruling Chiefs of Hawaii* (1961), from which the following account is taken.

One of the most striking differences between Kamakau's narrative and the English records—which all stress Captain Cook's egregious chastity —is the charge that the British explorer succumbed to the charms of a princess of Kauai. John F. G. Stokes, former curator of Polynesian ethnology at the Bishop Museum, has pointed out that the anti-Cook attitude may reflect the pro-American bias of Dibble, for native opinion previous to 1838 was quite friendly to Cook and remorseful about his death. Perhaps the chief value of Kamakau's legendary account lies in showing how the Hawaiians of his generation preferred to recollect the incursions of the first Europeans in their islands.

IT was eighty-eight years ago, in January, 1778, that Captain Cook first came to Hawaii. Kaeo was ruling chief of Kauai, Kahahana of Oahu and Molokai, and Kahekili of Maui, Lanai, and Kahoolawe. The ship was first sighted from Waialua and Waianae [on Oahu] sailing for the north. It anchored at night at Waimea, Kauai, that place being nearest at hand. A man named Moapu and his companions who were out fishing with heavy lines saw this strange thing move by and saw the lights on board. Abandoning their fishing gear, no doubt through fright, they hurried ashore and hastened to tell Kaeo and the other chiefs of Kauai about this strange apparition.

The next morning the ship lay outside Kaahe at Waimea. Chiefs and commoners saw the wonderful sight and marveled at it. Some were terrified and shrieked with fear. The valley of Waimea rang with the shouts of the excited people as they saw the boat with its masts and its sails shaped like a gigantic sting ray. One asked another, "What are those branching things?" and the other answered, "They are trees moving about on the sea." Still another thought, "A double canoe of the hairless ones of Mana!" A certain kahuna named Kuohu declared, "That can be nothing else than the heiau of Lono, the tower of Keolewa, and the place of sacrifice at the altar." The excitement became more intense, and louder grew the shouting.

The chief sent some men on board to see what the wonderful thing was. Those who went were Kaneakahoowaha, the kahuna Kuohu, wearing a whale-tooth ornament to show his rank, the chief Kiikiki, and some paddlers. When they drew near and saw how much iron there was along the side of the ship and on the rails, they said excitedly to each other, "Oh, how much dagger material (pahoa) there is here!" for they called iron "pahoa" because that was what they used in old days for their fighting daggers.

One of them went on board and saw many men on the ship with white foreheads, sparkling eyes, wrinkled skins, and angular heads [three-cornered hats], who spoke a strange language and breathed fire from their mouths. The chief Kiikiki and the kahuna Kuohu, each clothed in a fine girdle of tapa cloth about the loins and a red tapa garment caught about the neck, stepped forward with the left fist clenched and, advancing before Captain Cook, stepped back a pace and bowed as they murmured a prayer; then, seizing his hands, they knelt down and the tabu was freed. Captain Cook gave Kuohu a knife, and it was after this incident that Kuohu named his daughter Changed-into-a-dagger and The-feather-that-went-about-the-ship. This was the first gift given by Captain Cook to any native of Hawaii.

They called Captain Cook Lono (after the god Lono who had gone away promising to return). A man hoisting a flag they called Ku-of-the-colored-flag after the image that stood against the outer wall of the heiau. A lighted pipe in the mouth of another gave him the name of Lono-of-the-volcanic-fire. When they saw a heap of coconuts they said, "These are the fruits of Traveling-coconut; they must have killed this mischief-maker of the sea." Of a bullock's hide they said, "They must also have killed Ku-long-dog! Perhaps they have come here to kill all the mischief-makers of the sea." And they returned to shore and reported all they had seen, the men's acts and their speech; how they had killed the kupua of the sea, Niuolahiki and Kuilioloa, of which the coconuts and the hides were proof; how much iron there was lying about the floating heiau (for the Hawaiians had seen iron before); and how the men had fair skins, bright eyes, sharp noses, angular heads, and deep-set eyes. Then both chiefs and commoners, hearing this report, said to each other, "This is indeed Lono, and this is his heiau come across the sea from Moaulanuiakea across Manowainuikaioo!" When the priest's prayer had freed the tabu and his words were ended the chief asked, "Would there be any harm in going to the heiau of the god?" The kahuna reassured him, saying, "No harm at all, for I did my work well. Only do not meddle with the things belonging to the god."

The people made ready to go on board. When Kapupuu, a warrior of Kaeo's guard, heard of the quantity of iron on the ship, he said to the chief, "I shall go on board and take the iron." The chief answered, "The kahuna warned us not to take the god's property lest there be trouble." "Let my lands be surety for any trouble." "Just as you say," replied the chief.

Kapupuu went out to the ship and, seeing a quantity of iron objects lying about, he seized some hastily and threw them into his canoe. The stranger saw him taking the iron and shot him with a gun and killed him. Then all the men in the canoes paddled ashore and told the chiefs and the people how Kapupuu had died, and of the death-dealing thing which the white men used and which squirted out like the gushing forth of water. Some called the weapon a "water squirter" because of its squirting out like water from a bamboo; others called it a "water gusher."

The strangers asked where they could find water, pointing to water with their hands, and the people told them that there was abundant supply inland. The strangers therefore went ashore to draw water. The Hawaiians, observing the way they rowed, said, "They must be nursing babies the way they lean over!" and as the men swayed as they rowed, they exclaimed in surprise, "They row their canoe swaying back and forth and they seem to be bending back the tips of their paddles!" For this reason they called a boat a "doubling-up canoe." When the boat landed at the mouth of the Waimea River, the beach of Luhi and the opposite side of Laauakala were crowded with people. There was not a bare spot visible. Chiefs and commoners, old and young, came from Polihale, Napali, and Kipu, like a rushing stream.

Some chiefs cried, "Let us kill these people for killing Kapupuu!" but the kahuna Kuohu said, "That is not a good thought, for they were not to blame. The fault was ours for plundering, for Kapupuu went to plunder. I have told you that we live under a law; if any man rob or steal, his bones shall be stripped of flesh. The proper way to do is to treat these people kindly. For listen, you chiefs and people! I do not know whether these are gods or men. Here is the test of a god: if we tempt them and they do not open their gourd container which holds their ancestral gods, then they are themselves gods, but if they open the sacred gourds [that is, if they yield to the temptation of women] then they are not gods—they are foreigners, men from the land of Kaekae and Kukanaloa and their companions." Many of the old people felt doubtful, for they had heard of foreigners, but the majority of the people and the young men shouted, "A god! A god! Lono is a god! Lono is a god!" Thus the name Lono spread from Kauai to Hawaii.

The Floating Islands and the Return of Lono

When night fell, the men on the ship shot off guns and skyrockets, perhaps to express their joy in having discovered this first land of the group, Kauai. The people called the rockets "the fires of Lonomakua" and they named the flash of the gun "the lightning" and its report "Kane in the thunder."

The next day Captain Cook, his officers, and some of his men went ashore with their guns in readiness, and were taken before Kaeo, the ruling chief, the chiefess Kamakahelei, and the other chiefs. They greeted him well and gave him gifts of hogs, chickens, bananas, taro, potatoes, sugar cane, yams, fine mats, and bark cloth. Captain Cook accepted their gifts; it may be that he took them to show the British people what the products of Kauai were like. To the Hawaiians he gave gifts of cloth, iron, a sword, knives, necklaces, and mirrors. The cloth they called "foreign fiber" because it resembled coconut fiber. Glass they called "kilo" [from the practice of the kilo, or soothsayer, looking into a shallow bowl of water where he was supposed to see reflected the persons or acts about whom inquiry was made], and iron they called "dagger." They ceased to believe the foreigners to be gods. At first they had taken their cocked hats to be a part of their heads and their clothing to be wrinkled skin.

Kaeo gave to Captain Cook his wife's daughter Lelemahoalani, who was a sister of Kaumualii, and Captain Cook gave Kaeo gifts in exchange for Lelemahoalani. When the other women noticed that the chiefess had slept with foreigners, they too slept with foreigners in order to obtain cloth, iron, and mirrors.

Captain Cook left Kauai and sailed northwest of America through Bering Strait to seek lands to the north. To these islands he bequeathed such possessions as the flea, never known on them before his day, and prostitution with its results, syphilis and other venereal diseases. These serious diseases caused the dwindling of the population after the coming of Captain Cook....

[Having returned from his northern voyaging], Captain Cook sailed past Hamakua, Hilo, Puna, and Kau, and put in at Kealakekua Bay, and on January 17, 1779, he put in at Kaawaloa Bay. Kalaniopuu was fighting Kahekili on Maui at the time. Captain Cook arrived during the tabu time of the makahiki, when no man could paddle out to the ship without breaking the law and forfeiting all his possessions. But when Captain Cook appeared they declared that his name must be Lono, for Kealakekua was the home of that deity as a man, and it was a belief of the ancients that he had gone to Kahiki and would return. They were full of joy, all the more so that these were Lono's tabu days. Their happiness knew no bounds; they leaped for joy [shouting]: "Now shall our bones live; our aumakua has come back. These are his tabu days and he has returned!" This was a great mistake. He was a long-tailed god, a scorpion, a slayer of men. What a pity! But they believed in him and shouted, "Lono is a god! Lono is a god!"

Hikiau was the name of Lono's heiau at Kealakekua, and it lay close to the beach. The kahunas of the heiau were among the first, together with those who fed the god, to adopt the error of the rest of the people. The men hurried to the ship to see the god with their own eyes. There they saw a fair man with bright eyes, a high-bridged nose, light hair, and handsome features. Good-looking gods they were! They spoke rapidly. Red was the mouth of the god. When they saw the strangers letting out ropes, the natives called them Ku-of-the-tree-fern and Coverer-of-the-island. These were gods of the canoe builders in the forest. When they saw them painting the ship, they said, "There are Maikoha and Ehu (Fair-haired) daubing their canoe, and Lanahu (Charcoal) daubing on the black!" When they saw the strangers smoking, they said, "There are Lono-pele and his companions [of the volcano] breathing fire from their mouths!" Another sailor who put up a flag at the masthead they called Ku-of-the-colored-ensign.

When Captain Cook went ashore at Kealakekua the kahuna, believing him to be a god, led him to the heiau, and seated him above the altar where sacrifices were offered. The kahuna stepped back, and had a soft white tapa wrapped about his loins. Captain Cook was covered with a cloak of red tapa like that about the images. Then the kahuna prayed thus: "Your heavenly bodies, O Lono, are the long clouds, the short clouds, the peeping cloud, the peering cloud, the clouds gathering in clusters in the sky, from Uliuli, from Melemele, from Kahiki, from Ulunui, from Haehae, from Omaokuululu, from Hakauai, from the land that Lono split in twain, in the lower heavens, in the higher heavens, at the foundation of Laka of Lalohana, from the foundations of the earth. O Ku! O Lono!

The Floating Islands and the Return of Lono

O Kane! O Kanaloa! gods from the upper regions, from the lower regions, from Kahiki in the east and Kahiki in the west, here is an offering, a gift. Grant life to the chief, life to your children until they reach the world of light, the fruitful land. It is ended, it is freed."

Now it is doubtful whether Captain Cook consented to have worship paid to him by the priests. He may have thought they were worshiping as in his own land. But he was a Christian and he did wrong to consent to enter an idolator's place of worship. He did wrong to accept gifts offered before idols and to eat food dedicated to them. Therefore God smote him.

Some days later, many women went on board the ship to offer themselves to the sailors and received in return iron, mirrors, scissors, and beads. When the women looked into the mirrors and saw their own likenesses as if alive, they scraped the quicksilver off the backs of the mirrors, but when the glass could no longer reflect their images they regretted their act. The natives took hogs a fathom in length to trade for guns, for they liked the sound of the report. They said, "Trade, trade! we will trade the hogs for your shooting-water, your exploding-water; guns, guns, guns!" The strangers said, "No!" "Trade! Trade! Guns!" "No more." "The moa (fowl) are all gone from Molea in Hamakua," the natives said. "Ha! the white men know where the fish are hid. These long-tailed gods know well, for they are taking our women on board."

On Kalaniopuu's return with his chiefs and warriors from Maui on January 24, 1779, he landed at Awili in Kaawaloa and stayed in Hanamua at the home of Keaweaheulu, who had been with them on Maui fighting with Kahekili, and when he saw how many women went aboard the ship to prostitute themselves to the strangers, he forbade their going. When the strangers could get no more women on the ship, they came ashore at Napoopoo, at Kahauloa, and on this side of Kaawaloa, and numerous were the opala haole [foreign rubbish] born to the women. Kalaniopuu treated Captain Cook hospitably, giving him hogs, kalo, potatoes, bananas, and other provisions, as well as feather capes, helmets, kahili, feather leis, wooden bowls beautifully shaped, kapa cloths of every variety, finely woven mats of Puna, and some especially fine mats made of pandanus blossoms. In return Captain Cook gave Kalaniopuu some trifles. It is said that the hat Cook gave to Kalaniopuu is in the wrappings of the head of Keaweikekahialiiokamoku.

On February 4, Lono sailed away in his ship and had got beyond Kawaihae when he discovered that one of the masts was decayed and he had to put back to Kealakekua to repair it. The natives saw him return, and the women took up once more their association with the sailors, but not in such numbers as before. The natives had begun to be suspicious, and some said, "These are not gods; these are men, white men from the land of Kukanaloa." Others declared them to be gods. Still others said, "The legends of Kane, Kanaloa, Ku, and Lono say that they came from Kahiki; they do not lie with women. Lonoikamakahiki was a deified man, not a god." One man said, "The woman [Lelemahoalani] who was on the ship says that they groan when they are hurt. When the woman sticks her nails into them they say, 'You scratch like an owl; your nails are too long; you claw like a duck!' and more that she did not understand."

The natives tried to provoke Lono to wrath to see whether he would be angry. They reasoned, "Perhaps the god will not be angry because he has received offerings of hogs, clothing, red fish, bananas, and coconuts, and the god Lono has been propitiated." The natives accordingly went on board the ship and took some iron. The sailors caught them stealing it and shot them; then a fight began. One of the sailors grasped the canoe of a certain chief named Palea, who was an intimate friend of Kalaniopuu. Palea defied the sailor, thrusting him to one side. Another sailor ran toward them and struck Palea down with a club. The natives fell upon the sailor, but Palea recovered consciousness, and the fighting ceased. They were afraid lest Lono kill them, hence they stopped fighting.

Palea no longer believed in the divinity of Lono and he plotted to steal a boat. He and his men secretly took a boat from Lono's ship and, conveying it to Onouli, they broke it up in order to get the iron in it, also perhaps because they were angry with the white men for striking Palea with a club. It was this theft of a boat by Palea that led to the fight in which Captain Cook was killed. When Captain Cook and the sailors awoke in the morning and found their boat gone they were troubled; so Captain Cook went ashore at Kaawaloa to inquire about the boat of Kalaniopuu, the ruling chief.

The Floating Islands and the Return of Lono

Kalaniopuu denied any knowledge of the affair, saying, "I know nothing about it; perhaps the natives stole it and carried it away."

Possibly Captain Cook did not quite understand what Kalaniopuu said. He returned to the ship, and the officers discussed the affair and resolved to take the high chief Kalaniopuu on board and hold him there until the boat was found and restored, when he was to be given his liberty. It was resolved that an officer be chosen to fetch the chief; and an officer and some marines were selected and armed with swords and guns for the purpose of bringing the chief on board the next day. However, because on that day, Thursday, February 14, the officer appointed for the duty was ill, Captain Cook took his place.

Cook landed with his company at Kaawaloa between Kalaniopuu's place at Awili and Keaweaheulu's at Hanamua. As a result of the conference held in the men's eating house before Kalaniopuu, his older chiefs, and his sons, Kalaniopuu consented to go on board the ship.

Kekuhaupio, meanwhile, seeing Cook on his way to Kaawaloa, hastily set out from Keei with another chief named Kalimu. The strangers, seeing a man sitting at the outrigger of the canoe wearing a feather cape, shot at him. The shot struck Kalimu and killed him. Kekuhaupio then hurriedly turned back and landed at Kaawaloa. Just then Kalaniopuu and some of the chiefs dressed in chiefly array and carrying their war clubs appeared on the shore, ready to go on board the ship. Kekuhaupio cried: "O heavenly one! Stop! It is not safe on the sea; Kalimu is dead. Go back to the house."

When Kalola heard that Kalimu was dead, shot by the strangers, she ran out of the sleeping house, threw her arms about the shoulders of Kalaniopuu and said, "O heavenly one! Let us go back!" Kalaniopuu turned to go back. Captain Cook tried to grasp him by the hand, but Kalanimanookahoowaha stuck his club in the way, and Kalaniopuu was borne away by his chiefs and warriors to Maunaloia, and the fight began.

Captain Cook struck Kalanimanookahoowaha with his sword, slashing one side of his face from temple to cheek. The chief with a powerful blow of his club knocked Captain Cook down against a heap of lava rock. Captain Cook groaned with pain. Then the chief knew that he was a man and not a god, and, that mistake ended, he struck him dead together with four other white men.

The rest of the party fled to their boats and shot the gun, and many of the Hawaiians were killed. Some of those who were skillful with the sling shot stones after the boat. Of one of these named Moa the strangers said, "Mahimoa is a bad one. He twists his sling and the stone flies forth. He who flees, dies; he who stands still, lives."

When the strangers on the ship knew that their chief was dead, they shot their guns from the ship while the natives tried to ward off the shots with sleeping mats. The bodies of Captain Cook and the four men who died with him were carried to Kalaniopuu at Maunaloia, and the chief sorrowed over the death of the captain. He dedicated the body of Captain Cook, that is, he offered it as sacrifice to the god with a prayer to grant life to the chief (himself) and to his dominion. Then they stripped the flesh from the bones of Lono. The palms of the hands and the intestines were kept; the remains were consumed with fire. The bones Kalaniopuu was kind enough to give to the strangers on board the ship, but some were saved by the kahunas and worshiped.

Eight days after the death of Captain Cook, friendly relations were resumed with those on board the ship. On Monday, February 23, the ship sailed and it anchored at Kauai on the twenty-ninth of that month to get water and food supplies, then sailed to Niihau and got a supply of yams, potatoes, and hogs. On March 15, the ship sailed into the blue and disappeared. This was the end of Captain Cook's voyages of exploration among these islands.

Captain Cook was a [man] of Britain famous for his explorations in the Indian, Atlantic, and the Pacific Oceans. He discovered lands in the ocean which were [previously] unknown. He had been but a short time in Hawaii when God punished him for his sin. It was not the fault of the Hawaiian people that they held him sacred and paid him honor as a god worshiped by the Hawaiian people. But because he killed the people he was killed by them without mercy, and his entrails were used to rope off the arena, and the palms of his hands used for fly swatters at a cock fight. Such is the end of a transgressor. The seeds that he planted here have sprouted, grown, and become the parents of others that have caused the decrease of the native population of these islands. Such are gonorrhea, and other social diseases; prostitution; the illusion of his being a god [which led to] worship of him; fleas and mosquitoes [erroneous]; epidemics. All of these things have led to changes in the air which we breathe; the coming of things which weaken the body; changes in plant life; changes in religion; changes in the art of healing; and changes in the laws by which the land is governed.

John Nicol

The Cooper and the Kings

Born near Edinburgh, John Nicol (1755–1825) was a cooper on the *King George,* Nathaniel Portlock's flagship, in 1785–88, which along with the *Queen Charlotte* under George Dixon touched several times in the Hawaiian group. The crews of these ships were the first to land on the island of Oahu and to visit Waikiki.

Nicol had earlier served on British vessels in the American Revolution, and had been cooper on a whaler to Greenland. He had shipped on a previous voyage with Portlock, who appreciated him as "an excellent brewer of spruce beer," served out to prevent scurvy.

After the visits to Hawaii here chronicled, Nicol returned via China to England, but his sea adventures had only begun. His later career included a voyage to New South Wales on a convict ship, whaling in the South Seas, a mutiny, and action off Cape St. Vincent and at Aboukir Bay. In 1822, poor and feeble but still cheerful, he was met by John Howell, a writer who "thought of taking down a narrative of his life, from his own mouth. This I have done," adds Howell in a postscript, "as nearly as I could, in his own words." The book appearing that year was called *The Life and Adventures of John Nicol, Mariner.* Nicol's narrative, according to a later editor, Alexander Laing, is "surpassed in its kind by none but that of Melville."

THE first land we made was Hawaii, the island where Captain Cook was killed. The *King George* and *Queen Charlotte* were the first ships which had touched there since that melancholy event. The natives came on board in crowds, and were happy to see us; they recognized Portlock and others, who had been on the island before, along with Cook. Our decks were soon crowded with hogs, breadfruit, yams, and potatoes. Our deck soon resembled a shambles; our butcher had fourteen assistants. I was as busy and fatigued as I could be, cutting iron hoops into lengths of eight and nine inches, which the carpenter ground sharp. These were our most valuable commodity in the eyes of the natives. I was stationed down in the hold of the vessel, and the ladders were removed to prevent the natives from coming down to the treasury.

The king of Hawaii looked to my occupation with a wistful eye; he thought me the happiest man on board, to be among such vast heaps of treasure. Captain Portlock called to me to place the ladder, and allow the king to come down, and give him a good long piece. When the king descended he held up his hands, and looked astonishment personified. When I gave him the piece of hoop of twenty inches long, he retired a little from below the hatch into the shade, undid his girdle, bent the iron to his body, and, adjusting his belt in the greatest haste, concealed it. I suppose he thought I had stole it. I could not but laugh to see the king concealing what he took to be stolen goods.

We were much in want of oil for our lamps. The sharks abounding, we baited a hook with a piece of salt pork, and caught the largest I ever saw in any sea; it was a female, nineteen feet long; it took all hands to hoist her on board; her weight made the vessel heel. When she was cut up we took forty-eight young ones out of her belly, eighteen inches long; we saw them go into her mouth after she was hooked. The hook was fixed to a chain attached to our main brace, or we never would have kept her. It was evening when she snapped the bait; we hauled the head just above the surface, the swell washing over it. We let her remain thus all night, and she was quite dead in the morning. There were in her stomach four hogs, four full-grown turtles, besides the young ones. Her liver, the only part we wanted, filled a tierce.

Almost every man on board took a native woman for a wife while the vessel remained, the men thinking it an honor, or for their gain, as they got many presents of iron, beads, or buttons. The women came on board at night, and went on shore in the morning. In the evening they would call for their husbands by name. They often brought their friends to see their husbands, who were well pleased, as they were never allowed to go away empty. The fattest woman I ever saw in my life our gunner chose for a wife. We were forced to hoist her on board; her thighs were as thick as my waist; no hammock in the ship would hold her; many jokes were cracked upon the pair.

They are the worst people to pronounce the English of any I ever was among. Captain Portlock they called Potipoti. The nearest approach they could make to my name was Nittie; yet they would make the greatest efforts, and look so angry at themselves, and vexed at their vain efforts.

We had a merry facetious fellow on board called Dickson. He sang pretty well. He squinted, and the natives mimicked him. Opunui, king of Kauai ["Big Belly"—he was actually second in command under King Kaeo], could cock his eye like Dickson better than any of his subjects. Opunui called him Billicany, from his often singing "Rule, Britannia." Opunui learned the air, and the words as near as he could pronounce them. It was an amusing thing to hear the king and Dickson sing. Opunui loved him better than any man in the ship, and always embraced him every time they met on shore, or in the ship, and began to sing "Tule, Billicany! Billicany, tule," etc.

We had the chief on board who killed Captain Cook for more than three weeks. He was in bad health, and had a smelling bottle with a few drops in it, which he used to smell at; we filled it for him. There were a good many bayonets in possession of the natives, which they had obtained at the murder of Cook.

We left Hawaii, and stood down to Kauai, where we watered, and had a feast from Opunui the king. We took our allowance of brandy on shore, and spent a most delightful afternoon, the natives doing all in their power to amuse us; the girls danced, the men made a sham fight, throwing their spears; the women, standing behind, handed the spears to the men, the same as in battle, thus keeping up a continued shower of spears. No words can convey an adequate idea of their dexterity and agility. They thought we were bad with the rheumatism, our movements were so slow compared with their own. The women would sometimes lay us down, and chafe and rub us, making moan and saying "Lomilomi!" They wrestled, but the stoutest man in our ship could not stand a single throw with the least chance of success.

We stood next for Niihau, of which Opunui was king as well as of Kauai, to get yams. This island grows them in abundance, and scarce anything else. They have no wood upon the island, but exchange their yams for it to build their canoes. While lying here, it came to blow a dreadful gale; we were forced to cut our cables, and stand out to sea and leave sixteen men and boys. It was three weeks before we could return. When we arrived, we found them well and hearty; these kind people had lodged them two and two in their houses, gave them plenty of victuals, and liberty to ramble over the whole island. The only man who was in the least alarmed for his safety was an old boatswain; he was in continual fear. The innocent natives could not meet to divert themselves, or even a few talk together, but the old sinner would shake with horror, and called to his shipmates, "Now they are going to murder us; this is our last night." He was a perfect annoyance to the others; he scarce ever left the beach but to go to some height to look out for the ships, and after looking till he was almost blind he would seek out the other men to make his lamentations, and annoy them with his fears of the loss of the ships, or their being deserted by them. At length we returned, and took them on board, making presents to the king and his kind people for their unlimited hospitality. We now took an affectionate leave of these kind islanders. . . .

After waiting in Nootka Sound, our place of rendezvous, for some time, and [the *Queen Charlotte*] not appearing, we immediately set sail for Hawaii, but got no word of our consort until we came to Kauai, when we perceived Opunui in his single canoe, making her scud through the water, crying, "tattoo for Potipoti," as he jumped upon deck with a letter from Captain Dixon, which removed our fears and informed us he had discovered an island and got a very great number of skins, and had sailed for China. We watered and laid in our provisions as quick as we could, to follow her.

Opunui, soon after he came on board, told the captain he had seen Billicany, and squinted so like Dickson that we knew at once Meares had been there in the *Nootka*. Dickson afterward told us Meares would not have got anything from Opunui had he and Willis not been with him. Opunui had a son called Poinui—in English, "large pudding." I thought him well named. He had the largest head of any boy I ever saw. His father wished Captain Portlock to take him to England, but Poinui did not wish to go. He leaped overboard just as we sailed, and swam back to his father.

It was with a sensation of regret I bade a final adieu to the Sandwich Islands. Even now I would prefer them to any country I ever was in. The people so kind and obliging, the climate so fine, and provisions so abundant, all render it a most endearing place. Hawaii is the only place I was not ashore in. Captain Portlock never went himself, and would not allow his crew to go. The murder of Cook made him timorous of trusting too much to the islanders. At Kauai and Niihau we went on shore, one watch one day, the other the next.

John Bartlett

Attack on the *Gustavus III*

An American seaman, John Bartlett of Boston, visited the Islands in 1791 as a crew member of the square-rigger *Gustavus III*. This vessel, commanded by Thomas Barnett, was really the *Mercury* of London, but her name had been changed and she sailed under Swedish colors to evade the British monopoly held by the King George's Sound Company.

Those were the days when a fur-trading ship coming down from Nootka to get provisions on the way to the China market might still run the risk of being captured by Hawaiians seeking iron, muskets, and other treasure. Indeed, only a year before the arrival of the *Gustavus III*, the *Fair American* under Thomas Metcalfe had been seized off Hawaii and all except one of her crew were killed. Through an audacious plot, in which native women played the role of Delilah, the *Gustavus III* almost succumbed to a similar fate while anchored off Waikiki. Then, in retaliation for the theft of an anchor, the crew fired on a fleet of canoes and bombarded the village.

Bartlett, who wrote the account of this affray, later cruised Chinese waters, killed sea lions among the Kerguelen Islands of the Indian Ocean, chased whales in Mozambique Channel, and finally, when impressed into the British Navy, disappeared from our ken.

August 23, 1791

ALL the next day we lay with the main topsail to the mast and the courses held up, trading with the natives off Kealakekua Bay. We bought a great number of hogs, potatoes, breadfruit, grass lines, and kapa, which they make from the bark of trees and use for their clothing. It looks very much like calico but will not stand the water. We had upward of one hundred girls on board at a time, but not a man excepting one at a time. One of their chiefs came alongside with one of young Metcalfe's muskets. He was one of the stoutest men that I ever saw. Our captain compared his hindquarters to that of a bullock and would not suffer him to come aboard. Afterward the captain asked him for his musket and made signs for him to stand on the quarter bridge of our vessel, and when he did so the captain gave him his musket and at the same time fired a musket over his head, which made him jump overboard and swim ashore. At night every man took his girl and the rest jumped overboard to swim upward of three miles for the shore.

Early on the morning of August 25, we took our departure from the island of Hawaii, which is a very fine island with level land as far as we could see to the windward and with mountains on the lee shore with snow on them all the year round. At 10 A.M. saw the island of Maui. A great number of natives followed us from the island of Hawaii. At six o'clock the next morning we saw the island of Oahu and at 10 A.M. came to, in twenty fathoms of water. A great many natives came alongside with plenty of hogs, potatoes, yams, breadfruit, grass lines, spears, mats, mother-of-pearl beads, and a great number of curiosities. All hands were employed the next day in buying hogs and vegetables for a sea stock. During the morning the natives stole the buoy from our anchor and kept stealing and cutting all the hooks and thimbles they could get at.

The next day, Sunday, August 28, the king, his brother, and son came on board and made the captain a present of three red feather caps and some kapa cloth. Our captain gave them a musket and some powder. This day they sent all the handsomest girls they had on board and gave everyone their charge how to behave that night. When they gave the signal every one of them was to cling fast to the Europeans and to divert them while they cut our cable. At night every man in the ship took a girl and sent the remainder ashore. At 12 o'clock at night the watch perceived the ship adrift and at the same time every girl in the ship clung fast to her man in a very loving manner. All hands were called immediately. I had much to do to get clear of my loving mistress. The girls all tried to make their escape but were prevented by driving them all into the cabin. We found the cable cut about two fathoms from the hawsehole and made sail and stood off and on in the bay all night, and the next morning ran in and came to with the best bower. Saw a number of canoes trying to weigh our anchor. Three of the girls jumped overboard and two canoes came and picked them up. We fired a musket at one of them and a native turned up his backsides at us. We fired three or four more times, so they were glad to leave off and make for the shore.

The following morning a double war canoe came off with the men singing their war song. They paddled round our vessel and when abreast of the lee bow, seeing no anchor, they gave a shout and went on shore again. At eight o'clock forty or fifty canoes came off to trade but seemed shy of us. We bought some hogs and potatoes and sent several messages on shore to the king, but could not get our anchor from him. At twelve meridian the king sent a man off to dive for the anchor, pretending they had not stolen it. The boat was manned and two bars put in her as a reward for the native if he found the anchor. He dived several times but did not go to the bottom. He would stay under water longer than any man we ever saw. We could see him lie with his back against the bottom of the canoe for some minutes and then let himself sink down and come up again about three or four yards from the canoe, pretending that he had been to the bottom. Seeing this, we were fully convinced that they had our anchor ashore and meant to keep it, so we sent another message to the king and told him if he didn't send the anchor aboard that we should be obliged to fire on his town and lay it in ashes.

The next day we could not get a canoe to come alongside and could see natives running in from all parts of the island to assist the king if we attempted to land, which our mate was for doing, but our captain didn't approve of it and so at eleven o'clock we got under way and fired four or five broadsides into the village. We could see thousands of the natives running, one on top of the other. On the beach were a number of canoes off the lee bow, so we made for them and fired a broadside that stove a great many of them and sent the natives swimming and diving under water. We ran by two men swimming and shot one of them through the shoulder and killed him. We also ran alongside of a canoe with a man in her. We stood by with ropes to heave to him to get him on board, at the same time pointing six muskets at him if he refused to take hold of the rope. He laid hold of it and hauled himself aboard and let his canoe go adrift. We then hove about and came abreast of the village a second time, when the natives on the beach fired a musket and kept running along with white flags flying in defiance for us to land. Seeing no possibility of our getting our anchor we bore away and ran out to about two miles from the shore, where we gave the native on board six spikes and let him go to swim ashore. The seven girls on board we gave a number of beads and let them go likewise.

Blake Clark

Hawaiian Hospitality

Thomas Blake Clark, born in Tennessee in 1908, went to Hawaii directly from graduate study at Vanderbilt University, where he obtained a Ph.D. degree. From 1930 to 1942 he taught in the English Department of the University of Hawaii. On the scene when Japanese planes dropped their bombs on Oahu, Clark wrote the first book—*Remember Pearl Harbor!*—to describe the attack and the tense week that followed December 7, 1941. Later, as a journalist and free-lance writer in Washington, D. C., he published many articles and some half dozen books about Hawaii and other areas of the Pacific.

Having read widely in the accounts of early Pacific voyagers, Clark had come upon the journal of young Thomas Manby (1769–1834), who as master's mate under Captain George Vancouver visited Hawaii three times during 1792–94, and from it Clark composed the diverting narrative that follows.

EAGERLY Thomas Manby, master's mate on the good British ship *Discovery*, stood by the rail watching the great green island of Hawaii rise from a turquoise sea. Would these islands in the middle of the far Pacific prove to be the earthly paradise described by the sailors he had talked to in Liverpool? This first view met all expectations: a sky of the deepest blue in the world, masses of clean white clouds canopying the black volcanic peaks, the white flashes of tumbling waterfalls everywhere! It looked like a paradise, but what reception could they hope for from its people? Barely fifteen years had passed since England's great Captain Cook had been stabbed to death by angry natives on this pleasant-looking island.

The *Discovery* soon found a bay and brought to three miles from shore. There it prepared to wait for a visit from the island king, whose good will George III had instructed Captain Vancouver to cement for England. Even as early as 1793 the islands were attractive to English traders seeking a source of provisions.

Word of the great ship's arrival had flown quickly among the Hawaiians, so that now Manby became the joyful witness of a rare sight which ravished his sailor soul—a Hawaiian welcome. Natives swarmed on the white shore. From every side of the bay, hundreds of canoes were launched—canoes of all sizes, some large enough to hold forty people, some small and narrow, into which no more than two children could be wedged. Their paddles flashed in the sun as Manby watched the approach of the brown Hawaiians, men and women, old and young, handsome and hunchbacked. Laughing and shouting, crying, "Aloha, aloha!" they made a circle fifty canoes deep around the *Discovery*. The water was dotted with Hawaiians who had swum the three miles from the shore to the boat. As they trod water they held high in one hand gifts of aloha for the delighted sailors: live chickens, yellow yams, and some even clutched squealing little pigs!

The Englishmen were enchanted. Did their eyes deceive them, or was it true that hundreds of dark-eyed girls were swimming about in the water or sitting in canoes, eagerly looking up, beseeching, imploring to be invited to come on board? Their eyes were fine, black as jet, Manby said of the girls, "and when possessed by youth beam forth with languishing softness." The sailors leaned over the rail and selected the prettiest to ask aboard. "A slight beckon was a sufficient invitation, as they plunged like Sea Nymphs from their canoes, diving under every canoe that obstructed their passage to the ship. No incumbrance of clothes impeded their swimming, as they were in a state of nature except for a small strip of cloth applied like a fig leaf worn by our Grandmother Eve." Once they were on board, said the mate, "a towel absorbed the saline particles from their skin and left them cool as cucumbers. No bad thing in a tropical country. Our decks were crowded with young, good-natured girls, whilst the surface of the water around us was covered with some hundreds soliciting admittance. Our Bark instantly became a scene of Jollity and all was Pleasure and Delight."

"Oh, the elevation of spirit of the sailor attended by beautiful feminine companions!" philosophizes the enchanted mate. "It is them alone that can harmonize the soul, banish sorrows from the mind, and give mankind true felicity; even the uncivilized Brunette in a state of nature can do all this, and convinces that happiness is incomplete without them."

The sailors were shocked, however, upon getting their first close look at their chosen ones, to discover that virtually every one had had her two front teeth knocked out. They later learned that this was done in mourning for a king recently deceased, but at their first meeting, the happy Englishmen generously overlooked the detail. As Manby put it, ". . . being women, they were surely entitled to every civility and attention honest sailors could bestow."

At the height of the excitement, all uproar and confusion suddenly ceased. The Englishmen ran to the rail to discover the reason. Below them, they saw that the crowded canoes had cleft apart, leaving a wide straight lane from the ship to the shore. Their eyes followed the waterway, and there at the end of the three-mile path stood a Hawaiian of noble stature robed in a beautiful cloak of brilliant yellow feathers and wearing a splendid feather helmet. It was Kamehameha, king of the island of Hawaii.

The king stepped with dignity into the first and largest of fourteen double-outrigger canoes and commanded his forty-six warrior-paddlers to lead the way to the English ship. Kamehameha, spear in hand, stood proudly at the helm, an imposing masthead as his golden cloak and helmet gleamed in the tropic sun. The monarch and his squadron moved with dignity and precision, every man in all the fourteen canoes dipping his oar at exactly the same moment. They approached the *Discovery* and impressively passed three times around her before coming alongside.

The Hawaiians were quiet as shadows as they watched the pageant, but when their king boarded the big ship and exchanged the usual token of friendship with Captain Vancouver by touching noses, they set up an outcry that was deafening, so great was their joy. The uproar continued all the time the king was presenting Vancouver with the gifts he had brought—eighty large hogs, many chickens, pigs, coconuts, sweet potatoes, and all the island delicacies. The captain, in return, paid his compliments and informed Kamehameha that he had the honor to present His Majesty with a rare gift from the king of England to the king of Hawaii.

As they descended to the deck below, the Hawaiians on the ship, both men and girls, fled in panic, leaping overboard like schools of mullet. The startled Englishmen later learned that the mass exodus was caused by the fact that it was tabu for anyone, on pain of death, to stand or sit above the king.

In the hold lay the gift: a huge bull and five cows. As he presented them, Vancouver explained what they would do for Hawaii; how they would multiply and provide food and drink which he and King George hoped would make all the people of Hawaii healthier and happier. Kamehameha affected great pleasure, although actually he was somewhat afraid one of these "big hogs," as he called them, would bite. He timidly approached the bull, when suddenly the beast tossed its horned head and lunged to its feet. The king leaped back so recklessly that half of his retinue were sprawled on the deck.

In the captain's cabin, Vancouver threw about his guest's shoulders a long scarlet cloak, and stood him between two full-length mirrors where he could admire himself. The sight of himself in the gorgeous robe filled the king with such rapture that the cabin could not contain him. He capered about so that several persons were forced outside. Then he went up on the deck and posed with his arm against the mast where all could see and admire. When he climbed down the rope ladder into his canoe, it was with the sincerest good feelings toward Captain Vancouver and his crew.

The English king's gift cattle were put in the royal canoes and rowed ashore. As the natives flocked about the "big hogs," one of the cows, in her exuberance at feeling her hoofs on land again, unexpectedly began to cavort along the beach, kicking up her heels. Hawaiians fled as from a volcanic eruption. Thousands ran for the sea and plunged in. Others scrambled for safety on land. Every coconut tree was full in a moment. Some frightened natives jumped down precipices, others fled up rocks and houses, and not a man would reapproach the beach for half an hour. A few did not come back for two days.

Kamehameha, however, in spite of his early fears, was convinced of the worth of the cattle and placed a tabu upon them, which decreed death to any who dared harm them. And King George's "big hogs" flourished and multiplied for the future benefit of Hawaii.

For the Englishmen, these were halcyon days. Every man on the two ships, apparently, every common seaman, gunner, boatswain, mate, astronomer, botanist, and all the rest "folded youth and beauty in his arms." The girls stayed on board day and night. Their naïve delight in experiencing the pleasures of this new friendship with these white-skinned people charmed the Englishmen. How could anyone resist such creatures? they asked. Had Captain Cook really refused them? The celebrated navigator had achieved a kind of immortality among sea-going men as the only person reaching these South Sea islands who failed to indulge in the pleasure for which they were most famous. The captain's admirers always apologized for his singular abstinence on the grounds that he was very much in love with his wife. The boatswains and mates and sailors insisted indignantly that they, too, were in love with their wives, "but," they pointed out, "we are in Hawaii, whereas our wives are in England!"

When the time drew near to sail on to other islands, Kamehameha came on board to bid the Englishmen aloha. Was there not something they could give the king as a final token of their gratitude? Vancouver asked, and extracted from him a confession to a longing for a knife, fork, and plate. The utensils were presented ceremoniously to the proud king. "I shall now live like my brother-king, George," he boasted, and with many alohas left the ship.

In due time the two ships reached Kauai, three hundred miles and six islands north of Hawaii. After dinner Captain Vancouver, Manby, and a party of marines went ashore. Here they were received by the local chief, Enemoo, who was so helpful in directing the filling of the ship's water casks that Vancouver decided to leave a party on shore in order that the work might continue effectively in the morning. Manby, Lieutenant Puget, and six others he ordered to remain. Chief Enemoo, conscious of the high trust in his authority, allotted the men two large grass houses belonging to the king of the island.

At daybreak Enemoo emerged from his house with several of his wives, some of whom were extremely pretty. Manby thought it was a shame for them to be married to this old fellow. He was upward of fifty and disgusting to look at because of the quantities of awa he had consumed in his day. With Enemoo's party was "King George," the youthful son of the king of Kauai. The chief was inordinately proud of having the care of the boy.

The old gentleman was intrigued with desire to visit the *Discovery*, but loath to leave his wives and the king's son. After consultation with all his attendants, it was decided that he should go, take with him half his wives, and on his return permit "King George" with the other half to pay their respects to the *Discovery*. The stipulation was made that Manby should be left on shore as hostage in case anything should happen. Enemoo wept copiously for several minutes over "King George," and warned Manby that if harm came to the boy it would mean the white man's life. The mate "begg'd him to eradicate fear from his bosom by being perfectly at ease, promising at the same time I would amuse his little charge and divert his queens to the utmost of my abilities." (One of the younger wives had caught his fancy.) With this comforting assurance, Enemoo set off.

Soon after the excitement of Enemoo's departure was over, Manby conscientiously set out for the chief's household to keep his promise. Upon entering the walled enclosure, he was received by the young chiefess who had caught his eye. She was sitting under a tree, stringing beads. As if expecting him, she invited Manby to her side, sent for some fruit, and ordered fresh young coconuts to be gathered from a nearby tree.

Friendships grew apace in those islands, and soon the chiefess was amusing herself by tying and untying the Englishman's hair, which he wore long and clubbed behind. She wove yellow feathers into it, and decorated it with red hibiscus and white ginger blossoms.

Manby's white skin fascinated her. She all but undressed him to observe it closely. In the course of examining his left leg, she came upon some designs in tattoo which he had received in Tahiti. These delighted her. She sent for an old man, and the two examined the designs. Then ensued a conversation which produced a great deal of mirth. The mate explained the old man was able to interpret the Tahitian symbols. The artist who tattooed him, he said, "knew my disposition and how I was circumstanced at the moment; I conjecture he has imprinted some South Sea mark that will create a smile in most Islands in the Pacific Ocean."

Attracted by the laughter, the other wives of Enemoo joined the group. "Good natured souls!" the mate exclaims. "Without reluctance they yielded to the encircling arms of youth, so far superior to the loathsome embraces their situation obliges them to bear from the feeble and infirm Enemoo. Two hours I revilled in extatic enjoyment."

In the midst of his agreeable pastime, Manby was summoned to attend the young "King George." Although it was abominable to him to go, the mate had to admit that it was an extraordinary scene to which he was now introduced. This was the sight of "King George" at breakfast. He found the royal lad and his retinue sitting in the middle of the floor, surrounded by a semicircle of large, clean green leaves and calabashes. On the leaves rested four dogs, three hogs, and a number of fish; in the calabashes were poi and island fruit: breadfruit, bananas, and coconuts. No one but the youngster dared touch the food. He tore a steaming pig to pieces with his hands, making distributions to those around him, after first carefully selecting the choicest morsels for himself. Manby was accustomed to exhibitions of appetite from hearty English seamen, but they did not compare with that of this Hawaiian princeling. Alone he accounted for a whole dog within the space of a few minutes. Several fish, each weighing half a pound, followed the dog. They were in the same state as when taken from the sea, but down they went, scales, gills, and garbage.

Would Manby join him? The Englishman was game, and accepted a portion of pig and dog. "The hind leg of Bow-wow made an excellent breakfast," Manby claimed. "I picked the bone all but the Petty toes; them I made over to my next neighbor who was highly gratified with the delicious bit."

In spite of the fact that he was eating enough for three men, "King George" kept up a running fire of witty conversation. Did the king's sons in Beretani (Britain) have as much to eat as he had? Did they have as many wives as he was going to have? How did the princes' wives pass the time of day? On this general subject he made many facetious inquiries which created hearty laughter among the Hawaiians. They in turn passed the joke about with appropriate variations "with as much glee as the most accomplished courtiers," Manby found.

The meal over, "King George" proposed a walk. Manby observed, however, that everyone except the young prince did the walking. He preferred to be carried on the broad back of a Hawaiian attendant. He had asked Manby to bring his gun along, and was overjoyed when the Englishman brought down a duck. It amazed him that a flying bird could be speared at such a distance, and although Manby tried to explain, "King George" still thought the bayonet on the end of the gun was principally responsible for the duck's demise.

Returning from their excursion, they met old Enemoo just landing from his visit on board ship. He was highly pleased with the reception given him. He displayed the liberal presents that had been made him, presents chiefly of red cloth and ten-penny nails. He laid them out on the beach where the admiring Hawaiians might see the wealth and splendor of their chief. His wives he encouraged to display their gifts, too: ribbons and beads and trinkets, the most fascinating of which to everyone were numerous small mirrors.

That evening was spent in a manner designed to delight the hearts of English seamen. Enemoo, while keeping his own wives well within doors, collected a large group of ladies to entertain the visitors, and went off to bed. Manby and his companions passed a very jolly evening in the midst of these Hawaiian lasses "who," he says scornfully, "our fine gentlemen in England are pleased to denominate Savages."

The sailors vied with each other in diverting the Hawaiian girls. They tied knots in pieces of rope, and made Jacob's ladders with string. They danced the Highland Fling and executed lively Irish jigs. The most popular performer, however, was a marine who could make a penny disappear. Each time he concealed it he made it reappear from some most unexpected part of a lady's person. This mystifying performance completely captivated them.

As the hour grew late, the Englishmen, each having long ago selected a favorite, prepared to retire to the quarters provided for them by Enemoo in the king's houses. But no, the girls would not follow. The men were shocked and disappointed. In fact, they could not believe the girls were serious. Nevertheless, they would not be moved. All the sailors' tricks and entreaties were vain. "Tabu," the girls said, "tabu."

These sudden scruples were completely baffling. "Enemoo!" the Englishmen shouted. "Enemoo!" and roused their protector from the darkness of his grass house. The girls were right, explained the chief.

Hawaiian Hospitality

The tabu decreed death to any woman not a queen who entered a royal residence.

"An abominable prohibition!" declared the Englishmen; nevertheless the girls could not enter the sacred houses. Their friend, Enemoo, however, soon found a solution to the difficulty. He ordered snug little huts of sticks and mats to be quickly thrown up just outside the king's enclosure. The sailors never forgot this considerate kindness. These happy arbors were enough to inspire them to lyricism. Manby calls them "little bits of Paradise that excluded the Wind and Dew, accommodating at the same time three or four pretty females as the most effectual way of preventing the cold from penetrating. . . . Ten thousand execrations did I vent on the dawning day that compelled me to break from the arms of these bewitching girls so lovely and endearing."

But, execrations or no, the mate was summoned to attend the boats, and was forced to say farewell. "I displayed all my treasures before them, but could only prevail upon them each to except a pair of scissors and a small looking glass. They came down to the Boats to see me embark, and just before I left them they gave me two small pieces of Cloth folded up very curiously like a Ball which on opening I found to contain six pearls in each."

Nor was he forgotten by Enemoo's grateful wives and "King George," all of whom agreed he had fulfilled his promise to amuse and divert them. The prince presented him with ten finely woven mats. The women were more profuse in their donations. "One of the generous creatures gave me a supply of sixteen fowls and filled a canoe with young Cocoa Nuts ready to go off with me," he says. "I remained with these benevolent people to the last moment. The Boy kept his hand in mine to the last and cried at my bidding him farewell. Enemoo and each of the Royal Family took a friendly leave of me."

Manby found the ship preparing to sail. The decks were heaped with hogs, coconuts, bananas, and sweet potatoes. A great many canoes were alongside, too, carrying "good-natured Brunettes."

After dark, Manby was standing on deck, looking out toward the island, when suddenly a canoe appeared below. He was surprised to hear a woman's voice gently calling "Mappee, Mappee," the nearest the soft Hawaiian language could attain to "Manby." Instantly he knew the voice was that of Enemoo's pretty wife who had found so much to amuse her in his tattoo. She had slipped away from Enemoo's bed to say a final farewell and to bring her lover some handsome mats and rare pieces of kapa. The chiefess came aboard and lingered there with him for two hours. Then, "she again took a sorrowful adieu and left with a heavy heart."

The ship's prow turned toward the cold coasts of England, but the thoughts of the master's mate were with the green isle he was leaving behind. Before the crew of the *Discovery* had become acquainted with the Hawaiians, they had thought of the natives as a set of ferocious savages, the murderers of Captain Cook. Now their attitude was changed. Nowhere had they received such a welcome, such hospitality, as at the hands of the generous Hawaiians. If Captain Vancouver had fulfilled his mission of giving the islanders a good opinion of England, the islanders had completely charmed the sailors with Hawaii. "A warm, loving, sailor's paradise, indeed," said Manby, his face cooled by the trade winds that gently eased the *Discovery* into the tropical night.

John P. Marquand

You Can't Do That

A native of New England, John Phillips Marquand (1893–1960) also knew Hawaii. This author, winner of a Pulitzer Prize for his novel *The Late George Apley,* first resided in the Islands in the 1930's, when he began writing his "Mr. Moto" detective stories. During World War II Marquand served in Honolulu as a naval attaché in the Pacific theater.

In "You Can't Do That," one of his least-known stories, Marquand tells how a fabulous feather cloak came to be revered as one of the finest treasures in an aristocratic home above a New England seaport town. Young John March, on his first voyage into the Pacific, encounters the conflict between the trusting, trade-seeking Hawaiians of the sandalwood era and their exploiters, as represented by some ship captains. The drama of his decision is enhanced by Marquand's deep knowledge of the early Hawaiian scene.

SINCE the year 1806 a cloak of red and yellow feathers has hung in the hallway of the March house on the Ridge, with a helmet made from the same plumage suspended above it. These two articles have always held the same position on the wall, except for such times as they have been put away in camphor to protect them from the moths. The cloak was brought there by John March and indicates very accurately the first venture of the March ships in the fur-and-sandalwood trade with China. It was hung there by John March when he returned as supercargo on the brig *Polly,* Moses March, owner, and Elihu Griggs, master. A single glance at that cloak in the shady, spacious hallway of that square Federalist house is startling to anyone who is even remotely familiar with the curiosities of the South Seas.

It hangs there, an alien object, and yet, through association, somehow strangely suitable to a house like the old March house in a

New England seaport town. Granted that its presence there is known to many scholars, familiarity cannot avert a shock of surprise at a sight of that vivid garment, for it is one of the most beautiful objects ever conceived by the mind or executed by the hand of man. It is strange, too, to realize that if that cloak and the helmet above it were sold today, their price would probably equal the March profits in their precarious trade of another century. It is a long, fine cloak —and the Marches have always been careful of everything they have laid their hands on—one of the best of the hundred-and-some-odd feather garments which are known to be extant today, and there will never be another made. The o-o which supplied those yellow feathers, only one beneath each wing, a shy bird which once fluttered through the crimson-blossomed ohia and the tree-fern forests of the Hawaiian mountains, is virtually extinct, and the bird that wore the red plumage is in hardly a better case. He is vanishing from the face of this earth like the genial race whose ancestors collected and attached those feathers to their delicate base of fiber netting in a manner so admired by Captain Cook. Granted that the labor which went into the making of that garment is beyond all accurate calculation, the result was worth it. The reds and yellows are nearly as vivid as when the coat was new. They glisten there in the hallway, jewel-like, with a depth of luster and lacy velvet texture that is more vital than inanimate. On an evening when the lights are lit, John March's cloak glows like flame and there is an element of awe in its splendor.

This is not odd, for it was intended to indicate greatness. The red lozenge pattern upon the yellow marks it as belonging not alone to one of the alii but to a Hawaiian chief of a royal lineage that was very near to kingship. Its size and the amount of yellow is a sufficient indication of its former owner's greatness. If the shadow of a commoner were to touch the shadow of the man who wore it, that commoner would suffer death, for the man who wore it was sublimated in the complicated feudal ritual of his islands into a being more than human. The feather kahili was carried behind him; an attendant bore his calabash of koa wood to preserve his spittle, his nail parings, and his fallen hair, so that they might not fall into the hands of enemies whose kahunas, or witch doctors, might use them in fatal incantations. When the man who wore that cloak walked abroad, the populace assumed a prone position on pain of death. Some trace of the majesty of its first owner's presence still seems to linger about that feather cloak, incongruously, in a New England town.

The cloak was owned by the chieftain Kualai, as his name is spelled, probably incorrectly, in the March letter books and the log of the brig *Polly*, since there were no missionaries then to bring order to the Hawaiian phonetics—no missionaries, no mosquitoes, no red ants to kill the kou trees, no colds, and no disease. Kualai ruled his share of the Kona coast on what is now known as the Big Island under the protection of the great King Kamehameha in the days when John March was young. In Kualai's youth he had been one of the king's best warriors; in the war exercises he could evade six spears thrown at him simultaneously from varying directions; and he could trace his descent from one of the gods who had sailed with his attendants from the south.

Kualai gave his cloak and helmet to young John March when the *Polly* anchored in a bay on the Kona coast to exchange Yankee notions for sandalwood before proceeding to Canton. There is no doubt that John March valued the gift, for it is mentioned in his will. The clause reads:

"Item, the Feather Cloak that was given me by my friend Kualai on my first voyage to the Sandwich Islands, and the feather hat that goes with it, I leave to my daughter, Polly March, and I ask her to guard it carefully."

John March sailed other seas before he died and brought back other curious things, but there is every reason why the cloak should have had a value to him which was more than intrinsic; and his descendants have never sold that cloak because of the reason why it was given him, a reason that is closely connected with honor and integrity. John March was a shrewd trader, but he was an honest man.

In the New England harbor town which was the home port for the March ships, a voyage around the world was not an unusual matter when John March was young. As long as John March could remember, his town had been a port of travelers, although a part of it was cast in the narrow mold of puritanical tradition. When John March was young, no music was allowed in the white church with

the rooster on its spire, where merchants and clerks and shipwrights
and returned mariners listened for three hours each Sunday to discourses on original sin. Not even the note of a pipe was allowed,
to indicate the pitch for the singing of the psalms, because such a
concession was considered an encouragement to the idolatrous errors
of papacy. Yet in such surroundings of a Sunday one could see from
the square box of the March pew a distinctly cosmopolitan congregation, for the world across the seas was closer to the town in those
days than it has ever been since. Nearly every man and boy and
most of the women in the pews and the Reverend Thomas himself,
who thundered forth his nasal sermon while the sands ran from his
hourglass on the pulpit, knew their geography as well as they knew
the intricacies of their catechism. They could talk familiarly of the
Baltic ports and of St. Eustatius and St. Kitts. There were plenty
who knew the ivory factories and the slave pens on the Grain Coast
and the anchorages along Fernando Po. There were plenty who had
seen the sand upon the lead from soundings off Madagascar. The
weather off Cape Horn was common talk. A restless, burning energy that made the town a lively place, except on Saturday nights
and Sunday, had driven others to the factories at Canton. The townspeople were familiar with nearly every world port where money
could be gained, for the town lived from shipping. One had to go,
of necessity, a long way to make money then, what with European
wars and privateers and orders in council and blockades. It was a
time for gambling with lives and ships, a time of huge losses and
huge gains, and no one could judge which until the ships came in.

It seemed hardly more than a piece of everyday business to John
March when his father called him into the square parlor of the
March house on the Ridge. It was an evening in April; a bright,
fresh fire was burning in the parlor, and the candles were lighted on
the mahogany table in the center of the room. Moses March and a
man whom John March had never seen before were seated somewhat stiffly by the table with a punch bowl between them. When
John March saw the punch, he knew that they were discussing important business, for his father, particularly in his later years, was
abstemious with liquor. Moses March had not changed much since
John March could remember him. His brown hair, done in a queue,
was heavily streaked with gray, and the shrewd lines around his eyes

and mouth were deeper and more pronounced. There was an added stoop to his lanky shoulders, but his eyes were as bright as ever and his voice was vibrant, without any quaver of age.

"John," said Moses March, nodding at his guest, "this here is Captain Griggs from Boston. Captain Griggs, he's been sailing for the Perkinses in the fur trade."

In many ways it seemed to John March that Captain Griggs was a younger replica of his father. The captain had the same bony facial contours and the same slouch to his shoulders. When he spoke he had the same flat voice, but his eyes were different—more mobile and less steady. The captain raised a hand before his tight-lipped mouth and coughed, then he rose from his chair with a creaking of his joints, a tall, somber man who might have been a deacon in a church. His eyes met John's and looked away toward some invisible object on the floor, then darted back and looked away again.

"Pleased to meet you," he said.... "I compliment you, Mr. March; he's handy-looking, that's a fact."

"He's kind of peaked," said Moses March, "but John here's almighty quick at figures."

There was a silence. Captain Griggs ladled himself a fresh tumbler of punch, drank it at a gulp, and said, "He needs to be. It pays to be sharp, don't it, Mr. March?"

Moses March smiled in faint embarrassment. He had never been able to acquire a manner with his captains, nor to stop undue familiarity.

"Yes," he said, "I guess so.... John, Captain Griggs is taking out the *Polly*. You're sailing with him, supercargo."

John March looked at Captain Griggs again. The captain was staring intently at a lemon peel in the bottom of his glass. The news was entirely unexpected.

"Where to, Father?" he asked.

"Where you haven't been, son," said Moses March, "but you've heard the talk, I guess. Up along the Northwest Coast for sea otter, trading with the savages, then to these new islands you've heard Enoch Mayo talk about, to put aboard sandalwood, then the whole cargo sold at Canton for tea. The *Polly*, she's sailing the end of the month. You'll start in working over the cargo tomorrow. Your mother, she'll get your things packed."

John March nodded without speaking, and he showed no emotion. It was not the first time that his father had surprised him, because it was one of his father's maxims never to talk about what he proposed to do until he was ready. His father was always reaching for something new; his mind was always working. Probably he had been pondering over the matter all winter, and now, as though he were speaking about arrangements for hauling firewood, he was making plans to send one of his vessels where a March ship had never gone before.

It was strange to think that while he sat there, a homely, uncouth man, his mind could reach around the world and back. His life had never seemed so plain or matter-of-fact. The order of the March house, each piece of furniture exactly in its place, had never seemed so perfect as when he spoke of that voyage. That literal order of the letter books and the columns in the ledger were all a part of the business. There was no expression of doubt, because they all knew by then that a ship could go wherever there was water.

Captain Griggs ladled himself another tumbler of punch and blew his nose on a long blue handkerchief which seemed to have imparted some of its own color to his nose. Not having been asked to sit down, John March stood examining his new captain, comparing him with other seafaring men whom he had met. The captain was evidently a heavy and competent drinker and no doubt a capable master, but behind his lantern jaws and his high, narrow forehead there were hidden convolutions of character beyond John March's grasp. He only knew that by the time the voyage ended he would know the captain like a book. At the present time all John March could do was to stand staring at the pictures of his own imagination, striving to conjure up sights which he and Captain Griggs would see. Captain Griggs was staring at him moodily across the brim of his glass.

"He'll do. He'll fill out," he said. "He'll be aft with the mate and me, of course. Does he know navigation, sir?"

"Yes," said Moses March; "he ain't a fool, but I hadn't aimed to make him a sailor. He'll handle this business ashore when I get through."

Captain Griggs nodded in a melancholy way. "I hope he ain't squeamish," he said. "He'll see some rough sights, like as not. We have a saying on the coast: 'You hang your conscience on the Horn.' "

"Yes," said Moses March, "I've heard it, but you, Captain, I'd like for you to keep your conscience on your ship."

"God bless you, sir," Captain Griggs said quickly, "no owner's ever complained of me. I'm always in my owner's interest. It's just dealing with these here savages, I mean. They've killed crews on the coast and they're murdering thieves on the islands." He rose stiffly. "You'll be satisfied, Mr. March. You'll be pleased as punch with me. There ain't no tricks in the trade that I don't know thereabouts. Four four-pounders and a bow chaser will be enough, and the grape-shot and plenty of small arms, and thanking you, I'll pick my own mate, and now I'll be under way, and I'll wish you a very good evening, and you, mister." He nodded to John March.

When the captain was gone, Moses March called to John March again.

"John," he said, "set down. You've been to the Baltic; you've been to the Indies; and I'd proposed keeping you ashore, but I want for you to learn this trade when it's still new." Moses March paused and rubbed his jaw. "I hear tell there's money in it, and we're going where there's money."

"Yes, sir," said John March.

"It seems," his father continued, staring at the fire, "as how these savages put aboard furs, and these other savages put aboard sandalwood, for nothing more than notions and novelties in trading goods. Well, I got 'em for you; you and Griggs can get the rest. He'll try hard. He has his money and more than the usual prerequisites."

"Yes, sir," said John March.

"And sandalwood and furs are worth a mint of money in Canton."

"Yes, sir," said John March.

"You know about it, do you?"

"Yes, sir," said John March; "I've heard 'em talking."

His father smiled. "That's right," he said; "listen to 'em talk, but keep your own mouth shut. Have you anything to say?"

John March thought a moment. He had a number of things to say, but he kept them to himself. "No," he said. "I can obey orders, I guess. You know what you're doing, I guess, Father."

Moses March stroked his chin slowly, and then he asked a sudden question: "How did you like Griggs?"

"He looks too sharp to me," John March said, "but I guess we'll get along."

"Yes," said Moses March, "he's sharp, but maybe that's all right. But mind you watch him, John. I'm sharp, but I guess I'm honest. Mind you watch him."

Even when he was three thousand miles away from town and farther than that by water, something of the town was always with him. The *Polly* was a part of the town because she had been built in the yards by the river, a good tight brig of two hundred and fifty tons. The crew was a part of the town, because most of the men before the mast had been born within its limits. The sense of the nearness of things he knew gave John March a certain peace when everything else was strange. The emptiness of the Pacific coast, the incredible size of its fir trees, the frowning menace of its mountains would have oppressed him if it had not been for that sense of home. As it was, everyone stood together and behaved, in order to keep reputations intact when they got home.

John March was used to work. He was satisfactory to Captain Griggs, and he was treated well because he was the owner's son. Once they began bartering for furs off the Northwest Coast, there was no doubt that the captain knew his business, and John March admired in silence the way the captain worked. Martin Sprague, the mate, knew his business, too, in caring for the ship. The men were armed; there was a sharp lookout day and night. The four-pounders were loaded wth grapeshot, and the matches were kept burning. Only a definite number of the painted dugout canoes of the Indians were allowed alongside, and only a certain number of savages were permitted on deck to trade. There were very few ships off the coast that year, so that the selection of pelts was particularly fine. Sea-otter pelts came aboard in great quantity in exchange for powder, shot, nails, muskets, beads, and blankets. It was a pretty sight to see the captain read faces and weigh the desire to sell. He seemed to have an intuitive sense of when to bargain and when to buy immediately.

"If there's any trade goods left after the islands," he said, "we'll stand back here again and use 'em up. It's a pity to see this fine fur wasting here. I wish we had six ships."

John March could feel the excitement as small goods turned suddenly into a valuable cargo. It was better than any figuring in the countinghouse to see the fur pelts come aboard and to estimate their probable value in a Chinese port.

"Yes, sir," said Captain Griggs, "it seems a pity to haul off and leave this. We ought to buy the villages out and to the devil with the islands and the wood."

They were in the cabin at the time, the captain and Sprague, the mate, a heavy muscular man, and John March, a thin blond boy.

"Mr. Sprague," said the captain, "pass the rum. What do you think, mister? Shall we do all the trading here and simply water at the islands?"

Martin Sprague rubbed the palm of his left hand over the knuckles of his right. "I never seen trading so easy," he said. "Yes, sir, I think I should."

Then John March spoke up; it was the first time on the voyage that he'd made a positive statement. "We can't," he said.

Captain Griggs set down his glass and scowled. "Young man," he said, "I'm surprised at you. You ought to know better. You do know better. You've behaved yourself fine up till now, my boy. You've done your duty, and more, and I shall be pleased to report favorably to your father if you continue, but there's two things for you to get inside your head. The first is, you were sent here to learn to trade. You don't know this business, and don't you forget it. The second is, I'm captain, and this brig goes where I tell it to. I'm sorry to be obliged to tell you straight."

John March did not shift his position at the table. He knew that he was young and that he was green. He had interrupted solely from a conscientious sense inherited from his race. It had come over him that he was a representative of the March family and of the March cargo. Now that the eyes of the older men were upon him, he found himself stammering, because he was shy in those days, but his hesitation only made him the more determined to speak out.

"Captain," he said, "I understand what you say. This is your ship, of course, but you are under owner's orders, just as I am. A portion of these trade goods was allotted for furs and the rest for sandalwood. The owner's orders are to stop and trade at the Sandwich Islands. There may be more profit here, but we are to establish relations there. We may send out another ship."

Captain Griggs leaned half across the table. "Young man," he inquired, "are you insinuating I'm not looking after owner's interests? Because if you are, I will not tolerate it. I'm thinking of my owner all the time, and a sight better than you are, maybe. We'll make for the islands tomorrow, and there's an end to that, but if there's any trade goods left when we're through there, why, then, with your kind permission, we'll come back here. I hope that satisfies you."

"Yes," said John March, "it does, and I ask your pardon, Captain."

Mr. Sprague rose. "I must be up with the watch," he said, "if you'll excuse me, sir. . . . Will you come with me, Mr. March?"

It was a fine night on deck, clear, with bright stars and a faint, quivering circle of the northern lights. The night was cool, without a breath of wind. The ship, with her own small lights, was like an insignificant fragment of a distant world anchored there in space. The mate took out his pipe and tinderbox. There was a flash of spark as he expertly hit the flint against the steel, and then the tinder glowed.

"Johnny March," he said, "I've kind of got to like you. Now you listen to what I say. This kind of spark's all right, but not the kind that you were striking in the cabin. You leave the old man be. He's as good a master as there is, and he's honest with the owners, and that's all we have to care for. I've sailed with Griggs before. I don't need to tell you that a master's king aboard his ship, and you know it makes 'em queer. I've never seen a skipper yet who liked to be crossed. You better leave him be."

"Yes, sir," said John March.

"And listen, Johnny," the mate said, "the islands are a fine place. You'll like the islands. The islands are like heaven, pretty near. The captain will take you ashore, of course, to make the bargain. You'll see plenty of funny sights, but keep your mouth shut, Johnny, except to say 'Yes, sir,' to the captain. We got a long way yet to go."

"Yes, sir," said John March.

"That's right," said Sprague, "that's right. I like a tight-lipped boy."

It was said in the forecastle of the *Polly,* just as it was said aft, that Johnny March was taciturn. As a supercargo he had no fixed duties in working the ship, and few knew much about him except that he was March's son. They only saw him as a thin, brown-faced, gray-eyed boy with yellow hair who made no trouble or complaint. They did not know the impression which strange sights made upon him, because he was studiously silent on that voyage to the islands, hardly ever venturing a remark, only answering courteously when addressed. No one on the *Polly* knew—and perhaps it was just as well—that his thoughts were poetic, because there was no room for poetry on a Yankee trading brig.

The evening before they sighted land, he had a sense of the land's nearness. The banks of clouds off the port bow as the sun went down were pink and gold, and were more like land clouds than sea clouds. The *Polly* was moving in the steady breath of the trades, and the setting sun struck the bellying sails forward, making their colors soft and golden. The only sounds were the creaking of wood, the straining of ropes, and the splash of waves on the bow. He had seen many evenings like that one, but subtly this was different. There was a mystery in the warmth of the air, an intangible unreality in the cloud banks. Captain Griggs came and stood beside him, smelling strongly of rum.

"Mr. Sprague," he said, "you've got everything locked up, I hope. Tomorrow we'll be overrun by black thieves and their women. Clew up the courses and continue under topsails. Set a watch up in the crosstree and keep an eye out for breakers. We must not get in too close tonight.... And, Mr. March—"

"Yes, sir," said John.

"You and I will go ashore."

"Yes, sir," said Johnny March, and then he cleared his throat: "How will we speak to them, sir?"

"You'll soon learn, boy," said Captain Griggs. "You've got a lot to learn. These islands have kings, or chiefs, and the chiefs will have someone who can speak trading English. The sandalwood is up in the mountains. It will be the property of the king, or chief. We will agree to purchase so many piculs, and he'll send his people to cut it. The chief will come aboard to see our goods, and we will make a bargain for the cargo, payable when the wood is safe aboard, you understand. There's no need to make our crew work when the chief will make his people load it. The islanders are handy men on ships. We'll go to see the chief, and we'll make the chief a present. Break out that clock that strikes the hour, and two cutlasses. That will be enough, and maybe"—Captain Griggs paused and hesitated—"three yards of bright print calico; he ought to like it—paper's all they dress in."

"Yes, sir," said Johnny March. "Did you say that they dressed in paper?"

The hard lines of the captain's face wrinkled into an indulgent smile.

"Young man," he said, "it's a fact they dress in paper, when they dress at all, which isn't often. The women, they pound it out of the bark of a tree. They have nothing else on the islands, or almost nothing. Time was when they'd sell a pig for three tenpenny nails, and their women sell their virtue for less than that, which isn't strange, because they have no morals. Why, their menfolk bring 'em right aboard for the time we stay. Will you come below for a glass of rum?"

"No, thank you, sir," said Johnny March. "I'll stay on deck—that is, if you don't mind."

The sun had dipped out of sight behind a bank of clouds, and then suddenly the light was gone. Without a prelude of dusk, the dark came over them, like a warm black garment. It seemed only a second before that the sky had been red and gold. Then, in another second, the sky was a void of darkness, filled with the trade wind and with stars. He stood for a while listening to the wind singing through the ropes, and then he went below.

It was still dark when John March was awakened by a long-drawn-out call and by Mr. Sprague's voice shouting, "Where away?" and he knew that they had come in sight of land. Once he was up on deck, the topsails were slatting sleepily, and off the starboard bow there was a glow in the sky like fire.

"We've hit it to a second, sir," the mate was saying to Captain Griggs. "Yonder's the volcano; we're in the lee of the mountains."

Captain Griggs was a shadow in the starlight. It was too dark to see his face, but his voice was satisfied. "A pretty piece of navigating," he said, "if I do say so, mister. There'll be an inshore breeze by dawn, and then we'll make the bay." He sniffed the air. "We can't be far from land," he said, "but there's no use heaving lead. It shelves off here as deep as hell. There'll be an inshore breeze with dawn."

"Is that a light yonder, sir?" asked Johnny March.

Near the horizon there was a twinkling, glimmering point.

"Your eyesight's good," the captain said. "Yes, that will be a fire. We're close to land."

The dawn came as suddenly as the dark, in a swift rush of light, as though a hand had snatched away a veil, and John March saw the land. It was a solemn sight to see land which seemed to have risen out of nowhere. Off the bows of the *Polly* was a mountain, black and green, that rose in a gradual slope up into snow and clouds. The coast was dark from volcanic rock which made ugly black gashes between green forests. Close to the water's edge there was a fringe of palms and beaches between black lava headlands. The sea was smooth and calm and streaked with violet; the air was as soft as the air of spring at home and was subtly laden with the smells of land. All the colors were soft in a faint, early-morning haze. The black rocks merged into reds and purples. The greens of the upland forest blended subtly from shades of silver to emerald, and Captain Griggs was right—a soft breeze was filling the sails, moving the *Polly* gently along the coast.

"That's where the sandalwood comes from," Mr. Sprague was saying, "up yonder in the mountains. The coast hereabouts is the favorite place of the kings. Do you see the stone walls and the yellow thatch of the houses of the villages? The chiefs own straight from the tops of the mountains to the sea. How do you like it, son?"

The question made John March tongue-tied. "I think it's very handsome, sir," he said, "a very pleasant island."

The *Polly* was moving under topsails into a small bay. It opened out before them, a smooth amphitheater of water, surrounded by high cliffs. "Yonder's where the kings are buried," the mate said. "They scrape the flesh off their bones and tie them up in paper cloth and put them there in caves with their canoes."

At the head of the bay John March could see a beach fringed with tall palm trees, the leaves of which moved idly in the breeze, and he could see the thatch of houses beneath them. There was a dark crowd of people on the beach, pushing canoes into the water, log dugouts, balanced by an outrigger and manned by naked paddlers. Captain Griggs was wearing clean linen and a black broadcloth coat, although the day was hot.

"Mister," he said, "we'll anchor. Let go falls and clew up lower topsails and order the stern boat cleared. You can allow the women aboard, Mr. Sprague."

By the time the anchor struck the water, the *Polly* was surrounded by canoes and the water was full of swimmers who were pulling themselves up the anchor chain, smiling and laughing; men and women as beautiful as statues, their straight dark hair glistening with the water. Captain Griggs stared at his visitors sourly from the quarter-deck.

"They've got the minds of children," he said. "The chief's man should be here. Look at those shameless hussies, will you? There's no decency on these islands. They don't care for decency; no, they don't care."

As Captain Griggs finished speaking, a native pushed his way through the crowd at the waist and walked aft; evidently a man of importance, because the crowd gave way respectfully. He wore a pair of sailor's castoff trousers, and his skin was lighter than the others'. His voice rose above the babel of strange words in English.

"Mr. Captain," he called out, "I am Kualai's man."

"Who's he?" asked Captain Griggs. "The chief?"

The other nodded, bobbing his head up and down, still smiling. "Yes," he said, "yes, yes. And he sends me because I speak English good. I've been a sailor on a Boston boat. I speak English very good. Kualai sends me to say aloha. He is glad to see you. He asks you will you trade for wood?"

"Yes," said Captain Griggs, "we're here for wood. What's your name?"

"Moku," said the native. "Billy Adams Moku. Kualai ask what name."

The captain nodded condescendingly. "Captain Griggs," he said, "brig *Polly*. Moses March, owner. We're carrying very fine calicoes, ironware, tinware, lead and copper, and even a few muskets. Has your chief got wood?"

Moku nodded. "The wood is coming down. Kualai, he will see you." He pointed to a laden canoe. "Kualai sends you food."

Captain Griggs looked at the canoe carefully as it drew alongside. "Very good," he said. "When will he see me?"

"Now," said Moku. "He waits on the shore."

"Mister," the captain called, "have the stern boat lowered. Mr. March and I will go ashore, and, Mr. March, give that man a pocketknife and bring along the presents."

The dark sand of the beach at the head of the bay seemed insecure under John March's feet, since he had been so long on the water. In the sunshine like a warm June day at home, every sight and sound was new. The crowd of natives standing on the beach drew back from them shyly and smiled, but their tongues kept chattering busily; commenting, probably, on the way these strangers looked. The chief's man walked first, then Captain Griggs, nonchalant and cool, and then John March behind him. They walked along a path beneath a grove of coconut palms and beneath large broad-leafed trees such as he had never seen. They were threading their way through a settlement of houses made of dried grass, past small gardens enclosed between walls of black volcanic rock. His memory of that day always brought back living green against dark rock, and dark smiling faces and red hibiscus flowers. In his memory of the place a soft breeze was always blowing and there was always a strange dry rattle from the leaves of the coconut palms.

There was a group of larger houses not far back from the beach which evidently belonged to a man of importance. Natives were busying themselves about a fire in a pit; women and children were staring from open doorways. There was an open pavilion near the center of this group of buildings, and the chief's man led them toward it. Seated in a Cantonese armchair under the pavilion was one of the largest men that John March had ever seen. He was middle-aged and so corpulent that the chair seemed to creak beneath his weight. A single look at his face was enough to indicate that he was the ruler, Kualai, of whom the man had spoken. The face was set in benign lines that could only have come upon it through suave and complete authority. It was all that was necessary to indicate his rank, but he also had the exterior show of office. He was wearing a yellow-and-red cloak of feathers, dazzlingly bright, which fell below his waist, and an attendant stood behind him holding a large stick which bore a tuft of colored feathers on the end. Moku stopped dead still at the entrance of the pavilion, and the great man rose from his chair and stepped slowly forward, gracefully, in spite of his heavy paunch. It was plain that he had seen other white men and knew something of their manners, because he smiled graciously and held out his right hand. At the same time he spoke melodiously in a language that was all vowels, so that his words sounded like rippling water.

"What's he saying?" asked Captain Griggs.

"Kualai," Moku translated, "he say he's, oh, very glad to see you."

"Well, I guess we're glad to see him too," said Captain Griggs as he shook hands. Then John March saw that Kualai was looking at him.

"He wants to know," said Moku, "who is the other man?"

"Tell him he's the son of the man who owns the vessel," said Captain Griggs.

"He wants to know," said Moku, "is he a chief's son?"

"Tell him yes," said Captain Griggs.

"He would like," said Moku, "to feel his hair. He would like to know if it is real."

"Take off your hat," said Captain Griggs, "and let him feel your hair. Don't be afraid of him. He won't hurt you."

"All right," said Johnny March. He felt very much like a child as he walked toward Kualai, for the man, now that he was standing, must have been close to seven feet in height. His skin was glistening with coconut oil. He was stretching out his arm. He touched Johnny March's hair gently and then he pulled it softly. Johnny March looked up at him and smiled, and Kualai smiled back.

"Break out the presents," said Captain Griggs, "bow to him and put 'em on the ground."

Kaulai's face lighted up at the sight of the clock when John March held it toward him. It was evident that he had never seen such a mechanism—a battered ship's chronometer whose useful days were over. He touched it gingerly and imitated its sound.

"Tick-tick," he said, and John March nodded and repeated after him, "Tick-tick." That interchange of words always seemed to him ridiculous, but somehow there was an exchange of thought with the words which made them friends.

"He asks you to stay and eat," said Moku. "He will come on the ship tomorrow and see the goods, and he asks the young man to stay with him until the trade is over, to sleep inside his house."

Captain Griggs muttered something beneath his breath, and then he said, "March, you'd better stay."

"Yes sir," said John March, "I'd be very glad to stay." He turned to Moku. "Tell him I'll be glad."

Then Moku spoke again: "Kualai says he will trade with the young man."

"All right," said Captain Griggs, "as long as I'm there too. And tell him"—Captain Griggs's eyes shifted toward the bay and back—"you tell him I want the wood measured on the beach and put aboard by his people. Tell him my men are tired." And then he drew a bottle of rum from his pocket and added plaintively: "Ain't we had enough of this? Let's everybody have a drink, and bring on the dancing girls."

Some half-perceptible change in Captain Griggs's voice made John March turn to watch him. The captain's face was bleak and impassive, but his eyes were shifting from point to point, from the chief to John March, then away to the matting on the ground, then to the houses of the settlement. John March knew him well enough by then to know that the captain was turning over in his mind some thought which he wished entirely to conceal.

"Ah," he said suddenly, "here comes some wood." And he nodded toward a path which led upward to the mountains.

A dozen men and women were staggering down the path in single file, each bearing a burden of long sticks, and John March knew from hearsay that these were the chief's people, who had been sent to the upland forests where the sandalwood grew. The chief called out an order, which Moku ran to obey, and a few moments later a pile of the sandalwood lay on the matting before his chair, a heap of sticks which varied in size from a few inches to a foot in diameter. The bark had been stripped off, leaving a heavy wood of deep yellow which verged on orange. Captain Griggs ripped out his clasp knife, whittled at the sticks, and sniffed the shavings.

"It ain't bad," he said; "in fact, it's prime."

He was right that the wood was fine, since sandalwood was plentiful in the islands then, when the trade was new, and John March did not suspect that he would live to see the time when hardly a stick would be left standing on the entire island group. Captain Griggs stood there, staring at the pile of wood, apparently lost in thought.

"Tell him we'll pay him well for it," he said, and his voice was soft and almost kindly, "once he lands it on the deck."

But all the while John March was sure that Captain Griggs was concealing some other thought.

It took nearly two weeks to collect the wood and measure it, a space of time which moved in a peculiar series of days and nights, but it was strange to John March how soon the life there grew familiar. Though he could hardly understand a word which was spoken, though nearly every sight and sound in those two weeks was new, he became aware immediately of certain human values. Kualai, in his way, was a cultivated man of gentle breeding, who had developed his own taste for the arts, and qualities of understanding which were the same on that isolated island as they were elsewhere. He would sit for hours of an evening watching interpretive dances and listening to his minstrels sing of the exploits of his ancestors. He had a good eye for patterns in the kapa cloth, and a nice skill in various games of chance, which he played daily with his choice companions, but, above all, he had a sense of hospitality. He lost no occasion to make John March feel politely that he was a welcome guest. He took him fishing in his war canoe; he took him to the caves and the lava rocks; he took him to watch the young men perform feats of strength; he was even careful that John March's privacy should not be disturbed unduly. When he came aboard the *Polly,* he kept John March beside him. He was greatly pleased with the calico and nails and lead and copper in the trading cargo, but he went through the intricacies of the bargain in a detached way, like a gentleman. In those days trading was easy on the islands, before the chiefs were glutted with material possessions.

"He say he want you to be happy," Moku said the last time Kualai came aboard; "he want you to come again."

"Tell him we're happy," said Captain Griggs. "He understands when all the wood's aboard that we'll give out the goods."

Moku nodded. "He understands," he said; "he knows you're good men."

Captain Griggs coughed slightly. "I shall want Mr. March back with me," he said, "tomorrow morning. . . . Mr. March, you come here; I want to speak with you in the cabin."

It occurred to John March, when they were in the cabin, that it was the first time since they had been on the island that he and Captain Griggs had been alone. Captain Griggs rubbed his long hands together and poured himself a glass of rum.

"Young man," he said, "you've done fine. You've kept that old heathen happy, and that's all we needed—to keep him happy—and now we're all finished shipshape. We'll get the wood stowed tonight"—Captain Griggs smiled happily—"and tomorrow they can come and take off their goods, but I want you aboard first, understand?"

"Yes, sir," said John March, "but there's one thing I don't see. I don't see why you haven't put the goods ashore before this, sir."

Captain Griggs poured himself a second tumbler of rum.

"Young man," he said, "when you take a few more voyages you'll understand you can't trust natives. How do you know we'd get the wood if we put the goods ashore?"

"Because Kualai's honest," John March said.

Captain Griggs looked thoughtfully at the ceiling. "Maybe," he said, "and maybe not. Anyways, we've got the wood. You come aboard tomorrow." And Captain Griggs smiled genially, but even when he smiled, John March had a suspicion that something had been left unsaid, that there was some thought in the captain's mind of which he had not spoken.

Mr. Sprague came up to get him the next morning, carrying a bundle of small presents and perspiring in the heat of the early sun.

"Say good-by to the chief," he said. "The captain's orders are to leave right now. You're to stay aboard until we sail. The quarter boat's waiting at the beach."

John March was sorry, now that it was time to go. He walked to Kualai and held out his hand. "Thank you very much," he said, and the interpreter, Moku, gave him back the chief's answer:

"He say for you to come back soon."

The canoes were gathering about the *Polly* already, by the time he reached the beach. He and Mr. Sprague sat in the stern sheets of the quarter boat while two men rowed, helped by a light breeze offshore.

It was only when they were halfway out that John March was aware of something disturbing.

"Look," he said; "they're setting the lower topsails!"

"Yes," said Mr. Sprague shortly, "so they are. We've got a fair breeze, haven't we?"

"But it'll take a good six hours to put off those goods," said Johnny March.

Mr. Sprague put a heavy hand on his knee and smiled. "Don't you worry, boy," he said. "Captain Griggs will see about those goods."

They were beside the companion ladder by that time, and even John March was puzzled, but nothing more. He was not aware of Captain Griggs's idea until he was on the poop, then he saw that the tarpaulins were off the guns and that men were beside them with matches, and then he saw that the decks were clear and that the sandalwood and the trade goods were all back in the hold. Captain Griggs grinned at him.

"Safe and sound," he said. "You've done very well, Mr. March; your father will be very pleased, I think. . . . Mister, you can man the capstan now."

John March found himself stammering: "But what about the goods, Captain? We haven't put the goods ashore."

"No, boy," said Captain Griggs, "we ain't, and we ain't going to. What's the use when we've got the wood aboard? Those goods are going to go for skins."

Even then John March did not entirely understand him. "But you can't do that," he said. "We owe the chief the goods."

"Listen, boy," said Captain Griggs, "this ain't like home. There're plenty of other chiefs, and plenty of other islands. Let 'em come and get the goods, and I'll blow 'em out of water. There ain't no law out here. Now you be quiet, boy."

For a moment John March found it impossible to speak. Now that the whole matter was completely clear, he knew that he should have suspected long ago what must have been in the back of the captain's mind. Captain Griggs proposed sheer robbery, but he would not have called it that. He would have called it a clever piece of business in a place where there was no law.

"You see," Captain Griggs was saying, "it isn't as though they were white people, Mr. March. More fools they, that's all."

Then John March found his voice. "Captain," he said, "this is a March ship. You don't leave until you've set those goods on shore. We don't do things that way, Captain. You can't——"

Captain Griggs turned toward him quickly.

"That'll be enough from you," he said. "Who says I can't? I'm trying to make a profit on this voyage. I can, and I will, and I'm taking full responsibility. If you don't like it, get below."

John March's tongue felt dry and parched as he tried to speak. Even in that short while a hundred things were happening. The fore-and-aft staysails and the lower topsails were set by then, and the call came from forward, "Hawser short!" A glance toward the beach was enough to show him that the islanders were aware of the captain's trick. Men were running toward the water. He could hear the beating of a drum. Men in canoes were gesticulating and shouting. Men with spears and clubs and slings were hurrying to the beach.

"Break out anchor, mister," shouted Captain Griggs, "and stand by them guns! Forward there, pass out the small arms! By God, we'll show 'em!"

"Captain," said John March suddenly. He knew there was only one thing to do as he spoke. "If you go, you'll leave me here. I'm going back ashore."

Captain Griggs looked at him and laughed. "They'll kill you back ashore," he said. "Look at 'em on the beach."

John March spoke with difficulty. "You and I are different sorts of men," he said. "You can either set those goods ashore or I'm going."

"May I inquire," said Captain Griggs, "how you're going to go? Keep your mouth shut, boy!"

In the haste of getting under way, the quarter boat was still drifting alongside, and the captain must have perceived John March's intention from his glance.

He made a lunge at John March, but John March broke away, and then he went on the bulwarks.

"Get ahold of that damned fool!" shouted Captain Griggs. "Lay ahold of him!"

Two of the crew ran toward him, and he jumped crashing into the quarter boat. "Get in there after him!" Captain Griggs was shouting. "Don't let him go!"

And then John March cut the painter, and the quarter boat was drifting from the side.

"You damned fool!" shouted Captain Griggs. "You hear my orders! Come back here or they'll kill you, March!"

Once the boat was drifting from the side, John March was amazed at himself. His anger and his lack of fear amazed him. He was standing amidships in the quarter boat, shouting back at Captain Griggs.

"I'd rather be killed ashore," he shouted, "than stay aboard with you!" Then he picked up the oars and began to row ashore, slowly, because the boat was heavy for a single man to handle.

"You hear me?" Captain Griggs was shouting. "Stay there and be damned to you!"

John March saw that the anchor was aweigh and the *Polly* was standing slowly out to the open sea. His back was to the beach as he pulled toward it, but he heard the shouting and the beating of the drums. It must have been his anger at Captain Griggs that did not make him afraid, or an assurance within himself that he was right and Captain Griggs was wrong. A glance astern of the quarter boat as he strained at the oars showed him the *Polly* standing out to sea, but he did not look over his shoulder toward the beach. He did not look until the bottom of the quarter boat grated on the sand, then he shipped his oars carefully and stepped ashore. He found himself surrounded by shouting men who waved their spears and their fists in his face, but somehow they were not so real to him as the reality which lay inside himself. He only realized later that a single gesture of fear might have meant his death, but then he was so involved in his own preoccupation and with the single desire which was in him that he walked calmly enough across the beach toward the palm trees and the thatched houses; the crowd in front of him gave way as he walked, and then followed on his heels. He was taking the path to Kualai's house, and the shouting around him died away as he drew near it.

Then he saw Kualai walking toward him in the feather cloak

which he had worn the first day they had met, carrying a light throwing spear in his right hand. Kualai was shouting something to him —obviously a question which he could not understand—and Moku was standing near him.

"Tell Kualai," John March said, "that I come from honest people. Tell him that I have come here to stay until he is paid for his wood." He saw Kualai listening intently to his answer, and then Kualai raised his right arm and drove his spear into the earth.

"He says you are his son," Moku said. "He asks you: Will you please to shake his hand?"

The reaction from what he had done came over him when Kualai grasped his hand. He knew the harsh and accurate consequences of his action then, as the smells and sounds of that Polynesian village came over him like a wave. Captain Griggs had left him, and every vestige of home was gone. He was a stranger among savages, and he might be there forever, for anything he knew, yet even then he knew that he had done the only proper thing. Suddenly he found that he was homesick, because the chief was kind.

"Ask him if I can be alone," he said. "Tell him I want to be alone."

He was given a house of his own that night, next to where the chief slept. He was given a pile of woven mats for his bed and a piece of kapa cloth to cover him. He was given baked pig and sweet potatoes and the gray paste made from the kalo root, called poi, for his evening meal, and mullet from Kualai's fishpond. He was as comfortable as he could have hoped to be that night. For a moment, when he was awakened early the next morning, he thought he was at home, until he saw the rafters and the thatch above him. Moku was standing near him in his ragged sailor breeches, and Kualai himself was bending his head, just entering the door.

"Wake up!" Moku was saying. "The ship is back!"

John March sat up on his bed of mats and rubbed his arm across his face. Although he spoke to Moku, his eyes were on Kualai.

"The ship?" he asked. "What ship?"

"Your ship," said Moku. "She come back, and now the captain, he unloads the goods."

John March stood up. He had no great capacity for showing emotion.

"Ask Kualai if he is satisfied," he said.

Moku nodded. "He says, 'Yes, very much,' " he said, and Kualai nodded back. "He asks for you to stay a long time—always."

"Thank him, please," said John March, "but tell him it's my ship. Tell him I must go to see that the goods are right."

"Kualai," Moku answered, "says he will go with you to the beach."

Mr. Sprague had landed in the longboat by the time they had reached the shore, and the beach was already covered with bolts of calico and small goods and ironware and lead and copper. Mr. Sprague nodded to John March formally, as though nothing had happened. "The captain sends his compliments," he said, "and asks you to come aboard, so that he can resume the voyage." And then Sprague grinned and added, "It's damned lucky for you, John March, that you're the owner's son."

John March looked at the goods upon the shore. "You can thank the captain for me for coming back," he answered. "You can tell him that I hope we both can forget what has happened, but the complete consignment is not landed yet. I'll stay here until the list is checked."

"You're an accurate man," said Sprague.

John March nodded. "I've been taught to be," he said, and he stayed there on the beach until every item was verified. Then he turned to Kualai and his interpreter.

"Tell the chief," he said, "that I believe that everything is right. Ask his pardon for the delay, but tell him our house will make any mistakes correct. Thank him, and tell him that I am going."

Moku spoke quickly in the musical language of the islands while Kualai stood, looking first at John March and then at the ship that brought him. After Kualai had listened, he stood silently for a moment. Then he smiled and spoke swiftly. He raised a hand and took off his feather helmet, and one of his men very carefully removed his feather cloak from his shoulders.

"He says there will always be wood for you," said Moku. "He asks you to take his coat."

Archibald Campbell

A Scotsman in Honolulu, 1809

A minor classic among narratives of the sea as well as a primary source of information about life in early Hawaii before the coming of the missionaries is *Voyage Round the World, from 1806 to 1812* (1816), by Archibald Campbell. Born near Glasgow around 1787, Campbell received "the common rudiments of education," and while serving as a weaver's apprentice he ran away to sea at the age of fourteen. After making several voyages to various parts of the world, he joined the American ship *Eclipse* bound for the Russian outposts at Kamchatka and the Aleutian Islands. The ship was wrecked on a reef off the Alaskan coast, and while Campbell was attempting to get help from the nearest Russian settlement, both his feet were frozen and later had to be amputated. A returning ship carried him to Hawaii, where he was taken into the household of King Kamehameha the Great, to be the king's sailmaker. In this capacity he remained for over a year, in 1809 and part of 1810.

Making his way home after further adventures in South America, Campbell earned a meager living playing the violin for the amusement of steamboat passengers on the river Clyde until he published his book, which sold unusually well. With the proceeds he went to New York and started a small chandlery business, continuing there at least until 1821, when all trace of him disappears. A novel based on his adventures is *The Restless Voyage* (1948) by Stanley D. Porteus.

AT one time, during my stay, there were nearly sixty white people upon Oahu alone, but the number was constantly varying, and was considerably diminished before my departure. Although the great majority had been left by American vessels, not above one third of them belonged to that nation; the rest were almost all English, and of these six or eight were convicts who had made their escape from New South Wales.

Many inducements are held out to sailors to remain here. If they conduct themselves with propriety, they rank as chiefs, and are entitled to all the privileges of the order; at all events, they are certain of being maintained by some of the chiefs, who are always anxious to have white people about them. The king has a considerable number in his service, chiefly carpenters, joiners, masons, blacksmiths, and bricklayers; these he rewards liberally with grants of land. Some of these people are sober and industrious; but this is far from being their general character; on the contrary, many of them are idle and dissolute, getting drunk whenever an opportunity presents itself. They have introduced distillation into the island; and the evil consequences, both to the natives and whites, are incalculable. It is no uncommon sight to see a party of them broach a small cask of spirits and sit drinking for days till they see it out.

There were, however, a few exceptions to this. William Davis, a Welshman who resided with Isaac Davis, used to rise every morning at five and go to his fields, where he commonly remained till the same hour in the evening. This singularity puzzled the natives not a little; but they accounted for it by supposing that he had been one of their own countrymen who had gone to Tahiti or England after his death, and had now come back to his native land.

There were no missionaries upon the island during the time I remained in it, at which I was often much surprised.

Most of the whites have married native women, by whom they have families; but they pay little attention either to the education or to the religious instruction of their children. I do not recollect having seen any who knew more than the letters of the alphabet. . . .

The natives, although not tall, are stout and robust in their make, particularly those of the higher rank; their complexion is nut-brown, and they are extremely cleanly in their persons. They are distinguished by great ingenuity in all their arts and manufactures, as well as by a most persevering industry. They are divided into two great classes, the alii, or chiefs, and the Kanaka-maori, or people. The former are the proprietors of the land, the latter are all under the dominion of some chief, for whom they work or cultivate the ground, and by whom they are supported in old age. They are not, however, slaves, or attached to the soil, but at liberty to change masters when they think proper.

The supreme government is vested in the king, whose power seems to be completely absolute. He is assisted by the principal chiefs, whom he always keeps about his person; many of these have particular departments to attend to; one chief took charge of the household and appointed the different surveys to be performed by every individual; another, named Coweeoranee, acted as paymaster; his province was to distribute wages and provisions amongst the people in the king's service. An elderly chief, of the name of Naai, took a general charge of the whole and was, in fact, prime minister. He was commonly called Billy Pitt by the white people, and was by no means pleased when they addressed him by any other appellation.

The principal duties of the executive were, however, entrusted to the priests; by them the revenues were collected and the laws enforced. Superstition is the most powerful engine by which the latter purpose is effected, actual punishment being rare. I knew only one instance of capital punishment, which was that of a man who had violated the sanctity of the morai. Having got drunk, he quitted it during tabu time and entered the house of a woman. He was immediately seized and carried back to the morai, where his eyes were put out. After remaining two days in this state, he was strangled and his body exposed before the principal idol.

The method of detecting theft or robbery affords a singular instance of the power of superstition over their minds. The party who has suffered the loss applies to one of the priests, to whom he presents a pig and relates his story. The following ceremony is then performed: The priest begins by rubbing two pieces of green wood upon each other, till, by the friction, a kind of powderlike snuff is produced, which is so hot that on being placed in dry grass and blown upon it takes fire; with this a large pile of wood is kindled and allowed to burn a certain time. He then takes three nuts of an oily nature called kukui; having broken the shells, one of the kernels is thrown into the fire, at which time he says an anana, or prayer; and while the nut is crackling in the fire, repeats the words, *"Makeloa o kanaka aihue,"* that is, "Kill or shoot the fellow." The same ceremonies take place with each of the nuts, provided the thief does not appear before they are consumed. This, however, but seldom happens; the culprit generally makes his appearance with the stolen property, which is restored to the owner, and the offense punished by a fine of four pigs. He is then dismissed, with strict injunctions not to commit the like crime in future, under pain of a more severe penalty. The pigs are taken to the morai, where they are offered up as sacrifices and afterwards eaten by the priests.

Should it happen that the unfortunate criminal does not make his appearance during the awful ceremony, his fate is inevitable; had he the whole island to bestow, not one word of the prayer could be recalled, nor the anger of the Akua appeased. The circumstance is reported to the king, and proclamation made throughout the island that a certain person has been robbed and that those who are guilty have been prayed to death. So firm is their belief in the power of these prayers that the culprit pines away, refusing to take any sustenance, and at last falls a sacrifice to his credulity. . . .

I have but few particulars to give of their religious opinions. Their principal god, to whom they attribute the creation of the world, is called Akua; and they have seven or eight subordinate deities, whose images are in the morai, and to whom offerings are made as well as to the Akua. Their names I cannot recollect. . . . They have a tradition of a general deluge. According to their account, the sea once overflowed the whole world, except Mauna Kea, in Hawaii, and swept away all the inhabitants but one pair, who saved themselves on that mountain and are the parents of the present race of mankind.

Their morais, or places of worship, consist of one large house or temple, with some smaller ones round it, in which are the images of their inferior gods. The tabu'd, or consecrated, precincts are marked out by four square posts, which stand thirty or forty yards from the building. In the inside of the principal house there is a screen or curtain of white cloth hung across one end, within which the image of Akua is placed. When sacrifices are offered, the priests and chiefs enter occasionally within this space, going in at one side and out at the other. Although present on one occasion, I did not enter this recess, partly because I was doubtful of the propriety of doing so, and also on account of the difficulty I had in moving myself and the risk of getting my wounds injured among the crowd. On the outside are placed several images made of wood, as ugly as can be well imagined, having their mouths all stuck round with dogs' teeth. . . . Human sacrifices are offered upon their going to war, but nothing of the kind took place during my stay; unless in the case already mentioned, of the man punished for breaking the tabu, and whose body was exposed before the idol.

During the period called Makahiki, which lasts a whole month and takes place in November, the priests are employed in collecting the taxes, which are paid by the chiefs in proportion to the extent of their territories; they consist of mats, feathers, and the produce of the country. The people celebrate this festival by dancing, wrestling, and other amusements. The king remains in the morai for the whole period; before entering it, a singular ceremony takes place. He is obliged to stand till three spears are darted at him; he must catch the first with his hand, and with it ward off the other two. This is not a mere formality. The spear is thrown with the utmost force; and should the king lose his life, there is no help for it. . . .

The women are subject to many restrictions from which the men are exempted. They are not allowed to attend the morai upon tabu days, nor at these times are they permitted to go out in a canoe. They are never permitted to eat with the men, except when at sea, and then not out of the same dish. Articles of delicacy, such as pork, turtle, shark, coconuts, bananas or plantains, are also forbidden. Dogs' flesh and fish were the only kinds of animal food lawful for them to eat; but since the introduction of sheep and goats, which are not tabu'd, the ladies have less reason to complain.

Notwithstanding the rigor with which these ceremonies are generally observed, the women very seldom scruple to break them when it can be done in secret. They often swim off to ships at night during the tabu, and I have known them to eat of the forbidden delicacies of pork and sharks' flesh. What would be the consequence of a discovery I know not; but I once saw the queen transgressing in this respect and was strictly enjoined to secrecy, as she said it was as much as her life was worth.

Their ideas of marriage are very loose; either party may quit the other when they tire or disagree. The lower classes, in general, content themselves with one wife; but they are by no means confined to that number, and the chiefs have frequently several. Kamehameha had two, besides a very handsome girl, the daughter of a chief, educating for him. One elderly chief, Coweeoranee, had no fewer than fifteen. They are very jealous of any improper connection between natives and their wives; but the case is widely different with respect to their visitors, where connection of that kind is reckoned the surest proof of friendship, and they are always anxious to strengthen it by that tie.

The virtue of the king's wives is, however, most scrupulously guarded, each of them having a male and a female attendant whose duty it is to watch them on all occasions. Should it be discovered that any of the queens have been unfaithful, these attendants are punished with death unless they have given the first intimation.

Immediately after childbirth, women are obliged to retire to the woods, where they remain ten days, and must not be seen by the men. The queen, who had a daughter whilst I was there, had a house for the purpose of retirement; but, in general, they have no other shelter but what the woods afford. . . .

The dances are principally performed by women, who form themselves into solid squares, ten or twelve each way, and keep time to the sound of the drum, accompanied by a song in which they all join. In dancing they seldom move their feet, but throw themselves into a variety of attitudes, sometimes all squatting and at other times springing up at the same instant. A man in front, with strings of shells on his ankles and wrists, with which he marks time, acts as a fugleman. On these occasions the women display all their finery, particularly in European clothes, if they are so fortunate as to possess any. They receive great applause from the spectators, who frequently burst into immoderate fits of laughter at particular parts of the song.

They have a game somewhat resembling draughts, but more complicated. It is played upon a board about twenty-two inches by fourteen, painted black, with white spots, on which the men are placed; these consist of black and white pebbles, eighteen upon each side, and the game is won by the capture of the adversary's pieces. Kamehameha excels at this game. I have seen him sit for hours playing with his chiefs, giving an occasional smile, but without uttering a word. I could not play; but William Moxley, who understood it well, told me that he had seen none who could beat the king. The game of draughts is now introduced, and the natives play it uncommonly well.

Flying kites is another favorite amusement. They make them of kapa, of the usual shape, but of uncommon size, many of them being fifteen or sixteen feet in length and six or seven in breadth; they have often three or four hundred fathom of line, and are so difficult to hold that they are obliged to tie them to trees. The only employment I ever saw Tamena the queen engaged in was making these kites.

A theater was erected under the direction of James Beattie, the king's blockmaker, who had been at one time on the stage in England. The scenes representing a castle and a forest were constructed of different-colored pieces of kapa, cut out and pasted together.

I was present, on one occasion, at the performance of *Oscar and Malvina*. This piece was originally a pantomime, but here it had words written for it by Beattie. The part of Malvina was performed by the wife of Isaac Davis. As her knowledge of the English language was very limited, extending only to the words yes and no, her speeches were confined to these monosyllables. She, however, acted her part with great applause. The Fingalian heroes were represented by natives clothed in the Highland garb, also made out of kapa, and armed with muskets.

The audience did not seem to understand the play well, but were greatly delighted with the afterpiece, representing a naval engagement. The ships were armed with bamboo cannon; and each of them fired a broadside by means of a train of thread dipped in saltpeter, which communicated with each gun—after which one of the vessels blew up. Unfortunately the explosion set fire to the forest, and had nearly consumed the theater.

Otto von Kotzebue

The Russians Meet Kamehameha I

A memorable encounter between Kamehameha I and one of the round-the-world expeditions sent out by the Czar of Russia took place on November 24, 1816, a few miles north of Kealakekua Bay. Captain of the visiting brig *Rurik* was Otto von Kotzebue (1787–1846), who at seventeen had previously visited Hawaii while serving under his uncle, Adam Johann von Krusenstern.

Kotzebue, who inherited the writing aptitude of his father, the German dramatist August von Kotzebue, published in German an important account of the *Rurik* expedition. The English title is *A Voyage of Discovery into the South Sea and Behring's Strait* (1821), from which the present selection is taken. In 1823 Kotzebue was commissioned as commander of the ship *Predpiatie;* his account of this circumnavigation, appearing in English as *A New Voyage Round the World* (1830), gives an account of Hawaii in 1824.

The *Rurik* appeared off the stronghold of Kamehameha I in 1816 at a ticklish time in Russian–Hawaiian relations. Von Kotzebue was ignorant of the fact that a German adventurer, Dr. George Anton Scheffer, claiming to represent the Czar Alexander, had led a party of filibusters who were even then entrenched on the northwestern island of Kauai, with the consent of Kamehameha's rival King Kaumualii. Kamehameha feared at first that the *Rurik* had come as a warship to reinforce Scheffer.

Aboard the *Rurik* was John Elliot de Castro, who had joined the ship at San Francisco in order to return to the Hawaiian court. Botanist on the staff was Adelbert von Chamisso. Artist of the party was Louis Choris, who, under the difficulties described herein, sketched the only portraits of Kamehameha I made during his lifetime.

November 21. At one o'clock in the afternoon, we were distant only fifty miles from Hawaii, and were in sight of the mountain, Mauna Loa. By Elliot's advice, I determined first to sail around the north side of Hawaii, in order to obtain, in Kawaihae Bay, where the Englishman, Young, lived, information respecting both the situation of the island, and the present residence of the king. This precaution seemed to me to be the more necessary because, in case Kamehameha should happen to be dead, we ought to know how the people were disposed toward the Europeans. Besides this, the king often lives on the island of Oahu, and you save a considerable distance by avoiding the southern point of Hawaii, where the lofty Mauna Loa detains the navigator by calms. According to Elliot's assurance, provisions could not be obtained but by bargaining with the king himself; because the inhabitants have not the liberty of supplying the ships.

At sunset, we were near the island; sailed along the north part, kept to the east side during the night, and, at daybreak, steered toward the northern point, which, on the twenty-second, at noon, lay southwest at the distance of eleven miles. The northeast side of Hawaii affords to the mariner a picturesque, but not inviting, prospect. The land rises regularly and gradually to an elevation which loses itself in the clouds. It is said that the island is not fruitful on this side; but, to judge from the number of columns of smoke which we saw rise, it must be very populous. Elliot assured us that the piece of ground which he possessed on this side could only be used as a pasture for his hogs.

A canoe, with two men, rowed toward us; and as I lay to, in hopes of obtaining some information here, one of the islanders immediately came on board, who offered to sell us a fowl, and some ropes of his own manufacture. Elliot, who understood his language, was directly recognized by him as the Naja (so the king called him), and with much trouble drew from him the intelligence that the king was in the Bay of Kealakekua, and Young (Olohana) in the island of Oahu. The reserved and suspicious manner of the savage made us doubt the truth of his statement; and Elliot was of opinion that some disagreeable circumstance had occurred on the island which required the greatest precaution.

While we were engaged with the islander, the boat, which was fastened with a rope to the ship, was upset, and the man sitting in it fell out, but he immediately seized the rope, and suffered himself to be dragged behind the ship, though we were sailing very fast. We were astonished at the strength of this man; we lay to, and our dealer leaped into the sea to untie the boat; hereupon both the men had much trouble to right it, and to bale out the water, as the high waves continually dashed over it. As all this was done swimming, the reader may form some notion of their expertness in this art. They were at last seated, but they had no oars, having lost them when the boat upset. An European would not have known how to help himself; they were, however, not at all embarrassed, for they found their safety in their strength, and rowed with their hands, briskly forward.

At two o'clock in the afternoon, we doubled the north point and sailed, at a distance of three quarters of a mile, along the shore, to Kawaihae Bay. Ships which double the north point of Hawaii must be very careful not to lose the oars, as sudden gusts of wind generally come from shore: some Americans who were negligent have lost theirs in this place. We now plainly distinguished the objects on shore, and enjoyed a very pleasing prospect of green fields and many dwellings shaded by banana and palm trees. We saw here several morais, which belong to the chiefs of these parts, and may be recognized by the stone fence and the idols placed in them. Several canoes filled with girls rowed up to us; but as I had no time to show the politeness due to the fair sex, I sailed quickly on, in order to reach Kealakekua Bay as soon as possible, where I hoped to find Kamehameha.

The north point of Hawaii consists of low land, which rises in a straight line under an acute angle into the region of the clouds. As soon as you reach these parts, the monsoon has no longer any effect, and you may expect sea and land winds, frequently interrupted by total calms, and light breezes from every point of the compass; this was our case near Kawaihae Bay, where the wind entirely died away. We now saw Young's settlement of several houses built of white stone, after the European fashion, surrounded by palm and banana trees; the land has a barren appearance, and is said to be little adapted to agriculture, as it consists, for the most part, of masses of lava.

A canoe, with six people, took advantage of the calm to come on board; and, being the king's subjects (Kanakas, a name given to the lower class in the Sandwich Islands), they all recognized Mr. Elliot as the Naja; one of them, who had been a sailor on board an

American ship in Boston, spoke a little English, and was a clever fellow; he remained on board, at Elliot's request, to pilot our ship. He was of opinion that the king was in Kealakekua, and that Young had been sent on business to Oahu; he further told us that there were lying at anchor two ships at Oahu, and one at Kealakekua, all with the American flag, of which the latter had lost all her masts in a violent storm near the Sandwich Islands.

When our pilot learned that he was on board a Russian ship, he became very uneasy; and, on Mr. Elliot's questioning him about the ground of his apprehension, he stated as follows: Five months since, two Russian ships belonging to the American Company (the *Elemenia* and the *Discovery*) had stopped here; there had been some disputes between the Russians and the natives, in which the latter, according to the account of the relater, appeared in a very favorable light. When the ships left the Sandwich Islands, they had threatened to return very soon with a strong force, and had likewise mentioned a ship of war whose views were also hostile to the inhabitants.

We now understood the uneasiness shown by the first islander, and it was with much difficulty that Mr. Elliot prevented our savage, who wanted to escape us by jumping into the sea; while we assured him that we had come solely for the purpose of repairing the injury done by our countrymen to his people. I was very glad to have received all this information before my interview with Kamehameha, who, being incensed against the Russians, might easily take our ship for the expected hostile man-of-war. I now doubly felt how useful Elliot was to us, as he might become here, in some measure, our guardian genius. A perfect calm detained us this day on the same spot.

November 23. We made but little progress all this day for want of wind. Early in the morning we were visited by a canoe, for the purpose of inquiring what our vessel was. They brought us news, at the same time, that the king had left Kealakekua, and had gone to Kailua, a small bay a few miles to the north, where he would only remain for the night, and in the morning proceed farther northward along the coast to the bonito fishery. I therefore immediately dispatched the canoe to the king with the information that a Russian ship of war had come with friendly intentions, the commander of which wished to speak with His Majesty, and therefore requested him not to leave Kailua, where he hoped to arrive tomorrow: the Naja also announced his arrival to the king.

During the night a fresh breeze carried us near to Kailua. The current set by day toward the south, and at night toward the north, parallel with the coast, which is a consequence of the land and sea winds.

November 24. At daybreak we approached the bay; several boats, sent by the king, came to meet us, and I embraced this opportunity of sending Elliot and our gentlemen on shore, to acquaint the king with the object of our voyage. As the island of Hawaii does not afford a convenient harbor, I had determined, as soon as I had settled with the king respecting the delivery of the provisions, to sail to the island of Oahu, where Elliot assured me there was a very safe harbor, not mentioned by any preceding navigator.

I left the *Rurik,* got under sail, and made short tacks close in shore. We saw the American ship which had been lying at Kealakekua sailing to Kailua, where she cast anchor, though the bay is not secure, being open, and the bottom consisting of corals.

At eight o'clock in the morning Elliot had happily executed his commission advantageously for us, and came on board with two of the most distinguished chiefs of the country, of whom one was the queen's brother; and these welcomed us in the name of the king. They were two extremely tall Herculean figures, whose dress, in the newest fashion of Hawaii, struck us very much, as it merely consisted of a black frock and a small white straw hat. I learned from Elliot that the king had really expected the hostile ship of war, and had immediately given orders to station soldiers all along the coast; they were all prepared, and consisted already of four hundred men armed with muskets.

The king sent me word that he was very sorry not to be able to visit me on board my ship, as his mistrustful people would not suffer him, but for his own part he had a better opinion of us, after his Naja had acquainted him with the object of our voyage; and, as a proof of his friendly intentions, he invited me to his camp, where he would entertain me with a pig baked in the ground. He had ordered, for my security, that one of the chiefs should remain on board as long as I stayed on shore, and accordingly I rowed on shore at ten o'clock, accompanied by Messrs. Elliot and Schischmareff, and a chief named John Adams. The view of the king's camp was concealed only by a narrow tongue of land, consisting of naked rocks, but when we had sailed round we were surprised at the sight of the most beautiful landscape. We found ourselves in a small sandy bay of the smoothest water, protected against the waves of the sea; on the bank was a pleasant wood of palm trees, under whose shade were built several straw houses; to the right, between the green leaves of the banana trees, peeped two snow-white houses, built of stone, after the European fashion, on which account this place has the mixed appearance of an European and Hawaiian village, which afforded us a new but charming prospect. To the left, close to the water, on an artificial elevation, stood the morai of the king, surrounded by large wooden statues of his gods, representing caricatures of the human figure. The background of this valley is formed by the high, majestic Mauna Hualalai, the height of which, according to my estimation, is 1,687 toises. It rises on this side pretty steep; its ascent is varied by green fields and vales, with beautiful woods, between which you frequently perceive very large and overhanging rocks of lava, which give the whole landscape, by this mixture of wildness and cultivation, a most picturesque appearance.

A number of islanders armed with muskets stood on the shore. The king came to meet us as far as the landing place with some of his most distinguished warriors, and when we got out of the boat he came up to me and cordially shook me by the hand. Curiosity brought the people from all sides, but the greatest order prevailed, and no noise or importunity was permitted. I now stood at the side of the celebrated Kamehameha, who had attracted the attention of all Europe, and who inspired me with the greatest confidence by his unreserved and friendly behavior. He conducted me to his straw palace, which, according to the custom of the country, consisted only of one spacious apartment, and, like all the houses here, afforded a free draft both to the land and sea breezes, which alleviates the oppressive heat. They offered us European chairs, very neatly made, placed a mahogany table before us, and we were then in possession of all the furniture of the palace. Though the king has houses built of stone in the European fashion, he prefers this simple dwelling, not to forsake the customs of his country; he imitates everything he knows to be useful, and tries to introduce it among his people; palaces built of stone appeared to him superfluous, as the straw houses are convenient, and as he only wishes to increase the happiness and not the wants of his subjects.

Kamehameha's dress, which consisted of a white shirt, blue pantaloons, a red waistcoat, and a colored neckcloth, surprised me very much, for I had formed very different notions of the royal attire. He, however, sometimes dresses very splendidly, having several embroidered uniforms and other articles of dress. The distinguished personages present at our audience, who had all seated themselves on the ground, wore a still more singular costume than the king; for the black frocks look very ludicrous on the naked body; add to this that they seldom fit, being purchased of American ships, where the people are not always so tall and so robust as the chiefs of the Sandwich Islands. One of the ministers had the waist halfway up his back; the coat had been buttoned with the greatest difficulty; he perspired in his tight state dress; his distress was very evident, but fashion would not suffer him to relieve himself of this inconvenience. It is very singular that the savages should surpass the Europeans in bearing the inconveniencies which the power of fashion imposes on them. The sentinels at the door were quite naked; a cartridge box and a pair of pistols were tied round their waist, and they held a musket in their hand.

After the king had poured out some very good wine and had himself drunk to our health, I made him acquainted with my intention of taking in fresh provisions, water, and wood. A young man of the name of Cook, the only white whom the king had about him, was quick, not without education, and spoke fluently the language of the country; he had formerly served as pilot on board a ship, but had been settled on the island for several years. He was a favorite with the king, and was in possession of a considerable portion of land; he acted as interpreter between us. Kamehameha desired him to say to me as follows: "I learn that you are the commander of a ship of war, and are engaged in a voyage similar to those of Cook and Vancouver, and consequently do not engage in trade; it is therefore my intention not to carry on any with you, but to provide you gratis with everything that my islands produce. This affair is now settled, and no further mention need be made of it. I shall now beg you to inform me whether it is with the consent of your emperor that his subjects begin to disturb me in my old age? Since Kamehameha has been king of these islands, no European has had cause to complain of having suffered injustice here. I have made my islands an asylum for all nations, and honestly supplied with provisions every ship that desired them. Some time ago there came from the American settlement of Sitka some Russians, a nation with whom I never had any intercourse before; they were kindly received, and supplied with everything necessary; but they have ill rewarded me, for they behaved in a hostile manner to my subjects in the island of Oahu, and threatened us with ships of war, which were to conquer these islands; but this shall not happen as long as Kamehameha lives! A Russian physician, of the name of Scheffer, who came here some months ago, pretended that he had been sent by the Emperor Alexander to botanize on my islands; as I had heard much good of the Emperor Alexander and was particularly pleased with his bravery, I not only permitted M. Scheffer to botanize, but also promised him every assistance; made him a present of a piece of land, with peasants, so that he could never want for provisions; in short, I tried to make his stay as agreeable as possible, and to refuse none of his demands. But what was the consequence of my hospitality? Even before he left Hawaii, he repaid my kindness with ingratitude, which I bore patiently. Upon this, according to his own desire, he traveled from one island to another; and, at last, settled in the fruitful island of Oahu, where he proved himself to be my most inveterate enemy; destroying our sanctuary, the morai; and exciting against me, in the island of Kauai, King Kaumualii, who had submitted to my power years before. Scheffer is there at this very moment, and threatens my islands."

Such was the account given by the king; for the truth of which I can only say that Kamehameha highly distinguishes every European who settles in his islands, if his conduct be good; and that he is generally known to be an upright and honest man. I am not personally acquainted with M. Scheffer, but have since learned the manner in which he came to the Sandwich Islands. He had served as physician on board the *Suvarov*, belonging to the Russian American Company, which went, in 1814, from Kronstadt to Sitka, under the command of Lieutenant Lasaref. From motives unknown to me, Lieutenant Lasaref left Dr. Scheffer, in 1815, at Sitka, and returned to Europe without a physician. M. Baranof, who generally resides at Sitka, as director of all the Russian American colonies, and whose character is but indifferent, took him under his protection, and sent him to the Sandwich Islands; with what intention is not known. How he conducted himself there, the reader has been informed.

I assured Kamehameha that the bad conduct of the Russians here must not be ascribed to the will of our emperor, who never commanded his subjects to do an unjust act; but that the extent of his empire prevented him from being immediately informed of bad actions, which, however, never remained unpunished when they came to his knowledge. The king seemed very much pleased on my assuring him that our emperor never intended to conquer his island; the glasses were immediately filled, to drink the health of the emperor; he was even more cordial than before, and we could not have desired a more agreeable and obliging host. He conversed with a vivacity surprising at his age, asked us various questions respecting Russia, and made observations. Cook was not always able to translate the words that the king used, which were peculiar to the Hawaiian language and so witty that his ministers often laughed aloud.

One of Kamehameha's wives passed by our house, and in a friendly manner wished me a good morning through the door, but she was not allowed to enter, it being the king's eating house. With the king's permission, we took a walk, accompanied by Cook and a guard of honor of five naked soldiers. We visited the favorite queen Kaahumanu, mentioned by Vancouver; we found her with the two other wives, and were very politely received by all. The house which Kaahumanu inhabits is built very neatly, and is very cleanly in the interior; the entrance hall, in which the three wives were seated according to the Asiatic fashion, was covered with fine and elegant mats, and she herself was pretty closely wrapped up in the finest cloth of the country. Kaahumanu was seated in the middle, and the two other ladies on either side; and I had the honor to be invited to sit down opposite to them, likewise on the ground. They put to me several questions, which I answered to their satisfaction through Cook. Watermelons were brought and Kaahumanu was polite enough to cut one and hand me a piece.

The chief employment of the royal ladies consists in smoking tobacco, combing their hair, driving away the flies with a fan, and eating. Kamehameha himself does not smoke; otherwise this custom has become so general in the Sandwich Islands, within these few years, that young children smoke before they learn to walk, and grown-up people have carried it to such an excess that they have fallen down senseless, and often died in consequence. They do not want pipe tubes, but the pipe heads, which, according to the custom of the country, they have always hanging at their side, constitute a part of the royal ornaments; these were of the size of the largest German pipes, made of dark wood, and mounted with brass, but which only rich people can procure. Kaahumanu took a few whiffs with evident pleasure; she then swallowed a part of the smoke, and emitted the rest through her nostrils. Half dizzy, she gave me the pipe, and as I declined, she, astonished at my European stupidity, gave it to her neighbor, who, after a short enjoyment of it, gave it to the third wife. As soon as the pipe was emptied, a fresh one was filled, and went round in the same manner.

The second employment of the ladies is to dress their hair, which is cut short after their fashion; only over the forehead they let it grow a couple of inches long, smear it with a white sticky substance, and comb it back; the snow-white streaks which by this mode rise above the dark brown countenance give it a ludicrous appearance.

All the three queens were very large, corpulent women, who had lived to above half a century, and did not look as if they had ever been handsome. Their dress was distinguished from that of the other ladies by various silk handkerchiefs. Before the door, on a mat, was seated the king's daughter, a tolerably handsome girl; behind her stood a little Negro boy, holding a silk umbrella over her head to protect her from the rays of the sun; two other boys, with tufts of red feathers, drove away the flies from her: the whole group had a pleasing effect.

When I was about to rise, Kaahumanu held me back to inquire with much kindness after Vancouver, who, during his stay there, had found Kamehameha at variance with Kaahumanu, and had reconciled them. She seemed much affected at the news of his death.

After we had left the king's wives, we visited his son. Cook informed me that this prince, as successor to the throne, had already begun to exercise the rights of his father, which consist in the fulfilling of the most important tabus. Kamehameha has ordered this from political motives, that no revolution may arise after his death; for as soon as the son fulfills the most important tabu, he is sacred, is associated with the priests, and nobody dare dispute the throne with him. The prince, as soon as he is admitted into the rights of his father, receives the name of Liholiho, that is, dog of all dogs [erroneous; liholiho means "fiery"]; and such we really found him.

We entered a neat and small house, in which Liholiho, a tall, corpulent, and naked figure, was stretched out on his stomach, and just indolently raised his head to look at his guests; near him sat several naked soldiers armed with muskets, who guarded the monster; a handsome young native, with a tuft of red feathers, drove away the flies from him, and from his interesting countenance and becoming behavior, I should rather have taken him for the king's son. Kamehameha, who, by his wise government, has acquired permanent glory, and has laid the foundation for the civilization and improvement of his people, ought to have a successor capable of prosecuting with zeal and judgment the work which he has begun. It would be very important for navigation if the Sandwich Islands were on a level with Europe in civilization; and the English, who have taken these islands under their protection, should take care that after Kamehameha's death a sensible man may succeed and every revolution be avoided. Kamehameha deserves to have a monument erected to him.

The dog of all dogs at last rose very lazily, and gaped upon us with a stupid, vacant countenance. My embroidered uniform seemed to meet his approbation, for he held a long conversation about it with a couple of naked chamberlains. I could not learn his age, as no account is kept of it. I guess it may be about twenty-two years, and am of opinion that his enormous corpulency is occasioned by his constant lying on the ground.

At dinnertime, we returned to Kamehameha's residence, where I was surprised to see on the shore barges, sixty or seventy feet long, built quite in the European fashion, which are employed to convey provisions from one island to another. Kamehameha exerts himself to draw European shipwrights to his country, and pays them liberally for their instruction. During our walk, we were always accompanied by a number of men and women, joking and making much noise, but at the same time behaving with great propriety.

We were very kindly received by Kamehameha, who, after inquiring how I liked the place, ordered wine to be brought, and conducted us to a neat house, built near the morai, where we found the table already laid out, after the European fashion. He pretended that no pork was allowed to be eaten in the house in which we had first been, because his wives lived near it; but Young, who was perfectly acquainted with the king's character, gave me a very different reason: he was of opinion that the king had chosen the house near the morai, in which he generally holds his sacrificial repasts, for our house of entertainment because he desired to offer the hog baked for our repast to his gods, out of gratitude for the reconciliation with the Russians. The women dare not be present at the meals of the men, on pain of death; for which reason every family, besides their dwelling house, has two others, one for the repasts of the men, and one for those of the women.

The table was laid only for us Europeans, and the king and his ministers partook of nothing, though they were present; because, he said, that pork was tabu'd (forbidden) today. The hog, which was laid on a palm branch on the middle of the table, was cut up by one of the ministers, with various ceremonies; and besides this dish we had sweet potatoes, yams, and baked kalo roots. The king was very talkative during the entertainment; he sometimes conversed with me, and then with his ministers, who could not refrain from laughing at his conceits. He is fond of wine, but does not indulge in it to excess; and was always anxious to fill our glasses. After having severally drunk the health of all his guests, after the English fashion, he desired us to drink the health of our emperor in a bumper; and when this was done, one of his ministers presented me with a collar of colored feathers, of admirable workmanship, which the king had worn himself on solemn days; as, for example, in time of war. He then said to me, through Cook, though he speaks tolerably good English himself, "I have heard that your monarch is a great hero; I love him for it, because I am one myself; and I send him this collar, as a testimony of my regard."

After we had dined, and left the house, the king was very anxious that my rowers should be well entertained; he gave orders to this effect to one of the chiefs, and the table was immediately laid out again. They were obliged to sit down, and were served with the same attention as had been shown us. The sailors were certainly never in their lives treated with so much ceremony; for each of them had, like us, a Kanaka standing behind him, with a tuft of feathers to drive away the flies.

Kamehameha's first walk was to the morai; he embraced one of the statues, which was hung round more than the others with fruits and pieces of a sacrificed hog, saying, "These are our gods, whom I worship; whether I do right or wrong, I do not know; but I follow my faith, which cannot be wicked, as it commands me never to do wrong." This declaration from a savage, who had raised himself by his own native strength of mind to this degree of civilization, indicated much sound sense, and inspired me with a certain emotion.

While the king is gone into the morai, nobody is allowed to enter; and during that time we admired the colossal idols, cut in wood, and representing the most hideous caricatures. Kamehameha soon returned and conducted us to the house in which he had first received us; and we took our place as before, on chairs, while the distinguished personages seated themselves on the ground. It was now near the time in which Kamehameha was accustomed to dine; he made an apology for eating in our presence, and said, "I have seen how the Russians eat; now you may satisfy your curiosity and see how Kamehameha eats." The table was not set out; but the dinner was ready placed in a distant corner, on banana leaves, which served instead of dishes; particular attendants, bending very low, brought it near to the king, where it was received by a chief, and placed on the table. The repast consisted of boiled fish, yams, kalo roots, and a roasted bird, a little larger than a sparrow, which lives on the summits of the mountains. It is very rare, and is a dish only for the royal table.

The king ate very quick, and with a good appetite, conversing, however, all the time. Instead of bread, he ate the kalo dough [poi], which, when diluted with water, becomes a soft pap; and, though the king possesses very handsome table utensils, it stands in a gourd shell at his right hand, in which he dips his forefinger when he eats fish or flesh, and dexterously stuffs a good portion of it in his mouth; and this slovenly way of eating is observed from the king down to the lowest menial. Kamehameha, who during the whole repast had made use only of his fingers, perceived very well that I attentively observed his motions, and said to me, "This is the custom in my country, and I will not depart from it!"

The bearer of his spitting tray does not quit him a moment, as he always holds the tray ready, which is made of wood, in the form of a snuffbox, and provided with a lid, which is opened when the king intends to make use of it, and then immediately closed. This careful preservation of the royal saliva is in consequence of a superstition that so long as they are in possession of this treasure, their enemies are not able to send him any sickness by conjuration.

After the king had dined, it was at last agreed what provisions I was to receive from Oahu; they consisted of forty-three hogs, a proportionate number of fowl and geese, every kind of fruit which the island produces, and as much wood as I wished to have. Kamehameha told me that he had sent for a confidential friend who should accompany me to Oahu and see that his orders were punctually obeyed; besides this, that I must have a companion to be able to put into the harbor of Oahu, this not being permitted to any Russian ship. This highly generous conduct of a half-savage monarch exceeded my expectations, and I was now more fully convinced that, as a king, Kamehameha will not be easily replaced, his government being so greatly distinguished for justice, the instruction of his subjects, and the introduction of useful arts.

To give him some testimony of my gratitude, I presented him, in the name of the emperor, with two brass mortars (eight-pounders) with all their appendages, on the carriages of which the name *Rurik* was carved; a present which seemed to give him great pleasure. Besides this, I presented him with a quarter of a pipe of wine, as his stock was exhausted, and promised to send him some iron bars from Oahu, which were necessary to build boats. I was very happy in being able to return his presents with articles useful to him. Some very fine large apples, which I had brought with me from California, were quite new to the king. He immediately shared them with his ministers, and, as everybody found them very agreeable, the pips were preserved to make a trial whether these trees would thrive here, of which I make no doubt.

The skill of our painter was much admired, he having, with great rapidity, taken portraits of some of the chiefs, which were extraordinary likenesses. Even Kamehameha looked with surprise at the work of M. Choris, but long resisted my entreaties to suffer himself, as they here express it, to be transferred to paper: probably because he connected some idea of magic with this art. It was not till I had represented to him how happy our emperor would be to possess his likeness that he consented, and, to my great astonishment, M. Choris succeeded in taking a very good likeness of him, though Kamehameha, in order to embarrass him, did not sit still a moment, and made all kinds of faces, in spite of my entreaties.

At five o'clock in the afternoon we took leave of the king, who again repeated that we should want for nothing in the island of Oahu. As our companion had not yet arrived, I promised to lay to, near the coast, to wait for him. He considered as a great rarity a handsome tame horse, which the king had received from America, by an American ship, and which he suffered to run about unrestrained. A number of little boys had trodden the sand on the shore quite smooth, and with the assistance of a stick had with much skill drawn the *Rurik* under sail.

I was obliged, though with great regret, to part from Elliot de Castro, who had promised to accompany me to Oahu; but the king wished to have his physician and Naja again about him, and this request I could not refuse. Without the presence of Mr. Elliot, we should probably have fallen victims to the faults of others; and we indisputably owe to him the friendly reception that we met with here.

We had been cruising a couple of hours, and our companion did not yet appear; the sun set, and as our nearness to the coast might be dangerous in the dark, I fired some guns to put the king in mind of us. At eight o'clock Mr. Cook at length appeared, with our companion, who had been unable to come before, as he lived far in the interior of the island; he was a lively man, endowed with natural understanding, of the name of Manuja, who, though he was not one of the chief people of the country, was, however, honored in the highest degree with the confidence of the king, which was especially evinced by his entrusting to his care the most valuable European goods from his store. Cook told us that Kamehameha never regarded the rank of his subjects; that he generally chose his confidants from the lower classes, and was seldom deceived in his choice. He behaves to his great men with justice indeed, but with rigor, and as he places little confidence in them, they are obliged to accompany him on his journeys, by which he deprives them of the opportunity to throw off his authority by a conspiracy. They have not forgotten that Kamehameha is the conqueror of their lands, and is now sole monarch, and they would certainly attempt to conquer their property if he did not know so well how to keep them in his power.

Lucy Goodale Thurston

The Missionaries Arrive

Born in Marlborough, Massachusetts, daughter of a deacon of the Congregational Church, Lucy Goodale (1795–1876) was graduated from Bradford Academy and became a schoolteacher. At twenty-four she married Asa Thurston, a graduate of Yale College and Andover Theological Seminary, newly ordained as a minister and preparing to leave New England with the first company of missionaries to Hawaii. After a voyage of five months aboard the *Thaddeus,* a small trading vessel, the Thurstons settled at Kailua, on the island of Hawaii, and began their task of teaching and converting the Hawaiians. Many of the other early missionaries soon returned to New England, but the Thurstons remained in the Islands, and to them belongs much credit for the remarkable success of the Hawaiian mission. In her old age, when she was the last surviving member of the original missionary company, Lucy Thurston compiled her memoirs from journals and letters—*The Life and Times of Mrs. Lucy G. Thurston* (1882).

A few of the persons mentioned in the following selection should be identified here: Thomas Hopu was one of four Hawaiian youths, partly educated in New England, who accompanied the missionaries to Hawaii; Kamehameha I was the powerful king who had recently died; Kalanimoku was the chief councilor of the young new king, Liholiho or Kamehameha II.

AFTER sailing one hundred and fifty-seven days, we beheld, looming up before us, March 30, 1820, the long looked-for island of Hawaii. As we approached the northern shore, joy sparkled in every eye, gratitude and hope seemed to fill every heart. . . .

Soon the islanders of both sexes came paddling out in their canoes, with their island fruit. The men wore girdles, and the women a slight piece of cloth wrapped round them, from the hips downward. To a civilized eye their covering seemed to be revoltingly scanty. But we

The Missionaries Arrive

learned that it was a full dress for daily occupation. All was kapa, beaten out of the bark of a certain tree, and could ill bear washing. Kamehameha I as well understood how to govern as how to conquer, and strictly forbade foreign cloth from being assumed by his large plebeian family.

As I was looking out of a cabin window to see a canoe of chattering natives with animated countenances, they approached and gave me a banana. In return I gave them a biscuit. "Wahine maikai" ("Good woman") was the reply. I then threw out several pieces, and from my scanty vocabulary said, "Wahine" ("Woman"). They with great avidity snatched them up and again repeated, "Wahine maikai."

Thus, after sailing eighteen thousand miles, I met, for the first time, those children of nature alone. Although our communications by look and speech were limited, and simple, friendly pledges received and given, yet that interview through the cabin window of the brig *Thaddeus* gave me a strengthening touch in crossing the threshold of the nation.

Approaching Kawaihae, Hopu went ashore to invite on board some of the highest chiefs of the nation. Kindly regarding the feelings of the ladies, he suggested that they put on garments. So they prepared for the occasion. Kalanimoku was the first person of distinction that came. In dress and manners he appeared with the dignity of a man of culture. He was first introduced to the gentlemen, with whom he shook hands in the most cordial manner. He then turned to the ladies, to whom, while yet at a distance, he respectfully bowed, then came near, and being introduced, presented to each his hand. The effects of that first warm appreciating clasp I feel even now. To be met by *such* a specimen of heathen humanity on the borders of their land was to "stay us with flagons, and comfort us with apples."

Kalakua, with a sister queen, next welcomed us with similar civilities. They were two out of five dowager queens of Kamehameha. They had limbs of giant mold. I was taught to estimate their weight at three hundred pounds and even more. Kalakua was the mother of three of the wives of the young king. Two wives of Kalanimoku followed. They were all attired in a similar manner, a dress, then the pa-u, which consisted of ten thicknesses of the bark cloth three or four yards long and one yard wide, wrapped several times round the middle, and confined by tucking it in on one side. The two queens had loose dresses over these.

Trammeled with clothes and seated on chairs, the queens were out of their element. They divested themselves of their outer dresses. Then the one stretched herself full length upon a bench, and the other sat down upon the deck. Mattresses were then brought for them to recline in their own way.

After reaching the cabin, the common sitting room for ladies and gentlemen, one of the queens divested herself of her only remaining dress, simply retaining her pa-u. While we were opening wide our eyes, she looked as self-possessed and easy as though sitting in the shades of Eden.

Kalanimoku dined with our family, eating as others ate. The women declined sitting with us. After we rose from table they had their own food brought on, raw fish and poi, eating with their fingers.

From Kawaihae the chiefs and their large retinue all sailed with us to Kailua, where the king resided. They all slept on deck on their mats. While passing in the gray of evening between two rows of native men in Hawaiian costume, the climax of queer sensations was reached.

Kalakua brought a web of white cambric to have a dress made for herself in the fashion of those of our ladies, and was very particular in her wish to have it finished while sailing along the western side of the island before reaching the king.

Monday morning, April 3, the first sewing circle was formed that the sun ever looked down upon in his Hawaiian realm. Kalakua, queen dowager, was directress. She requested all the seven white ladies to take seats with them on mats, on the deck of the *Thaddeus*. Mrs. Holman and Mrs. Ruggles were executive officers, to ply the scissors and prepare the work. As the sisters were very much in the habit of journalizing, every one was a self-constituted recording secretary. The four native women of distinction were furnished with calico patchwork to sew, a new employment to them.

The dress was made in the fashion of 1819. The length of the skirt accorded with Brigham Young's rule to his Mormon damsels —*have it come down to the tops of the shoes*. But in the queen's case, where the shoes were wanting, the bare feet cropped out very prominently. . . .

The Missionaries Arrive

April 4, Tuesday, A.M., one hundred and sixty-three days from Boston, the *Thaddeus* was anchored before Kailua. The queen dowager, Kalakua, assumed a new appearance. In addition to her newly made white dress, her person was decorated with a lace cap having on a wreath of roses, and a lace half-neckerchief, in the corner of which was a most elegant sprig of various colors. They were presents we had brought her from some American friends. When she went ashore, she was received by hundreds with a shout.

Captain Blanchard, Messrs. Bingham and Thurston, together with Hopu went ashore and called on the king in his grass-thatched house. They found him eating dinner with his five wives, all of them in the free, cool undress of native dishabille. Two of his wives were his sisters, and one the former wife of his father.

After completing their meal, four of the wives, with apparent sisterly affection and great pleasure, turned to a game of cards. As was the custom, one wife was ever the close attendant of her regal lord.

Hopu then introduced Messrs. Bingham and Thurston as priests of the Most High God who made heaven and earth.

The letters were then read to the king from Dr. Worcester of Boston, and from the Prudential Committee, and the object for which they came to live among them was explained. The visitors then retired, leaving the subject for royal consideration.

April 6, the king and family dined with us by invitation. They came off in a double canoe with waving kahilis and twenty rowers, ten on each side, and with a large retinue of attendants. The king was introduced to the first white women, and they to the first king, that each had ever seen.

His dress on the occasion was a girdle, a green silk scarf put on under the left arm, brought up and knotted over the right shoulder, a chain of gold around his neck and over his chest, and a wreath of yellow feathers upon his head.

We honored the king, but we loved the cultivated manhood of Kalanimoku. He was the only individual Hawaiian that appeared before us with a full civilized dress.

After dining with the royal family, all were gathered on the quarter-deck. There the mission family, the captain and officers sang some hymns, aided by the bass viol played by Kaumualii, a young native chief returning with us.

The king appeared with complacency, and retired with that friendly "aloha" that left behind him the quiet hope that he would be gracious.

The next day several of the brothers and sisters of the mission went ashore, hoping that social intercourse might give weight to the scale that was then poising. They visited the palace. Ten or fifteen armed soldiers stood without, and although it was ten or eleven o'clock in the forenoon, we found him on whom devolved the government of a nation, three or four of his chiefs, and five or six of his attendants prostrate on their mats, wrapped in deep slumber.

The king had just put down one religion. In doing it his throne had tottered. It was a grave question for him to accept a new one. Hopu, who was apt to teach, had told them that our religion allowed neither polygamy nor incest. So when Kamamalu, the sister and marked favorite out of five queens, urged the king to receive the mission, he replied: "If I do they will allow me but one wife, and that will not be you." His royal father had twenty-one wives.

Nor did the king seem to understand about learning what kind of a thing it was, and whether it would be good for his people. He asked a missionary to write his name on a piece of paper. He wrote it *Liholiho*. The king looked at it and said: "It looks neither like myself nor any other man."

After various consultations, fourteen days after reaching the Islands, April 12, permission, simply for one year, was obtained from the king for all the missionaries to land upon his shores. Two gentlemen, with their wives, and two native youth were to stop at Kailua. The rest of the mission were to pass on forthwith to Honolulu.

Such an early separation was unexpected and painful. But broad views of usefulness were to be taken, and private feelings sacrificed.

At evening twilight we sundered ourselves from close family ties, from the dear old brig, and from civilization. We went ashore and entered, as our home, an abode of the most uncouth and humble character. It was a thatched hut, with one room, having two windows made simply by cutting away the thatch, leaving the bare poles. On the ground for the feet was first a layer of grass, then of mats. Here

The Missionaries Arrive

we found our effects from the *Thaddeus;* but no arrangement of them could be made till the house was thoroughly cleansed.

On the boxes and trunks, as they were scattered about the room, we formed a circle. We listened to a portion of scripture, sang a hymn, and knelt in prayer. The simple natural fact speaks for itself. It was the first family altar ever reared on this group of islands to the worship of Jehovah.

Flat-topped trunks and chests served admirably in accommodating us to horizontal positions for the night. Honest Dick, a native who had been with us while lying in port, sat within, and the king sent soldiers to keep sentinel without. Notwithstanding all, the night proved to be nearly a sleepless one. There was a secret enemy whose name was legion lying in ambush; or rather we had usurped their rights and taken possession of their own citadel. It was the flea. Thus the night passed. But bright day visited us with its soft climate and gentle sea breeze....

The two American missionaries rolled up their shirt sleeves above their elbows and went to work in good earnest, removing from the house all their effects brought from the *Thaddeus,* conveying away all old mats and grass, giving a thorough sweeping to the thatch above and the ground below, spreading down new grass and new mats, putting up two high-post bedsteads of Chinese manufacture lent them by Kamamalu, the queen, and bringing in such articles as would be a substitute for furniture. A large chest in the middle of the room served for a dining table, small boxes and buckets for dining chairs, and trunks for settees. We had block-tin tumblers, which answered well in receiving hot tea, and likewise served to impress the mind with the philosophical fact, through the lips and tips of the fingers, that metal is a good conductor of heat.

We trimmed the high-post bedsteads with curtains; then added one from the foot corner to the side of the house, thereby forming at the back of each bed a spot perfectly retired. The two native youth were added to the king's retinue. In twenty-four hours we found ourselves in circumstances comparatively neat and comfortable.

For three days the king's steward kept three pewter platters liberally supplied with fish, taro, and sweet potato, cooked in the native manner.

For several days we received calls from the queens and their whole train of attendants, three or four times in a day, and at each time were solicited to hear them read. When the queens were at our house, we sisters were Marys; when they were away, we were Marthas. . . .

April 29. For two days we heard one continued yell of dogs. I visited their prison. Between one and two hundred were thrown in groups on the ground, utterly unable to move, having their forelegs brought over their backs and bound together. Some had burst the bands that confined their mouths, and some had expired. Their piteous moans would excite the compassion of any feeling heart. Natives consider baked dog a great delicacy, too much so in the days of their idolatry ever to allow it to pass the lips of women. They never offer it to foreigners, who hold it in great abhorrence. Once they mischievously attached a pig's head to a dog's body, and thus inveigled a foreigner to partake of it to his great acceptance.

The above-mentioned dogs were collected for the grand feast which is this day made to commemorate the death of Kamehameha I. The king departed from his usual custom and spread a table for his family and ours. There were many thousand people present. The king appeared in a military dress with quite an exhibition of royalty. Kamamalu, his favorite queen, applied to me for one of my dresses to wear on the occasion; but as it was among the impossibles for her to assume it, the request happily called for neither consent nor denial. She, however, according to court ceremony so arranged a native-cloth pa-u, a yard wide, with ten folds, as to be enveloped round the middle with seventy thicknesses. To array herself in this unwieldy attire, the long cloth was spread out on the ground, when, beginning at one end, she laid her body across it, and rolled herself over and over till she had rolled the whole around her. Two attendants followed her, one bearing up the end of this cumbrous robe of state, and the other waving over her head an elegant nodding fly-brush of beautiful plumes, its long handle completely covered with little tortoise-shell rings of various colors.

Her head was ornamented with a graceful yellow wreath of elegant feathers of great value, from the fact that after a mountain bird had been caught in a snare, but just two small feathers of rare beauty, one under each wing, could be obtained from it. A mountain vine, with green leaves, small and lustrous, was the only drapery which went to deck and cover her neck and the upper part of her person. Thus this noble daughter of nature, at least six feet tall and of comely bulk in proportion, presented herself before the king and the nation, greatly to their admiration. After this presentation was over, her majesty lay down again upon the ground and unrolled the cloth by reversing the process of clothing.

The first time that Mr. Thurston preached before the king through an interpreter was from these words: "I have a message from God unto thee." The king, his family, and suite listened with attention. When prayer was offered, they all knelt before the white man's God.

The king's orders were that none should be taught to read but those of rank, those to whom he gave special permission, and the wives and children of white men. For several months his majesty kept foremost in learning, then the pleasures of the cup caused his books to be quite neglected. Some of the queens were ambitious, and made good progress, but they met with serious interruptions, going from place to place with their intoxicated husband. The young prince, seven years of age, the successor to the throne, attended to his lessons regularly. Although the king neglected to learn himself, yet he was solicitous to have his little brother apply himself, and threatened chastisement if he neglected his lessons. He told him that he must have learning for his father and mother both,—that it would fit him for governing the nation, and make him a wise and good king when old.

The king brought two young men to Mr. Thurston, and said: "Teach these, my favorites, Ii and Kahuhu. It will be the same as teaching me. Through them I shall find out what learning is." To do *his* part to distinguish and make them respectable scholars, he dressed them in a civilized manner. They daily came forth from the king, entered the presence of their teacher, clad in white, while his majesty and court continued to sit in their girdles. Although thus distinguished from their fellows, in all the beauty and strength of ripening manhood, with what humility they drank in instruction from the lips of their teacher, even as the dry earth drinks in water!

(After an absence of some months, the king returned, and called at our dwelling to hear the two young men, his favorites, read. He was delighted with their improvement, and shook Mr. Thurston most cordially by the hand—pressed it between both his own—then kissed it.)

For three weeks after going ashore, our house was constantly surrounded, and our doors and windows filled with natives. From sunrise to dark there would be thirty or forty at least, sometimes eighty or a hundred. For the sake of solitude, I one day retired from the house and seated myself beneath a shade. In five minutes I counted seventy companions. In their curiosity they followed the ladies in crowds from place to place, with simplicity peering under bonnets, and feeling articles of dress. It was amusing to see their efforts in running and taking a stand, that so they might have a full view of our faces. As objects of curiosity, the ladies were by far the most prominent. White men had lived and moved among them for a score of years. In our company were the first white women that ever stepped on these shores. It was thus the natives described the ladies: "They are white and have hats with a spout. Their faces are round and far in. Their necks are long. They look well.". . .

We could command only green brushwood, brought two miles on the backs of men, for cooking and heating our one iron, for smoothing all our light, thin, tropical dresses, which had been so abundantly prepared for us. But to such dresses we were limited. Every quart of water was brought to us from two to five miles in large gourd shells, on the shoulders of men. The natives were too ignorant to wash without superintendence. A new article was sent to be washed at the fountain, but five holes were made in it by being rubbed on sharp lava. We had entered a pathway that made it wisdom to take things as they came—and to take them by the smooth handle.

William Ellis

Missionaries Climb Kilauea

Born in London of a poor family, William Ellis (1794–1872) was trained as a gardener before he felt a call to offer himself to the London Missionary Society, which had opened stations in the Marquesas, Tonga, and Society Islands. Ellis was ordained in 1815 and worked for six years in the Society group, becoming the most proficient missionary ethnologist in Polynesia. A deputation of the London Missionary Society, headed by the Reverend Daniel Tyerman and George Bennet, visited the islands in 1822, and when they decided to extend their journey to observe the activities of the American missionaries in Hawaii, Ellis accompanied them. In Honolulu, Ellis's knowledge of the Tahitian language enabled him to learn Hawaiian quickly, and he was the first person to preach a sermon in that tongue.

The American missionaries were so pleased with Ellis that they invited him to work with them permanently. He agreed, and after returning to Huahine for his family, he began his labors in the Hawaiian Islands in February, 1823. At that time no mission stations had been opened on the island of Hawaii, the largest and most populous of the group, and a party was sent there to seek suitable sites. Ellis, with the Reverend Asa Thurston, the Reverend Artemas Bishop, and Joseph Goodrich began in June a two-month tour. They were the first white men to make a circuit of the island and the first to ascend the volcano of Kilauea.

A copy of their report, recommending eight possible sites for missions, was printed in Boston in 1825. Ellis, who because of his wife's health had returned to England in 1824, rewrote his journal as a personal narrative and added various observations. This was published in 1825 as *A Narrative of a Tour Through Hawaii* and went into five printings by 1828. In his introduction to a modern edition, Lorrin A. Thurston terms Ellis's narrative "the clearest, most accurate, and detailed account extant of the physical and social conditions existing in Hawaii in 1823. . . . The poet Coleridge is reported to have stated that he considered Ellis's *Tour* to be the most interesting and instructive book of travel that he had ever read."

Ellis in later life served as a missionary in Madagascar and wrote a history of that island. Nearing the age of eighty, having survived the rigors of primitive conditions in far-off lands, he died of a chill caught in an English railway carriage.

REFRESHED by a comfortable night's sleep, we arose before daylight on the morning of the first of August, and after stirring up the embers of our fire rendered, with grateful hearts, our morning tribute of praise to our almighty Preserver.

As the day began to dawn, we tied on our sandals, ascended from the subterraneous dormitory, and pursued our journey, directing our course toward the column of smoke, which bore east-northeast from the cavern.

The path for several miles lay through a most fertile tract of country, covered with bushes, or tall grass and fern, frequently from three to five feet high, and so heavily laden with dew that before we had passed it we were as completely wet as if we had walked through a river. The morning air was cool, the singing of birds enlivened the woods, and we traveled along in Indian file nearly four miles an hour, although most of the natives carried heavy burdens, which were tied on their backs with small bands over their shoulders, in the same manner that a soldier fastens on his knapsack. Having also ourselves a small leather bag containing a Bible, inkstand, notebook, compass, etc., suspended from one shoulder, a canteen of water from the other, and sometimes a light portfolio, or papers, with specimens of plants besides, our whole party appeared, in this respect at least, somewhat *en militaire*.

After traveling a short distance over the open country we came to a small wood, into which we had not penetrated far before all traces of a path entirely disappeared. We kept on some time, but were soon brought to a stand by a deep chasm, over which we saw no means of passing. Here the natives ran about in every direction searching for marks of footsteps, just as a dog runs to and fro when he has lost the track of his master.

After searching about half an hour, they discovered a path, which led some distance to the southward, in order to avoid the deep chasm in the lava. Near the place where we crossed over, there was an extensive cavern. The natives sat down on the top of the arch by which it was formed, and began eating their sugar cane, a portable kind of provision usually carried on their journeys, while we explored the cavern in hopes of finding fresh water. In several places drops of water, beautifully clear, constantly filtered through the vaulted arch and fell into calabashes placed underneath to receive it. Unfortunately for us, these were all nearly empty. Probably some thirsty traveler had been there but a short time before.

Leaving the wood, we entered a waste of dry sand, about four miles across. The traveling over it was extremely fatiguing, as we sank in to our ankles at every step. The sand was of a dark olive color, fine and sparkling, parts of it adhering readily to the magnet, and being raised up in heaps in every direction, presented a surface resembling, color excepted, that of drifted snow.

It was undoubtedly volcanic; but whether thrown out of any of the adjacent craters in its present form, or made up of small particles of decomposed lava and the crystalline olivine we had observed so abundant in the lava of the southern shore and drifted by the constant trade wind from the vast tract of lava to the eastward, we could not determine.

When we had nearly passed through it, we sat down on a heap of lava to rest and refresh ourselves, having taken nothing since the preceding noon. About ten o'clock, Messrs. Bishop and Goodrich reached the place where we were sitting. They had heard by some travelers that two or three days would elapse before Makoa would overtake them, and deeming it inexpedient to wait so long had procured a guide, and early this morning set out from Kapapala to follow the rest of the party.

Having refreshed ourselves, we resumed our journey, taking a northerly direction toward the columns of smoke, which we could now distinctly perceive. Our way lay over a wide waste of ancient lava, of a black color, compact and heavy, with a shining vitreous surface, sometimes entirely covered with obsidian, and frequently thrown up, by the expansive force of vapor or heated air, into conical mounds from six to twelve feet high, which were, probably, by the same power rent into a number of pieces, from the apex to the base. The hollows between the mounds and long ridges were filled with volcanic sand and fine particles of olivine, or decomposed lava.

This vast tract of lava resembled in appearance an inland sea, bounded by distant mountains. Once it had certainly been in a fluid state, but appeared as if it had become suddenly petrified, or turned into a glassy stone while its agitated billows were rolling to and fro. Not only were the large swells and hollows distinctly marked, but in many places the surface of these billows was covered by a smaller ripple, like that observed on the surface of the sea at the first springing up of a breeze, or the passing currents of air which produce what the sailors call a cat's-paw. The billows may have been raised by the force which elevated the mounds or hills, but they look as if the whole mass, extending several miles, had, when in a state of perfect fusion, been agitated with a violent undulating or heaving motion.

The sun had now risen in his strength, and his bright rays, reflected from the sparkling sand and undulated surface of the vitreous lava, dazzled our sight and caused considerable pain, particularly as the trade wind blew fresh in our faces and continually drove into our eyes particles of sand. This part of our journey was unusually laborious, not only from the heat of the sun and the reflection from the lava, but also from the unevenness of its surface, which obliged us constantly to tread on an inclined plane, in some places as smooth and almost as slippery as glass, where the greatest caution was necessary to avoid a fall. Frequently we chose to walk along on the ridge of a billow of lava, though considerably circuitous, rather than pass up and down its polished sides. Taking the trough, or hollow between the waves, was found safer, but much more fatiguing, as we sunk every step ankle-deep into the sand. The natives ran along the ridges, stepping like goats from one ridge to another. They, however, occasionally descended into the hollows, and made several marks with their feet in the sand at short distances, for the direction of two or three native boys with our provisions, and some of their companions, who had fallen behind early in the morning, not being able to keep up with the foremost party.

Between eleven and twelve we passed a number of conical hills on our right, which the natives informed us were craters. A quantity of sand was collected round their base, but whether thrown out by them, or drifted thither by the wind, they could not inform us. In their vicinity we also passed several deep chasms, from which, in a number of places, small columns of vapor arose, at frequent and irregular intervals. They appeared to proceed from Kilauea, the great volcano, and extended toward the sea in a southeast direction. Probably they are connected with Ponahohoa, and may mark the course of a vast subterraneous channel leading from the volcano to the shore. The surface of the lava on both sides was heated, and the vapor had a strong sulphureous smell.

We continued our way beneath the scorching rays of a vertical sun till about noon, when we reached a solitary tree growing in a bed of sand, spreading its roots among the crevices of the rocks, and casting its grateful shade on the barren lava. Here we threw ourselves down on the sand and fragments of lava, stretched out our weary limbs, and drank the little water left in our canteens.

In every direction we observed a number of pieces of spumous lava, of an olive color, extremely cellular, and as light as sponge. They appeared to have been drifted by the wind into the hollows which they occupied. The high bluff rocks on the northwest side of the volcano were distinctly seen; the smoke and vapors driven past us, and the scent of the fumes of sulphur, which, as we approached from the leeward we had perceived ever since the wind sprang up, becoming very strong, indicated our proximity to Kilauea.

Impatient to view it we arose, after resting about half an hour, and pursued our journey. In the way we saw a number of low bushes bearing beautiful red and yellow berries in clusters, each berry being about the size and shape of a large currant. The bushes on which they grew were generally low, seldom reaching two feet in height. The native name of the plant is ohelo. The berries looked tempting to persons experiencing both hunger and thirst, and we eagerly plucked and ate all that came in our way. They are juicy, but rather insipid to the taste. As soon as the natives perceived us eating them, they called out aloud, and begged us to desist, saying we were now within the precincts of Pele's dominions, to whom they belonged, and by whom they were rahuiia (prohibited) until some had been offered to her, and permission to eat them asked. We told them we were sorry they should feel uneasy on this account—that we acknowledged Jehovah as the only divine proprietor of the fruits of the earth, and felt thankful to him for them, especially in our present circumstances. Some of them then said, "We are afraid. We shall be overtaken by some calamity before we leave this place." We advised them to dismiss their fears and eat with us, as we knew they were thirsty and faint. They shook their heads, and perceiving us determined to disregard their entreaties, walked along in silence.

We traveled on, regretting that the natives should indulge notions so superstitious, but clearing every ohelo bush that grew near our path, till about 2 P.M., when the Crater of Kilauea suddenly burst upon our view. We expected to have seen a mountain with a broad base and rough indented sides, composed of loose slags or hardened streams of lava, and whose summit would have presented a rugged wall of scoria, forming the rim of a mighty caldron. But instead of this, we found ourselves on the edge of a steep precipice, with a vast plain before us, fifteen or sixteen miles in circumference, and sunk from two hundred to four hundred feet below its original level. The surface of this plain was uneven, and strewed over with large stones and volcanic rocks, and in the center of it was the great crater, at the distance of a mile and a half from the precipice on which we were standing. Our guides led us round toward the north end of the ridge, in order to find a place by which we might descend to the plain below. As we passed along, we observed the natives, who had hitherto refused to touch any of the ohelo berries, now gather several bunches and, after offering a part to Pele, eat them very freely. They did not use much ceremony in their acknowledgment; but when they had plucked a branch containing several clusters of berries, they turned their faces toward the place whence the greatest quantity of smoke and vapor issued and, breaking the branch they held in their hand in two, they threw one part down the precipice, saying at the same time, *"E Pele, eia ka ohelo 'au; e taumaha aku wau ia oe, e ai hoi au tetahi."* "Pele, here are your ohelos: I offer some to you, some I also eat." Several of them told us, as they turned round from the crater, that after such acknowledgments they might eat the fruit with security. We answered we were sorry to see them offering to an imaginary deity the gifts of the true God; but hoped they would soon know better, and acknowledge Jehovah alone in all the benefits they received.

We walked on to the north end of the ridge, where, the precipice being less steep, a descent to the plain below seemed practicable. It

Missionaries Climb Kilauea

required, however, the greatest caution, as the stones and fragments of rock frequently gave way under our feet, and rolled down from above; but, with all our care, we did not reach the bottom without several falls and slight bruises.

The steep which we had descended was formed of volcanic matter, apparently a light-red and gray kind of lava, vesicular, and lying in horizontal strata, varying in thickness from one to forty feet. In a small number of places the different strata of lava were also rent in perpendicular or oblique directions, from the top to the bottom, either by earthquakes or other violent convulsions of the ground connected with the action of the adjacent volcano. After walking some distance over the sunken plain, which in several places sounded hollow under our feet, we at length came to the edge of the great crater, where a spectacle, sublime and even appalling, presented itself before us—"We stopped, and trembled."

Astonishment and awe for some moments rendered us mute, and, like statues, we stood fixed to the spot, with our eyes riveted on the abyss below. Immediately before us yawned an immense gulf, in the form of a crescent, about two miles in length, from northeast to southwest, nearly a mile in width, and apparently eight hundred feet deep. The bottom was covered with lava, and the southwest and northern parts of it were one vast flood of burning matter, in a state of terrific ebullition, rolling to and fro its "fiery surge" and flaming billows. Fifty-one conical islands of varied form and size, containing so many craters, rose either round the edge or from the surface of the burning lake. Twenty-two constantly emitted columns of gray smoke, or pyramids of brilliant flame, and several of these at the same time vomited from their ignited mouths streams of lava, which rolled in blazing torrents down their black indented sides into the boiling mass below.

The existence of these conical craters led us to conclude that the boiling caldron of lava before us did not form the focus of the volcano, that this mass of melted lava was comparatively shallow, and that the basin in which it was contained was separated, by a stratum of solid matter, from the great volcanic abyss, which constantly poured out its melted contents through these numerous craters into this upper reservoir. We were further inclined to this opinion from the vast columns of vapor continually ascending from the chasms in the vicinity of the sulphur banks and pools of water, for they must have been produced by other fire than that which caused the ebullition in the lava at the bottom of the great crater; and also by noticing a number of small craters, in vigorous action, situated high up the sides of the great gulf, and apparently quite detached from it. The streams of lava which they emitted rolled down into the lake and mingled with the melted mass there, which, though thrown up by different apertures, had perhaps been originally fused in one vast furnace.

The sides of the gulf before us, although composed of different strata of ancient lava, were perpendicular for about four hundred feet, and rose from a wide horizontal ledge of solid black lava of irregular breadth, but extending completely round. Beneath this ledge the sides sloped gradually toward the burning lake, which was, as nearly as we could judge, three hundred or four hundred feet lower. It was evident that the large crater had been recently filled with liquid lava up to this black ledge and had, by some subterranean canal, emptied itself into the sea, or upon the low land on the shore; and in all probability this evacuation had caused the inundation of the Kapapala coast, which took place, as we afterward learned, about three weeks prior to our visit. The gray, and in some places apparently calcined, sides of the great crater before us, the fissures which intersected the surface of the plain on which we were standing, the long banks of sulphur on the opposite side of the abyss, the vigorous action of the numerous small craters on its borders, the dense columns of vapor and smoke that rose at the north and south end of the plain, together with the ridge of steep rocks by which it was surrounded, rising probably in some places three hundred or four hundred feet in perpendicular height, presented an immense volcanic panorama, the effect of which was greatly augmented by the constant roaring of the vast furnace below.

After the first feelings of astonishment had subsided, we remained a considerable time contemplating a scene which it is impossible to describe, and which filled us with wonder and admiration at the almost overwhelming manifestation it affords of the power of that dread Being who created the world, and who has declared that by fire he will one day destroy it. We then walked along the west side of the crater, and in half an hour reached the north end.

While walking over the plain, which was covered with a thin layer of what appeared like indurated sand, but which we afterward found to be decomposed lava, the natives requested us not to *"kaha, a heru ka one,"*—strike, scratch, or dig the sand—assuring us it would displease Pele, and be followed by an irruption of lava or other expression of vengeance from this goddess of the volcano, of whose power and displeasure they had manifested the greatest apprehensions ever since our approach to Kilauea.

At the north end of the crater we left the few provisions and little baggage that we had, and went in search of water, which we had been informed was to be found in the neighborhood of a number of columns of vapor, which we saw rising in a northerly direction. About half a mile distant, we found two or three small pools of perfectly sweet, fresh water; a luxury which, notwithstanding the reports of the natives, we did not expect to meet with in these regions of fire. It proved a most grateful refreshment to us after traveling not less than twenty miles over a barren thirsty desert.

These pools appeared great natural curiosities. The surface of the ground in the vicinity was perceptibly warm, and rent by several deep irregular chasms, from which steam and thick vapors continually arose. In some places these chasms were two feet wide, and from them a volume of steam ascended, which was immediately condensed by the cool mountain air and driven, like drizzling rain, into hollows in the compact lava on the leeward side of the chasms. The pools, which were six or eight feet from the chasms, were surrounded and covered by flags, rushes, and tall grass. Nourished by the moisture of the vapors, these plants flourished luxuriantly and, in their turn, sheltered the pools from the heat of the sun and prevented evaporation. We expected to find the water warm, but in this we were also agreeably disappointed. When we had quenched our thirst with water thus distilled by nature, we directed the natives to build a hut in which we might pass the night, in such a situation as to command a view of the burning lava; and while they were thus employed, we prepared to examine the many interesting objects around us. Mr. Bishop returned, with a canteen of water, to meet Mr. Harwood, who had not yet come up.

Mr. Thurston visited the eastern side of the great crater, and I went with Mr. Goodrich to examine some extensive beds of sulphur at the northeast end. After walking about three quarters of a mile over a tract of decomposed lava, covered with ohelo bushes and ferns, we came to a bank about a hundred and fifty yards long, and in some places upward of thirty feet high, formed of sulphur, with a small proportion of red clay or ocher. The ground was very hot, its surface rent by fissures; and we were sometimes completely enveloped in the thick vapors that continually ascended from these cracks. A number of apertures were visible along the whole extent of the bank of sulphur; smoke and vapors arose from these fissures also; and the heat of the sulphur around them was more intense than in any other part. Their edges were fringed with fine crystals in various combinations, like what are called flowers of sulphur. We climbed about halfway up the bank and endeavored to break off some parts of the crust, but soon found it too hot to be handled. However, by means of our walking sticks, we detached some curious specimens. Those procured near the surface were crystallized in beautiful acicular prisms, of a light-yellow color; while those found three or four inches deep in the bank were of an orange-yellow, generally in single or double tetrahedral pyramids, and full an inch in length. A singular hissing and cracking noise was heard among the crystals whenever the outside crust of the sulphur was broken and the atmospheric air admitted. The same noise was produced among the fragments broken off, until they were quite cold. The adjacent stones and pieces of clay were frequently incrusted, either with sulphate of ammonia, or volcanic sal ammoniac. Considerable quantities were also found in the crevices of some of the neighboring rocks, which were much more pungent than that exposed to the air. Along the bottom of the sulphur bank we found a number of pieces of tufa, or clay stone, which appeared to have been fused, extremely light and cellular. It seemed as if sulphur, or some other inflammable substance, had formerly occupied the cells in these stones. A thick fog now came over, which, being followed by a shower of rain, obliged us to leave this interesting laboratory of nature and return to our companions.

On the eastern side of the crater, we saw banks of sulphur less pure, but apparently more extensive, than those we had visited; but their distance from us, and the unfavorable state of the weather, prevented our examining them. On our way to the sulphur banks, we saw two flocks of wild geese [nene], which came down from the mountains and settled among the ohelo bushes, near the pools of water. They were smaller than the common goose, had brown necks, and their wings were tipped with the same color. The natives informed us there were vast flocks in the interior, although they were never seen near the sea.

Just as the sun was setting we reached the place where we had left our baggage, and found Messrs. Bishop and Harwood sitting near the spot, where the natives, with a few green branches of trees, some fern leaves, and rushes, had erected a hut. We were none of us pleased with the site which they had chosen. It was at the northeast end of the crater, on a pile of rocks overhanging the abyss below and actually within four feet of the precipice. When we expressed our disapprobation, they said it was the only place where we might expect to pass the night undisturbed by Pele, and secure from earthquake and other calamity, being the place in which alone Pele allowed travelers to build a hut. We told them it was unnecessarily near and, being also unsafe, we wished to remove. They answered that as it was within the limits prescribed by Pele for safe lodging, *they* should be unwilling to sleep anywhere else, and had not time to build another hut for *us*.

We then directed them to collect a quantity of firewood, as we expected the night would be cold, although the thermometer then stood at 69°. We were the more anxious to have the fuel collected before the shades of night should close upon us, as traveling in some places was extremely dangerous. The ground sounded hollow in every direction, frequently cracked, and, in two instances, actually gave way while we were passing over it. Mr. Bishop was approaching the hut when the lava suddenly broke under him. He instantly threw himself forward, and fell flat on his face over a part that was more solid. A boy, who followed me with a basket to the sulphur banks, and walked about a yard behind Mr. Goodrich and myself, also fell in. There was no crack in the surface of the lava over which he was walking, neither did it bend under his weight, but broke suddenly, when he sank in up to his middle. His legs and thighs were considerably bruised, but providentially he escaped without any other injury. The lava in both places was about two inches in thickness and broke short, leaving the aperture regular and defined, without even cracking the adjoining parts. On looking into the holes, we could see no bottom, but on both sides, at a short distance from the aperture, the lava was solid, and they appeared to have fallen into a narrow chasm covered over by a thin crust of lava, already in a state of decomposition.

When night came on, we kindled a good fire, and prepared our frugal supper. Mr. Thurston, however, had not yet returned, and, as the darkness of the night increased, we began to feel anxious for his safety. The wind came down from the mountains in violent gusts, dark clouds lowered over us, and a thick fog enveloped every object; even the fires of the volcano were but indistinctly seen. The darkness of the night advanced, but no tidings reached us of Mr. Thurston.

About seven o'clock we sent out the natives with torches and firebrands, to search for him. They went as far as they durst, hallooing along the border of the crater, till their lights were extinguished, when they returned, without having seen or heard anything of him. We now increased our fire, hoping it might serve as a beacon to direct him to our hut.

Eight o'clock came, and he did not appear. We began seriously to fear that he had fallen into the crater itself, or some of the deep and rugged chasms by which it was surrounded. In this state of painful suspense we remained till nearly half past eight, when we were happily relieved by his sudden appearance. He had descended, and walked along the dark ledge of lava on the east side of the crater, till a chasm obliged him to ascend. Having with difficulty reached the top, he traveled along the southern and western sides, till the light of our fire directed him to our encampment. The extent of the crater, the unevenness of the path, the numerous fissures and rugged surface of the lava, and the darkness of the night had prevented his earlier arrival.

We now partook with cheerfulness of our evening repast, and afterward, amidst the whistling of the winds around, and the roaring of the furnace beneath, rendered our evening sacrifice of praise, and committed ourselves to the secure protection of our God. We then spread our mats on the ground, but as we were all wet through with the rain, against which our hut was but an indifferent shelter, we preferred to sit or stand round the fire, rather than lie down on the ground. Between nine and ten, the dark clouds and heavy fog that since the setting of the sun had hung over the volcano gradually cleared away, and the fires of Kilauea, darting their fierce light athwart the midnight gloom, unfolded a sight terrible and sublime beyond all we had yet seen.

The agitated mass of liquid lava, like a flood of melted metal, raged with tumultuous whirl. The lively flame that danced over its undulating surface, tinged with sulphureous blue, or glowing with mineral red, cast a broad glare of dazzling light on the indented sides of the insulated craters, whose roaring mouths, amidst rising flames and eddying streams of fire shot up, at frequent intervals, with very loud detonations, spherical masses of fusing lava, or bright ignited stones.

The dark, bold outline of the perpendicular and jutting rocks around formed a striking contrast with the luminous lake below, whose vivid rays, thrown on the rugged promontories and reflected by the overhanging clouds, combined to complete the awful grandeur of the imposing scene. We sat gazing at the magnificent phenomena for several hours, when we laid ourselves down on our mats, in order to observe more leisurely their varying aspect; for, although we had traveled upward of twenty miles since the morning and were both weary and cold, we felt but little disposition to sleep. This disinclination was probably increased by our proximity to the yawning gulf and our conviction that the detachment of a fragment from beneath the overhanging pile on which we were reclining, or the slightest concussion of the earth, which everything around indicated to be no unfrequent occurrence, would perhaps precipitate us, amidst the horrid crash of falling rocks, into the burning lake immediately before us.

The natives, who probably viewed the scene with thoughts and feelings somewhat different from ours, seemed, however, equally interested. They sat most of the night talking of the achievements of Pele, and regarding with a superstitious fear, at which we were not surprised, the brilliant exhibition. They considered it the primeval abode of their volcanic deities. The conical craters, they said, were their houses, where they frequently amused themselves by playing at konane; the roaring of the furnaces and the crackling of the flames were the kani of their hula (music of their dance), and the red flaming surge was the surf wherein they played, sportively swimming on the rolling wave. . . .

Some months after our visit to Kilauea, a priestess of Pele came to Lahaina, in Maui, where the principal chiefs of the islands then resided. The object of her visit was noised abroad among the people and much public interest excited. One or two mornings after her arrival in the district, arrayed in her prophetic robes, having the edges of her garments burned with fire and holding a short staff or spear in her hand, preceded by her daughter, who was also a candidate for the office of priestess, and followed by thousands of the people, she came into the presence of the chiefs; and having told who she was, they asked what communications she had to make. She replied that, in a trance or vision, she had been with Pele, by whom she was charged to complain to them that a number of foreigners had visited Kilauea, eaten the sacred berries, broken her houses, the craters, thrown down large stones, etc.; to request that the offenders might be sent away and to assure them that if these foreigners were not banished from the islands, Pele would certainly, in a given number of days, take vengeance by inundating the country with lava and destroying the people. She also pretended to have received, in a supernatural manner, Liholiho's approbation of the request of the goddess. The crowds of natives who stood waiting the result of her interview with the chiefs were almost as much astonished as the priestess herself when Kaahumanu and the other chiefs ordered all her paraphernalia of office to be thrown into the fire, told her the message she had delivered was a falsehood, and directed her to return home, cultivate the ground for her subsistence, and discontinue her journeys of deception among the people.

This answer was dictated by the chiefs themselves. The missionaries at the station, although they were aware of the visit of the priestess and saw her, followed by the thronging crowd, pass by their habitation on her way to the residence of the chiefs, did not think it necessary to attend or interfere, but relied entirely on the enlightened judgment and integrity of the chiefs to suppress any attempts that might be made to revive the influence of Pele over the people; and in the result they were not disappointed, for the natives returned to their habitations and the priestess soon after left the island and has not since troubled them with the threatenings of the goddess.

On another occasion, Kapiolani, a pious chief-woman, the wife of Naihe, chief of Kaawaloa, was passing near the volcano and expressed her determination to visit it. Some of the devotees of the goddess met her and attempted to dissuade her from her purpose; assuring her that though foreigners might go there with security, yet Pele would allow no Hawaiian to intrude. Kapiolani, however, was not to be thus diverted, but proposed that they should all go together; and declaring that if Pele appeared, or inflicted any punishment, she would then worship the goddess, but proposing that if nothing of the kind took place, they should renounce their attachment to Pele, and join with her and her friends in acknowledging Jehovah as the true God. They all went together to the volcano; Kapiolani, with her attendants, descended several hundred feet toward the bottom of the crater, where she spoke to them of the delusion they had formerly labored under in supposing it inhabited by their false gods; they sung a hymn, and after spending several hours in the vicinity, pursued their journey. What effect the conduct of Kapiolani, on this occasion, will have on the natives in general remains yet to be discovered.

Samuel L. Clemens

Mark Twain on the Kona Coast

Samuel L. Clemens, appearing on the passenger list of the steamer *Ajax* under his recently assumed pseudonym of Mark Twain, arrived in Honolulu on March 18, 1866, and remained in the Islands for four months. He came to write a series of travel letters for the Sacramento, California, *Union*. This young man from Missouri, with drooping mustache and flaming-red hair, rode around on a rented horse, talking and waving his arms and observing the Hawaii of a century ago with a keen repertorial eye. He visited not only the capital island of Oahu but also Maui, where he climbed to the edge of the giant crater of Haleakala, rode into Iao Valley, and then embarked on a schooner to the island of Hawaii, as described in the following selection.

The twenty-five letters sent to the *Union* (edited in one volume in 1966 by A. Grove Day) were later the basis for Chapters 74 through 78 of Clemens' book *Roughing It* (1872). These Hawaii chapters, sometimes omitted in recent reprints, were more smoothly written than the letters, and avoided some remarks that had caused offense to the people of Hawaii. The present account of the rigors of sailing between the islands on a crowded schooner, and of observations during a visit to the scene where Captain Cook was killed, reveals the young Mark Twain both as humorist and as zestful traveler.

BOUND for Hawaii (a hundred and fifty miles distant), to visit the great volcano and behold the other notable things which distinguish that island above the remainder of the group, we sailed from Honolulu on a certain Saturday afternoon, in the good schooner *Boomerang*.

The *Boomerang* was about as long as two streetcars, and about as wide as one. She was so small (though she was larger than the majority of the interisland coasters) that when I stood on her deck

I felt but little smaller than the Colossus of Rhodes must have felt when he had a man-of-war under him. I could reach the water when she lay over under a strong breeze. When the captain and my comrade (a Mr. Billings), myself, and four other persons were all assembled on the little afterportion of the deck which is sacred to the cabin passengers, it was full—there was not room for any more quality folks. Another section of the deck, twice as large as ours, was full of natives of both sexes, with their customary dogs, mats, blankets, pipes, calabashes of poi, fleas, and other luxuries and baggage of minor importance. As soon as we set sail the natives all lay down on the deck as thick as Negroes in a slavepen, and smoked, conversed, and spit on each other, and were truly sociable.

The little low-ceiled cabin below was rather larger than a hearse, and as dark as a vault. It had two coffins on each side—I mean two bunks. A small table, capable of accommodating three persons at dinner, stood against the forward bulkhead, and over it hung the dingiest whale-oil lantern that ever peopled the obscurity of a dungeon with ghostly shapes. The floor room unoccupied was not extensive. One might swing a cat in it, perhaps, but not a long cat. The hold forward of the bulkhead had but little freight in it, and from morning till night a portly old rooster, with a voice like Baalam's ass, and the same disposition to use it, strutted up and down in that part of the vessel and crowed. He usually took dinner at six o'clock, and then, after an hour devoted to meditation, he mounted a barrel and crowed a good part of the night. He got hoarser and hoarser all the time, but he scorned to allow any personal consideration to interfere with his duty, and kept up his labors in defiance of threatened diphtheria.

Sleeping was out of the question when he was on watch. He was a source of genuine aggravation and annoyance. It was worse than useless to shout at him or apply offensive epithets to him—he only took these things for applause, and strained himself to make more noise. Occasionally, during the day, I threw potatoes at him through an aperture in the bulkhead, but he only dodged and went on crowing.

The first night, as I lay in my coffin, idly watching the dim lamp swinging to the rolling of the ship, and snuffing the nauseous odors of bilge water, I felt something gallop over me. I turned out promptly. However, I turned in again when I found it was only a rat. Presently something galloped over me once more. I knew it was not a rat this time, and I thought it might be a centipede, because the captain had killed one on deck in the afternoon. I turned out. The first glance at the pillow showed me a repulsive sentinel perched upon each end of it—cockroaches as large as peach leaves—fellows with long, quivering antennae and fiery, malignant eyes. They were grating their teeth like tobacco worms, and appeared to be dissatisfied about something. I had often heard that these reptiles were in the habit of eating off sleeping sailors' toenails down to the quick, and I would not get in the bunk any more. I lay down on the floor. But a rat came and bothered me, and shortly afterward a procession of cockroaches arrived and camped in my hair. In a few moments the rooster was crowing with uncommon spirit, and a party of fleas were throwing double somersaults about my person in the wildest disorder, and taking a bite every time they struck. I was beginning to feel really annoyed. I got up and put my clothes on and went on deck.

The above is not overdrawn; it is a truthful sketch of interisland schooner life. There is no such thing as keeping a vessel in elegant condition when she carries molasses and Kanakas.

It was compensation for my sufferings to come unexpectedly upon so beautiful a scene as met my eye—to step suddenly out of the sepulchral gloom of the cabin and stand under the strong light of the moon—in the center, as it were, of a glittering sea of liquid silver—to see the broad sails straining in the gale, the ship keeled over on her side, the angry foam hissing past her lee bulwarks, and sparkling sheets of spray dashing high over her bows and raining upon her decks; to brace myself and hang fast to the first object that presented itself, with hat jammed down and coattails whipping in the breeze, and feel that exhilaration that thrills in one's hair and quivers down his backbone when he knows that every inch of canvas is drawing and the vessel cleaving through the waves at her utmost speed. There was no darkness, no dimness, no obscurity there. All was brightness, every object was vividly defined. Every prostrate Kanaka, every coil of rope, every calabash of poi, every puppy, every seam in the flooring, every bolthead—every object, however minute, showed sharp and distinct in its every outline; and the shadow of the broad mainsail lay black as a pall upon the deck, leaving Billings's white upturned face glorified and his body in a total eclipse.

Monday morning we were close to the island of Hawaii. Two of its high mountains were in view—Mauna Loa and Hualalai. The latter is an imposing peak, but being only ten thousand feet high is seldom mentioned or heard of. Mauna Loa is said to be sixteen thousand feet high. The rays of glittering snow and ice that clasped its summit like a claw looked refreshing when viewed from the blistering climate we were in. One could stand on that mountain (wrapped up in blankets and furs to keep warm), and while he nibbled a snowball or an icicle to quench his thirst he could look down the long sweep of its sides and see spots where plants are growing that grow only where the bitter cold of winter prevails; lower down he could see sections devoted to productions that thrive in the temperate zone alone; and at the bottom of the mountain he could see the home of the tufted coco palms and other species of vegetation that grow only in the sultry atmosphere of eternal summer. He could see all the climes of the world at a single glance of the eye, and that glance would only pass over a distance of four or five miles as the bird flies!

By and by we took boat and went ashore at Kailua, designing to ride horseback through the pleasant orange and coffee region of Kona and rejoin the vessel at a point some leagues distant. This journey is well worth taking. The trail passes along on high ground—say a thousand feet above sea level—and usually about a mile distant from the ocean, which is always in sight, save that occasionally you find yourself buried in the forest in the midst of a rank tropical vegetation and a dense growth of trees, whose great boughs overarch the road and shut out sun and sea and everything, and leave you in a dim, shady tunnel, haunted with invisible singing birds and fragrant with the odor of flowers. It was pleasant to ride occasionally in the warm sun and feast the eye upon the ever changing panorama of the forest (beyond and below us), with its many tints, its softened lights and shadows, its billowy undulations sweeping gently down from the mountain to the sea. It was pleasant also, at intervals, to leave the sultry sun and pass into the cool, green depths of this forest and indulge in sentimental reflections under the inspiration of its brooding twilight and its whispering foliage.

We rode through one orange grove that had ten thousand trees in it! They were all laden with fruit.

At one farmhouse we got some large peaches of excellent flavor. This fruit, as a general thing, does not do well in the Sandwich Islands. It takes a sort of almond shape, and is small and bitter. It needs frost, they say, and perhaps it does; if this be so, it will have a good opportunity to go on needing it, as it will not be likely to get it. The trees from which the fine fruit I have spoken of came had been planted and replanted *sixteen times,* and to this treatment the proprietor of the orchard attributed his success.

We passed several sugar plantations—new ones and not very extensive. The crops were, in most cases, third rattoons. [NOTE.—The first crop is called "plant cane"; subsequent crops which spring from the original roots, without replanting, are called "rattoons."] Almost everywhere on the island of Hawaii, sugar cane matures in twelve months, both rattoons and plant, and although it ought to be taken off as soon as it tassels, no doubt, it is not absolutely necessary to do it until about four months afterward. In Kona, the average yield of an acre of ground is *two tons* of sugar, they say. This is only a moderate yield for these islands, but would be astounding for Louisiana and most other sugar-growing countries. The plantations in Kona being on pretty high ground—up among the light and frequent rains—no irrigation whatever is required.

At four o'clock in the afternoon we were winding down a mountain of dreary and desolate lava to the sea, and closing our pleasant land journey. This lava is the accumulation of ages; one torrent of fire after another has rolled down here in old times, and built up the island structure higher and higher. Underneath, it is honeycombed with caves. It would be of no use to dig wells in such a place; they would not hold water—you would not find any for them to hold, for that matter. Consequently, the planters depend upon cisterns.

The last lava flow occurred here so long ago that there are none now living who witnessed it. In one place it enclosed and burned down a grove of coconut trees, and the holes in the lava where the trunks stood are still visible; their sides retain the impression of the bark: the trees fell upon the burning river, and becoming partly submerged left in it the perfect counterpart of every knot and branch and leaf and even nut, for curiosity seekers of a long-distant day to gaze upon and wonder at.

There were doubtless plenty of Kanaka sentinels on guard hereabouts at that time, but they did not leave casts of their figures in the lava as the Roman sentinels at Herculaneum and Pompeii did. It is a pity it is so, because such things are so interesting; but so it is. They probably went away. They went away early, perhaps. However, they had their merits; the Romans exhibited the higher pluck, but the Kanakas showed the sounder judgment.

Shortly we came in sight of that spot whose history is so familiar to every schoolboy in the wide world—Kealakekua Bay—the place where Captain Cook, the great circumnavigator, was killed by the natives, nearly a hundred years ago. The setting sun was flaming upon it, a summer shower was falling, and it was spanned by two magnificent rainbows. Two men who were in advance of us rode through one of these and for a moment their garments shone with a more than regal splendor. Why did not Captain Cook have taste enough to call his great discovery the Rainbow Islands? These charming spectacles are present to you at every turn; they are common in all the Islands; they are visible every day, and frequently at night also—not the silvery bow we see once in an age in the States, by moonlight, but barred with all bright and beautiful colors, like the children of the sun and rain. I saw one of them a few nights ago. What the sailors call "rain dogs"—little patches of rainbow—are often seen drifting about the heavens in these latitudes, like stained cathedral windows.

Kealakekua Bay is a little curve like the last kink of a snail shell, winding deep into the land, seemingly not more than a mile wide from shore to shore. It is bounded on one side—where the murder was done—by a little flat plain, on which stands a coconut grove and some ruined houses; a steep wall of lava, a thousand feet high at the upper end and three or four hundred at the lower, comes down from the mountain and bounds the inner extremity of it. From this wall the place takes its name, Kealakekua, which in the native tongue signifies "The Pathway of the Gods." They say (and still believe, in spite of their liberal education in Christianity) that the great god Lono, who used to live upon the hillside, always traveled that causeway when urgent business connected with heavenly affairs called him down to the seashore in a hurry.

As the red sun looked across the placid ocean through the tall, clean stems of the coconut trees, like a blooming whiskey bloat through the bars of a city prison, I went and stood in the edge of the water on the flat rock pressed by Captain Cook's feet when the blow was dealt which took away his life, and tried to picture in my mind the doomed man struggling in the midst of the multitude of exasperated savages—the men in the ship crowding to the vessel's side and gazing in anxious dismay toward the shore—the—but I discovered that I could not do it.

It was growing dark, the rain began to fall, we could see that the distant *Boomerang* was helplessly becalmed at sea, and so I adjourned to the cheerless little box of a warehouse and sat down to smoke and think, and wish the ship would make the land—for we had not eaten much for ten hours and were viciously hungry.

Toward midnight a fine breeze sprang up and the schooner soon worked herself into the bay and cast anchor. The boat came ashore for us, and in a little while the clouds and the rain were all gone. The moon was beaming tranquilly down on land and sea, and we two were stretched upon the deck sleeping the refreshing sleep and dreaming the happy dreams that are only vouchsafed to the weary and the innocent.

In the breezy morning we went ashore and visited the ruined temple of the last god Lono. The high chief cook of this temple—the priest who presided over it and roasted the human sacrifices—was uncle to Obookia [Opukahaia] and at one time that youth was an apprentice priest under him. Obookia was a young native of fine mind who, together with three other native boys, was taken to New England by the captain of a whale ship during the reign of Kamehameha I, and they were the means of attracting the attention of the religious world to their country. This resulted in the sending of missionaries there. And this Obookia was the very same sensitive savage who sat down on the church steps and wept because his people did not have the Bible. That incident has been very elaborately painted in many a charming Sunday school book—aye, and told so plaintively and so tenderly that I have cried over it in Sunday school myself, on general principles, although at a time when I did not know much and could not understand why the people of the Sandwich Islands needed to worry so much about it as long as they did not know there was a Bible at all.

Obookia was converted and educated, and was to have returned to his native land with the first missionaries, had he lived. The other native youths made the voyage, and two of them did good service, but the third, William Kanui, fell from grace afterward, for a time, and when the gold excitement broke out in California he journeyed thither and went to mining, although he was fifty years old. He succeeded pretty well, but the failure of Page, Bacon & Co. relieved him of six thousand dollars, and then, to all intents and purposes, he was a bankrupt in his old age and he resumed service in the pulpit again. He died in Honolulu in 1864.

Quite a broad tract of land near the temple, extending from the sea to the mountaintop, was sacred to the god Lono in olden times —so sacred that if a common native set his sacrilegious foot upon it, it was judicious for him to make his will, because his time had come. He might go around it by water, but he could not cross it. It was well sprinkled with pagan temples and stocked with awkward, homely idols carved out of logs of wood. There was a temple devoted to prayers for rain—and with fine sagacity it was placed at a point so well up on the mountainside that if you prayed there twenty-four times a day for rain you would be likely to get it every time. You would seldom get to your Amen before you would have to hoist your umbrella.

And there was a large temple near at hand which was built in a single night, in the midst of storm and thunder and rain, by the ghastly hands of dead men! Tradition says that by the weird glare of the lightning a noiseless multitude of phantoms were seen at their strange labor far up the mountainside at dead of night—flitting hither and thither and bearing great lava blocks clasped in their nerveless fingers—appearing and disappearing as the pallid luster fell upon their forms and faded away again. Even to this day, it is said, the natives hold this dread structure in awe and reverence, and will not pass by it in the night.

At noon I observed a bevy of nude native young ladies bathing in the sea, and went and sat down on their clothes to keep them from being stolen. I begged them to come out, for the sea was rising, and I was satisfied that they were running some risk. But they were not afraid, and presently went on with their sport. They were finished swimmers and divers, and enjoyed themselves to the last degree. They swam races, splashed and ducked and tumbled each other about, and filled the air with their laughter. It is said that the first thing an Islander learns is how to swim; learning to walk, being a matter of smaller consequence, comes afterward. One hears tales of native men and women swimming ashore from vessels many miles at sea—more miles, indeed, than I dare vouch for or even mention. And they tell of a native diver who went down in thirty- or forty-foot waters and brought up an anvil! I think he swallowed the anvil afterward, if my memory serves me. However, I will not urge this point. . . .

Only a mile or so from Kealakekua Bay is a spot of historic interest—the place where the last battle was fought for idolatry. Of course we visited it, and came away as wise as most people do who go and gaze upon such mementos of the past when in an unreflective mood.

While the first missionaries were on their way around the Horn, the idolatrous customs which had obtained in the island, as far back as tradition reached, were suddenly broken up. Old Kamehameha I was dead, and his son, Liholiho, the new king, was a free liver, a roistering, dissolute fellow, and hated the restraints of the ancient tabu. His assistant in the government, Kaahumanu, the queen dowager, was proud and high-spirited, and hated the tabu because it restricted the privileges of her sex and degraded all women very nearly to the level of brutes. So the case stood. Liholiho had half a mind to put his foot down, and Kaahumanu had a whole mind to badger him into doing it, and whiskey did the rest. It was probably the first time whiskey ever prominently figured as an aid to civilization. Liholiho came up to Kailua as drunk as a piper, and attended a great feast; the determined queen spurred his drunken courage up to a reckless pitch, and then, while all the multitude stared in blank dismay, he moved deliberately forward and sat down with the women! They saw him eat from the same vessel with them, and were appalled! Terrible moments drifted slowly by, and still the king ate, still he lived, still the lightnings of the insulted gods were withheld! Then conviction came like a revelation—the superstitions of a hundred generations passed from before the people like a cloud, and a shout went up, "The tabu is broken! The tabu is broken!"

Thus did King Liholiho and his dreadful whiskey preach the first sermon and prepare the way for the new gospel that was speeding southward over the waves of the Atlantic.

The tabu broken and destruction failing to follow the awful sacrilege, the people, with that childlike precipitancy which has always characterized them, jumped to the conclusion that their gods were a weak and wretched swindle, just as they formerly jumped to the conclusion that Captain Cook was no god, merely because he groaned, and promptly killed him without stopping to inquire whether a god might not groan as well as a man if it suited his convenience to do it; and satisfied that the idols were powerless to protect themselves they went to work at once and pulled them down—hacked them to pieces—applied the torch—annihilated them!

The pagan priests were furious. And well they might be; they had held the fattest offices in the land, and now they were beggared; they had been great—they had stood above the chiefs—and now they were vagabonds. They raised a revolt; they scared a number of people into joining their standard, and Bekuokalani [Kekuaokalani], an ambitious offshoot of royalty, was easily persuaded to become their leader.

In the first skirmish the idolaters triumphed over the royal army sent against them, and full of confidence they resolved to march upon Kailua. The king sent an envoy to try and conciliate them, and came very near being an envoy short by the operation; the savages not only refused to listen to him, but wanted to kill him. So the king sent his men forth under Major General Kalaimoku and the two hosts met at Kuamoo. The battle was long and fierce—men and women fighting side by side, as was the custom—and when the day was done the rebels were flying in every direction in hopeless panic, and idolatry and the tabu were dead in the land!

The royalists marched gaily home to Kailua glorifying the new dispensation. "There is no power in the gods," said they; "they are a vanity and a lie. The army with idols was weak; the army without idols was strong and victorious!"

The nation was without a religion.

The missionary ship arrived in safety shortly afterward, timed by providential exactness to meet the emergency, and the gospel was planted as in a virgin soil.

Isabella Bird

Impressions of Honolulu, 1873

One of the most intrepid of nineteenth-century women travelers, Isabella Bird (Mrs. J. F. Bishop, 1832–1904), spent half a year in the "Sandwich Islands" in 1873. A diminutive but tireless woman about five feet tall, she shocked the Victorian inhabitants of Honolulu by riding astride on horseback over the hazardous trails of the Islands in a sort of bloomer-girl costume of Scottish tartan. She first recounted her experiences and observations in a series of letters to her sister in Scotland, a fact that accounts in part for the freshness and directness of her book.

Eventually Isabella Bird—whose marriage to Dr. John F. Bishop when he was forty and she was fifty did not greatly interrupt her world travels—visited not only Hawaii but also the Rocky Mountains of America, Japan, Malaya, Korea, the upper Yangtze River, the vale of Kashmir, the tablelands of Tibet, and the deserts of Morocco. She wrote engaging and perceptive books about all these places, and was the first woman to be accepted as a fellow of the Royal Geographical Society.

The present selection comes from her volume, *The Hawaiian Archipelago: Six Months among the Palm Groves, Coral Reefs, and Volcanoes of the Sandwich Islands* (1875), which has been reprinted many times, most recently in an attractive illustrated edition in Honolulu in 1964. Isabella Bird's first, undulled impressions of Honolulu and its society nearly a century ago reflect her uncommon capacity for enjoying new scenes and experiences.

Hawaiian Hotel, Honolulu, January 26, 1873.

YESTERDAY morning at six-thirty I was aroused by the news that "The Islands" were in sight. Oahu in the distance, a group of gray, barren peaks rising verdureless out of the lonely sea, was not an exception to the rule that the first sight of land is a disappointment.

Owing to the clear atmosphere, we seemed only five miles off, but in reality we were twenty, and the land improved as we neared it. It was the fiercest day we had had, the deck was almost too hot to stand upon, the sea and sky were both magnificently blue, and the unveiled sun turned every minute ripple into a diamond flash. As we approached, the island changed its character. There were lofty peaks, truly—gray and red, sun-scorched and wind-bleached, glowing here and there with traces of their fiery origin; but they were cleft by deep chasms and ravines of cool shadow and entrancing green, and falling water streaked their sides—a most welcome vision after eleven months of the desert sea and the dusty browns of Australia and New Zealand. Nearer yet, and the coastline came into sight, fringed by the feathery coconut tree of the tropics, and marked by a long line of surf. The grand promontory of Diamond Head, its fiery sides now softened by a haze of green, terminated the wavy line of palms; then the Punchbowl, a very perfect extinct crater, brilliant with every shade of red volcanic ash, blazed against the green skirts of the mountains. We were close to the coral reef before the cry, "There's Honolulu!" made us aware of the proximity of the capital of the island kingdom, and then, indeed, its existence had almost to be taken upon trust, for besides the lovely wooden and grass huts, with deep verandas, which nestled under palms and bananas on soft greensward, margined by the bright sea sand, only two church spires and a few gray roofs appeared above the trees.

We were just outside the reef, and near enough to hear that deep sound of the surf which, through the ever serene summer years, girdles the Hawaiian Islands with perpetual thunder, before the pilot glided alongside, bringing the news which Mark Twain had prepared us to receive with interest, that "Prince Bill" [Lunalilo] had been unanimously elected to the throne. The surf ran white and pure over the environing coral reef, and as we passed through the narrow channel, we almost saw the coral forests deep down under the *Nevada*'s keel; the coral fishers plied their graceful trade; canoes with outriggers rode the combers and glided with inconceivable rapidity round our ship; amphibious brown beings sported in the transparent waves; and within the reef lay a calm surface of water of a wonderful blue, entered by a narrow, intricate passage of the deepest indigo. And beyond the reef and beyond the blue, nestling among coconut trees and bananas, umbrella trees and breadfruits, oranges, mangoes, hibiscus, algarroba, and passionflowers, almost hidden in the deep, dense greenery, was Honolulu. Bright blossom of a summer sea! Fair Paradise of the Pacific!

Inside the reef the magnificent ironclad *California* (the flagship) and another huge American war vessel, the *Benicia,* are moored in line with the British corvette *Scout,* within two hundred yards of the shore; and their boats were constantly passing and repassing, among countless canoes filled with natives. Two coasting schooners were just leaving the harbor, and the interisland steamer *Kilauea,* with her deck crowded with natives, was just coming in. By noon the great decrepit *Nevada,* which has no wharf at which she can lie in sleepy New Zealand, was moored alongside a very respectable one in this enterprising little Hawaiian capital.

We looked down from the towering deck on a crowd of two or three thousand people—whites, Kanakas, Chinamen—and hundreds of them at once made their way on board, and streamed over the ship, talking, laughing, and remarking upon us in a language which seemed without backbone. Such rich brown men and women they were, with wavy, shining black hair, large, brown, lustrous eyes, and rows of perfect teeth like ivory. Everyone was smiling. The forms of the women seem to be inclined toward obesity, but their drapery, which consists of a sleeved garment which falls in ample and unconfined folds from their shoulders to their feet, partly conceals this defect, which is here regarded as beauty. Some of these dresses were black, but many of those worn by the younger women were of pure white, crimson, yellow, scarlet, blue, or light green. The men displayed their lithe, graceful figures to the best advantage in white trousers and gay Garibaldi shirts. A few of the women wore colored handkerchiefs twined round their hair, but generally both men and women wore straw hats, which the men set jauntily on one side of their heads, and aggravated their appearance yet more by bandanna handkerchiefs of rich bright colors round their necks, knotted loosely on the left side, with a grace to which, I think, no Anglo-Saxon dandy could attain. Without an exception the men and women wore wreaths and garlands of flowers, carmine, orange, or pure white, twined round their hats, and thrown carelessly round their necks, flowers unknown to me, but redolent of the tropics in fragrance and color. Many of the young beauties wore the gorgeous blossom of the red hibiscus among their abundant, unconfined black hair, and many, besides the garlands, wore festoons of a sweet-scented vine, or of an exquisitely beautiful fern, knotted behind and hanging halfway down their dresses. These adornments of natural flowers are most attractive. Chinamen, all alike, very yellow, with almond-shaped eyes, youthful, hairless faces, long pigtails, spotlessly clean clothes, and an expression of mingled cunning and simplicity, "foreigners," half-whites, a few Negroes, and a very few dark-skinned Polynesians from the far-off South Seas, made up the rest of the rainbow-tinted crowd.

The "foreign" ladies, who were there in great numbers, generally wore simple light prints or muslins and white straw hats, and many of them so far conformed to native custom as to wear natural flowers round their hats and throats. But where were the hard, angular, careworn, sallow, passionate faces of men and women, such as form the majority of every crowd at home, as well as in America and Australia? The conditions of life must surely be easier here, and people must have found rest from some of its burdensome conventionalities. The foreign ladies, in their simple, tasteful, fresh attire, innocent of the humpings and bunchings, the monstrosities and deformities of ultrafashionable bad taste, beamed with cheerfulness, friendliness, and kindliness. Men and women looked as easy, contented, and happy as if care never came near them. I never saw such healthy, bright complexions as among the women, or such "sparkling smiles," or such a diffusion of feminine grace and graciousness anywhere.

Outside this motley, genial, picturesque crowd about two hundred saddled horses were standing, each with the Mexican saddle, with its lassoing horn in front, high peak behind, immense wooden stirrups, with great leathern guards, silver or brass bosses, and colored saddlecloths. The saddles were the only element of the picturesque that these Hawaiian steeds possessed. They were sorry, lean, undersized beasts, looking in general as if the emergencies of life left them little time for eating or sleeping. They stood calmly in the broiling sun, heavy-headed and heavyhearted, with flabby ears and pendulous lower lips, limp and rawboned, a doleful type of the "creation which groaneth and travaileth in misery." All these belonged to the natives, who are passionately fond of riding. Every now and then a flower-wreathed Hawaiian woman, in her full radiant garment, sprang on one of these animals astride, and dashed along the road at full gallop, sitting on her horse as square and easy as a hussar. In the crowd and outside of it, and everywhere, there were piles of fruit for sale—oranges, guavas, strawberries, papayas, bananas (green and golden), coconuts, and other rich, fantastic productions of a prolific climate, where nature gives of her wealth the whole year round. Strange fishes, strange in shape and color—crimson, blue, orange, rose, gold—such fishes as flash like living light through the coral groves of these enchanted seas, were there for sale, and coral divers were there with their treasures—branch coral, as white as snow, each perfect specimen weighing from eight to twenty pounds. But no one pushed his wares for sale—we were at liberty to look and admire, and pass on unmolested. No vexatious restrictions obstructed our landing. A sum of two dollars for the support of the Queen's Hospital is levied on each passenger, and the examination of ordinary luggage, if it exists, is a mere form. From the demeanor of the crowd it was at once apparent that the conditions of conquerors and conquered do not exist. On the contrary, many of the foreigners there were subjects of a Hawaiian king, a reversal of the ordinary relations between a white and a colored race which it is not easy yet to appreciate.

Two of my fellow passengers, who were going on to San Francisco, were anxious that I should accompany them to the Pali, the great excursion from Honolulu; and leaving Mr. M——— to make all arrangements for the Dexters and myself, we hired a buggy, destitute of any peculiarity but a native driver, who spoke nothing but Hawaiian, and left the ship. This place is quite unique. It is said that fifteen thousand people are buried away in these low-browed, shadowy houses, under the glossy, dark-leaved trees, but except in one or two streets of miscellaneous, old-fashioned-looking stores, arranged with a distinct leaning toward native tastes, it looks like a large village, or rather like an aggregate of villages. As we drove through the town we could only see our immediate surroundings, but each had a new fascination. We drove along roads with overarching trees, through whose dense leafage the noon sunshine only trickled in dancing, broken lights; umbrella trees, caoutchouc, bamboo, mango, orange, breadfruit, candlenut, monkey pod, date and coco palms, alligator pears, "prides" of Barbary, India, and Peru, and huge-leaved, wide-spreading trees, exotics from the South Seas, many of them rich in parasitic ferns, and others blazing with bright, fantastic blossoms. The air was heavy with odors of gardenia, tuberose, oleanders, roses, lilies, and great white trumpet flower, and myriads of others whose names I do not know, and verandas were festooned with a gorgeous trailer with magenta blossoms, passionflowers, and a vine with masses of trumpet-shaped, yellow, waxy flowers. The delicate tamarind and the feathery algarroba intermingled their fragile grace with the dark, shiny foliage of the South Sea exotics, and the deep-red, solitary flowers of the hibiscus rioted among dear familiar fuchsias and geraniums, which here attain the height and size of large rhododendrons.

Few of the new trees surprised me more than the papaya. It is a perfect gem of tropical vegetation. It has a soft, indented stem, which runs up quite straight to a height of from fifteen to thirty feet, and is crowned by a profusion of large, deeply indented leaves, with long foot-stalks, and among, as well as considerably below, these are the flowers or the fruit, in all stages of development. This, when ripe, is bright yellow, and the size of a muskmelon. Clumps of bananas, the first sight of which, like that of the palm, constitutes a new experience, shaded the native houses with their wonderful leaves, broad and deep green, from five to ten feet long. The breadfruit is a superb tree, about sixty feet high, with deep-green, shining leaves a foot broad, sharply and symmetrically cut, worthy, from their exceeding beauty of form, to take the place of the acanthus in architectural ornament, and throwing their pale-green fruit into delicate contrast. All these, with the exquisite rose apple, with a deep-red tinge in its young leaves, the fan palm, the cherimoya, and numberless others, and the slender shafts of the coco palms rising high above them, with their waving plumes and perpetual fruitage, were a perfect festival of beauty.

In the deep shade of this perennial greenery the people dwell. The foreign houses show a very various individuality. The peculiarity in which all seem to share is that everything is decorated and festooned with flowering trailers. It is often difficult to tell what the architecture is, or what is house and what is vegetation; for all angles, and lattices, and balustrades, and verandas are hidden by jessamine or passionflowers, or the gorgeous flamelike bougainvillea. Many of the dwellings straggle over the ground without an upper story, and have very deep verandas, through which I caught glimpses of cool, shady rooms, with matted floors. Some look as if they had been transported from the old-fashioned villages of the Connecticut Valley, with their clapboard fronts painted white and jalousies painted green; but then the deep veranda in which families lead an open-air life has been added, and the chimneys have been omitted, and the New England severity and angularity are toned down and draped out of sight by these festoons of large-leaved, bright-blossomed, tropical climbing plants. Besides the frame houses there are houses built of blocks of a cream-colored coral conglomerate laid in cement; of adobe, or large sun-baked bricks, plastered; houses of grass and bamboo; houses on the ground and houses raised on posts; but nothing looks prosaic, commonplace, or mean, for the glow and luxuriance of the tropics rest on all. Each house has a large garden or yard, with lawns of bright perennial greens and banks of blazing, many-tinted flowers, and lines of dracaena, and other foliage plants, with their great purple or crimson leaves, and clumps of marvelous lilies, gladiolas, ginger, and many plants unknown to me. Fences and walls are altogether buried by passionflowers, the night-blowing cereus, and the tropaeolum, mixed with geraniums, fuchsia, and jessamine, which cluster and entangle over them in indescribable profusion. A soft air moves through the upper branches, and the drip of water from miniature fountains falls musically on the perfumed air. This is midwinter! The summer, they say, is thermometrically hotter, but practically cooler, because of the regular trades which set in in April, but now, with the shaded thermometer at 80° and the sky without clouds, the heat is not oppressive.

The mixture of the neat grass houses of the natives with the more elaborate homes of the foreign residents has a very pleasant look. The "aborigines" have not been crowded out of sight, or into a special "quarter." We saw many groups of them sitting under the trees outside their houses, each group with a mat in the center, with calabashes upon it containing poi, the national Hawaiian dish, a fermented paste made from the root of the kalo, or *arum esculentum*. As we emerged on the broad road which leads up the Nuuanu Valley to the mountains, we saw many patches of this kalo, a very handsome tropical plant, with large leaves of a bright, tender green. Each plant was growing on a small hillock, with water round it. There were beautiful vegetable gardens also, in which Chinamen raise for sale not only melons, pineapples, sweet potatoes, and other edibles of hot climates, but the familiar fruits and vegetables of the temperate zones. In patches of surpassing neatness there were strawberries, which are ripe here all the year, peas, carrots, turnips, asparagus, lettuce, and celery. I saw no other plants or trees which grow at home, but recognized as hardly less familiar growths the Victorian eucalyptus, which has not had time to become gaunt and straggling, the Norfolk Island pine, which grows superbly here, and the handsome Moreton Bay fig.

But the chief feature of this road is the number of residences; I had almost written of pretentious residences, but the term would be a base slander, as I have jumped to the conclusion that the twin vulgarities of ostentation and pretense have no place here. But certainly for a mile and a half or more there are many very comfortable-looking dwellings, very attractive to the eye, with an ease and imperturbable serenity of demeanor as if they had nothing to fear from heat, cold, wind, or criticism. Their architecture is absolutely unostentatious, and their one beauty is that they are embowered among trailers, shadowed by superb exotics and surrounded by banks of flowers, while the stately coconut, the banana, and the candlenut, the aborigines of Oahu, are nowhere displaced. One house with extensive grounds, a perfect wilderness of vegetation, was pointed out as the summer palace of Queen Emma, or Kaleleonalani, widow of Kamehameha IV, who visited England a few years ago, and the finest garden of all is that of a much respected Chinese merchant named Afong. Oahu, at least on this leeward side, is not tropical-looking, and all this tropical variety and luxuriance which delight the eye result from foreign enthusiasm and love of beauty and shade.

When we ascended above the scattered dwellings and had passed the tasteful mausoleum, with two tall kahilis, or feather plumes, at the door of the tomb in which the last of the Kamehamehas received Christian burial, the vegetation ceased. At that height a shower of rain falls on nearly every day in the year, and the result is a greensward which England can hardly rival, a perfect sea of verdure, darkened in the valley and more than halfway up the hillsides by the foliage of the yellow-blossomed and almost impenetrable hibiscus, brightened here and there by the pea-green candlenut. Streamlets leap from crags and ripple along the roadside, every rock and stone is hidden by moist-looking ferns, as aerial and delicate as marabou feathers, and when the windings of the valley and the projecting spurs of mountains shut out all indications of Honolulu, in the cool green loneliness one could imagine oneself in the temperate zones. The peculiarity of the scenery is that the hills, which rise to a height of about four thousand feet, are wall-like ridges of gray or colored rock, rising precipitously out of the trees and grass, and that these walls are broken up into pinnacles and needles.

At the Pali (wall-like precipice), the summit of the ascent of a thousand feet, we left our buggy, and passing through a gash in the rock, the celebrated view burst on us with overwhelming effect. Immense masses of black and ferruginous volcanic rock, hundreds of feet in nearly perpendicular height, formed the pali on either side, and the ridge extended northward for many miles, presenting a lofty, abrupt mass of gray rock broken into fantastic pinnacles, which seemed to pierce the sky. A broad, umbrageous mass of green clothed the lower buttresses and fringed itself away in clusters of coco palms on a gardenlike stretch below, green with grass and sugar cane, and dotted with white houses, each with its palm and banana grove, and varied by eminences which looked like long-extinct tufa cones. Beyond this enchanted region stretched the coral reef, with its white wavy line of endless surf, and the broad blue Pacific, ruffled by a breeze whose icy freshness chilled us where we stood. Narrow streaks on the landscape, every now and then disappearing behind intervening hills, indicated bridle tracks connected with a frightfully steep and rough zigzag path cut out of the face of the cliff on our right. I could not go down this on foot without a sense of insecurity, but mounted natives driving loaded horses descended with perfect impunity into the dreamland below.

This pali is the scene of one of the historic tragedies of this island. Kamehameha the Conqueror, who after fierce fighting and much ruthless destruction of human life united the island sovereignties in his own person, routed the forces of the King of Oahu in the Nuuanu Valley and drove them in hundreds up the precipice from which they leaped in despair and madness, and their bones lie bleaching eight hundred feet below.

The drive back here was delightful, from the wintry height—where I must confess that we shivered—to the slumbrous calm of an endless summer, the glorious tropical trees, the distant view of cool chasmlike valleys, with Honolulu sleeping in perpetual shade, and the still, blue ocean, without a single sail to disturb its profound solitude. Saturday afternoon is a gala day here, and the broad road was so thronged with brilliant equestrians that I thought we should be ridden over by the reckless laughing rout. There were hundreds of native horsemen and horsewomen, many of them doubtless on the dejected quadrupeds I saw at the wharf, but a judicious application of long-rowelled Mexican spurs, and a degree of emulation, caused these animals to tear along at full gallop. The women seemed perfectly at home in their gay, brass-bossed, high-peaked saddles, flying along astride, barefooted, with their orange and scarlet riding dresses streaming on each side beyond their horses' tails, a bright kaleidoscopic flash of bright eyes, white teeth, shining hair, garlands of flowers and many-colored dresses; while the men were hardly less gay, with fresh flowers round their jaunty hats and the vermilion-colored blossoms of the ohia round their brown throats. Sometimes a troop of twenty of these free-and-easy female riders went by at a time, a graceful and exciting spectacle, with a running accompaniment of vociferation and laughter. Among these we met several of the *Nevada*'s officers, riding in the stiff, wooden style which Anglo-Saxons love, and a horde of jolly British sailors from H.M.S. *Scout,* rushing helter-skelter, colliding with everybody, bestriding their horses as they would a topsail yard, hanging on to manes and lassoing horns, and enjoying themselves thoroughly. In the shady tortuous streets we met hundreds more of native riders, dashing at full gallop without fear of the police. Many of the women were in flowing riding dresses of pure white, over which their unbound hair and wreaths of carmine-tinted flowers fell most picturesquely.

Charles Warren Stoddard

On the Reef

Born in Rochester, New York, Charles Warren Stoddard (1843–1909) went to California as a boy and became one of the leading writers in San Francisco during the 1860's, along with the young Mark Twain, Bret Harte, and Ambrose Bierce. Stoddard made his first trip to the Hawaiian Islands in 1864. This and subsequent visits to those islands and Tahiti provided the material for his first and best-known book, *South-Sea Idyls* (1873), a collection of stories and sketches which William Dean Howells hailed as the "freshest things that ever were written about the life of that summer ocean."

Later, during a residence in Hawaii in 1881–1884, when he became concerned that the generous, life-enjoying Hawaiians were being corrupted by civilization, he composed an edged indictment in his story of Kane-pihi. Giving it the ambiguous title of "On the Reef," Stoddard included it in two of his books, *Hawaiian Life* (1894) and *The Island of Tranquil Delights* (1904).

ONCE upon a time—it was on one of those nights when without apparent reason the spirit of mortal is filled with vague unrest—I strode into the starlight and sought with a kind of desperation the least frequented paths, such as lead away out of the borders of the town toward the shadowy hills.

On such a night the superstitious note with awe the faintest articulation, and too often attribute the least sound to a preternatural cause. I remember that the hedges seemed to shudder at intervals and shadows to move noiselessly before me, while the water that trickled in the shallow stream muttered a refrain that was almost like human speech.

When I stumbled in the darkness I was vexed, and the still air, heavily charged with electricity, was irritating and aggressive.

I had got beyond the reach of voices, as I thought, and was groping in the deep shade of clustering kamani trees, when a dull murmur, like the drone of the hive, fell upon my ear. I paused to listen. The crickets were chirping bravely, the rill fell with a hollow note into the pool below, and from far away came the solemn suspiration of the sea.

Then I saw a light dimly flickering among the branches in the path and I advanced with some caution, for I was in no mood to discover myself to anyone in that seeming solitude.

A few paces distant stood a rude grass hut such as the Hawaiian formerly inhabited, but which, alas, has been suffered to fall into disuse. A door, its only aperture, stood open. Upon a broad, flat stone within the center of the hut flamed a handful of faggots, and over these bowed the withered forms of two venerable Hawaiians, who may have been the last representatives of the ancient race. They were squatted upon their lean haunches, their fleshless arms were extended, their clawlike fingers clasped above the flames. They were both nude, and the light that played about them exaggerated their wrinkles so that the face of each—I say it in all seriousness—resembled a baked apple. They were chanting in turn one of those weird meles now seldom heard and soon to be utterly forgotten. Their thin voices gathered strength as they recounted the triumphs of departed heroes and the glory that has passed forever. The quivering voices were at times blended, and the ancient bards locked in a tremulous embrace; but at last, profoundly agitated, while the tears coursed their hollow cheeks, they folded their arms above their bowed foreheads, and, shaken with tremors, rocked to and fro in the fading firelight and were dumb.

They were bewailing the fate of their people—a fate that in very many respects is to be deplored. Never again can aught be made of them, for their doom is accomplished. And how? We shall see.

Years ago I sat under the eaves of a grass house which stood upon this sand dune and looked out upon the reef as I am looking now; the afternoon was waning; the wind, that had for hours been whirling the fine sand in eddies around the corner of the house, began to fail, and the sea, with all its waves, subsided upon the reef. It was as if the little island world was about to compose itself in sleep; on

On the Reef

the contrary, we were but beginning to recover from the inertia induced by the tireless activity of the elements.

On my lap lay the only volume I was able to discover in the vicinity, an ill-used copy of *The Evidences of Christianity*. How it came into the possession of Pilikia, my host, I know not, but that he had found it of great service was evident. At least half of the pages had already been disposed of and the remnant—a catacomb of white ants and such other vermin as affect literature in the tropics—was sure to follow in due course.

Pilikia politely offered me this precious volume at an early stage of our acquaintance, for we were quite unable to communicate with one another, he being stone deaf and I as good as dumb in those days. The truth is, I was awaiting the return of Kane-pihi, the man-fish, with whom I proposed to pass a night upon the reef practicing the art which had already distinguished him and had won for him the admiration and the envy of his fellow craftsmen.

Anon I closed the volume with decision; the evidences were incomplete and I was impatient for the arrival of the man-fish, who was certainly more interesting than the antiquated specimen of humanity who sat in the corner of the hut, like an idol, and whose blue-black, weatherbeaten figurehead looked as if it had been carved out of a walrus' tusk and smoked.

I arose impetuously, shook off my ennui, and strolled along the beach. There was a joyous sparkle upon the sea; little windy waves slid up the sloping sands, curled crisply and retired in a white litter of explosive bubbles; diminutive crabs rushed pell-mell before my feet; at intervals I felt the sting of the flying sand, but the heat and the burden of the day were about over and I began to lift up my heart, when, in the hollow of the shore, sheltered only by sand ridges, I saw a dark object stretched motionless at full length. Flotsam or jetsam, the prize was mine, and I hastened forward. It was a youth just out of his teens, a slim, sleek creature, unconscious, unclad, sprawled inartistically, absorbing sunshine and apparently steeped to the toes in it; it was Kane-pihi, the man-fish, stark asleep.

Retiring a little distance, I tossed a pebble upon his motionless body; then another and another, and finally a whole handful of them. At last he turned, with a serpentine movement, lifting his head like a lizard, swaying it slowly to and fro and looking listlessly upon the sand and the sea. When he espied me, he coiled his limbs under him and was convulsed with riotous laughter.

I approached him and exhausted my vocabulary in five minutes, but I learned meanwhile that the fellow had been lying there on the hot sand in the blazing sun for a good portion of the day, and that now he was ready to eat. Two things on earth were necessary to the existence of this superior animal—to eat and to sleep; but for pleasure and profit, for life and all that makes it livable and lovable, the man-fish sought the waters under the earth. He was amphibious.

Pilikia—born to trouble, as his name implies, and like all who are never out of it living to the age of the prophets—Pilikia still sat in his corner when we returned to the grass house, but upon the appearance of Kane-pihi, the apple of his eye, the child of his old age, peradventure, his face changed suddenly, as if about to weep. This simulation of tearless agony was his method of showing joy. The range of facial expression had grown limited with him and he now seemed to be gradually assuming the fixed, blank stare of the dead. Pilikia crawled out of his obscurity and we all gathered about a calabash of poi in the door of the hut as the sun shot suddenly into the sea.

Kane-pihi began to awaken as the twilight deepened; his eyes—he had bronze eyes that were opaque in the sunshine—grew limpid and lustrous; he began to search the wave as if he could pluck from it the heart of its mystery. Perhaps he could; perhaps its color and texture imparted to him secrets unknown to us. Now and again he sang to himself fragments of meles that sounded like invocations and added sacredness to an hour exquisitely beautiful and pathetic.

The sea advanced and retreated noiselessly along the shelving sand; each wavelet, unrolling like a scroll, told its separate story and was withdrawn into the deep. For a moment the shore was glossed where the waters had passed over it, but this varnish immediately grew clouded, like a mirror that has been breathed upon, and then vanished, leaving only a dark shadow in the moist sand. Long, luminous bars lay upon the more distant water, and beyond these the rough edges of the reef, now exposed to the air, were lightly powdered with filmy and prismatic spray. It was dark when we set forth in Kane-pihi's canoe. Pilikia, who also revived under the beneficent influence of the stars, followed us to the water's edge and even made

On the Reef

a feint of aiding us in the launch of our canoe. Our course lay down the coast, within the reef. We might easily have waded throughout the length and breadth of the lagoon but for the shoals of sharp coral and the jagged hills among them, of which I knew nothing, though each coral prong was familiar to the man-fish, it having been his chief end to chart every inch of the lagoon at an early stage in his career.

Oh, heavenly night! We floated upon an element that seemed a denser atmosphere; this delicious air was like the spirit of God moving upon the face of the waters. We were both silent, for the earth and sea were silent, but now and again we heard a *glug* under our bow, where a bewildered fish had swum into the air by mistake and dived back in dismay.

The mysterious voyage filled me with a kind of awe, such as a surprised soul might feel after sudden death, upon finding itself propelled slowly across the Styx by an almost invisible Charon. In this mood we rounded the lagoon, and lo, the sea radiant with flaming torches and peopled by a race of shadowy fishers—bronzed, naked, statuesque! The superb spectacle inspired Kane-pihi; with an exclamation of delight he plunged his paddle into the water and a half dozen vigorous strokes brought us where he was at once recognized and received with every demonstration of affection.

In the charmed circle all things were transformed; the earth and the very stars were forgotten; the sea was like wine, ripples of perfume played upon its surface; the torches above it were imaged in the water below, where the coral glowed resplendently and the bewildered fish darted to their doom in basket-nets or at the point of the glancing spear. The fishers were for the most part dumb as statues; with a thousand exquisite poses they searched the luminous depths for the fleet prey that shone like momentary sunbeams and were as speedily captured and transferred to their canoes. In this graceful art the women, costumed like fabled sea nymphs, were as skillful as the men, and even when we had drifted in the shallows, and they, descending into the sea, were wandering apart, each with a torch in one hand, a net in the other, and a sack hanging upon the hip, they were as fearless and as active as the best man among them. But this kind of fishing was mere child's play in the eyes of Kane-pihi and only the diversion of a night.

Hour after hour the flotilla dazzled upon the tideless lagoon; it was only when the waters seemed to have been robbed of their last vestige of finny life that we separated and soared like meteors into outer darkness. Then I became conscious of fatigue, and throwing myself upon a mat in the corner of Pilikia's grass house I slept while Kane-pihi sang into the dawn.

In those days a barren plain, relieved here and there by stretches of salt-marsh land, lay between the fishing grounds and the seaport. It was seldom that Kane-pihi entered the town. A gentle savage, whose childhood had been passed upon the shore of the least civilized of the islands of the group, his unconventional life had scarcely fitted him for anything so confining as a pavement or a trim garden spot, hedged or fenced about in individual exclusiveness.

He had lounged in the fish market, where his fame had preceded him, but the clamoring crowd soon drove him forth, and when he had sat for an hour in silent contemplation of the street traffic, he strode soberly back to the hut on the sand dunes and dreamed away the disgust with which such method and industry invariably inspired him.

We sat together one morning looking far off upon the town and far off upon the sea in comfortable idleness. We had hoped for a change in the spirit of our dream and it came presently, for it was observed that a school of fish was making for the shore. In an instant several canoes were slid into the water and a dozen excited natives went in hot pursuit of the spoil.

Before the day of dynamite, deep-sea fishing was an art in which few excelled, but with Kane-pihi it was a specialty, and when we had weathered the breakers and were out upon the swell beyond the reef, he dropped a handful of bait into the water and watched it as it slowly sank; then he cautiously climbed out of the canoe and with fearless resignation sank after it. It was as if he were braving all the laws of nature—as if he were defying death itself.

Breathlessly I watched him as he sank feet foremost into the depths; I saw his motionless body slowly descending, growing dimmer in outline all the while; I saw the fish circling suspiciously about him, attracted by the bait, which they were greedily devouring, and evidently filled with curiosity as to the nature of the man-fish in their midst, who, like a corpse, was fading in the horrible obscurity of the sea; then, at the moment when it seemed that life must have deserted him, with a sudden lunge he buried a knife in the body of a huge fish and rose like a water-nymph out of the waves. It was the work of a moment only, but it seemed to me an age since I had seen the sea close over him.

Several times he repeated the act successfully, and it became difficult to see through the bloodstained water, but by moving the canoes cautiously from point to point, we still kept within reach of the shoal and avoided the crimson cloud that marked the scene of Kane-pihi's recent marine combat. A highly successful catch was the reward of his prowess, and with our canoe well laden, we headed for the shore.

Those who were watching us from the beach must have lost sight of us at intervals as we rose and sank upon the rollers. Sometimes the comber that broke between us and the land looked like a precipitated avalanche of snow, and the mass behind us swelled and burst, darting forward with an impetuosity that threatened the destruction of our frail craft. But into the wilderness of this tumultuous sea it was Kane-pihi's intention to venture, and through the midst of it lay our perilous course. With a paddle that was never at rest, we hovered upon the outer edges of the reef, hastening over the brow of a billow before it broke, for it was only upon the bosom of one of these monsters that we could hope for safety, and *the* one had not yet arrived. Like a bird's pinion, the paddle held us poised—suspended in midair, I had almost written—until, with an impulse which was an inspiration, Kane-pihi plowed the sea with swift, impetuous strokes. I felt the canoe leap forward before a wave that seemed rising to overwhelm us; we rose with it, on the inner slope of it, just out of reach of the torrent of foam that hissed and roared behind us. How we sped onward in that mad chase! The very canoe seemed instilled with life; nervous tremors seized it; it was almost as if some invisible power were about to sweep it from under us; so fast it fled over the oily slope of the huge wave, at the top of which tumbled a world of foam—and thus, with hardly so much as a stroke of the paddle, after we were well settled on the down grade, we sprang like a flying fish into the tranquil waters of the lagoon and then turned to one another with a half-gasp, as if we had been delivered from sudden death.

This was the life of the man-fish; if he had been upset in the breakers he would have come to shore none the worse for it, but my blood would have stained the reef for a moment and my bones found coral sepulture.

Thus he played with the elements—having not so much vanity as a child, nor so much wisdom either, though he was weatherwise, knew all about the moods of the wind and waves, could do everything but shape them—and there I left him to sleep away the hot hours in the hot sun and sand; to eat when he listed and wait upon the turning of the tides, or the advent of those fishy episodes that were events in his life; a perfectly constituted creature, whose highest ambition he could himself satisfy at almost any moment; who, I venture to affirm, never did harm to anyone, and who unquestionably was, in his line, a complete and unqualified success—in brief, a perfect human animal, who was doing in his own way and in his own good time what he could toward destroying the last vestiges of *The Evidences of Christianity*.

In revisiting an inconsiderable community nothing is more natural than for one to pick up the threads where they were dropped and then seek to work out the story of the lives of those with whom he has been associated in former years, and in this wise I was busy enough for some weeks upon my return to Honolulu.

I soon began to familiarize myself with all that had transpired in the intervening decade, and was making lazy pilgrimages to various points of interest, when it occurred to me that the prison was still unvisited.

In the delectable kingdom of which I write, the lawbreakers in former times were condemned to a period of servitude upon the reef. There, at low water, they hewed out the coral blocks of which many of the early buildings were constructed, and to this day a convict is spoken of as being "on the reef," although coral has given place to brick and stone and timber, and the reef is comparatively deserted.

At once, or as nearly on the instant as one ever gets in an easygoing land, I made application at the gate of the neatest, coziest, cleanest and most cheerful house of correction in the world. In form and color only is it outwardly severe, and even this is the kind of severity affected by those suburban residents who build angular, gray monuments of masonry and inhabit them in an uncomfortably medieval frame of mind. It stands upon a coral ridge and is almost surrounded by fishponds, mud flats, and salt marshes. It is approached by a well-kept, but unsheltered, coral-dusted drive that glares in the sunshine and moonlight as if to magnify the shadow of him who is being led away captive, or to cast a glory about the feet of the one who is set free. I knocked with a knocker surmounted by a British lion in bronze; the gate was immediately opened by a native guard in a dark uniform, who, like all natives in dark uniforms, looked exceedingly stuffy and uncomfortable. I asked leave to enter. He seemed to think I had done him a favor and honor in calling upon such a very warm day and at once waved me gracefully across a court that was as trim and complete as a modern stage setting for an act in a society drama. There was, I confess, a superfluity of very neat stonework in wall and pavement; but there were flower plots quite like stage flower plots and a moderate perspective which seemed heightened by exaggerated foreshortening, all of which was so obviously evident to the naked eye.

Other guards, perched in picturesque nooks and corners, smiled a welcome as I advanced. The original stuffed one, who had backed mechanically into his little sentry box out of the sun, was also smiling, and smiling very broadly for a man on serious duty.

Might I come in and inspect the prison? Assuredly. Would I only be good enough to look at everything, see everybody, go everywhere, and then graciously inscribe my name in the finest of visitors' books, with the very whitest of paper and a very brave array of signatures? I went in and out, up and down, over and across and back again. The valley of Rasselas could not have been more peaceful than was the inner court of that island jail, with its spreading kamani tree in the midst thereof. The keeper apologized for the smallness of his family at the moment; he begged to assure me that there were more than I found present; that the house was always full; those whom I saw were the lame, the halt, and the blind; the able-bodied were all out at work on the road, clad in garments of two colors—half and half, like a chorus in *Boccaccio*—at the expense of the amiable government.

If those of the infirmary, sunning themselves in the court, were so merry, what must be the state of the able-bodied, thought I. I had seen detachments of them at their work—work which they evidently did not take to heart, but, on the contrary, regarded in the light of a somewhat tedious joke.

While I was absorbed in the legends of the local museum, illustrated with celebrated shackles, bits of hangman's rope, bloodstained implements of destruction, and a whole rogue's gallery of interesting criminals, there was a sound of revelry, and lo! the prisoners who had had their outing were returning joyously to this haven of rest, and some of them without a keeper.

Chief among the Ishmaelitish crew was one who wore his prison garb jauntily, who betrayed a tendency to good-natured bravado and who kept his fellows on a roar. The warden presently claimed my attention and told me something of the prisoner's history. He had been reared among a primitive people; was superstitious, ingenuous, confiding; knew little or nothing of foreign ways and manners and cared little to hear of them. The simplicity of his life assured his perpetual happiness, but of course there was no hope of his development—he must forever remain contented with his lot and perish like the beast of the field, if nature were to take her course; but nature was not permitted to take her course; she seldom, or never, is nowadays.

An itinerant evangelist arrived in Honolulu and began his work. The Hawaiian is nothing if not emotional. You may rouse him to the pitch of frenzy, and he will subside without having achieved anything more than a thrill; but the thrill is very much to him and is worth striving for. The natives became as wax in the presence of this magnetic exhorter. Prayer meetings were held night and day. There was a corner in New Testament and hymn books. Prophets —whether true or false you will decide for yourselves—arose in numbers, and the Scriptures were very freely interpreted. Yet, if out of the mouths of babes and sucklings cometh forth wisdom, it may be that these dark ones were wiser in that day than the children of light. Natives were gathering from far and near, attracted by the rumors which surcharged the atmosphere and by the "messenger of the Lord," who ran to and fro gathering the lost sheep into the fold of Kaumakapili. This youth who, while we discussed him, was regaling the prisoners in the courtyard with a hula-hula, was finally seduced into the town and ultimately into the fold.

Kaumakapili, whatever may be said of its evasive order of architecture, has a reputation established beyond question, and the evening meetings held in that trysting place are ever popular with the young. Hither came this child of nature, and here, listening to the experiences most eloquently detailed of those who had turned from the error of their ways and found salvation under the eaves of Kaumakapili, he in his turn repented—of what it is not easy to conjecture—and was baptized in the name of the eternal Trinity.

It is my belief that the native modesty of the Hawaiians, and of all unclad races, is extinguished the moment they are slipped under cover. They put on vice as a garment and with knowledge comes the desire for evil; so when this youth got into foreign clothing he straightway began to backslide. He picked up bits of English, grew sharp at a bargain, learned to lie a little when necessary, and to cheat now and again. He took that which was not his, not because he meant to defraud the owner of it, but because he needed it himself, and finding it in his way laid hands on it. This he used to do before he knew it was a sin, and in those days he expected you to take of his possessions in like manner according to your need, but now there was a new pleasure in doing it; the excitement of secrecy added an interest to the act which he had never known until this hour. God pity him! Many and various experiences sharpened the convert's wits, and he became one of the cleverest boys in town—one on whom its mild-eyed constabulary bent loving glances; but his career was shortened for having shattered one of the commandments—the only one of the ten whose number shall be nameless—he was arrested, tried, convicted, and was now serving out his time with charming abandon. His story touched you, though it was not without parallel in the kingdom. There, indeed, it is an oft-told tale.

We descended into the courtyard, where the young rascal was beguiling his fellows, and I saw—I had suspected it—that he was none other than my young friend of yore completely transformed by civilization—in other words, Kane-pihi, the man-fish, out of his element. We had a few moments' conversation; these few were sufficient to convince me that his case was hopeless. He could never again return to the life to which he was born and in which it seemed that he could do no guile; for those with whom he was associated were as guileless as he, and they were alike subject to no temptations and no snares; but he must now go on to the bitter end, for he had eaten of the tree of knowledge and fallen in its shade.

As for the ancient Pilikia, it was pau pilikia with him; his troubles were over. When he saw the fate of his idol and that no pleading and no incantation could bring the lad to his right mind, the old man turned his face to the wall and gave up the ghost; he tasted death and found it sweeter than the new life which had defrauded him of his own. The boy spoke of it as a matter of course; all who live must die, and, Heaven knows, as the boy implied, he had lived long enough; and with this he returned to the dance.

The chains of the jailbirds rang gayly over the battlements as I bade farewell to the keeper and the kept. Among the latter are several of the graduates of Lahainaluna, the Protestant Theological Seminary of the kingdom. The little sentinel showed me out, full of pride and good cheer and swelling bravely in his stuffed jacket; and the key clanked musically in the big lock as I set my face toward town. It is said that this prison is the despair of the rising generation; that those who are turned from it pine until they once more enjoy its inexpensive hospitality; for here the merriest and the mildest people in the world are prisoners.

Courage, my children! If you can only be naughty enough you, too, in the course of time, shall inherit the penitentiary.

Again I look upon the reef, but now from a hill slope skirted by a belt of perennial verdure; between us a vein of water, the pulse of the sea, throbs languidly. The reef, an amber shoal, seems to rise and float twice in the four and twenty hours—as the tide falls— and to slowly subside meanwhile, until much of it is submerged, but there is always a visible strip of rank green grass, and upon it is perched a cluster of low whitewashed hovels just above high-water mark—the whited sepulchers of the lazaretto.

It is possible to drive through the shallows that ripple between the reef and the mainland when the tide is out. Indeed, one may wade through it then without much difficulty, but the lazaretto is zealously guarded when pestilence has filled it with tenants, and it

On the Reef

is rare indeed that anyone succeeds in escaping from this desolate, wind-swept strand. They are pretty enough when seen from shore, these small white hovels, and especially so when, looking from a distant hilltop, one sees the sun launch from a rent cloud his golden bolts upon them, or a rainbow precipitates its curved torrent in their midst, flooding them with prismatic splendor. The reef, or rather that part of the reef—for it is all one, though a ship may pass through the cleft in it at long intervals—seems like a phantom island to most of us, for there are times when it has well-nigh disappeared and when even the little huts are almost obscured by dark cloud shadows, and then again it shines in glory and the silver surf beyond it leaps against a wall of sapphire, and the sands glisten like refined gold.

It was during my third visit to the Hawaiian capital when, having looked off upon the reef night and morning, and at midday and moonlight, from a serene height, I grew to know it as a theme capable of infinite variation, a kind of poem to which every day, and almost every hour, added a new stanza; a picture that was always complete, though never finished.

About this time it was publicly announced that a great luau would be given at the lazaretto, the occasion being the anniversary of the staying of the plague. Now there is no absolute necessity for the introduction of smallpox into the Hawaiian kingdom; among the natives the measles are sufficiently destructive; but the smallpox has appeared and desolated the people more than once. In such cases it is hard to segregate the victims, for love is stronger than death, and too often the seeds of death are nourished in the bosom of love. But a year or more before my third visit, by persistent energy the authorities gathered some hundreds of natives, and not a few foreigners, upon the reef, and of these no small proportion perished, and the bodies of the natives were interred in the sand. I think of that sad season when I look upon the reef of an evening and behold the watch fires of the quarantine twinkling across the sea, and when, by daylight, the sequestered coolies swarm like ants upon the sand, yearning, no doubt, as souls in purgatory, for the heavenly hills which we inhabit.

In common with the masses, I crossed the ford on the day appointed and joined them at the luau on the reef. A temporary lanai, or marquee, had been erected for the feast; the feast is the foundation of a luau. Musicians were there and hula dancers, for without these no luau is worthy of the name.

There was eating, overmuch of it, and temperate drinking and music almost incessantly. Many of the songs were composed for the occasion. The *improvisatori* were chanting the requiems for the dead, the eulogies on the living, and in each case stirring the hearts of the listeners to pathetic raptures.

Long meles in praise of those who imperiled their lives for the sake of the suffering ones were droned to the dolorous accompaniment of mourners vociferously wailing among the tombs. It was when the foreign element, drawn thither by curiosity, had returned to town—when the sun had sunk into the golden flood and the rich twilight was melting into darkness—that the natives began to abandon themselves to those rites which we call heathen, and which, though forbidden by Christian law and to some extent obsolete, still sway them irresistibly in their more emotional moods. It was the hula-hula that alone satisfied them, and rhythmical refrains from a mythology that defies translation, and mysterious invocations to the unforgotten gods. Call it orgy if you will; there was in it an expression of feeling, momentary it may be, but nevertheless profound; a display of emotion that was contagious. The ecstasies of the dancers mingled strangely with the agonies of the bereaved, and when the music and dancing had finally ceased and the sea seemed to have parted to let the multitude pass dry-shod to the shore, there were those who lingered yet among the lonely graves, their foreheads prone upon the sand, their hearts broken, and their throats hoarse with the howl of despair. Among these were some who came to weep for one who had passed too rapidly from the simplicity of the savage to the duplicity of civilized man. I had known him in his prime and in his degeneracy, and now I knew that somewhere among the bleaching, sea-washed sands lay the bones of Kane-pihi, who early fell a victim to the scourge.

Nothing was more natural than that he should absorb the seeds of disease, for caution is unknown of his race and he would not be likely to desert a comrade in affliction. He took the smallpox with avidity and never for a moment, so I am credibly informed, thought of letting it go again. Fatalism was the foundation of his faith and not all the Scriptures in Christendom could rob him of one jot or tittle of it. He could enjoy the religious diversions at Kaumakapili, and distinguish himself in the afterglow of the periodical revival; he could abandon his birthright of health, happiness, and wholesome liberty for the shams which were offered him in their stead; he could play fast and loose, false and true with the best of them, for this art is easily acquired by the ingenious, and once acquired is never again forgotten or neglected; but he could not survive the great change—the change of heart, the change of diet and of air and water and all the elements, and he went to his death like a bird in a snare without so much as a hope of rescue. It chanced to be the smallpox that finished him; had it not been this, doubtless it would shortly have been something else as unpremeditated.

The luau—the feast—was perhaps not entirely appropriate, it is true; it may never recur on that lonely slip of sand, and if it should, the bones of the dead will have been ground to powder in the pitiless mills of the sea; yet it cannot be said of him that he perished unwept, unhonored, and unsung, and there is some satisfaction in that. It was only the smallpox, but it was enough; I don't note the fact as being one of the evidences of Christianity as applied to the Hawaiian race, though for the most part Puritanism touches them like a frost. The epidemic merely precipitated the inevitable climax. One has only to glance at a comparative table of the census during the last threescore years, or to take the dimensions of the numerous and now almost vacant Protestant churches scattered through the length and the breadth of the land to draw a conclusion by no means flattering to any Board of Missions. Having spied the gentlest of savages out of the lonely sea for the purpose of teaching them how to die, the American missionary calmly folds his hands over the grave of the nation and turns his attention to affairs more private and peculiar.

James A. Michener and A. Grove Day

Gibson, the King's Evil Angel

James Michener suggested in 1954 to A. Grove Day that they collaborate on a volume of true accounts from the lives of violent and picturesque characters who had played roles in Pacific history. The result was *Rascals in Paradise* (1957), containing the biographies of nine men and one woman. Among those chosen was Walter Murray Gibson (1822–1888), whose adventures and intrigues strongly influenced Hawaiian history during the reign of Kalakaua, the "merry monarch," last king of Hawaii.

ONE of the most engaging rascals who ever plied the Pacific was an amazing gentleman from South Carolina. Tall, handsome, dressed in black, with sharp, deep-set eyes and a patriarchal beard, he commanded an orotund speaking style, a fine gift for quoting the Bible, and a vision of himself as the savior of all the native peoples in the Pacific.

"My heart is with the Oceanican races," he once cried in the oratory that marks even his simplest statements. "I was born on the ocean and I have felt a sort of brotherhood with islanders." He constantly dreamed of uniting the entire Pacific, and incredible as it seems, came reasonably close to doing so.

Think of what he accomplished solely through the exercise of a glib tongue. He plotted a Sumatran war of liberation from the Dutch. He rescued himself from a Java jail after more than a year of doleful imprisonment. Almost singlehandedly he brought Holland and the United States to the brink of war. Then, shifting ground, he became one of the most potent missionaries in the Pacific, from which job he was ousted because of public scandal. He thereupon became an extremely wealthy man, and then he entered upon his greatest adventure.

With little more than his charm and cunning to support him, he became prime minister of a sovereign Polynesian kingdom, held at one time or another all the cabinet positions, and from this point of vantage launched his grandiose scheme for uniting the Pacific. As the power behind the throne for more than a decade, he was indeed the evil angel of the Hawaiian king who reveled in the title of "the merry monarch." And then Gibson boldly challenged the armed might of Germany, Great Britain, and the United States, and initiated one of the most hilarious episodes of naval history.

Even in his declining years he was spectacular, involving himself in a notorious breach-of-promise suit. In addition to all this, he was a vehement writer, a philosopher, a dreamer, a self-appointed expert on tropical medicine, an energetic sea captain, a skillful editor, a fine farmer, a good businessman, a superb orator and a distinguished linguist.

In fact, Walter Murray Gibson was one of the most high-blown, dignified, and utterly delightful adventurers in history; and if he had not simultaneously accepted two separate bribes totaling $151,000 for an opium monopoly, he might have ruled a fair portion of the Pacific until he died.

As he boasted, Gibson was truly a child of the ocean. Appropriately, he began his adventurous life by being born at sea, during a raging storm in the Bay of Biscay on January 16, 1822. He was the third son of English emigrants bound from Northumberland to the United States.

Growing up in New York and New Jersey, young Walter was fired by the tales of an uncle who had mysteriously returned from long voyages to Malaysia and who was then in the service of an Arab merchant of Muscat. This romantic relative announced that he was making the boy his heir. "And then he spoke," Gibson later recalled, "of a great city in the center of the island [of Sumatra], a city once of mighty extent and population, whose sultans had given laws to all the rest of the Malay nations. But this great city had decayed, and its empire had been divided into many small and feeble portions. Now the Malays looked for the restoration of the sacred city, and their traditions had pointed to fair-skinned men from the

West, who should come with wisdom and great power, and who should destroy the robbers of Islam, the evil genii of the woods, and a great plunderer called Jan Company." It is clear that from then on, Walter Murray Gibson was determined to be the fair-skinned man who would restore this romantic city and save Sumatra.

As if such an uncle were not enough to inflame a boy's mind, young Gibson also went to school to a teacher who had been a missionary among the Indians of the American Northwest, and this man's lurid tales committed the lad to a life of high adventure.

When his parents moved to the backwoods of South Carolina, the wild outdoor life gave Walter "independence of spirit and an impatience of restraint." He ran away from home at fourteen and for a while dwelt among the Indians. He went to New York and then back to South Carolina, where he met a Miss Lewis, daughter of a planter. For a sample of Gibsonian prose at its best, no better excerpt could be found than his account of his wooing:

When I was yet a boy, I met in my wanderings in the backwoods of South Carolina with a fair gentle girl of my own age, who had never been more than half a day's ride from the plantation of her father. We often sauntered together in the still woods of Milwee on summer days; we would wade, barefooted, the shallow pebbly streams; cross the deep and rapid creeks, with mutual help of hands to our tottering steps, as we walked the unsteady swinging trunk that bridged them over. We rambled hand in hand to gather wild grapes and the muscadine, then we would rest beneath the dense shade, and at the foot of some great tree, and talk of our boyish and girlish fancies; and then without any thought as to mutual tastes, character, or fitness, or any thing that had to do with the future—but listening only to the music of our young voices, to the alluring notes of surrounding nature, and having only our young faces to admire—we loved; and long ere I was a man, we were married.

The early death of his wife left him a widower at the age of twenty-one, with three children—a girl, Talula, and two boys, John and Henry. The father of this brood then went to sea, according to one account, as master of the first iron steamship ever built in the United States, which ran from Savannah to Florida. After a year or so he turned up in New York as a commission merchant, and then joined the gold rush to California.

Afterward he traveled in Mexico, and he seems to have won many influential people there by the charm of his personality. Still feeling his way, he dropped down to Central America, where his pulse quickened, for he became involved in the intrigue of the banana countries. On a secret mission, of the kind he loved, he returned to the United States and in 1851 bought the cutter *Flirt*, a 96-foot schooner of less than a hundred tons' burden. But before he could smuggle it out of the harbor, the *Flirt* was seized by the revenue service and found to be loaded with arms and ammunition for General Carrera of Guatemala.

Deprived of his chance to become an admiral in the Guatemalan Navy, Gibson nevertheless spirited the *Flirt* out to sea with a crew of eight and a ballast cargo of eighty tons of ice. After a few weeks of Atlantic weather, a mutiny aboard caused Gibson to put into Porto Praia in the Cape Verde island of São Tiago, owned by Portugal. There he avoided confiscation of his ship as the property of a filibuster by entertaining some officials with "gracious gentility and rare old wine."

Out of Porto Praia, with his cargo of ice rapidly melting in the warmer seas, Captain Gibson found that somebody had vengefully smashed his chronometer and other nautical instruments, and sailing blind, he headed for Brazil to get some new ones. There, to raise funds, he sold one or two tons of ice, all that was left of his melting cargo. For the rest of this unbelievable voyage the *Flirt* sailed completely unladen. At the port of Maceió the death of a crew member in a drunken brawl almost brought confiscation once more, but Gibson's appeal to the British vice-consul enabled him to escape arrest.

Gibson then sailed the empty *Flirt* eastward around the Cape of Good Hope. He said that the magic islands he now passed in the Indian Ocean—Madagascar, Mauritius, Cocos-Keeling—held no allure for him, as he was drawn almost magnetically on toward the great island of Sumatra, about which he had dreamed since youth. His rhapsody upon his first sight of it is still moving:

On Christmas eve, we were sailing with a gentle wind over a smooth sea. We were nearing thick masses of land-clouds, when there came a faint aroma of sweet woody scents, wafted on the breeze; as we sped through the yielding vapory banks, the fragrant air came strong and pleasurable, like distant strains of song; then the retreating clouds presented to our gaze a dark blue peak, piercing the skyey blue above; the wood, and blossoms, and gum-scented breeze came stronger and more thrilling, rivaling in pleasure sweet melody on the waters; and the peak, and the odor-laden winds, were the first sight and first welcome breath of the land of long dreams, the island of Sumatra.

But he was tempted to leave Sumatra by prospects of a trip to nearby Singapore, where his storytelling uncle, now dead, had supposedly left him a fortune. Unable to go because the Dutch would not clear his ship, he turned with a profound uplifting of spirit to his main job of setting Sumatra free from Dutch rule. Accordingly he steered the *Flirt* into one of the most sensitive and spy-ridden ports of the Dutch colonial empire, the tin depot of Muntok on the metal-rich island of Bangka.

There followed a hilarious interlude. One practical Dutch official after another tried to figure out what an empty ship, seeking no cargo, was doing in the East Indies. Did Mynheer come halfway around the world for a shipment of tin? No? Then perhaps coffee? No? Then surely he seeks pepper? Cloves? Cinnamon? Good, then the captain wishes a cargo of lumber? No? Then maybe arrack? Perhaps tobacco for the China trade? Ah, yes! Mynheer has come for a boatload of our wild animals for the zoos of America. The great elephant? The fierce tiger? The rhinoceros? The curious tapir? Perhaps the musk deer?

The questioning went on day after day, and one can imagine the frustrating reports filed by the Dutch secret police. At one point it was suspected that Gibson was after a restricted and highly lucrative cargo of birds' nests for the Chinese soup trade, and after half a dozen similarly exotic suggestions had proved vain, the patient Dutch started to repeat the litany. Did Mynheer come for tin, for coffee, for pepper? Gently Captain Gibson gave reply:

I reached out my hand over the rail of the veranda where we sat, and drew towards me the limb of a jessamine bush, which becomes a tree of twenty and thirty feet high in these islands. I inhaled the sweet fragrance of its blossoms. I then pointed to some banana and coconut trees, loaded with their fruit; to a tame musk deer, running about in the yard; to a bird of bright plumage....

These were the things, he said grandiloquently, that he had come around the world in an empty boat to see.

The Dutch gave up and concluded that Gibson must be a wealthy yachtsman traveling solely for pleasure.

A local guide, a native of Bali, now offered to lead Gibson to Palembang, the largest town of Sumatra, a floating city known as the Venice of the East. This was a ticklish proposal, because Englishmen were stirring up native revolts against Dutch rule; and when Gibson indicated that he might go inland, the Dutch concluded that he was a supersmart secret agent. They began to suspect him of being an American spy or deserter, and kept an increasingly attentive eye on his activities.

Gibson, meanwhile, was reflecting upon the success of James Brooke, about whom he had read back in the United States. On the island of Borneo, to the east of Sumatra, Brooke had succeeded in setting up a personal kingdom as Raja of Sarawak. Gibson felt that he was as good a man as Brooke and began looking around for a similar opportunity in Sumatra.

Trying to get in touch with the Sultan of Djambi, a native prince of the region, Gibson made the mistake of writing a message to that potentate in Malayan, offering to supply weapons and ships to free the natives from Dutch domination. Unluckily, the translator he chose happened to be a Malay spy who had been planted on him by the Dutch government police. Gibson's sailing master, Graham, was sent to deliver this incriminating letter, which was found on his person when he was quickly captured by the vigilant Dutch.

Gibson was clapped into the Dutch prison of Weltevreden at Batavia, Java, on a charge of fomenting rebellion. He always claimed that the innocent letter of greeting he had dictated had been replaced with an incriminating document. He refused several chances to escape and hoped for rescue by the American government, even though there was at the time no American consul near at hand. His trial was postponed indefinitely, because if he were convicted the penalty had to be death, and his execution might lead to trouble with the United States.

Gibson endured sixteen months of imprisonment with fortitude. He learned the Dutch and Javanese languages, invented a brickmaking machine, and studied for hours with Sahyeepah, "the winged one," a native princess who visited him often in the free-and-easy Dutch jail.

He was finally brought to trial on February 14, 1852, and judged not guilty of high treason, but was ordered to be put in the pillory for two hours and then to be jailed for twelve years, paying his own board bill during his imprisonment. Other Dutch authorities, trusting that America had decided to abandon her erring son, ignored the sentence, and in April, 1853, a secret tribunal condemned him to death.

Yet the practical Dutch hoped that he would escape and thus solve the problem for them, and so a complicated scheme to get Gibson away from prison with the aid of the princess—who had fallen in love with him—was finally worked out. An American schooner, the *N. B. Palmer*, was fortunately being repaired in the vicinity and it was arranged, probably by the Dutch themselves, for Captain C. P. Low to take the fugitive aboard on April 24, 1853. According to Gibson's later account of his escape, the *Palmer* while leaving the roadstead was fired on by the Dutch cruiser *Boreas*, and after retaliating crowded on sail and evaded pursuit. This seems highly unlikely, for the ship passed easily through the Straits of Sunda next morning, leaving behind the confiscated *Flirt*, as well as Gibson's hopes of becoming a second Raja Brooke.

Two years later Gibson published an excellently written account of his attempt to free Sumatra, *The Prison of Weltevreden*, in which he adopts the device of recounting to the passengers on his rescue ship, the *Palmer*, the incidents of his complicated adventure. Like a male Scheherazade, for fifty-four days of the flight from Java he thus entertains the people of the *Palmer*, and if any modern reader longs for the old days of high-flown style, lofty sentiment, and rich description, this narrative is recommended. His cell in the state prison he portrayed thus:

A narrow den, a foul sweltering oven; ten feet in length and eight in width, half filled by a coarse platform, its only furniture. No light or air, but from one double-barred grating in front. The cell stank, the air was dead and still; I sat down with sickened feeling, on the platform; the foulness and heat of that place was fearful. . . . The door was closed, the dead air felt deadlier and stiller, one quaff alone of the breezy air of the morning was prayed for; and then water, not thought of when the keeper was in the cell, water, water, I called for between those bars, but the brutal sentinel paid no heed; a little water, and a little air, were the craving wants of a dreadful night passed in the Stad prison of Batavia.

When the *Palmer* arrived in England, Gibson sought out the American consul at Liverpool and asked for a loan to enable him to return to the United States. He proclaimed grandly that he was going to demand high indemnities from the Dutch government for his mistreatment at Batavia.

The consul, whose name adds luster to the Gibson legend, listened to tales that threatened to put the consul's own volumes of romance in the shade. After the interview he reported that he found Gibson to be

a gentleman of refined manner, handsome figure, and remarkably intellectual aspect.... Literally, from his first hour, he had been tossed upon the surges of a most varied and tumultuous existence, having been born at sea, of American parentage, but on board of a Spanish vessel, and spending many of the subsequent years in voyages, travels, and outlandish incidents and vicissitudes which, methought, had hardly been paralleled since the days of Gulliver or Defoe. When his dignified reserve was overcome, he had the faculty of narrating these adventures with wonderful eloquence, working up his descriptive sketches with such intuitive perception of the picturesque points that the whole affair was thrown forward with a positively illusive effect, like matters of your own visual experience. In fact, they were so admirably done that I could not more than half believe them, because the genuine affairs of life are not apt to transact themselves so artistically. Many of his scenes were laid in the East, and among those seldom-visited archipelagoes of the Indian Ocean, so that there was an Oriental fragrance breathing through his talk, and an odor of the Spice Islands still lingering in his garments. He had much to say of the delightful qualities of the Malay pirates, who, indeed, carry on a predatory warfare against the ships of all civilized nations, and cut every Christian throat among their prisoners; but (except for deeds of that character, which are the rule and habit of their life, and a matter of religion and conscience with them) they are a gentle-natured people, of primitive innocence and integrity.

Those are the opinions of Nathaniel Hawthorne as recorded in his book of English observations, *Our Old Home*.

Then Hawthorne describes briefly one of the most completely typical of the Gibson antics. "Meanwhile," he writes,

> since arriving in England on his way to the United States, he had been providentially led to inquire into the circumstances of his birth on shipboard, and had discovered that not himself alone, but another baby, had come into the world during the same voyage of the prolific vessel, and that there were almost irrefragable reasons for believing that these two children had been assigned to the wrong mothers. Many reminiscences of his early days confirmed him in the idea that his nominal parents were aware of the exchange. The family to which he felt authorized to attribute his lineage was that of a nobleman, in the picture-gallery of whose country seat (whence, if I mistake not, our adventurous friend had just returned) he had discovered a portrait bearing a striking resemblance to himself. As soon as he should have reported to President Pierce and the Secretary of State, and recovered the confiscated property, he proposed to return to England and establish his claim to the nobleman's title and estate.... The English romance was among the latest communications that he entrusted to my private ear; and as soon as I heard the first chapter,—so wonderfully akin to what I might have wrote out of my own head, not unpractised in such figments,—I began to repent having made myself responsible for the future nobleman's passage homeward in the next Collins steamer.

Nevertheless, Hawthorne advanced $150 with which Gibson was able to travel to Washington, D. C.

There he persuaded the United States to present a formal claim against the Dutch for $100,000 in damages. When the Dutch refused to pay, the United States virtually threatened war, and conflict seemed imminent. Gibson meanwhile had obtained a post as attaché of the American Legation in Paris, and during rambles around Europe he "read the record of glorious adventure" and dreamed of further feats of daring. His favorite here was Prince Henry the Navigator. The Emperor Napoleon III, hearing of his exploits, offered Gibson a place in the New Caledonian expedition then forming, but the adventurer declined. He still wanted to fight the Dutch.

Returning to the United States, Gibson aroused public sympathy for his claim by lectures and by the publication of his book, *The Prison of Weltevreden*. But when his case was to be put before Congress, an important letter was found to be missing from the State

Department files on his case. Since Gibson himself, who had been given access to the file, was the only person who could have abstracted it, suspicion fell on him.

It just so happened that the Dutch diplomats had a duplicate of this purloined letter and they made it public. Written by Gibson, dated at Batavia on February 25, 1852, and addressed to the Governor of the Netherlands Indies, the letter begged for its writer's release and admitted making "vainglorious remarks" to the natives of Sumatra while under the influence of liquor. Gibson also confessed, "I have too often been led away in life by some high-colored romantic idea," and he admitted having indulged in "bravadoes that I would become a potentate in the East." Writing this letter and then pilfering it from the files destroyed Gibson's claim in the eyes of Congress. War with the Dutch was thus fortunately averted.

Throughout the rest of his life Gibson mourned Sumatra as his lost empire, and we can believe that, like Queen Mary Tudor's Calais, its name was engraved upon his heart. But his rajadom being irretrievably lost, he spruced up and looked around for other conquests.

It was in Washington that he became interested in the Mormons, or Latter-Day Saints, and observing their difficulties with the United States Government, he advocated settling all of them on some Pacific isle of Eden. But his plan was rejected by officials because the cost, five million dollars, was prohibitive. As he often pointed out later, the futile Mormon War subsequently cost the United States three times that amount.

Still, an idea had struck fire in his febrile brain, and he betook himself out to Salt Lake City, where on October 29, 1859, he suggested to Brigham Young that he sell Utah to the United States and move the Mormon state—lock, stock, and barrel—to Papua or New Guinea. He told Brother Brigham that his high object was to do good to the natives of those lands, as he had reason to believe they were the Lost Tribes of Israel. Instead of accepting this bizarre plan, Young countered with the suggestion that Gibson become a Mormon and perhaps go to the Pacific islands to convert the natives to that sect.

After some heart searching, Walter Murray Gibson on January 15, 1860, became a member of the Saints. He lectured for a while in Utah and then went to some of the eastern states to recruit converts, but he soon wearied and raised money to bring himself back to Utah, along with his three children. On arrival he heard the joyous news. His great desire had been realized—he had been cleared as a preacher and was appointed to carry the Mormon gospel to all the Pacific islands.

Accompanied by his daughter Talula (the two sons remained for the while in Salt Lake), Gibson headed west, and lectured in California, where because of high tensions he found it expedient to deny being a Mormon. Nor did he admit his affiliation when he landed on July 4, 1861, in the Hawaiian capital of Honolulu after a voyage on the ship *Yankee*. There he gave lectures on Malaysia and passed himself off as a world traveler on his way to the East Indies.

The Civil War had now broken out in the States, and the king of independent Hawaii, Kamehameha IV, had proclaimed his country's neutrality. Union sympathizers in Hawaii quickly became suspicious of this mysterious, energetic, glib-talking Captain Gibson of South Carolina. They guessed that he was planning a privateering venture. On September 2, while calling at the United States Legation, Gibson was prodded into a fiery defense of Jeff Davis, and Union spies were convinced they had their man. But two hours later he confounded everyone by leaving with his daughter on the steamer *Kilauea* for the island of Maui.

The United States consul on Maui was alerted regarding the suspicious Southerner and had him followed. He uncovered some highly perplexing data, for Gibson was accompanied by two worthies —one an ex-bartender—whom he had picked up on the ship from California. These two were now found to be wandering around Maui trying to peddle a compendium called *Dr. Warren's Household Physician*. The Union spies were utterly confused and no one knew what to do about Gibson; then suddenly he stepped forth as a full-blown Mormon missionary. His first act was, characteristically, to devise a Mormon flag with individual stars for the eight Hawaiian islands. The Union forces, withdrawing from the field, sneered at it as a "secession flag."

Gibson began his missionary labors among the native Mormon Church members, who had lacked a white leader for three years. Within a few weeks he was presiding over a conference of Mormons on Maui. But now the Hawaiian government became suspicious of him, and the cabinet council minute book shows that fifty dollars was authorized for obtaining any information regarding what Brother Walter was really up to. The missionary forestalled them, however, by giving a solemn promise that he would never take any Hawaiian subjects away to New Guinea. Somehow this made everything all right.

Meanwhile Gibson, in a whaleboat owned by a native, had visited the little island of Lanai. Here the heads of the Mormon Church had decided in 1853 to establish a stronghold. A tract of five thousand acres was obtained, a town site was laid out, houses were built and farms started, and slowly the City of Joseph rose. Gibson, viewing the scene, the site of his future grandiose operations, said sententiously: "I will plant my stakes here and make a home for the rest of my days."

He began to work to build up the Mormon settlements on Lanai, and by November 5 he and Talula were living at Palawai on that island. He was now head of a colony of about 180 Hawaiians, ruling under the title of "Priest of Melchizedec and Chief President of the Isles of the Sea," and this robust title seems to have awakened once more the dreams of his youth, for he wrote in his diary on January 31, 1862: "O smiling Palawai, thou infant hope of my glorious kingdom! Blessed is Lanai among the isles of the sea." From that moment, he was on his way to empire.

To further his plans, the Priest of Melchizedec began making a study of Hawaiian history, customs, and language, and soon became so proficient that he was venerated by the natives. His style became even more florid: "This is the time when the gentiles of America shall be swept from the face of the earth, as has been foretold in the prophecies of the Prophet, Joseph Smith. As for Zion, her time has come to be set free, and the Prophet, Brigham Young, is to become as the King of Kings. . . . You, the red-skinned children of Abraham, have attained the joy of preparing to found the New Jerusalem."

To build Zion on Lanai and advance the farming projects there, the faithful children of Abraham donated goats, fowls, donkeys, furniture, and cash. Gibson supplemented these funds by selling offices in his church; a post as one of the twelve apostles under him went for a price of $150, but other positions could be purchased for as low as fifty cents. At this point Gibson seems to have become more interested in wealth and political power than in erecting a religious Utopia, for in a revealing communication he assured the government that he could influence 2,500 votes in the kingdom.

Gibson had his troubles. The two cronies he had picked up on the ship ungratefully denounced him, called him a "blackhearted schemer," and accused him of sympathy with the Confederate cause. What was worse, a drought and a worm pest threatened the harvest in March, 1862, but Gibson resolutely ordered that teams of natives be harnessed to the plough to break new land, and under similar conditions of slavery most of the crop was saved. Although the Gibson diary now referred to "windy, desolate Lanai," success in raising cattle and sheep helped the colony prosper.

But now a few doubting natives began to wonder if what they were suffering was really the Lord's way, and a committee complained to Salt Lake City about their pastor's methods. In April a grim-faced delegation of Mormon elders arrived at Lahaina, Maui, where their investigations showed conclusively that the church had been betrayed. Gibson had diverted its funds to the purchase of about half the island of Lanai, and all the church property was in his name.

The elders were apoplectic, and Robert Louis Stevenson claimed some years later that "there is evidence to the effect that he was followed to the islands by Mormon assassins." But no avenging angel laid Gibson low for his theft and sacrilege. It does seem certain, however, that Elder Joseph F. Smith told the backslider: "Gibson, you will die in a gutter!"

Gibson was excommunicated by the Mormon Church within a month, and he ceased calling himself a Mormon. Most of the settlers left Lanai and went to build the New Jerusalem somewhere else. A much more promising site was chosen at Laie, Oahu, where after some years of hard work the community established a thriving sugar plantation which brought funds that enabled the erection of the imposing Mormon Temple that today glistens among the fields of waving cane. Gibson, however, stayed on Lanai with his fraudulent acres. In 1864 he was joined by his two sons, and thereafter he increased his island estates and flourished.

To the consternation of his enemies, the fruits of his wickedness seemed to multiply, and in a moving passage he recorded his reactions to his new home and its people:

They are material for a very little kingdom. They would not affect the course of trade nor change much the earth's balances of power. They are not material for a Caesar, nor a cotton lord, nor a railroad contractor. They would not be very potent secessionists and surely will seem but small material for me, after all the hope and grasp of my heart. But they are thorough, what they are. There is no cant among the kanakas. They bring a chicken or some yams to make up for their deficiencies in courtesy in approaching me.... I hope to influence the government to let us have all of this valley and most of the island to develop, and then we will dig and tunnel and build and plant and make a waste place a home for rejoicing thousands. I could make a glorious little kingdom out of this or any such chance, with such people, so loving and obedient. I would make a port and a commerce, a state and a civilization. I would make millions of fruits where one was never thought of. I would fill this lovely crater with corn and wine and oil and babies and love and health and brotherly rejoicing and sisterly kisses and the memories of me for evermore.

Gibson, realizing that at last he had a good thing, became a naturalized citizen of Hawaii on March 26, 1866. He made a trip back to New York in the fall of 1868, where he turned up as the "commercial agent to the colony of Singapore," trying to encourage the idea of Malaysian immigration into Hawaii, where labor was badly needed on the spreading sugar plantations. He also journeyed to Washington on his own account, where he lobbied for a reciprocity treaty between the United States and Hawaii that would break down the tariff wall on sugar and other articles exchanged by the two countries. Ignoring his Hawaiian citizenship, he tried to get himself a job on an American commission concerned with Oriental immigrants in the United States. And in his spare time he looked for good mainland farmers to bring back with him to the islands, but the few families he brought home to Lanai did not want to work very hard and the idea was a failure.

Gibson moved to Honolulu in September, 1872, and, supported by his hefty income from Lanai, entered politics. His first move was the promotion of a scheme for repopulating Hawaii. He advised importing people from the Orient or Malaysia—he strongly recommended Sumatra—to replace the declining Hawaiians and to supply labor in the fields. He founded a Hawaiian Immigration Society which advised the government on such matters, and the fact that Hawaii is today so strongly Oriental stems partly from his activity.

But sending memorials to the government was not his idea of politics. He had a much grander field of operation in mind, but for such achievement he required that the Hawaiian throne be occupied by the kind of king who would fit in with his grandiose plans. The present king, Kamehameha V, had not the commanding mind of the great ruler whose name he bore, but even so, Gibson could not make any headway with him. Fortunately for Gibson, Kamehameha V died without having named his successor, so Hawaii was free to elect a king.

Gibson looked over the two candidates, Prince William C. Lunalilo, a high-born chief with liberal opinions, and Colonel David Kalakaua, a politician and newspaper editor. Apparently he thought highly of neither, for there is some evidence that before the election he tried to organize a revolution which would have established a republic with Gibson as President; but this scheme failed, so he came out strongly for Lunalilo, and his candidate won overwhelmingly.

Yet Gibson had made a poor choice, for Lunalilo proved himself to be a fairly good king and one quite unprepared to follow Gibson's leadership in anything. Gibson, now fifty-two years old, a wealthy, influential man with a handsome black beard and commanding presence, decided to attain power without the king's assistance. His skill in oratory, and especially his mastery of the Hawaiian language, gave him command over the popular imagination, aided by his editorship of a paper called *Nuhou,* or *"Gossip."* He appealed to the natives' fear of foreigners and missionaries, and for his own ends stirred up racial hatred. Ironically, the cry of this Caucasian messiah was "Hawaii for the Hawaiians!" and his demagogic articles and lectures poured scorn on the "grasping and unscrupulous whites." Clearly aiming at the private goal of "Hawaii for Gibson!" he stirred up hatred of all non-Hawaiians, but particularly those who had long resided in the islands and were prominent in business and social life.

Then Lunalilo died after less than thirteen months of sovereignty, and Gibson had another chance to pick himself a king. This time he made no mistakes. Backing David Kalakaua vigorously, he opposed the more logical candidate, Queen Emma, a brilliant woman and widow of Kamehameha IV. Of her Gibson shouted piously that she should refrain from running, for "the Hawaiian people will love her as a benefactress and hate her as a politician." When the legislators met, thirty-nine voted for Kalakaua and only six for Emma. The queen's supporters attacked the Courthouse and a riot broke out that was quelled only by the landing of forces from British and American warships in the harbor.

At last Gibson had the king he wanted. Kalakaua, destined to be the last male monarch of the Hawaiian kingdom, was truly a "merry monarch," but also a visionary, one who believed in Hawaii's high destiny. Fourteen years younger than Gibson, he had been born on November 16, 1836, in Honolulu; but he came of a prominent family of the Big Island—Hawaii—and could trace his ancestry back to legendary times when chiefs had reached there from Tahiti. He was a practiced public speaker and writer in both English and Hawaiian, and had once edited a newspaper, *Star of the Pacific*. In 1888 his name was to appear as author of *Legends and Myths of Hawaii*, edited by R. M. Daggett, the first important book in English dealing with these old tales. He also loved music, and composed the words of the national anthem, "Hawaii Ponoi."

Kalakaua started his reign auspiciously, and won wide popularity by attaining a reciprocity treaty with the United States. To aid the cause he made a visit to that country, and thus became the first king of any nation to do so. Americans, of course, have always gone mad over royalty, and King Kalakaua was widely hailed as a democratic king. But he dreamed of restoring the strong personal rule of the early Hawaiian monarchs, and his reign was marked by an increasing march toward autocracy.

Burly in figure, with luxuriant side whiskers, Kalakaua Rex was imposing in the glittering uniforms in which he loved to dress. He was a living paradox, both kingly and democratic. Stevenson, who spent six months in the islands in 1889, called Kalakaua "the finest gentleman I ever met" and "a very fine intelligent fellow," but added, after the king had lunched on the writer's yacht *Casco*, "what a crop for the drink! He carries it, too, like a mountain with a sparrow on its shoulders." Henry Adams, whose education was advanced by a visit to Hawaii in 1890, noted that Kalakaua "talked of Hawaiian archaeology and arts as well as though he had been a professor." Charles Warren Stoddard, another author, remarked: "Oh, what a king was he! Such a king as one reads of in nursery tales. He was all things to all men, a most companionable person. Possessed of rare refinement, he was as much at ease with a crew of 'rollicking rams' as in the throne room." John Cameron, who as master of a steamer running to Kauai often found His Majesty seated among his retainers on mats on the afterdeck, termed him "easy to approach and difficult to leave; unfailingly genial; kind to high and low alike; beloved by his subjects. . . . It was not strange, I think, that many adventurers took advantage of Kalakaua's liberality and joviality to intrigue for their own miserable ends." The chief intriguer was Walter Murray Gibson.

Under Kalakaua, as under Lunalilo, Gibson continued his intrigues to obtain favorable leases on more Lanai lands. He was elected to the Legislative Assembly in 1878 from Lahaina, and took an active part as a supporter of the king and a champion of the natives. He worked for sanitation and better care of lepers.

Further, Gibson supported an appropriation to build a more commodious palace, observing in his rich prose that it was "essential to the dignity and security of a throne that it should be upheld by appropriate surroundings of domain and mansion." He also took the lead in proposing a fitting celebration of the centenary of the discovery of the islands by Captain James Cook, and an appropriation of $10,000 was made for a statue of Kamehameha I to be erected in Honolulu. Some people commended Gibson's efforts in this session, but the *Hawaiian Gazette* sourly wrote: "He got up more special committees, made more reports, and by his officiousness and vanity kept the legislature in a continual ferment of excitement, merely to enable him to air his inordinate ambition to shine as a leader of the Assembly; and par excellence, the special friend and protector-general of the remnants of the Hawaiian race."

The statue turned out to be a typical Gibson project. As committee head, he felt he had to go to the United States, and from Boston commissioned the sculptor Thomas R. Gould to design an idealized statue of Kamehameha the Great, which would be erected across from the new palace in downtown Honolulu. Somehow, the expense of this statue ran into big money; the pedestal alone cost the kingdom $4,500, and the statue itself sank when the ship that carried it caught fire off South America.

Now occurred one of those accidents which try the politician's soul. And Gibson must often have contemplated wryly the irony of a situation in which he introduced into Hawaii his own worst enemy. Some years before, while knocking around Washington, he had met an ingratiating Italian adventurer, Celso Caesar Moreno, whom he had casually invited to Hawaii. Long after the invitation had been forgotten, Moreno turned up brightly on the Honolulu docks. He immediately charmed King Kalakaua, and with Gibson's support wangled $24,000 for a steamship line to be run by Moreno, showed how an opium concession in Hawaii would make millions, tried to borrow $1,000,000 to lay a transpacific cable to China, and set up a plan for educating likely Hawaiian boys at overseas universities at government expense.

This was the kind of big thinking that appealed to King Kalakaua, and startling as it seems, exactly 274 days after the enterprising Celso Caesar Moreno landed in Hawaii, the king prorogued the assembly, forced his entire cabinet to resign, and appointed Moreno premier of Hawaii!

A tornado of protest at once arose against the interloper. Various people advocated the crowning of Emma, the abdication of Kalakaua, the lynching of Moreno, or immediate annexation of the kingdom by the United States. Under this storm of indignation, the king reluctantly dismissed Moreno, but to save face gave him the position of escorting some young Hawaiians abroad to study in Italy. Moreno departed, suspected of some sinister mission.

Gibson must have breathed a sigh of enormous relief when the gallant Italian disappeared, for Moreno had done exactly what Gibson wanted to do, and only the popular revolution against the appointment made it possible for Gibson himself to attain the post of premier. His election, however, was to come more slowly than Moreno's dazzling rise.

Posing as the savior of the declining Hawaiian race, Gibson had been busy giving medical advice toward that end. He rightly asserted that the race "which cared not for the chastity of its females must not hope for independence or perpetuity." Completely without the aid of the medical profession, he wrote a book of sanitary instructions for the native Hawaiians, which would help them avoid malaria, smallpox, and leprosy. The main source of his rules was, as he wrote to one editor, "the first and most eminent writer on sanitary conditions known to us—and that is Moses." Gibson made a good deal of money on this volume and obtained a post on the Board of Health.

Gibson's real power began to accumulate when he acquired the influential newspaper, *Pacific Commercial Advertiser,* in whose columns he continued to play the champion of the Hawaiian people, the enemy of grasping Caucasians, and the only logical savior of the islands. He had plenty of space in which to advance these views, for all the respectable business leaders had pulled their ads out of his paper.

Kalakaua Rex departed in January, 1881, on a trip around the world, the first king to make such a tour. He was accompanied by his chamberlain, Colonel C. H. Judd, and his attorney general, W. N. Armstrong. His valet Robert, a decayed German baron who was an accomplished linguist, went along as interpreter. The king went abroad presumably to study the immigration problem, but one of his ministers said his only object was to gratify his curiosity and that it was "pure poppycock and Gibsonese" to say otherwise. Kalakaua went first to San Francisco and then visited Japan, China, Siam, India, Egypt, and the capitals of Europe. In all of these places he was given royal honors and hearty entertainment, and in Tokyo nearly succeeded in arranging a marriage between his lovely niece, the Princess Kaiulani, and one of the imperial princes of Japan.

During the king's absence, Gibson built up his political power and came to be considered a public leader. He was appointed a member of the privy council, and when Kalakaua returned, Gibson continued to instill in him a love of pomp and aggrandizement, for the king was easily dazzled by show.

While in England the king had ordered two golden crowns, set with precious jewels. On February 12, the ninth anniversary of Kalakaua's election to the throne, the coronation was held in a pavilion on the grounds of the new Iolani Palace. While eight thousand people watched, the elected king, Napoleon-style, put on his own head and that of his queen the royal crowns. Years later, runs the legend, on the night the Hawaiian monarchy was overthrown, an officer of the Provisional Government forces found his men in the palace basement throwing dice for jewels gouged out of these royal diadems. The biggest diamond was sent by an Irish sergeant to his Indiana sweetheart, who always considered it just a lump of glass.

During the election of 1882, Gibson's opponents tried to overwhelm him by publishing a satirical exposé entitled *The Shepherd Saint of Lanai*. It revealed in lurid detail the shadiness of his early career and predicted a revolution if Gibson continued to stir up hatred. This pamphlet failed to ruin him, however, because it was printed in English, and few of his native supporters could read it! Again his political cunning and his oratory enabled him to be elected by a large majority.

The 1882 session of the legislature was one of the most corrupt that had ever met in Honolulu. One of its first acts was to convey to Claus Spreckels, a California sugar magnate, a large tract of crown lands at Wailuku, Maui, to settle a claim he had bought from a local princess for $10,000. Gibson supported an opium-licensing bill, another big loan bill, a bill to permit sale of spirituous liquors to natives and another for nonsegregation of lepers. Another bill led to the minting of the silver coins which in 1884 were put in circulation bearing the bust of Kalakaua; on this coinage deal, Spreckels made a profit of $150,000, and the dumping of silver currency for a time threatened the entire Hawaiian economy.

Such flagrant misgovernment could not be tolerated by sensible men, and Kalakaua's entire cabinet resigned. This was Gibson's supreme chance, and he prevailed upon the king to appoint him premier and minister of foreign affairs. Thereafter, until his sudden downfall five years later, Gibson had everything his own way. He proved himself an adroit politician and held each of the cabinet posts in turn, occasionally several at once. Whenever the conservative elements in the kingdom tried to unseat him, he threatened them with his staunch Hawaiian supporters, and made his position secure by continuing to flatter the hula-loving, poker-playing king.

The Gibson rule was one of utter confusion, but slowly a Reform party, solidly organized, began to coagulate and it managed to defeat some of the wildest Gibson measures, even though the premier used patronage and government funds shamelessly to support his program. He favored his son-in-law with sinecures and showered the young man's father with building contracts. Among the more trivial scandals of the Gibson regime were the sale of public offices, the ruination of the civil service by purges, misuse of royal privilege to defraud the customs revenue, illegal leasing of lands to the king, neglect of the roads of the kingdom and the sale of exemptions to lepers, who could thereby escape confinement on Molokai.

Now Gibson was in a position where he could revive the dreams of his youth, and he launched a systematic program of corrupting Kalakaua's judgment and subtly introducing his own grand design. Hawaii must head a vast coalition of island states including Tahiti, Samoa, Tonga, the New Hebrides, the Solomons, the Gilberts and all the islands in between—and the king of Hawaii would become the emperor of the Pacific.

Gibson's studies had shown him that in the past, the Hawaiian Islands had not only striven for their independence but had at times tried to play a bigger role in Pacific politics and to annex other regions. He recalled that Kamehameha the Great, the "Napoleon of the Pacific," had dreamed of going far beyond his unique achievement of uniting the baronial, war-torn Hawaiian Islands under himself as ruler. During the last years of his reign that powerful monarch, who died in 1819, was reported to have opened negotiations with King Pomare II of Tahiti on the project of having a son and daughter of Kamehameha marry Pomare's offspring. An alliance of that kind might have been the first step in organizing a spreading Polynesian League in the Pacific before too many islands had been grabbed by European powers.

Gibson also remembered the disastrous expedition of Governor Boki and his two Hawaiian brigs in search of a sandalwood island in the New Hebrides in 1830. Trying to recoup his lost fortunes, Boki and nearly five hundred of his followers had mysteriously disappeared in the South Seas. Gibson deduced that Boki had probably carried secret orders to annex some of those islands to the Hawaiian kingdom. Could Boki's tragic trip be used as an excuse for annexation?

But most of all, Gibson was familiar with the exploits of one of the strangest men in Hawaiian history. Charles St. Julian never saw the Islands, probably never saw a Hawaiian. He was an underpaid law-court reporter in Sydney, Australia, with little schooling and only an inordinate personal vanity to build upon. As a result of writing innumerable letters to different governments, he was—almost accidentally—allowed to serve as *de facto* consular agent for Hawaii in Sydney.

That was all the purchase he needed, for he thereupon launched a veritable blizzard of reports, fantastic plans, involved negotiations and scatterbrained attempts at consolidating most of the island groups in the Pacific under Hawaiian rule. With his own money he purchased a lovely atoll just east of the Solomons called Sikaiana, and tried to give it to Hawaii. It is doubtful if any kingdom ever had a more loyal servant than Charles St. Julian. For twenty years he tried to get the Hawaiian kings to accept the "Primacy of the Pacific" and take the lead in establishing protectorates over islands that had not yet been seized by the great powers.

But Hawaii, without a Walter Murray Gibson on hand at the time to appreciate the Australian's energy, treated St. Julian badly. He got little or no pay, no support. Not even his atoll was accepted, but he did enjoy moments of grandeur. He was allowed to design his own uniforms, and by all accounts was one of the handsomest and most glittering consuls ever to operate in the Southern Hemisphere. He also initiated, on his own account, a florid, bejeweled decoration, the Order of Arossi, which he gave to himself for extraordinary services to the people of Polynesia.

Usually such dreamers reach a bad end, but Charles St. Julian gladdens the heart by his accomplishments. Despairing of getting anywhere with the unimaginative Hawaiian kingdom, he transferred his cyclonic talents to Fiji, where he appeared grandly as "Charles, Muara of Arossi and Sovereign Chief of Sikaiana." He completely bedazzled that island group and talked himself into the job of lord high chief justice. Then, as he was about to leave Sydney for his new post, he received notice that Hawaii, whom he had pestered for years seeking some kind of honors, had finally awarded him "a Cross and Diploma as Knight Commander of the Order of Kamehameha I." With tears of gratitude overflowing upon the paper, he reported that he would accept the offer, because he would now be able to appear in Fiji as Sir Charles, which would "look better" and be "more fitting."

We see St. Julian for the last time as he enters the judicial chambers of Fiji. It is said that this flamboyant man, who was totally unschooled in law, appeared in a tremendous scarlet gown, a full-bottomed wig, and all the glittering accouterments of a proper English judge.

Walter Murray Gibson, who became premier eight years after St. Julian died in Fiji, was apparently haunted by the Australian's concept of what might be accomplished in the Pacific by a determined Hawaiian leader. He would be that leader. Accordingly he began to indoctrinate King Kalakaua with the idea of empire, and in 1880 the astonished United States Minister at Honolulu reported to his superiors that Kalakaua's imagination was actually "inflamed with the idea of gathering all the cognate races of the Islands of the Pacific into a great Polynesian Confederacy, over which he will reign." On June 28, Gibson had inserted into the preamble of a resolution adopted by the Legislative Assembly a statement that "the Hawaiian kingdom by its geographic position and political status is entitled to claim a Primacy in the family of Polynesian States." But this statement passed unnoticed by the press, and nothing further was done until Gibson came to power as head of the cabinet in 1882.

In this year Gibson received an inquiry from the chief of Makin, one of the Gilbert Islands, concerning a possible protectorate. He answered favorably and the upshot was that this chief and one from Abiang were invited to come to Kalakaua's coronation, but they were unable to do so.

As might be expected, Gibson's first overt act of empire was a disaster. Hearing that Captain A. N. Tripp, of the blackbirding ship *Julia,* was about to leave Honolulu for a native-stealing expedition to the New Hebrides, Gibson officially appointed him as "Special Commissioner for Central and Western Polynesia," with the job of inquiring whether any Gilbert Islands kings wanted to affiliate with Hawaii.

The *Julia* was wrecked on a Gilbert Islands reef while the captain was spying out the prospects, and the ship was a total loss; but when Special Commissioner Tripp beat his way back to Hawaii in another ship, he was quite excited about the prospects for a United Gilbert Islands nation under Hawaiian protection. The only lasting result of his mission, however, was the introduction into Hawaii of grass skirts from the Gilberts to adorn the palace hula dancers.

Soon after sending Tripp on his mission, Gibson took the first big step toward empire on August 23, 1883, when the Hawaiian government issued, in the form of a protest to the representatives of twenty-six nations, what was really a sort of Monroe Doctrine of Oceania. It proclaimed that Hawaii as a free Polynesian state should take the lead in guiding less fortunate neighbors. Only eight nations even bothered to reply. The document had no immediate effect, except to give Gibson's enemies a chance to ridicule the idea of his "calabash empire," referring to the Hawaiian expression of "calabash cousin" to indicate a non-blood relationship.

Tired of fooling around with paper measures, in 1886 Gibson decided that a likely region to begin in was the war-torn Samoan Islands, south of Hawaii, and he proposed that these islands should be taken under King Kalakaua's protection. Accordingly, he requested a $30,000 appropriation to send a government mission to Samoa and the South Pacific to demonstrate Hawaii's right to take the lead among Polynesian states. Opponents said it was "a policy of sentiment, show, and nonsense," and that "it was a ridiculous farce for this one-horse kingdom to maintain consular offices in all parts of the world." Gibson responded: "What was Rome but a one-horse state at its beginning? . . . The Great Powers never think of us as a one-horse state." Using steam-roller tactics, Gibson put through a final appropriation of $35,000 for the purpose, and in a gesture which he no doubt later regretted added on $100,000 for the purchase of a steamboat to overawe the other Polynesians and $50,000 for its running expenses.

The mission, which was about to stumble blindly into the fury of Prince Otto von Bismarck, chancellor of Germany, was appointed on December 22, 1886. Its totally inadequate head, John Edward Bush, a Caucasian-Hawaiian, was created "Envoy Extraordinary and Minister Plenipotentiary to the King of Tonga and High Commissioner to the Sovereign Chiefs and Peoples of Polynesia." He was accompanied by his wife; his daughter; some servants, at least one of whom could play a guitar; Henry Poor as secretary; and the artist Joseph D. Strong, husband of Robert Louis Stevenson's stepdaughter. Strong was commissioned to paint Polynesian portraits and scenes. The group left on Christmas Day on the S. S. *Zeelandia*. A fancy carriage, a gift to Malietoa, the leading chief of Samoa, was unfortunately left behind on the wharf at Honolulu.

Rarely has a mission headed so hopefully for an arena where only disaster could result. Not only was Samoa torn by internecine strife between two claimants to power, Malietoa and Tamasese, but Great Britain, the United States, and Germany were also involved in the bickering, and the last, a late-comer on the imperial scene, was determined on a showdown. Samoa would be German, or there would be war. It is pitiful to contemplate John Bush's fumbling group as it prepared to back into the German lawn mower.

Of all the places in the Pacific to which such a mission could have been sent, Samoa was in many respects the most appropriate, for there a heady brew of intrigue, romance, assassination, and adultery was provided in a rich tropical setting, of which Stevenson's wife was to write,

Socially, Samoa was certainly not dull. Diplomats and officials, many of them accompanied by their families, rented houses in the vicinity of Apia and entertained as they would at home. I have known Apia to be convulsed by a question of precedence between two officials from the same country, who each claimed the place of honour at public functions; burning despatches on the subject were written, and their respective governments appealed to. Well has Apia been called "the kindergarten of diplomacy."

With the arrival of the Bush party, the children in the kindergarten were going to play rough.

On arrival in Apia, Bush began building a spacious house that would serve as a permanent Hawaiian legation. In a show of glittering splendor he decorated Malietoa, the warring chieftain whom he had decided to support, with the "Grand Cross of the Royal Order of the Star of Oceania," a knightly order that Gibson had whipped up in imitation of St. Julian's abortive Order of Arossi. Bush then confided to Malietoa his breath-taking design: Samoa and Hawaii would form a federation under King Kalakaua. Then Tonga and the Cook Islands would join up, followed no doubt by Tahiti, whereupon the Gilberts would be annexed outright. In celebration, Malietoa and his supporting chiefs were given their first taste of Ambassador Bush's secret weapon: large bottles of square-face gin. The party lasted till five in the morning.

The Treaty of Confederation between Hawaii and Samoa was actually signed by Malietoa on February 17, 1887, and Bush celebrated the occasion with another all-night party. Stevenson, who arrived in Samoa two years later, wrote in *A Footnote to History* that Malietoa withdrew at an early hour, but "by those that remained, all decency appears to have been forgotten; high chiefs were seen to dance; and day found the house carpeted with slumbering grandees, who must be roused, doctored with coffee, and sent home. As a first chapter in the history of Polynesian Confederation, it was hardly cheering, and Laupepe [Malietoa] remarked to one of the embassy, 'If you have come here to teach my people to drink, I wish you had stayed away.'"

Bush went ahead to establish a virtual protectorate over the naïve Samoans. He obtained the defection of one of Malietoa's chief enemies, the father-in-law of rival Tamasese. Of this man Poor wrote that he had become "a generous admirer of our cheap gin and has even offered me his virgin daughter." Moreover, Tamasese's position was greatly weakened when his wife left him, and having "become charmed with the guitar music and songs" of one of Bush's Hawaiian servants, went to live with the latter as her paramour. In early March, Malietoa himself even proposed marriage to Bush's daughter Molly, offering to make her Queen Molly of Samoa, but unfortunately for her own future, the young lady declined that honor.

This extraordinary sequence of events infuriated the Germans, who had already secretly decided to back Tamasese and under his chieftainship to incorporate Samoa directly into the German Empire. But for the present Captain Brandeis, in charge of the German manipulating, had no clear-cut commission from Bismarck, and so had to fight off the Bush mission as slyly as he could. He had reason to believe, however, that when a squadron of the German Imperial Navy reached Apia, things would be different.

But Ambassador Bush also had a rather terrifying trump card up his sleeve. The Hawaiian fleet was about to appear in Samoan waters, and Bush felt certain that this redoubtable force would sway the balance of power definitely away from Germany and toward Hawaii.

The fleet consisted of one wormy ship, the 171-ton British steamer *Explorer*, which Gibson had bought for $20,000. It had been launched in Scotland in 1871 and had since seen good service in the guano trade. The government got possession of this vessel on January 21, 1887, and for $14,000 more fitted her out ostensibly as a naval training ship. Gibson's detractors hailed it as an expensive folly to "saddle the country with a toy ship for which she had as much need as a cow has for a diamond necklace."

The ship, whose name had been translated into Hawaiian as *Kaimiloa*, was armed with four muzzle-loading six-pounder saluting guns from Iolani Barracks, and two Gatling guns. Among the sixty-three-man crew it was decided to include twenty-four boys from the Oahu Reformatory School, twenty-one of whom would comprise a ship's band to "awe the natives with martial strains." Not much was known about the captain of the gunboat, George E. Gresley Jackson, except that he claimed to have been a British naval officer, was lately master of the reform school, and was indubitably one of the worst habitual drunkards in all Hawaii.

After many delays, H.H.M.S. *Kaimiloa* departed from Honolulu on May 18. She had been commissioned March 28 by Gibson "for the Naval Service of the Kingdom." Criticism arose against the use of the reform-school boys and this vessel of the Hawaiian navy, which critics ironically predicted would "shortly strike terror into the hearts of the natives, and teach the pigmy national ships of France, Germany, and Great Britain, in those waters, a necessary lesson."

Even before sailing, a disturbance on board upset discipline, and led to the dismissal of three officers. A marine officer was drinking with some sailors; he refused to return to his cabin, and called his marines into action to aid him. This was the first of the *Kaimiloa* mutinies.

That the *Kaimiloa* ever reached Apia to challenge Germany's imperial might was a miracle, for during the first eleven days at sea

Captain Jackson hid out in his cabin, blind drunk. None of the other officers knew anything about navigation, but they kept the ship in what they thought to be a southerly direction, so that when their captain finally staggered out to shoot the sun he found that his loyal crew had wasted not more than a week. A journal entry runs: "The captain took sights occasionally but never attempted to work out his longitude."

By some miracle, he and his crew sighted Apia on June 15, 1887, after a sickly twenty-nine-day passage. The German gunboat *Adler* was found at the anchorage and signaled inquiry as to the Hawaiian ship's identity, but the *Kaimiloa,* unaware of naval courtesies, drove gaily onward until checked by a shot across her bows.

The *Kaimiloa*'s first function was the presentation to Malietoa of a gorgeous uniform, which he wore when inspecting the ship, where a twenty-one-gun salute was offered. To everyone's astonishment, the guns fired.

Then came intrigue of the highest order. The German corvette *Adler,* which had been met in the harbor, was ordered to maintain constant vigil upon the intruding Hawaiian gunboat until the German squadron, which was on its way, had time to arrive and take command of the situation. A game of hide-and-seek developed when Ambassador Bush dispatched his warship to the neighboring island of Tutuila, where it was trailed by the suspicious *Adler*. But halfway to Pago Pago the *Kaimiloa* suddenly hove to and sent up a distress signal. Here was a chance for the Germans to board and inspect the Hawaiian menace!

But what the *Kaimiloa* wanted was a doctor. Captain Jackson, after having lived exclusively on gin for weeks, had finally eaten some food and it had given him galloping dysentery. Accordingly, a German medical officer, commissioned on the spot to spy out Hawaii's intentions, was rowed over to the wallowing *Kaimiloa,* where Captain Jackson was found doubled up in his bunk. For the remainder of the cruise the German officer more or less took charge.

Early in July, the second mutiny took place on board the *Kaimiloa*. A gunner, returning drunk, decided to rush the magazine and blow up the ship, just for the hell of it. Since trouble seemed inevitable, three officers promptly went ashore and presented their resignations to Captain Jackson, who was drinking gin, as usual. Ambassador Bush convinced them it was their duty to stay in service and quell the mutiny. But to safeguard his navy, he took the precaution of sending Poor and Jackson on board to see what they could do to save the *Kaimiloa*. Apparently the peacemakers got rough handling; according to Stevenson, "for a great part of the night she was in the hands of mutineers, and the secretary lay bound upon the deck."

After Poor had been chained for three hours and it seemed that the ship might actually be blown up, the Germans intervened. The *Adler* hove alongside and restored order. Her captain warned that if the uprising did not end, he would have to take over the rebellious ship and sail it back to Honolulu with the mutineers in irons. Where Poor and Jackson had failed, the Germans succeeded, and finally quelled the disturbance on the vessel sent to overawe European gunboats in Samoan waters.

Later Bush took the *Kaimiloa* on a cruise to the large island of Savaii to impress the outlying chiefs. He used up seven cases of gin, and the only result, according to one observer, was "to gratify the several chiefs visited by a sight of the ship, and by having the band sent ashore to entertain the people."

Now the Bush mission began to experience those heartaches which at times overtake even the best-planned operations. It was discovered that the ambassador had built his imposing legation on the wrong piece of ground and that it no longer belonged to him. Consequently a protracted lawsuit was initiated, which annoyed him greatly. Then an enemy secretly reported to Gibson in Hawaii that Bush was "the most dissipated man who has held a high position at this place for many years. His associates here are mostly of the lowest kind of half-castes and whites." Later Bush found that the instigator of this canard was his own secretary, Poor, but in a dispatch that must be unique in diplomatic history, he explained everything away by pointing out that Poor was living with Bush's daughter Molly and had got her pregnant and was thus somewhat irritated with her father, the ambassador.

As if the troubles ashore were not enough, the *Kaimiloa* now produced its third mutiny, for on July 22 the marines refused to load coal without being paid a bonus. Secretary Poor later called the vessel "a disgrace to her flag. . . . There was a state of continuous insubordination on the ship and utter disregard of all order and discipline. With a few exceptions the marines and white officers behaved badly, the marines continually breaking liberty by swimming ashore and disturbing the town with their drunken conduct." In fact, impartial observers reported that, if one took into consideration the behavior of the captain, the officers and the marines, the only people aboard the *Kaimiloa* who behaved even reasonably decently were the reform-school boys; but this was probably due to the fact that early in the visit to Samoa all the troublesome boys deserted the ship and were never heard of again.

Ambassador Bush's cup of trouble was brimming, for he found that his underlings had spent far more money than he could supply, and Apia merchants refused to do business on credit. The Germans were becoming stronger and more arrogant, and it seemed only a matter of time until Hawaii's friend, Malietoa, would be thrown out of power. Consequently it was a gloomy delegation that Bush led to say farewell to Chief Malietoa on the last night ashore; but the evening was made lively by Captain Jackson, who fell into a violent attack of delirium tremens.

That was enough. In disgust Ambassador Bush ordered the captain to take his warship back to Honolulu, and that, presumably, was the last of the *Kaimiloa*. Henry Poor wrote in his diary on August 8, "It was with a feeling of intense relief that I watched her disappear from sight."

But a few days later when Bush and his party, who had borrowed and scraped up enough money to pay their steamer fares back to Honolulu, reached Pago Pago on the way home, they found the *Kaimiloa* snugly berthed in that majestic anchorage. The enlisted men, fearing that they might have inadequate food for the trip north if their captain got drunk again and lost the way, were bartering all the ship's muskets for pigs, while Captain Jackson, also dubious about his own comforts on what might turn out to be a long voyage, was hocking the ship's silverware for bananas and other food.

In later years, when the *Kaimiloa*—which had once defied simultaneously the three greatest nations of the earth—was an inglorious hulk rotting on the Honolulu water front, Captain George E. Gresley Jackson turned up in various American ports. He dressed like an admiral and accorded himself that title. He was utterly contemptuous of the Hawaiians as sailors. "They were," he snorted bitterly, "far too fond of gin."

Thus ended Walter Murray Gibson's boyhood dream of a South Seas empire. The recall of the Bush mission and the abandonment of "gin diplomacy" occurred just in time, for Otto von Bismarck had endured enough. Around the end of July the Iron Chancellor confided to an associate: "We should not have put up with insolence of the Hawaiians any longer; if a German squadron were at anchor before Samoa, it could sail to Hawaii, and King Kalakaua could be told that, unless he desisted from his insolent intrigues in Samoa, we should shoot his legs in two, despite his American protection."

On August 19, only eleven days after the *Kaimiloa* had departed, a squadron of four German warships did arrive at Apia. The American consul there believed that, had the Hawaiian ship lingered until that time, it might well have been blown out of the water. Even Hawaii itself, as Bismarck had threatened, might have been attacked. On August 25, the squadron proclaimed Tamasese as King of Samoa, and unlucky Malietoa was deported. The Germans proclaimed martial law, and they threatened war with Hawaii if it aided the Malietoa faction in any way. Gibson's vision of Hawaiian empire had led to a very real danger to Hawaii's home islands from German cannons.

But Gibson was not around for the final debacle. Weeks before the collapse of empire, the man's follies had come home to roost, and his own neck was in danger. Had Germany known the true state of affairs, she might well have thought of armed intervention in Hawaii, for a revolution was simmering there. Gibson's attempts to use Kalakaua for his own selfish ends, plus his cabinet machinations and his stirring up of racial prejudice for political purposes, made pilikia—trouble—inevitable.

The election campaign of 1886 had been a riot of vilification by both parties. Gibson's royalists had the edge, however, because they could use the king's privilege of importing liquor duty free. Their henchmen served waiting lines of thirsty voters from a galvanized washtub full of straight gin, poured into tumbles from a coconut-shell ladle. The going price for votes was five dollars. Gibson won.

During the legislature of 1886, Gibson found the government heavily in debt to Spreckels and faced by the need to mortgage its revenue to the man who was being called "the second king of Hawaii." Public money continued going down the drain. The appropriations bill passed in 1886 exceeded four and a half millions. As the *Gazette* wrote: "The money borrowed has been used for every folly that the brains of a vain and foolish man could invent."

Now a worse scandal was about to break. For many years Gibson had abetted Kalakaua in reviving native customs and traditions, which opened the leaders to charges that they were "licensing sorcery and the hula and sacrificing black pigs." They had also founded a society which, it was charged, was set up "for the propagation of idolatry and sorcery." This was the Hale Naua or House of Ancient Science, a secret society combining aspects of Masonry with the rites of pagan chiefs. According to its charter from the privy council, it was organized forty quadrillions of years after the foundation of the world and 24,750 years after Lailai, the Hawaiian Eve. One historian believed that it was intended "partly as an agency for the revival of heathenism, partly to pander to vice, and indirectly to serve as a political machine."

The king dabbled in "scientific" theories such as the notion that Hawaii was the remains of a large Atlantislike continent which his race had once dominated—a theory that would appeal to the Mu enthusiasts of today but which evoked contemporary laughter. Kalakaua also founded a "Hawaiian Board of Health" which his critics termed an organized body of kahunas, medicine men. Gossips whispered of palace orgies at which the heathen pastimes were revived, including the hale ume, in which the companion of a night's pleasure was chosen by rolling a ball of twine in the direction of the selected charmer.

Other gossip concerned the private life of Gibson, who was still the Lothario. The sixty-four-year-old premier was courting a twenty-eight-year-old widow, Flora Howard St. Clair, who had come with her sister from their home state of California in February, 1886. She was a book agent and while canvassing for sales soon met Gibson. They immediately found a common interest in British painters. He told her that his life was lonely and remarked, "There is nothing like a true, loving heart." A day or two after Christmas, according to her testimony in court, he proposed marriage to her on the veranda of his home; but later he denied the engagement, and in May, 1887, when Gibson had his hands full with politics rather than with affairs of the heart, her lawyers brought a suit for breach of promise and asked $25,000 in damages. The suit did not come to trial until after Gibson's downfall, and in October, 1887, a jury awarded Mrs. St. Clair the sum of $10,000 heart balm.

As if no collapse were imminent, on November 16, 1886, Gibson had helped to celebrate King Kalakaua's fiftieth birthday with a grand hookupu, or gift-giving. Each guest brought a present suitable to his station. Premier Gibson led off with a pair of elephant tusks on a koa-wood stand with the inscription: "The horns of the righteous shall be exalted." The police department, more practical, tendered a bank check for $570. The ensuing jubilee pageantry and hula performances lasted more than a week.

Such scandals and the drain on public funds hopelessly alienated most of the white residents as well as many of the natives. Early in 1887 a secret society called the Hawaiian League had been formed to fight for a less autocratic constitution. Hundreds of islanders joined, and as a last resort were ready to overthrow the monarchy, set up a republic, and apply for annexation by the United States. The League members obtained arms and drilled regularly, and were ready to fight if necessary to obtain their rights.

The immediate occasion for the Revolution of 1887 was an act of blatant corruption. A disgruntled rice merchant named Tong Kee, alias Aki, disclosed that he had paid a bribe of $71,000 to cabinet officials for an opium monopoly in the kingdom, but that the license had been given to the Chun Lung syndicate, who had paid a bribe of $80,000. Both Gibson and the king were unquestionably involved. When the news broke, one firebrand advocated a march on the palace by the Honolulu Rifles, the armed militia of the League. Instead, the aroused citizenry held a mass meeting on June 30. Unanimous resolutions were passed demanding that the king dismiss his cabinet and other official concerned, and that he pledge himself never again to interfere in politics.

There was no bloodshed. Most of Kalakaua's troops had deserted him, and the battery of field guns he had bought in Austria on his world tour for $21,000 was of little value in defending him from his irate subjects. Hurriedly he fired Gibson and appointed a new cabinet, which drew up a less imperious constitution that he signed on July 6. The unfortunate Aki never got his money back, for the supreme court decreed that the king could not be sued.

What happened to the deposed premier? Taking advantage of the fear and confusion of the revolution, his opponents came within an ace of lynching him. The leader of the Honolulu Rifles dragged Gibson down to the docks and announced that he must hang from the yardarm of one of the vessels at the wharf, as a horrible example to those who would seek to overthrow the new government. But at the last minute the British consul intervened and the aging ex-premier was rescued from hanging.

He was hurried off to jail, where he remained until brought to trial on July 12 on charges of embezzlement, but the government decided not to prosecute. To save embarrassment, Gibson was allowed to leave Hawaii on a ship headed for the United States. His dreams of empire had vanished.

If Gibson's sense of drama had inspired him to seek out a proper death, he would have died in a California gutter, in accordance with the Mormon malediction directed against him. Instead, he died comfortably in bed, in St. Mary's Hospital, San Francisco, on January 21, 1888.

His body was embalmed and returned to Honolulu, where it was put on view at his late residence on King Street. Hordes of mourners came to pay their respects to the dreamer of the Pacific. "Native Hawaiians," reported a newspaper, "exceeded all other nationalities in numbers, and their manifestations of sorrow and grief were touching." A solemn funeral was then held at the Catholic Cathedral. Among the dignitaries who attended in formal attire were diplomatic representatives of the United States, Great Britain, and Portugal. The bishop who conducted the services, aware of the tensions accompanying this funeral, ended his peroration with an admonition: "Let him who is without fault among you cast the first stone." Gibson's estate, according to local rumor, totaled more than a million dollars.

In writing of Gibson, one is constantly tempted to dismiss him as another of the confused visionaries who have tormented the

Pacific, but to do so is to blind oneself to the authentic magnificence of this foolish man. True, he was the gaunt dreamer; but he was also an inspired prophet.

It is amazing how often Gibson was right, and if we tick off the areas in which he clearly foresaw the future, we find ourselves in the presence of a remarkable man.

The people of Sumatra won their independence from the Dutch in much the way that Gibson had envisaged. The Malaysian islands he loved have confederated into a powerful nation, as he predicted. The Malays of neighboring Malaysia have also done the same.

Hawaii has developed pretty much along the lines he predicted. The role of the native Hawaiian has diminished under the very pressures he foresaw and warned against. Concurrently, the Oriental population has achieved a status which in some respects he anticipated, for it was he who paved the way for their entrance. If he did not foresee the dominant role to be attained by these Chinese and Japanese immigrants, he was aware that energy like theirs was needed if Hawaii was to prosper.

He was right in his theories about the need for treatment of leprosy, in his general ideas on the health of native peoples, and in many of his advanced views on agriculture. He also foreshadowed the essential role to be played by Caucasians in politics—at least during the early years—and was one of the ablest practitioners of this difficult art of convincing full-blooded Hawaiians that they should elect a Caucasian immigrant to represent them. That he held power so long proves his gift of persuasion.

In one nebulous but increasingly important field he was spectacularly correct. With unexpected insight he explained the precautions that ought to be taken by a white, highly organized, mechanized, capitalistic society to preserve the existence of a primitive, non-mechanized, communal group. Gibson was one of the first to see that the native cultures of the Pacific were threatened with extinction, and although he himself did many things contrary to his own preachments, he clearly perceived that the native Hawaiians would have to be supported and protected in many psychological ways if they were to maintain themselves. He advocated the preservation of ancient Hawaiian artifacts, the cultivation of Hawaiian culture, and the study of indigenous songs and chants. The museums of the Pacific and the work of various cultural commissions exemplify his dreams.

Gibson's vision of a united Pacific under the leadership of Hawaii has not come to pass, but if he were alive today he would applaud the logic of America's governing hundreds of the islands west of Hawaii, some of them from naval headquarters in Honolulu. This is close to what he advocated.

The important South Pacific Commission operating out of New Caledonia in the interests of the entire South Pacific is a fulfillment of his plans, and within the next hundred years we can expect some kind of South Pacific federation similar to the one he envisaged, although it will probably not depend upon Hawaiian leadership.

Curiously, even the Mormon Church, which he abused so badly, has developed its Pacific missions largely as he predicted it would; and the church, in spite of the hurt Gibson did it, has accomplished about what he had originally hoped for it.

In view of Gibson's excellent foresight, and his accomplishments as a practical politician and his marked success in business, one might expect him to have enjoyed the reputation such attainments merit. Instead, by most people except his beloved Hawaiians, he was hated during his lifetime and ridiculed in death. Two grave defects in character nullified his accomplishments. First, he was cursed with an intemperate enthusiasm and imagination. The modern reader shares Nathaniel Hawthorne's amusement as he watches Gibson in England, his mind inflamed by the obsession that in infancy he had been swapped for a baby of noble lineage. We can also imagine the self-delusion in which Gibson dispatched the pathetic *Kaimiloa* to ensnare Samoa. His ridiculous enthusiasm constantly invited ridicule. Second, he was driven by an insatiable personal vanity. Most of his political excesses stemmed from this, as did most of his bitter enmities.

Time and again in his stormy career, Gibson allowed these two defects to seduce him into real folly. His mistakes then became so blatant as to invite condemnation, and his real accomplishments were overlooked.

Gibson's day in court will come when his voluminous and elegantly written diaries are published. They will disclose a poetic dreamer, an Old Testament prophet, and a contentious man whose ambition destroyed him. No more moving passage will be found than a prophecy he uttered at the age of forty on the island of Lanai. A powerful conspiracy of his enemies had humbled him momentarily and in his despair he caught a glimpse of his destiny: "There will be treasons as now, I shall die in the isles by the deed of an island foe, but I shall love them to the end, and it shall be said of me he was a worker of good among his fellow men and above all a lover of the weak island races that had no friend."

R. L. Stevenson

The Bottle Imp

One of the major authors who have written of the Pacific, Robert Louis Stevenson (1850–1894) was born and grew up in Edinburgh. He studied first engineering and then law at the University of Edinburgh, but despite his father's objections began to follow a literary career. Affected with tuberculosis, he made many journeys in search of health. In San Francisco in 1888 he chartered the yacht *Casco* and set sail for the South Seas with his wife Fanny and stepson Lloyd Osbourne. For two years they cruised the Pacific, stopping at many of the islands of Micronesia, Melanesia, and Polynesia, including Hawaii, where they remained for five months in 1889 and revisited in 1893. At Vailima on the Samoan island of Upolu, Stevenson bought land and built a house, deciding that this would be his final home. Here, at forty-four, while writing the novel that promised to be his masterpiece, *Weir of Hermiston,* he died of a cerebral hemorrhage.

Among Stevenson's writings that deal with Hawaii are *The Wrecker* (1892), a novel written in collaboration with Lloyd Osbourne; a series of travel sketches entitled "The Eight Islands" (1893); and two of the stories in *Island Nights' Entertainment* (1893), one of which is "The Bottle Imp." Stevenson called this story "one of my best works, and ill to equal," and it is indeed one of the finest short stories in English. Shortly after appearing in *Black and White* in the spring of 1891, "The Bottle Imp" was translated into Samoan and printed as a serial in a missionary paper, earning its author the title of Tusitala (teller of tales).

THERE was a man of the island of Hawaii, whom I shall call Keawe; for the truth is, he still lives, and his name must be kept secret; but the place of his birth was not far from Honaunau, where the bones of Keawe the Great lie hidden in a cave. This man was poor, brave, and active; he could read and write like a schoolmaster; he was a first-rate mariner besides, sailed for some time in the island steamers, and steered a whaleboat on the Hamakua coast. At length it came in Keawe's mind to have a sight of the great world and foreign cities, and he shipped on a vessel bound to San Francisco.

This is a fine town, with a fine harbor, and rich people uncountable; and, in particular, there is one hill which is covered with palaces. Upon this hill Keawe was one day taking a walk with his pocket full of money, viewing the great houses upon either hand with pleasure. "What fine houses these are!" he was thinking, "and how happy must those people be who dwell in them, and take no care for the morrow!" The thought was in his mind when he came abreast of a house that was smaller than some others, but all finished and beautified like a toy; the steps of that house shone like silver, and the borders of the garden bloomed like garlands, and the windows were bright like diamonds; and Keawe stopped and wondered at the excellence of all he saw. So stopping, he was aware of a man that looked forth upon him through a window so clear that Keawe could see him as you see a fish in a pool upon the reef. The man was elderly, with a bald head and a black beard, and his face was heavy with sorrow, and he bitterly sighed. And the truth of it is that, as Keawe looked in upon the man, and the man looked out upon Keawe, each envied the other.

All of a sudden, the man smiled and nodded, and beckoned Keawe to enter, and met him at the door of the house.

"This is a fine house of mine," said the man, and bitterly sighed. "Would you not care to view the chambers?"

So he led Keawe all over it, from the cellar to the roof, and there was nothing there that was not perfect of its kind, and Keawe was astonished.

"Truly," said Keawe, "this is a beautiful house; if I lived in the like of it, I should be laughing all day long. How comes it, then, that you should be sighing?"

"There is no reason," said the man, "why you should not have a house in all points similar to this, and finer, if you wish. You have some money, I suppose?"

"I have fifty dollars," said Keawe; "but a house like this will cost more than fifty dollars."

The man made a computation. "I am sorry you have no more,"

said he, "for it may raise you trouble in the future; but it shall be yours at fifty dollars."

"The house?" asked Keawe.

"No, not the house," replied the man; "but the bottle. For, I must tell you, although I appear to you so rich and fortunate, all my fortune, and this house itself and its garden, came out of a bottle not much bigger than a pint. This is it."

And he opened a lockfast place, and took out a round-bellied bottle with a long neck; the glass of it was white like milk, with changing rainbow colors in the grain. Withinsides something obscurely moved, like a shadow and a fire.

"This is the bottle," said the man; and, when Keawe laughed, "You do not believe me?" he added. "Try, then, for yourself. See if you can break it."

So Keawe took the bottle up and dashed it on the floor till he was weary; but it jumped on the floor like a child's ball, and was not injured.

"This is a strange thing," said Keawe. "For by the touch of it, as well as by the look, the bottle should be of glass."

"Of glass it is," replied the man, sighing more heavily than ever; "but the glass of it was tempered in the flames of hell. An imp lives in it, and that is the shadow we behold there moving: or so I suppose. If any man buy this bottle the imp is at his command; all that he desires—love, fame, money, houses like this house, ay, or a city like this city—all are his at the word uttered. Napoleon had this bottle, and by it he grew to be the king of the world; but he sold it at the last, and fell. Captain Cook had this bottle, and by it he found his way to so many islands; but he, too, sold it, and was slain upon Hawaii. For, once it is sold, the power goes and the protection; and unless a man remain content with what he has, ill will befall him."

"And yet you talk of selling it yourself?" Keawe said.

"I have all I wish, and I am growing elderly," replied the man. "There is one thing the imp cannot do—he cannot prolong life; and, it would not be fair to conceal from you, there is a drawback to the bottle; for if a man die before he sells it, he must burn in hell forever."

"To be sure, that is a drawback and no mistake," cried Keawe. "I would not meddle with the thing. I can do without a house, thank God; but there is one thing I could not be doing with one particle, and that is to be damned."

"Dear me, you must not run away with things," returned the man. "All you have to do is to use the power of the imp in moderation, and then sell it to someone else, as I do to you, and finish your life in comfort."

"Well, I observe two things," said Keawe. "All the time you keep sighing like a maid in love, that is one; and, for the other, you sell this bottle very cheap."

"I have told you already why I sigh," said the man. "It is because I fear my health is breaking up; and, as you said yourself, to die and go to the devil is a pity for anyone. As for why I sell so cheap, I must explain to you there is a peculiarity about the bottle. Long ago, when the devil brought it first upon earth, it was extremely expensive, and was sold first of all to Prester John for many millions of dollars; but it cannot be sold at all, unless sold at a loss. If you sell it for as much as you paid for it, back it comes to you again like a homing pigeon. It follows that the price has kept falling in these centuries, and the bottle is now remarkably cheap. I bought it myself from one of my great neighbors on this hill, and the price I paid was only ninety dollars. I could sell it for as high as eighty-nine dollars and ninety-nine cents, but not a penny dearer, or back the thing must come to me. Now, about this there are two bothers. First, when you offer a bottle so singular for eighty-odd dollars, people suppose you to be jesting. And second—but there is no hurry about that—and I need not go into it. Only remember it must be coined money that you sell it for."

"How am I to know that this is all true?" asked Keawe.

"Some of it you can try at once," replied the man. "Give me your fifty dollars, take the bottle, and wish your fifty dollars back into your pocket. If that does not happen, I pledge you my honor I will cry off the bargain and restore your money."

"You are not deceiving me?" said Keawe.

The man bound himself with a great oath.

"Well, I will risk that much," said Keawe, "for that can do no harm." And he paid over his money to the man, and the man handed him the bottle.

"Imp of the bottle," said Keawe, "I want my fifty dollars back." And sure enough he had scarce said the word before his pocket was as heavy as ever.

"To be sure this is a wonderful bottle," said Keawe.

"And now good morning to you, my fine fellow, and the devil go with you for me!" said the man.

"Hold on," said Keawe, "I don't want any more of this fun. Here, take your bottle back."

"You have bought it for less than I paid for it," replied the man, rubbing his hands. "It is yours now; and, for my part, I am only concerned to see the back of you." And with this he rang for his Chinese servant, and had Keawe shown out of the house.

Now, when Keawe was in the street, with the bottle under his arm, he began to think. "If all this is true about this bottle, I may have made a losing bargain," thinks he. "But perhaps the man was only fooling me." The first thing he did was to count his money; the sum was exact—forty-nine dollars American money, and one Chile piece. "That looks like the truth," said Keawe. "Now I will try another part."

The streets in that part of the city were as clean as a ship's decks, and though it was noon, there were no passengers. Keawe set the bottle in the gutter and walked away. Twice he looked back, and there was the milky, round-bellied bottle where he left it. A third time he looked back, and turned a corner; but he had scarce done so, when something knocked upon his elbow, and behold! it was the long neck sticking up; and as for the round belly, it was jammed into the pocket of his pilot coat.

"And that looks like the truth," said Keawe.

The next thing he did was to buy a corkscrew in a shop, and go apart into a secret place in the fields. And there he tried to draw the cork, but as often as he put the screw in, out it came again, and the cork as whole as ever.

"This is some new sort of cork," said Keawe, and all at once he began to shake and sweat, for he was afraid of that bottle.

On his way back to the port side, he saw a shop where a man sold shells and clubs from the wild islands, old heathen deities, old coined money, pictures from China and Japan, and all manner of things that sailors bring in their sea chests. And here he had an idea.

So he went in and offered the bottle for a hundred dollars. The man of the shop laughed at him at the first, and offered him five; but, indeed, it was a curious bottle—such glass was never blown in any human glassworks, so prettily the colors shone under the milky white, and so strangely the shadow hovered in the midst; so, after he had disputed awhile after the manner of his kind, the shopman gave Keawe sixty silver dollars for the thing, and set it on a shelf in the midst of his window.

"Now," said Keawe, "I have sold that for sixty which I bought for fifty—or, to say truth, a little less, because one of my dollars was from Chile. Now I shall know the truth upon another point."

So he went back on board his ship, and, when he opened his chest, there was the bottle, and had come more quickly than himself. Now Keawe had a mate on board whose name was Lopaka.

"What ails you," said Lopaka, "that you stare in your chest?"

They were alone in the ship's forecastle, and Keawe bound him to secrecy, and told all.

"This is a very strange affair," said Lopaka; "and I fear you will be in trouble about this bottle. But there is one point very clear—that you are sure of the trouble, and you had better have the profit in the bargain. Make up your mind what you want with it; give the order, and if it is done as you desire, I will buy the bottle myself; for I have an idea of my own to get a schooner, and go trading through the islands."

"That is not my idea," said Keawe; "but to have a beautiful house and garden on the Kona Coast, where I was born, the sun shining in at the door, flowers in the garden, glass in the windows, pictures on the walls, and toys and fine carpets on the tables, for all the world like the house I was in this day—only a story higher, and with balconies all about like the king's palace; and to live there without care and make merry with my friends and relatives."

"Well," said Lopaka, "let us carry it back with us to Hawaii; and if all comes true, as you suppose, I will buy the bottle, as I said, and ask a schooner."

Upon that they were agreed, and it was not long before the ship returned to Honolulu, carrying Keawe and Lopaka and the bottle. They were scarce come ashore when they met a friend upon the beach, who began at once to condole with Keawe.

"I do not know what I am to be condoled about," said Keawe.

"Is it possible you have not heard," said the friend, "your uncle—that good old man—is dead, and your cousin—that beautiful boy—was drowned at sea?"

Keawe was filled with sorrow, and, beginning to weep and to lament, he forgot about the bottle. But Lopaka was thinking to himself, and presently, when Keawe's grief was a little abated: "I have been thinking," said Lopaka. "Had not your uncle lands in Hawaii, in the district of Kau?"

"No," said Keawe, "not in Kau; they are on the mountainside—a little way south of Hookena."

"These lands will now be yours?" asked Lopaka.

"And so they will," says Keawe, and began again to lament for his relatives.

"No," said Lopaka, "do not lament at present. I have a thought in my mind. How if this should be the doing of the bottle? For here is the place ready for your house."

"If this be so," cried Keawe, "it is a very ill way to serve me by killing my relatives. But it may be, indeed; for it was in just such a station that I saw the house with my mind's eye."

"The house, however, is not yet built," said Lopaka.

"No, nor like to be!" said Keawe; "for though my uncle has some coffee and awa and bananas, it will not be more than will keep me in comfort; and the rest of that land is the black lava."

"Let us go to the lawyer," said Lopaka; "I have still this idea in my mind."

Now, when they came to the lawyer's, it appeared Keawe's uncle had grown monstrous rich in the last days, and there was a fund of money.

"And here is the money for the house!" cried Lopaka.

"If you are thinking of a new house," said the lawyer, "here is the card of a new architect, of whom they tell me great things."

"Better and better!" cried Lopaka. "Here is all made plain for us. Let us continue to obey orders."

So they went to the architect, and he had drawings of houses on his table.

"You want something out of the way," said the architect. "How do you like this?" and he handed a drawing to Keawe.

Now, when Keawe set eyes on the drawing, he cried out aloud, for it was the picture of his thought exactly drawn.

"I am in for this house," thought he. "Little as I like the way it comes to me, I am in for it now, and I may as well take the good along with the evil."

So he told the architect all that he wished, and how he would have that house furnished, and about the pictures on the wall and the knickknacks on the tables; and he asked the man plainly for how much he would undertake the whole affair.

The architect put many questions, and took his pen and made a computation; and when he had done he named the very sum that Keawe had inherited.

Lopaka and Keawe looked at one another and nodded.

"It is quite clear," thought Keawe, "that I am to have this house, whether or no. It comes from the devil, and I fear I will get little good by that; and of one thing I am sure, I will make no more wishes as long as I have this bottle. But with the house I am saddled, and I may as well take the good along with the evil."

So he made his terms with the architect, and they signed a paper; and Keawe and Lopaka took ship again and sailed to Australia; for it was concluded between them they should not interfere at all, but leave the architect and the bottle imp to build and to adorn that house at their own pleasure.

The voyage was a good voyage, only all the time Keawe was holding in his breath, for he had sworn he would utter no more wishes, and take no more favors from the devil. The time was up when they got back. The architect told them that the house was ready, and Keawe and Lopaka took a passage in the *Hall*, and went down Kona way to view the house, and see if all had been done fitly according to the thought that was in Keawe's mind.

Now, the house stood on the mountainside, visible to ships. Above, the forest ran up into the clouds of rain; below, the black lava fell in cliffs, where the kings of old lay buried. A garden bloomed about that house with every hue of flowers; and there was an orchard of papaya on the one hand and an orchard of breadfruit on the other, and right in front, toward the sea, a ship's mast had been rigged up and bore a flag. As for the house, it was three stories high, with great chambers and broad balconies on each. The windows were of glass, so excellent that it was as clear as water and as bright as day. All manner of furniture adorned the chambers. Pictures hung upon the wall in golden frames: pictures of ships, and men fighting, and of the most beautiful women, and of singular places; nowhere in the world are there pictures of so bright a color as those Keawe found hanging in his house. As for the knickknacks, they were extraordinary fine; chiming clocks and musical boxes, little men with nodding heads, books filled with pictures, weapons of price from all quarters of the world, and the most elegant puzzles to entertain the leisure of a solitary man. And as no one would care to live in such chambers, only to walk through and view them, the balconies were made so broad that a whole town might have lived upon them in delight; and Keawe knew not which to prefer, whether the back porch, where you got the land breeze, and looked upon the orchards and the flowers, or the front balcony, where you could drink the wind of the sea, and look down the steep wall of the mountain and see the *Hall* going by once a week or so between Hookena and the hills of Pele, or the schooners plying up the coast for wood and awa and bananas.

When they had viewed all, Keawe and Lopaka sat on the porch.

"Well," asked Lopaka, "is it all as you designed?"

"Words cannot utter it," said Keawe. "It is better than I dreamed, and I am sick with satisfaction."

"There is but one thing to consider," said Lopaka; "all this may be quite natural, and the bottle imp have nothing whatever to say to it. If I were to buy the bottle, and got no schooner after all, I should have put my hand in the fire for nothing. I gave you my word, I know; but yet I think you would not grudge me one more proof."

"I have sworn I would take no more favors," said Keawe. "I have gone already deep enough."

"This is no favor I am thinking of," replied Lopaka. "It is only to see the imp himself. There is nothing to be gained by that, and so nothing to be ashamed of; and yet, if I once saw him, I should be sure of the whole matter. So indulge me so far, and let me see the imp; and, after that, here is the money in my hand, and I will buy it."

"There is only one thing I am afraid of," said Keawe. "The imp may be very ugly to view; and if you once set eyes upon him you might be very undesirous of the bottle."

"I am a man of my word," said Lopaka. "And here is the money betwixt us."

"Very well," replied Keawe. "I have a curiosity myself. So come, let us have one look at you, Mr. Imp."

Now as soon as that was said, the imp looked out of the bottle, and in again, swift as a lizard; and there sat Keawe and Lopaka turned to stone. The night had quite come before either found a thought to say or voice to say it with; and then Lopaka pushed the money over and took the bottle.

"I am a man of my word," said he, "and had need to be so, or I would not touch this bottle with my foot. Well, I shall get my schooner and a dollar or two for my pocket; and then I will be rid of this devil as fast as I can. For, to tell you the plain truth, the look of him has cast me down."

"Lopaka," said Keawe, "do not you think any worse of me than you can help; I know it is night, and the roads bad, and the pass by the tombs an ill place to go by so late, but I declare since I have seen that little face, I cannot eat or sleep or pray till it is gone from me. I will give you a lantern, and a basket to put the bottle in, and any picture or fine thing in all my house that takes your fancy; and be gone at once, and go sleep at Hookena with Nahinu."

"Keawe," said Lopaka, "many a man would take this ill, above all, when I am doing you a turn so friendly as to keep my word and buy the bottle; and for that matter, the night and the dark, and the way by the tombs, must be all tenfold more dangerous to a man with such a sin upon his conscience, and such a bottle under his arm. But for my part, I am so extremely terrified myself, I have not the heart to blame you. Here I go then; and I pray God you may be happy in your house, and I fortunate with my schooner, and both get to heaven in the end in spite of the devil and his bottle."

So Lopaka went down the mountain; and Keawe stood in his front balcony, and listened to the clink of the horse's shoes, and watched the lantern go shining down the path, and along the cliff of caves where the old dead are buried; and all the time he trembled and clasped his hands, and prayed for his friend, and gave glory to God that he himself was escaped out of that trouble.

But the next day came very brightly, and that new house of his was so delightful to behold that he forgot his terrors. One day followed another, and Keawe dwelt there in perpetual joy. He had his place on the back porch; it was there he ate and lived, and read the stories in the Honolulu newspapers; but when anyone came by, they would go in and view the chambers and the pictures. And the fame of the house went far and wide; it was called Ka Hale Nui—the Great House—in all Kona; and sometimes the Bright House, for Keawe kept a Chinaman, who was all day dusting and furbishing; and the glass, and the gilt, and the fine stuffs, and the pictures shone as bright as the morning. As for Keawe himself, he could not walk in the chambers without singing, his heart was so enlarged; and when ships sailed by upon the sea, he would fly his colors on the mast.

So time went by, until one day Keawe went upon a visit as far as Kailua to certain of his friends. There he was well feasted; and left as soon as he could the next morning, and rode hard, for he was impatient to behold his beautiful house; and besides, the night then coming on was the night in which the dead of old days go abroad in the sides of Kona, and having already meddled with the devil, he was the more chary of meeting with the dead. A little beyond Honaunau, looking far ahead, he was aware of a woman bathing in the edge of the sea; and she seemed a well-grown girl, but he thought no more of it. Then he saw her white shift flutter as she put it on, and then her red holoku; and by the time he came abreast of her she was done with her toilet, and had come up from the sea, and stood by the trackside in her red holoku, and she was all freshened with the bath, and her eyes shone and were kind. Now Keawe no sooner beheld her than he drew rein.

"I thought I knew everyone in this country," said he. "How comes it that I do not know you?"

"I am Kokua, daughter of Kiano," said the girl, "and I have just returned from Oahu. Who are you?"

"I will tell you who I am in a little," said Keawe, dismounting from his horse, "but not now. For I have a thought in my mind, and if you knew who I was, you might have heard of me, and would not give me a true answer. But tell me, first of all, one thing: Are you married?"

At this Kokua laughed out aloud. "It is you who ask questions," she said. "Are you married yourself?"

"Indeed, Kokua, I am not," replied Keawe, "and never thought to be until this hour. But here is the plain truth. I have met you here at the roadside, and I saw your eyes, which are like the stars, and my heart went to you as swift as a bird. And so now, if you want none of me, say so, and I will go to my own place; but if you think me no worse than any other young man, say so, too, and I will turn aside to your father's for the night, and tomorrow I will talk with the good man."

Kokua said never a word, but she looked at the sea and laughed.

"Kokua," said Keawe, "if you say nothing, I will take that for the good answer; so let us be stepping to your father's door."

She went on ahead of him, still without speech; only sometimes she glanced back and glanced away again, and she kept the strings of her hat in her mouth.

Now, when they had come to the door, Kiano came out on his veranda, and cried out and welcomed Keawe by name. At that the girl looked over, for the fame of the great house had come to her ears; and, to be sure, it was a great temptation. All that evening they were very merry together; and the girl was as bold as brass under the eyes of her parents, and made a mock of Keawe, for she had a quick wit. The next day he had a word with Kiano, and found the girl alone.

"Kokua," said he, "you made a mock of me all the evening, and it is still time to bid me go. I would not tell you who I was because I have so fine a house, and I feared you would think too much of that house and too little of the man who loves you. Now you know all, and if you wish to have seen the last of me, say so at once."

"No," said Kokua; but this time she did not laugh, nor did Keawe ask for more.

This was the wooing of Keawe; things had gone quickly, but so an arrow goes, and the ball of a rifle swifter still, and yet both may strike the target. Things had gone fast, but they had gone far also, and the thought of Keawe rang in the maiden's head; she heard his voice in the breach of the surf upon the lava, and for this young man that she had seen but twice she would have left father and mother and her native islands. As for Keawe himself, his horse flew up the path of the mountain under the cliff of tombs, and the sound of the hoofs, and the sound of Keawe singing to himself for pleasure, echoed in the caverns of the dead. He came to the Bright House, and still he was singing. He sat and ate in the broad balcony, and the Chinaman wondered at his master, to hear how he sang between the mouthfuls. The sun went down into the sea, and the night came; and Keawe walked the balconies by lamplight high on the mountains, and the voice of his singing startled men on ships.

"Here am I now upon my high place," he said to himself. "Life may be no better; this is the mountaintop; and all shelves about me toward the worse. For the first time I will light up the chambers, and bathe in my fine bath with the hot water and the cold, and sleep alone in the bed of my bridal chamber."

So the Chinaman had word, and he must rise from sleep and light the furnaces; and as he wrought below, beside the boilers, he heard his master singing and rejoicing above him in the lighted chambers. When the water began to be hot the Chinaman cried to his master; and Keawe went into the bathroom; and the Chinaman heard him sing as he filled the marble basin; and heard him sing, and the singing broken, as he undressed; until of a sudden, the song ceased. The Chinaman listened, and listened; he called up the house to Keawe to ask if all were well, and Keawe answered him, "Yes," and bade him go to bed; but there was no more singing in the Bright House; and all night long the Chinaman heard his master's feet go round and round the balconies without repose.

Now the truth of it was this: as Keawe undressed for his bath, he spied upon his flesh a patch like a patch of lichen on a rock, and it was then that he stopped singing. For he knew the likeness of that patch, and knew that he was fallen in the Chinese Evil [leprosy].

Now, it is a sad thing for any man to fall into this sickness. And it would be a sad thing for anyone to leave a house so beautiful and so commodious, and depart from all his friends to the north coast of Molokai between the mighty cliff and the sea breakers. But what was that to the case of the man Keawe, he who had met his love but yesterday, and won her but that morning, and now saw all his hopes break in a moment, like a piece of glass?

Awhile he sat upon the edge of the bath; then sprang, with a cry, and ran outside; and to and fro, to and fro, along the balcony, like one despairing.

"Very willingly could I leave Hawaii, the home of my fathers," Keawe was thinking. "Very lightly could I leave my house, the high-placed, the many-windowed, here upon the mountains. Very bravely could I go to Molokai, to Kalaupapa by the cliffs, to live with the smitten and to sleep there, far from my fathers. But what wrong have I done, what sin lies upon my soul, that I should have encountered Kokua coming cool from the sea water in the evening? Kokua, the soul ensnarer! Kokua, the light of my life! Her may I never wed, her may I look upon no longer, her may I no more handle with my loving hand; and it is for this, it is for you, O Kokua! that I pour my lamentations!"

Now you are to observe what sort of a man Keawe was, for he might have dwelt there in the Bright House for years, and no one been the wiser of his sickness; but he reckoned nothing of that, if he must lose Kokua. And again, he might have wed Kokua even as he was; and so many would have done, because they have the souls of pigs; but Keawe loved the maid manfully, and he would do her no hurt and bring her in no danger.

A little beyond the midst of the night there came in his mind the recollection of that bottle. He went round to the back porch, and called to memory the day when the devil had looked forth; and at the thought ice ran in his veins.

"A dreadful thing is the bottle," thought Keawe, "and dreadful is the imp, and it is a dreadful thing to risk the flames of hell. But what other hope have I to cure my sickness or to wed Kokua? What!" he thought, "would I beard the devil once, only to get me a house, and not face him again to win Kokua?"

Thereupon he called to mind it was the next day the *Hall* went by on her return to Honolulu. "There must I go first," he thought, "and see Lopaka. For the best hope that I have now is to find that same bottle I was so pleased to be rid of."

Never a wink could he sleep; the food stuck in his throat; but he sent a letter to Kiano, and about the time when the steamer would be coming, rode down beside the cliff of the tombs. It rained; his horse went heavily; he looked up at the black mouths of the caves, and he envied the dead that slept there and were done with trouble; and called to mind how he had galloped by the day before, and was astonished. So he came down to Hookena, and there was all the country gathered for the steamer as usual. In the shed before the store they sat and jested and passed the news; but there was no matter of speech in Keawe's bosom, and he sat in their midst and looked without on the rain falling on the houses and the surf beating among the rocks, and the sighs arose in his throat.

"Keawe of the Bright House is out of spirits," said one to another. Indeed, and so he was, and little wonder.

Then the *Hall* came, and the whaleboat carried him on board. The afterpart of the ship was full of haoles who had been to visit the volcano, as their custom is; and the midst was crowded with Kanakas, and the forepart with wild bulls from Hilo and horses from Kau; but Keawe sat apart from all in his sorrow, and watched for the house of Kiano. There it sat, low upon the shore in the black rocks, and shaded by the coco palms, and there by the door was a red holoku, no greater than a fly, and going to and fro with a fly's busyness. "Ah, queen of my heart," he cried, "I'll venture my dear soul to win you!"

Soon after, darkness fell, and the cabins were lit up, and the haoles sat and played at the cards and drank whiskey as their custom is; but Keawe walked the deck all night; and all the next day, as they steamed under the lee of Maui or of Molokai, he was still pacing to and fro like a wild animal in a menagerie.

Toward evening they passed Diamond Head and came to the pier of Honolulu. Keawe stepped out among the crowd and began to ask for Lopaka. It seemed he had become the owner of a schooner —none better in the islands—and was gone upon an adventure as far as Pola-Pola or Kahiki; so there was no help to be looked for from Lopaka. Keawe called to mind a friend of his, a lawyer in the town (I must not tell his name), and inquired of him. They said he had grown suddenly rich, and had a fine new house upon Waikiki shore; and this put a thought in Keawe's head, and he called a hack and drove to the lawyer's house.

The house was all brand new, and the trees in the garden no greater than walking sticks, and the lawyer, when he came, had the air of a man well pleased.

"What can I do to serve you?" said the lawyer.

"You are a friend of Lopaka's," replied Keawe, "and Lopaka purchased from me a certain piece of goods that I thought you might enable me to trace."

The lawyer's face became very dark. "I do not profess to misunderstand you, Mr. Keawe," said he, "though this is an ugly business to be stirring in. You may be sure I know nothing, but yet I have a guess, and if you would apply in a certain quarter, I think you might have news."

And he named the name of a man, which, again, I had better not repeat. So it was for days, and Keawe went from one to another, finding everywhere new clothes and carriages, and fine new houses and men everywhere in great contentment, although, to be sure, when he hinted at his business their faces would cloud over.

"No doubt I am upon the track," thought Keawe. "These new clothes and carriages are all the gifts of the little imp, and these glad faces are the faces of men who have taken their profit and got rid of the accursed thing in safety. When I see pale cheeks and hear sighing, I shall know that I am near the bottle."

So it befell at last that he was recommended to a haole in Beretania Street. When he came to the door, about the hour of the evening meal, there were the usual marks of the new house, and the young garden, and the electric light shining in the windows; but when the owner came, a shock of hope and fear ran through Keawe; for here was a young man, white as a corpse, and black about the eyes, the hair shedding from his head, and such a look in his countenance as a man may have when he is waiting for the gallows.

"Here it is, to be sure," thought Keawe, and so with this man he no ways veiled his errand. "I am come to buy the bottle," said he.

At the word, the young haole of Beretania Street reeled against the wall.

"The bottle!" he gasped. "To buy the bottle!" Then he seemed to choke, and seizing Keawe by the arm carried him into a room and poured out wine in two glasses.

"Here is my respects," said Keawe, who had been much about with haoles in his time. "Yes," he added, "I am come to buy the bottle. What is the price by now?"

At that word the young man let his glass slip through his fingers, and looked upon Keawe like a ghost.

"The price," says he: "the price! You do not know the price?"

"It is for that I am asking you," returned Keawe. "But why are you so much concerned? Is there anything wrong about the price?"

"It has dropped a great deal in value since your time, Mr. Keawe," said the young man, stammering.

"Well, well, I shall have the less to pay for it," says Keawe. "How much did it cost you?"

The young man was as white as a sheet. "Two cents," said he.

"What?" cried Keawe, "two cents? Why, then, you can only sell it for one. And he who buys it—" The words died upon Keawe's tongue; he who bought it could never sell it again, the bottle and the bottle imp must abide with him until he died, and when he died he must carry him to the red end of hell.

The young man of Beretania Street fell upon his knees. "For God's sake, buy it!" he cried. "You can have all my fortune in the bargain. I was mad when I bought it at that price. I had embezzled money at my store; I was lost else: I must have gone to jail."

"Poor creature," said Keawe, "you would risk your soul upon so desperate an adventure, and to avoid the proper punishment of your own disgrace; and you think I could hesitate with love in front of me. Give me the bottle, and the change which I make sure you have all ready. Here is a five-cent piece."

It was as Keawe supposed; the young man had the change ready in a drawer; the bottle changed hands, and Keawe's fingers were no sooner clasped upon the stalk than he had breathed his wish to be a clean man. And, sure enough, when he got home to his room and stripped himself before a glass, his flesh was whole like an infant's. And here was the strange thing: he had no sooner seen this miracle than his mind was changed within him, and he cared naught for the Chinese Evil, and little enough for Kokua; and had but the one thought—that here he was bound to the bottle imp for time and for eternity, and had no better hope but to be a cinder forever in the flames of hell. Away ahead of him he saw them blaze with his mind's eye, and his soul shrank, and darkness fell upon the light.

When Keawe came to himself a little, he was aware it was the night when the band played at the hotel. Thither he went, because he feared to be alone; and there, among happy faces, walked to and fro, and heard the tunes go up and down, and saw Berger beat the measure, and all the while he heard the flames crackle and saw the red fire burning in the bottomless pit. Of a sudden the band played *"Hiki-ao-ao"*; that was a song that he had sung with Kokua, and at the strain courage returned to him.

"It is done now," he thought, "and once more let me take the good along with the evil."

So it befell that he returned to Hawaii by the first steamer, and as soon as it could be managed, he was wedded to Kokua and carried her up the mountainside to the Bright House.

Now it was so with these two, that when they were together Keawe's heart was stilled; but so soon as he was alone he fell into a brooding horror and heard the flames crackle and saw the red fire burn in the bottomless pit. The girl, indeed, had come to him wholly; her heart leaped in her side at sight of him, her hand clung to his and she was so fashioned from the hair upon her head to the nails upon her toes that none could see her without joy. She was pleasant in her nature. She had the good word always. Full of song she was, and went to and fro in the Bright House, the brightest things in its three stories, caroling like the birds. And Keawe beheld and heard her with delight, and then must shrink upon one side, and weep and groan to think upon the price that he had paid for her; and then he must dry his eyes, and wash his face, and go and sit with her on the broad balconies, joining in her songs and, with a sick spirit, answering her smiles.

There came a day when her feet began to be heavy and her songs more rare; and now it was not Keawe only that would weep apart, but each would sunder from the other and sit in opposite balconies with the whole width of the Bright House betwixt. Keawe was so sunk in his despair he scarce observed the change, and was only glad he had more hours to sit alone and brood upon his destiny, and was not so frequently condemned to pull a smiling face on a sick heart. But one day, coming softly through the house, he heard the sound of a child sobbing, and there was Kokua rolling her face upon the balcony floor, and weeping like the lost.

"You do well to weep in this house, Kokua," he said. "And yet I

The Bottle Imp

would give the head off my body that you, at least, might have been happy."

"Happy!" she cried. "Keawe, when you lived alone in your Bright House you were the word of the island for a happy man; laughter and song were in your mouth, and your face was as bright as the sunrise. Then you wedded poor Kokua; and the good God knows what is amiss in her—but from that day you have not smiled. Oh!" she cried, "what ails me? I thought I was pretty, and I knew I loved him. What ails me that I throw this cloud upon my husband?"

"Poor Kokua," said Keawe. He sat down by her side, and sought to take her hand; but that she plucked away. "Poor Kokua," he said again. "My poor child—my pretty. And I had thought all this while to spare you. Well, you shall know all. Then, at least, you will pity poor Keawe; then you will understand how much he loved you in the past—that he dared hell for your possession—and how much he loves you still (the poor condemned one), that he can yet call up a smile when he beholds you."

With that, he told her all, even from the beginning.

"You have done this for me?" she cried. "Ah, well, then what do I care!"—and she clasped and wept upon him.

"Ah, child!" said Keawe; "and yet, when I consider of the fire of hell, I care a good deal!"

"Never tell me," said she; "no man can be lost because he loved Kokua, and no other fault. I tell you, Keawe, I shall save you with these hands, or perish in your company. What! you loved me, and gave your soul, and you think I will not die to save you in return?"

"Ah, my dear! you might die a hundred times, and what difference would that make?" he cried, "except to leave me lonely till the time comes of my damnation?"

"You know nothing," said she. "I was educated in a school in Honolulu; I am no common girl. And I tell you, I shall save my lover. What is this you say about a cent? But all the world is not American. In England they have a piece they call a farthing, which is about half a cent. Ah! sorrow!" she cried, "that makes it scarcely better, for the buyer must be lost, and we shall find none so brave as my Keawe! But, then, there is France; they have a small coin there which they call a centime, and these go five to the cent or thereabouts. We could not do better. Come, Keawe, let us go to the

French islands; let us go to Tahiti, as fast as ships can bear us. There we have four centimes, three centimes, two centimes, one centime; four possible sales to come and go on; and two of us to push the bargain. Come, my Keawe! kiss me, and banish care. Kokua will defend you."

"Gift of God!" he cried. "I cannot think that God will punish me for desiring aught so good! Be it as you will, then; take me where you please: I put my life and my salvation in your hands."

Early the next day Kokua was about her preparations. She took Keawe's chest that he went with sailoring; and first she put the bottle in a corner; and then packed it with the richest of their clothes and the bravest of the knickknacks in the house. "For," said she, "we must seem to be rich folks, or who will believe in the bottle?" All the time of her preparation she was as gay as a bird; only when she looked upon Keawe, the tears would spring in her eye, and she must run and kiss him. As for Keawe, a weight was off his soul; now that he had his secret shared, and some hope in front of him, he seemed like a new man, his feet went lightly on the earth, and his breath was good to him again. Yet was terror still at his elbow; and ever and again, as the wind blows out a taper, hope died in him, and he saw the flames toss and the red fire burn in hell.

It was given out in the country they were gone pleasuring to the States, which was thought a strange thing, and yet not so strange as the truth, if any could have guessed it. So they went to Honolulu in the *Hall,* and thence in the *Umatilla* to San Francisco with a crowd of haoles, and at San Francisco took their passage by the mail brigantine, the *Tropic Bird,* for Papeete, the chief place of the French in the South Islands. Thither they came, after a pleasant voyage, on a fair day of the trade wind, and saw the reef with the surf breaking, and Motu Iti with its palms, and the schooner riding withinside, and the white houses of the town low down along the shore among green trees, and overhead the mountains and the clouds of Tahiti, the wise island.

It was judged the most wise to hire a house, which they did accordingly, opposite the British consul's, to make a great parade of money, and themselves conspicuous with carriages and horses. This it was very easy to do, so long as they had the bottle in their possession; for Kokua was more bold than Keawe, and, whenever she had a mind, called on the imp for twenty or a hundred dollars. At this rate they soon grew to be remarked in the town; and the strangers from Hawaii, their riding and their driving, the fine holokus and the rich lace of Kokua became the matter of much talk.

They got on well after the first with the Tahitian language, which is indeed like to the Hawaiian, with a change of certain letters; and as soon as they had any freedom of speech, began to push the bottle. You are to consider it was not an easy subject to introduce; it was not easy to persuade people you were in earnest when you offered to sell them for four centimes the spring of health and riches inexhaustible. It was necessary besides to explain the dangers of the bottle; and either people disbelieved the whole thing and laughed, or they thought the more of the darker part, became overcast with gravity, and drew away from Keawe and Kokua, as from persons who had dealings with the devil. So far from gaining ground, these two began to find they were avoided in the town; the children ran away from them screaming, a thing intolerable to Kokua; Catholics crossed themselves as they went by, and all persons began with one accord to disengage themselves from their advances.

Depression fell upon their spirits. They would sit at night in their new house, after a day's weariness, and not exchange one word, or the silence would be broken by Kokua bursting suddenly into sobs. Sometimes they would pray together; sometimes they would have the bottle out upon the floor, and sit all the evening watching how the shadow hovered in the midst. At such times they would be afraid to go to rest. It was long ere slumber came to them, and if either dozed off, it would be to wake and find the other silently weeping in the dark, or, perhaps, to wake alone, the other having fled from the house and the neighborhood of that bottle, to pace under the bananas in the little garden, or to wander on the beach by moonlight.

One night it was so when Kokua awoke. Keawe was gone. She felt in the bed and his place was cold. Then fear fell upon her, and she sat up in bed. A little moonshine filtered through the shutters. The room was bright, and she could spy the bottle on the floor. Outside it blew high, the great trees of the avenue cried aloud, and the fallen leaves rattled in the veranda. In the midst of this Kokua was aware of another sound; whether of a beast or of a man she could scarce tell, but it was as sad as death, and cut her to the soul. Softly she arose, set the door ajar, and looked forth into the moonlit yard. There, under the bananas, lay Keawe, his mouth in the dust, and as he lay he moaned.

It was Kokua's first thought to run forward and console him; her second potently withheld her. Keawe had borne himself before his wife like a brave man; it became her little in the hour of weakness to intrude upon his shame. With the thought she drew back into the house.

"Heavens!" she thought, "how careless have I been—how weak! It is he, not I, that stands in this eternal peril; it was he, not I, that took the curse upon his soul. It is for my sake, and for the love of a creature of so little worth and such poor help, that he now beholds so close to him the flames of hell—ay, and smells the smoke of it, lying without there in the wind and moonlight. Am I so dull of spirit that never till now I have surmised my duty, or have I seen it before and turned aside? But now, at least, I take up my soul in both the hands of my affection; now I say farewell to the white steps of heaven and the waiting faces of my friends. A love for a love, and let mine be equaled with Keawe's! A soul for a soul, and be it mine to perish!"

She was a deft woman with her hands, and was soon apparelled. She took in her hands the change—the precious centimes they kept ever at their side; for this coin is little used, and they had made provision at a government office. When she was forth in the avenue, clouds came on the wind and the moon was blackened. The town slept, and she knew not whither to turn till she heard one coughing in the shadows of the trees.

"Old man," said Kokua, "what do you here abroad in the cold night?"

The old man could scarce express himself for coughing, but she made out that he was old and poor, and a stranger in the island.

"Will you do me a service?" said Kokua. "As one stranger to another, and as an old man to a young woman, will you help a daughter of Hawaii?"

"Ah," said the old man. "So you are the witch from the eight islands, and even my old soul you seek to entangle. But I have heard of you, and defy your wickedness."

The Bottle Imp

"Sit down here," said Kokua, "and let me tell you a tale." And she told him the story of Keawe from the beginning to the end.

"And now," said she, "I am his wife, whom he bought with his soul's welfare. And what should I do? If I went to him myself and offered to buy it, he would refuse. But if you go, he will sell it eagerly; I will await you here: you will buy it for four centimes, and I will buy it again for three. And the Lord strengthen a poor girl!"

"If you meant falsely," said the old man, "I think God would strike you dead."

"He would!" cried Kokua. "Be sure he would. I could not be so treacherous—God would not suffer it."

"Give me the four centimes and await me here," said the old man.

Now when Kokua stood alone in the street, her spirit died. The wind roared in the trees, and it seemed to her the rushing of the flames of hell; the shadows tossed in the light of the street lamp, and they seemed to her the snatching hands of evil ones. If she had had the strength she must have run away, and if she had had the breath she must have screamed aloud; but, in truth, she could do neither, and stood and trembled in the avenue like an affrighted child.

Then she saw the old man returning, and he had the bottle in his hand.

"I have done your bidding," said he. "I left your husband weeping like a child; tonight he will sleep easy." And he held the bottle forth.

"Before you give it me," Kokua panted, "take the good with the evil—ask to be delivered from your cough."

"I am an old man," replied the other, "and too near the gate of the grave to take a favor from the devil. But what is this? Why do you not take the bottle? Do you hesitate?"

"Not hesitate!" cried Kokua. "I am only weak. Give me a moment. It is my hand resists, my flesh shrinks back from the accursed thing. One moment only!"

The old man looked upon Kokua kindly. "Poor child!" said he, "you fear; your soul misgives you. Well, let me keep it. I am old, and can never more be happy in this world, and as for the next—"

"Give it me!" gasped Kokua. "There is your money. Do you think I am so base as that? Give me the bottle."

"God bless you, child," said the old man.

Kokua concealed the bottle under her holoku, said farewell to the old man, and walked off along the avenue, she cared not whither. For all roads were now the same to her, and led equally to hell. Sometimes she walked, and sometimes ran; sometimes she screamed out aloud in the night, and sometimes lay by the wayside in the dust and wept. All that she had heard of hell came back to her; she saw the flames blaze, and she smelled the smoke, and her flesh withered on the coals.

Near day she came to her mind again, and returned to the house. It was even as the old man said—Keawe slumbered like a child. Kokua stood and gazed upon his face.

"Now, my husband," said she, "it is your turn to sleep. When you wake it will be your turn to sing and laugh. But for poor Kokua, alas! that meant no evil—for poor Kokua no more sleep, no more singing, no more delight, whether in earth or heaven."

With that she lay down in the bed by his side, and her misery was so extreme that she fell in a deep slumber instantly.

Late in the morning her husband woke her and gave her the good news. It seemed he was silly with delight, for he paid no heed to her distress, ill though she dissembled it. The words stuck in her mouth, it mattered not; Keawe did the speaking. She ate not a bite, but who was to observe it? for Keawe cleared the dish. Kokua saw and heard him, like some strange thing in a dream; there were times when she forgot or doubted, and put her hands to her brow; to know herself doomed and hear her husband babble seemed so monstrous.

All this while Keawe was eating and talking, and planning the time of their return, and thanking her for saving him, and fondling her, and calling her the true helper after all. He laughed at the old man that was fool enough to buy that bottle.

"A worthy old man he seemed," Keawe said. "But no one can judge by appearances. For why did the old reprobate require the bottle?"

"My husband," said Kokua, humbly, "his purpose may have been good."

Keawe laughed like an angry man.

"Fiddledeedee!" cried Keawe. "An old rogue, I tell you; and an old ass to boot. For the bottle was hard enough to sell at four centimes; and at three it will be quite impossible. The margin is not broad enough, the thing begins to smell of scorching—brrr!" said he, and shuddered. "It is true I bought it myself at a cent, when I knew not there were smaller coins. I was a fool for my pains; there will never be found another: and whoever has that bottle now will carry it to the pit."

"Oh, my husband!" said Kokua. "Is it not a terrible thing to save oneself by the eternal ruin of another? It seems to me I could not laugh. I would be humbled. I would be filled with melancholy. I would pray for the poor holder."

Then Keawe, because he felt the truth of what she said, grew the more angry. "Hoity-toity!" cried he. "You may be filled with melancholy if you please. It is not the mind of a good wife. If you thought at all of me, you would sit shamed."

Thereupon he went out, and Kokua was alone.

What chance had she to sell that bottle at two centimes? None, she perceived. And if she had any, here was her husband hurrying her away to a country where there was nothing lower than a cent. And here—on the morrow of her sacrifice—was her husband leaving her and blaming her.

She would not even try to profit by what time she had, but sat in the house, and now had the bottle out and viewed it with unutterable fear, and now, with loathing, hid it out of sight.

By-and-by, Keawe came back, and would have her take a drive.

"My husband, I am ill," she said. "I am out of heart. Excuse me, I can take no pleasure."

Then was Keawe more wroth than ever. With her, because he thought she was brooding over the case of the old man; and with himself, because he thought she was right, and was ashamed to be so happy.

"This is your truth," cried he, "and this your affection! Your husband is just saved from eternal ruin, which he encountered for the love of you—and you can take no pleasure! Kokua, you have a disloyal heart."

He went forth again furious, and wandered in the town all day. He met friends, and drank with them; they hired a carriage and drove into the country, and there drank again. All the time Keawe was ill at ease, because he was taking his pastime while his wife was sad, and because he knew in his heart that she was more right than he; and the knowledge made him drink the deeper.

Now there was an old brutal haole drinking with him, one that had been a boatswain of a whaler, a runaway, a digger in gold mines, a convict in prisons. He had a low mind and a foul mouth; he loved to drink and to see others drunken; and he pressed the glass upon Keawe. Soon there was no more money in the company.

"Here, you!" says the boatswain. "You are rich, you have been always saying. You have a bottle or some foolishness."

"Yes," says Keawe, "I am rich; I will go back and get some money from my wife, who keeps it."

"That's a bad idea, mate," says the boatswain. "Never you trust a petticoat with dollars. They're all as false as water; you keep an eye on her."

Now, this word stuck in Keawe's mind; for he was muddled with what he had been drinking.

"I should not wonder but she was false, indeed," thought he. "Why else should she be so cast down at my release? But I will show her I am not the man to be fooled. I will catch her in the act."

Accordingly, when they were back in town, Keawe bade the boatswain wait for him at the corner, by the old calaboose, and went forward up the avenue alone to the door of his house. The night had come again; there was a light within, but never a sound, and Keawe crept about the corner, opened the back door softly, and looked in.

There was Kokua on the floor, the lamp at her side; before her was a milk-white bottle, with a round belly and a long neck; and as she viewed it, Kokua wrung her hands.

A long time Keawe stood and looked in the doorway. At first he was struck stupid; and then fear fell upon him that the bargain had been made amiss, and the bottle had come back to him as it came at San Francisco; and at that his knees were loosened, and the fumes of the wine departed from his head like mists off a river in the morning. And then he had another thought; and it was a strange one, that made his cheeks to burn.

"I must make sure of this," thought he.

So he closed the door, and went softly round the corner again, and then came noisily in, as though he were but now returned. And, lo! by the time he opened the front door no bottle was to be seen; and Kokua sat in a chair and started up like one awakened out of sleep.

"I have been drinking all day and making merry," said Keawe. "I have been with good companions, and now I only come back for money, and return to drink and carouse with them again."

Both his face and voice were as stern as judgment, but Kokua was too troubled to observe.

"You do well to use your own, my husband," said she, and her words trembled.

"Oh, I do well in all things," said Keawe, and he went straight to the chest and took out money. But he looked besides in the corner where they kept the bottle, and there was no bottle there.

At that the chest heaved upon the floor like a sea billow, and the house span about him, like a wreath of smoke, for he saw he was lost now, and there was no escape. "It is what I feared," he thought; "it is she who has bought it."

And then he came to himself a little and rose up; but the sweat streamed on his face as thick as the rain and as cold as the well water.

"Kokua," said he, "I said to you today what ill became me. Now I return to carouse with my jolly companions," and at that he laughed a little quietly. "I will take more pleasure in the cup if you forgive me."

She clasped his knees in a moment; she kissed his knees with flowing tears.

"Oh," she cried, "I asked but a kind word!"

"Let us never one think hardly of the other," said Keawe, and was gone out of the house.

Now, the money that Keawe had taken was only some of that store of centime pieces they had laid in at their arrival. It was very sure he had no mind to be drinking. His wife had given her soul for him, now he must give his for hers; no other thought was in the world with him.

At the corner, by the old calaboose, there was the boatswain waiting.

"My wife has the bottle," said Keawe, "and, unless you help me to recover it, there can be no more money and no more liquor tonight."

"You do not mean to say you are serious about that bottle?" cried the boatswain.

"There is the lamp," said Keawe. "Do I look as if I was jesting?"

"That is so," said the boatswain. "You look as serious as a ghost."

"Well, then," said Keawe, "here are two centimes; you must go to my wife in the house and offer her these for the bottle, which, if I am not much mistaken, she will give you instantly. Bring it to me here, and I will buy it back from you for one; for that is the law with this bottle, that it still must be sold for a less sum. But whatever you do, never breathe a word to her that you have come from me."

"Mate, I wonder are you making a fool of me?" asked the boatswain.

"It will do you no harm if I am," returned Keawe.

"That is so, mate," said the boatswain.

"And if you doubt me," added Keawe, "you can try. As soon as you are clear of the house, wish to have your pocket full of money, or a bottle of the best rum, or what you please, and you will see the virtue of the thing."

"Very well, Kanaka," says the boatswain. "I will try; but if you are having your fun out of me, I will take my fun out of you with a belaying pin."

So the whaler man went off up the avenue; and Keawe stood and waited. It was near the same spot where Kokua had waited the night before; but Keawe was more resolved, and never faltered in his purpose; only his soul was bitter with despair.

It seemed a long time he had to wait before he heard a voice singing in the darkness of the avenue. He knew the voice to be the boatswain's; but it was strange how drunken it appeared upon a sudden.

Next, the man himself came stumbling into the light of the lamp. He had the devil's bottle buttoned in his coat; another bottle was in his hand; and even as he came in view he raised it to his mouth and drank.

"You have it," said Keawe. "I see that."

"Hands off!" cried the boatswain, jumping back. "Take a step near me, and I'll smash your mouth. You thought you could make a cat's-paw of me, did you?"

"What do you mean?" cried Keawe.

"Mean?" cried the boatswain. "This is a pretty good bottle, this is; that's what I mean. How I got it for two centimes I can't make out; but I'm sure you shan't have it for one."

"You mean you won't sell?" gasped Keawe.

"No, *sir!*" cried the boatswain. "But I'll give you a drink of the rum, if you like."

"I tell you," said Keawe, "the man who has that bottle goes to hell."

"I reckon I'm going anyway," returned the sailor; "and this bottle's the best thing to go with I've struck yet. No, sir!" he cried again, "this is my bottle now, and you can go and fish for another."

"Can this be true?" Keawe cried. "For your own sake, I beseech you, sell it me!"

"I don't value any of your talk," replied the boatswain. "You thought I was a flat; now you see I'm not; and there's an end. If you won't have a swallow of the rum, I'll have one myself. Here's your health, and good night to you!"

So off he went down the avenue toward town, and there goes the bottle out of the story.

But Keawe ran to Kokua light as the wind; and great was their joy that night; and great, since then, has been the peace of all their days in the Bright House.

R. L. Stevenson

Open Letter to the Reverend Dr. Hyde of Honolulu

One of the most scathing philippics in English since the days of Alexander Pope is Stevenson's "Open Letter to the Reverend Dr. Hyde," attacking this Protestant clergyman for remarks he had made concerning Father Damien, "martyr of Molokai."

Joseph Damien de Veuster (1840–1889), born in Belgium, spent several years in mission work in other Pacific islands before settling in 1873 at Kalawao, a small peninsula on the northern coast of the Hawaiian island of Molokai. Here the Board of Health of the Kingdom had set up an isolation station for lepers, and here Damien labored until he died of leprosy in 1889. (Scientists still do not know how this affliction, now usually referred to as "Hansen's disease," is transmitted.)

Stevenson, who spent seven days at the Kalawao settlement shortly after the death of Damien, admired the selfless priest greatly. While sojourning in Sydney, Australia, Stevenson heard that the project for a proposed monument to Damien had been abandoned because a letter from the Reverend Dr. C. M. Hyde of Honolulu, sent to another minister in California, had aroused doubts about Damien's personal habits. After reading this letter in the *Presbyterian* (Sydney) for October 26, 1889, Stevenson sat down and penned his invective, which sought as much to destroy Hyde as to defend Damien. Knowing that he risked financial ruin if Hyde should bring suits for libel, Stevenson consulted with his family, who agreed nevertheless that it should be published. It first appeared as a pamphlet in Sydney on March 27, 1890, and in the *Scots Observer* for May 3 and 10. The pamphlet became a collectors' item, and was reprinted many times, but Stevenson refused to take any payment. As he once wrote to a London publisher: "The letter to Dr. Hyde is yours, or any man's. I will never touch a penny of remuneration. I do not stick at murder; I draw the line at cannibalism. I could not eat a penny roll that piece of bludgeoning brought me."

Seven months after writing it, when his anger had cooled, Stevenson called his attack "barbarously harsh," and said that "if I did it now I would defend Damien no less well, and give less pain to those who are alive.... On the whole, it was virtuous to defend Damien; but it was harsh to strike so hard at Dr. Hyde."

Father Damien

AN OPEN LETTER TO THE REVEREND DR. HYDE OF HONOLULU

SYDNEY, *February 25, 1890*

SIR,—It may probably occur to you that we have met, and visited, and conversed; on my side, with interest. You may remember that you have done me several courtesies, for which I was prepared to be grateful. But there are duties which come before gratitude, and offenses which justly divide friends, far more, acquaintances. Your letter to the Reverend H. B. Gage is a document which, in my sight, if you had filled me with bread when I was starving, if you had sat up to nurse my father when he lay a-dying, would yet absolve me from the bonds of gratitude. You know enough, doubtless, of the process of canonization to be aware that, a hundred years after the death of Damien, there will appear a man charged with the painful office of the devil's advocate. After that noble brother of mine, and of all frail clay, shall have lain a century at rest, one shall accuse, one defend him. The circumstance is unusual that the devil's advocate should be a volunteer, should be a member of a sect immediately rival, and should make haste to take upon himself his ugly office ere the bones are cold; unusual, and of a taste which I shall leave my readers free to qualify; unusual, and to me inspiring. If I have at all learned the trade of using words to convey truth and to arouse emotion, you have at last furnished me with a subject. For it is in the interest of all mankind, and the cause of public decency in every quarter of the world, not only that Damien should be righted, but that you and your letter should be displayed at length, in their true colors, to the public eye.

To do this properly, I must begin by quoting you at large: I shall then proceed to criticize your utterance from several points of view, divine and human, in the course of which I shall attempt to draw again, and with more specification, the character of the dead saint whom it has pleased you to vilify: so much being done, I shall say farewell to you for ever.

HONOLULU, *August* 2, 1889

Reverend H. B. GAGE.

Dear Brother,—In answer to your inquiries about Father Damien, I can only reply that we who knew the man are surprised at the extravagant newspaper laudations, as if he was a most saintly philanthropist. The simple truth is, he was a coarse, dirty man, headstrong and bigoted. He was not sent to Molokai, but went there without orders; did not stay at the leper settlement (before he became one himself), but circulated freely over the whole island (less than half the island is devoted to the lepers), and he came often to Honolulu. He had no hand in the reforms and improvements inaugurated, which were the work of our Board of Health, as occasion required and means were provided. He was not a pure man in his relations with women, and the leprosy of which he died should be attributed to his vices and carelessness. Others have done much for the lepers, our own ministers, the government physicians, and so forth, but never with the Catholic idea of meriting eternal life.— Yours, etc.,

C. M. HYDE.

To deal fitly with a letter so extraordinary, I must draw at the outset on my private knowledge of the signatory and his sect. It may offend others; scarcely you, who have been so busy to collect, so bold to publish, gossip on your rivals. And this is perhaps the moment when I may best explain to you the character of what you are to read: I conceive you as a man quite beyond and below the reticences of civility: with what measure you mete, with that shall it be measured you again; with you, at last, I rejoice to feel the button off the foil and to plunge home. And if in aught that I shall say I should offend others, your colleagues, whom I respect and remember with affection, I can but offer them my regret; I am not free, I am inspired by the consideration of interests far more large; and such pain as can be inflicted by anything from me must be indeed trifling when compared with the pain with which they read your letter. It is not the hangman, but the criminal, that brings dishonor on the house.

Open Letter to the Reverend Dr. Hyde of Honolulu

You belong, sir, to a sect—I believe my sect, and that in which my ancestors labored—which has enjoyed, and partly failed to utilize, an exceptional advantage in the islands of Hawaii. The first missionaries came; they found the land already self-purged of its old and bloody faith; they were embraced, almost on their arrival, with enthusiasm; what troubles they supported came far more from whites than from Hawaiians; and to these last they stood (in a rough figure) in the shoes of God. This is not the place to enter into the degree or causes of their failure, such as it is. One element alone is pertinent, and must here be plainly dealt with. In the course of their evangelical calling, they—or too many of them—grew rich. It may be news to you that the houses of missionaries are a cause of mocking on the streets of Honolulu. It will at least be news to you that when I returned your civil visit, the driver of my cab commented on the size, the taste, and the comfort of your home. It would have been news certainly to myself had anyone told me that afternoon that I should live to drag such matter into print. But you see, sir, how you degrade better men to your own level; and it is needful that those who are to judge betwixt you and me, betwixt Damien and the devil's advocate, should understand your letter to have been penned in a house which could raise, and that very justly, the envy and the comments of the passers-by. I think (to employ a phrase of yours which I admire) it "should be attributed" to you that you have never visited the scene of Damien's life and death. If you had, and had recalled it, and looked about your pleasant rooms, even your pen perhaps would have been stayed.

Your sect (and remember, as far as any sect avows me, it is mine) has not done ill in a worldly sense in the Hawaiian Kingdom. When calamity befell their innocent parishioners, when leprosy descended and took root in the Eight Islands, a *quid pro quo* was to be looked for. To that prosperous mission, and to you, as one of its adornments, God had sent at last an opportunity. I know I am touching here upon a nerve acutely sensitive. I know that others of your colleagues look back on the inertia of your Church, and the intrusive and decisive heroism of Damien, with something almost to be called remorse. I am sure it is so with yourself; I am persuaded your letter was inspired by a certain envy, not essentially ignoble, and the one human trait to be espied in that performance. You were thinking of the lost chance, the past day; of that which should have been conceived and was not; of the service due and not rendered. *Time was,* said the voice in your ear, in your pleasant room, as you sat raging and writing; and if the words written were base beyond parallel, the rage, I am happy to repeat—it is the only compliment I shall pay you—the rage was almost virtuous. But, sir, when we have failed, and another has succeeded; when we have stood by, and another has stepped in; when we sit and grow bulky in our charming mansions, and a plain, uncouth peasant steps into the battle, under the eyes of God, and succors the afflicted, and consoles the dying, and is himself afflicted in his turn, and dies upon the field of honor—the battle cannot be retrieved as your unhappy irritation has suggested. It is a lost battle, and lost forever. One thing remained to you in your defeat—some rags of common honor; and these you have made haste to cast away.

Common honor—not the honor of having done anything right, but the honor of not having done aught conspicuously foul; the honor of the inert: that was what remained to you. We are not all expected to be Damiens; a man may conceive his duty more narrowly, he may love his comforts better; and none will cast a stone at him for that. But will a gentleman of your reverend profession allow me an example from the fields of gallantry? When two gentlemen compete for the favor of a lady, and the one succeeds and the other is rejected, and (as will sometimes happen) matter damaging to the successful rival's credit reaches the ear of the defeated, it is held by plain men of no pretensions that his mouth is, in the circumstance, almost necessarily closed. Your Church and Damien's were in Hawaii upon a rivalry to do well: to help, to edify, to set divine examples. You having (in one huge instance) failed, and Damien succeeded, I marvel it should not have occurred to you that you were doomed to silence; that when you had been outstripped in that high rivalry, and sat inglorious in the midst of your well-being, in your pleasant room—and Damien, crowned with glories and horrors, toiled and rotted in that pigsty of his under the cliffs of Kalawao—you, the elect who would not, were the last man on earth to collect and propagate gossip on the volunteer who would and did.

I think I see you—for I try to see you in the flesh as I write these sentences—I think I see you leap at the word pigsty, a hyperbolical expression at the best. "He had no hand in the reforms," he was "a coarse, dirty man"; these were your own words; and you may think it possible that I am come to support you with fresh evidence. In a sense, it is even so. Damien has been too much depicted with a conventional halo and conventional features; so drawn by men who perhaps had not the eye to remark or the pen to express the individual; or who perhaps were only blinded and silenced by generous admiration, such as I partly envy for myself—such as you, if your soul were enlightened, would envy on your bended knees. It is the least defect of such a method of portraiture that it makes the path easy for the devil's advocate, and leaves for the misuse of the slanderer a considerable field of truth. For the truth that is suppressed by friends is the readiest weapon of the enemy. The world, in your despite, may perhaps owe you something, if your letter be the means of substituting once for all a credible likeness for a wax abstraction. For, if that world at all remember you, on the day when Damien of Molokai shall be named Saint, it will be in virtue of one work: your letter to the Reverend H. B. Gage.

You may ask on what authority I speak. It was my inclement destiny to become acquainted, not with Damien, but with Dr. Hyde. When I visited the lazaretto, Damien was already in his resting grave. But such information as I have I gathered on the spot in conversation with those who knew him well and long: some indeed who revered his memory; but others who had sparred and wrangled with him, who beheld him with no halo, who perhaps regarded him with small respect, and through whose unprepared and scarcely partial communications the plain, human features of the man shone on me convincingly. These gave me what knowledge I possess; and I learned it in that scene where it could be most completely and sensitively understood—Kalawao, which you have never visited, about which you have never so much as endeavored to inform yourself; for, brief as your letter is, you have found the means to stumble into that confession. *"Less than one-half* of the island," you say, "is devoted to the lepers." Molokai—"Molokai ahina," the "gray," lofty, and most desolate island—along all its northern side plunges a front of precipice into a sea of unusual profundity. This range of cliff is, from east to west, the true end and frontier of the island. Only in one spot there projects to the ocean a certain triangular and rugged down, grassy, stony, windy, and rising in the midst into a hill with a dead crater: the whole bearing to the cliff that overhangs it somewhat the same relation as a bracket to a wall. With this hint you will now be able to pick out the leper station on a map; you will be able to judge how much of Molokai is thus cut off between the surf and precipice, whether less than a half, or less than a quarter, or a fifth, or a tenth—or, say, a twentieth; and the next time you burst into print you will be in a position to share with us the issue of your calculations.

I imagine you to be one of those persons who talk with cheerfulness of that place which oxen and wainropes could not drag you to behold. You, who do not even know its situation on the map, probably denounce sensational descriptions, stretching your limbs the while in your pleasant parlor on Beretania Street. When I was pulled ashore there one early morning, there sat with me in the boat two sisters, bidding farewell (in humble imitation of Damien) to the lights and joys of human life. One of these wept silently; I could not withhold myself from joining her. Had you been there, it is my belief that nature would have triumphed even in you; and as the boat drew but a little nearer, and you beheld the stairs crowded with abominable deformations of our common manhood, and saw yourself landing in the midst of such a population as only now and then surrounds us in the horror of a nightmare—what a haggard eye you would have rolled over your reluctant shoulder toward the house on Beretania Street! Had you gone on; had you found every fourth face a blot upon the landscape; had you visited the hospital and seen the butt ends of human beings lying there almost unrecognizable, but still breathing, still thinking, still remembering; you would have understood that life in the lazaretto is an ordeal from which the nerves of a man's spirit shrink, even as his eye quails under the brightness of the sun; you would have felt it was (even today) a pitiful place to visit and a hell to dwell in. It is not the fear of possible infection. That seems a little thing when compared with the pain, the pity, and the disgust of the visitor's surroundings, and the atmosphere of affliction, disease, and physical disgrace in which he breathes. I do not think I am a man more than usually timid; but I never recall the days and nights I spent upon that island promontory (eight days and seven nights), without heartfelt thankfulness that I am somewhere else. I find in my diary that I speak of my stay as a "grinding experience." I have once jotted in the margin, "*harrowing* is the word," and when the *Mokolii* bore me at last toward the outer world, I kept repeating to myself, with a new conception of their pregnancy, those simple words of the song: " 'Tis the most distressful country that ever yet was seen."

And observe: that which I saw and suffered from was a settlement purged, bettered, beautified; the new village built, the hospital and the Bishop Home excellently arranged; the sisters, the doctor, and the missionaries, all indefatigable in their noble tasks. It was a different place when Damien came there and made his great renunciation, and slept that first night under a tree amidst his rotting brethren, alone with pestilence and looking forward (with what courage, with what pitiful sinkings of dread, God only knows) to a lifetime of dressing sores and stumps.

You will say, perhaps, I am too sensitive, that sights as painful abound in cancer hospitals and are confronted daily by doctors and nurses. I have long learned to admire and envy the doctors and the nurses. But there is no cancer hospital so large and populous as Kalawao and Kalaupapa, and in such a matter every fresh case, like every inch of length in the pipe of an organ, deepens the note of the impression; for what daunts the onlooker is that monstrous sum of human suffering by which he stands surrounded. Lastly, no doctor or nurse is called upon to enter once for all the doors of that Gehenna; they do not say farewell, they need not abandon hope on its sad threshold; they but go for a time to their high calling, and can look forward as they go to relief, to recreation, and to rest. But Damien shut to with his own hand the doors of his own sepulcher.

I shall now extract three passages from my diary at Kalawao.

Damien is dead and already somewhat ungratefully remembered in the field of his labors and sufferings. "He was a good man, but very officious," says one. Another tells me he had fallen (as other priests so easily do) into something of the ways and habits of thought of a Kanaka; but he had the wit to recognize the fact, and the good sense to laugh at [over] it. A plain man it seems he was; I cannot find he was a popular.

After Ragsdale's death [Ragsdale was a famous luna, or overseer, of the unruly settlement] there followed a brief term of office by Father

Damien which served only to publish the weakness of that noble man. He was rough in his ways, and he had no control. Authority was relaxed; Damien's life was threatened, and he was soon eager to resign.

Of Damien I begin to have an idea. He seems to have been a man of the peasant class, certainly of the peasant type: shrewd, ignorant and bigoted, yet with an open mind, and capable of receiving and digesting a reproof if it were bluntly administered; superbly generous in the least thing as well as in the greatest, and as ready to give his last shirt (although not without human grumbling) as he had been to sacrifice his life; essentially indiscreet and officious, which made him a troublesome colleague; domineering in all his ways, which made him incurably unpopular with the Kanakas, but yet destitute of real authority, so that his boys laughed at him and he must carry out his wishes by the means of bribes. He learned to have a mania for doctoring; and set up the Kanakas against the remedies of his regular rivals: perhaps (if anything matter at all in the treatment of such a disease) the worst thing that he did, and certainly the easiest. The best and worst of the man appear very plainly in his dealings with Mr. Chapman's money; he had originally laid it out [intended to lay it out] entirely for the benefit of Catholics, and even so not wisely; but after a long, plain talk, he admitted his error fully and revised the list. The sad state of the boys' home is in part the result of his lack of control; in part, of his own slovenly ways and false ideas of hygiene. Brother officials used to call it Damien's Chinatown. "Well," they would say, "your Chinatown keeps growing." And he would laugh with perfect good-nature, and adhere to his errors with perfect obstinacy. So much I have gathered of truth about this plain, noble human brother and father of ours; his imperfections are the traits of his face, by which we know him for our fellow; his martyrdom and his example nothing can lessen or annul; and only a person here on the spot can properly appreciate their greatness.

I have set down these private passages, as you perceive, without correction; thanks to you, the public has them in their bluntness. They are almost a list of the man's faults, for it is rather these that I was seeking: with his virtues, with the heroic profile of his life, I and the world were already sufficiently acquainted. I was besides a little suspicious of Catholic testimony; in no ill sense, but merely because Damien's admirers and disciples were the least likely to be critical. I know you will be more suspicious still; and the facts set down above were one and all collected from the lips of Protestants who had opposed the father in his life. Yet I am strangely deceived, or they build up the image of a man, with all his weaknesses, essentially heroic, and alive with rugged honesty, generosity, and mirth.

Take it for what it is, rough private jottings of the worst sides of Damien's character, collected from the lips of those who had labored with and (in your own phrase) "knew the man"—though I question whether Damien would have said that he knew you. Take it, and observe with wonder how well you were served by your gossips, how ill by your intelligence and sympathy; in how many points of fact we are at one, and how widely our appreciations vary. There is something wrong here—either with you or me. It is possible, for instance, that you, who seem to have so many ears in Kalawao, had heard of the affair of Mr. Chapman's money and were singly struck by Damien's intended wrongdoing. I was struck with that also, and set it fairly down; but I was struck much more by the fact that he had the honesty of mind to be convinced. I may here tell you that it was a long business; that one of his colleagues sat with him late into the night, multiplying arguments and accusations; that the father listened as usual with "perfect good-nature and perfect obstinacy"; but at the last, when he was persuaded—"Yes," said he, "I am very much obliged to you; you have done me a service; it would have been a theft." There are many (not Catholics merely) who require their heroes and saints to be infallible; to these the story will be painful; not to the true lovers, patrons, and servants of mankind.

And I take it, this is a type of our division—that you are one of those who have an eye for faults and failures, that you take a pleasure to find and publish them, and that, having found them, you make haste to forget the overvailing virtues and the real success which had alone introduced them to your knowledge. It is a dangerous frame of mind. That you may understand how dangerous, and into what a situation it has already brought you, we will (if you please) go hand-in-hand through the different phrases of your letter, and candidly examine each from the point of view of its truth, its appositeness, and its charity.

Damien was coarse.

It is very possible. You make us sorry for the lepers, who had only a coarse old peasant for their friend and father. But you, who were so refined, why were you not there, to cheer them with the lights of culture? Or may I remind you that we have some reason to doubt if John the Baptist were genteel; and in the case of Peter, on whose career you doubtless dwell approvingly in the pulpit, no doubt at all he was a "coarse, headstrong" fisherman! Yet even in our Protestant Bibles, Peter is called Saint.

Damien was dirty.

He was. Think of the poor lepers annoyed with this dirty comrade! But the clean Dr. Hyde was at his food in a fine house.

Damien was headstrong.

I believe you are right again; and I thank God for his strong head and heart.

Damien was bigoted.

I am not fond of bigots myself, because they are not fond of me. But what is meant by bigotry, that we should regard it as a blemish in a priest? Damien believed his own religion with the simplicity of a peasant or a child; as I would I could suppose that you do. For this, I wonder at him some way off; and had that been his only character, should have avoided him in life. But the point of interest in Damien, which has caused him to be so much talked about and made him at last the subject of your pen and mine, was that, in him, his bigotry, his intense and narrow faith, wrought potently for good, and strengthened him to be one of the world's heroes and exemplars.

Damien was not sent to Molokai, but went there without orders.

It this a misreading? Or do you really mean the words for blame? I have heard Christ, in the pulpits of our Church, held up for imitation on the ground that His sacrifice was voluntary. Does Dr. Hyde think otherwise?

Damien did not stay at the settlement, etc.

It is true he was allowed many indulgences. Am I to understand that you blame the father for profiting by these, or the officers for granting them? In either case, it is a mighty Spartan standard to issue from the house on Beretania Street; and I am convinced you will find yourself with few supporters.

Damien had no hand in the reforms, etc.

I think even you will admit that I have already been frank in my description of the man I am defending; but before I take you up

Open Letter to the Reverend Dr. Hyde of Honolulu 257

upon this head, I will be franker still, and tell you that perhaps nowhere in the world can a man taste a more pleasurable sense of contrast than when he passes from Damien's "Chinatown" at Kalawao to the beautiful Bishop Home at Kalaupapa. At this point, in my desire to make all fair for you, I will break my rule and adduce Catholic testimony. Here is a passage from my diary about my visit to the Chinatown, from which you will see how it is (even now) regarded by its own officials:

> We went round all the dormitories, refectories, etc.—dark and dingy enough, with a superficial cleanliness, which he [Mr. Dutton, the lay-brother] did not seek to defend. "It is almost decent," said he; "the sisters will make that all right when we get them here."

And yet I gathered it was already better since Damien was dead, and far better than when he was there alone and had his own (not always excellent) way. I have now come far enough to meet you on a common ground of fact; and I tell you that, to a mind not prejudiced by jealousy, all the reforms of the lazaretto, and even those which he most vigorously opposed, are properly the work of Damien. They are the evidence of his success; they are what his heroism provoked from the reluctant and the careless. Many were before him in the field; Mr. Meyer, for instance, of whose faithful work we hear too little: there have been many since; and some had more worldly wisdom, though none had more devotion, than our saint. Before his day, even you will confess, they had effected little. It was his part, by one striking act of martyrdom, to direct all men's eyes on that distressful country. At a blow, and with the price of his life, he made the place illustrious and public. And that, if you will consider largely, was the one reform needful, pregnant of all that should succeed. It brought money; it brought (best individual addition of them all) the sisters; it brought supervision, for public opinion and public interest landed with the man at Kalawao. If ever any man brought reforms, and died to bring them, it was he. There is not a clean cup or towel in the Bishop Home but dirty Damien washed it.

Damien was not a pure man in his relations with women, etc.

How do you know that? Is this the nature of the conversation in that house on Beretania Street which the cabman envied, driving past?—racy details of the misconduct of the poor peasant priest, toiling under the cliffs of Molokai?

Many have visited the station before me; they seem not to have heard the rumor. When I was there I heard many shocking tales, for my informants were men speaking with the plainness of the laity; and I heard plenty of complaints of Damien. Why was this never mentioned? And how came it to you in the retirement of your clerical parlor?

But I must not even seem to deceive you. This scandal, when I read it in your letter, was not new to me. I had heard it once before; and I must tell you how. There came to Samoa a man from Honolulu; he, in a public house on the beach, volunteered the statement that Damien had "contracted the disease from having connection with the female lepers"; and I find a joy in telling you how the report was welcomed in a public house. A man sprang to his feet; I am not at liberty to give his name, but from what I heard I doubt if you would care to have him to dinner in Beretania Street. "You miserable little ———" (here is a word I dare not print, it would so shock your ears). "You miserable little ———," he cried, "if the story were a thousand times true, can't you see you are a million times a lower ——— for daring to repeat it?" I wish it could be told of you that when the report reached you in your house, perhaps after family worship, you had found in your soul enough holy anger to receive it with the same expressions; ay, even with that one which I dare not print; it would not need to have been blotted away, like Uncle Toby's oath, by the tears of the recording angel; it would have been counted to you for your brightest righteousness. But you have deliberately chosen the part of the man from Honolulu, and you have played it with improvements of your own. The man from Honolulu—miserable, leering creature—communicated the tale to a rude knot of beachcombing drinkers in a public house, where (I will so far agree with your temperance opinions) man is not always at his noblest; and the man from Honolulu had himself been drinking—drinking, we may charitably fancy, to excess. It was to your "Dear Brother, the Reverend H. B. Gage," that you chose to communicate the sickening story; and the blue ribbon which adorns your portly bosom forbids me to allow you the extenuating plea that you were drunk when it was done. Your "dear brother"—a brother indeed—made haste to deliver up your letter (as a means of grace, perhaps) to the religious papers; where, after many months, I found and read and wondered at it, and whence I have now reproduced it for the wonder of others. And you and your dear brother have, by this cycle of operations, built up a contrast very edifying to examine in detail. The man whom you would not care to have to dinner, on the one side; on the other, the Reverend Dr. Hyde and the Reverend H. B. Gage: the Apia bar-room, the Honolulu manse.

But I fear you scarce appreciate how you appear to your fellow men; and to bring it home to you, I will suppose your story to be true. I will suppose—and God forgive me for supposing it—that Damien faltered and stumbled in his narrow path of duty; I will suppose that, in the horror of his isolation, perhaps in the fever of incipient disease, he, who was doing so much more than he had sworn, failed in the letter of his priestly oath—he, who was so much a better man than either you or me, who did what we have never dreamed of daring—he too tasted of our common frailty. "O, Iago, the pity of it!" The least tender should be moved to tears; the most incredulous to prayer. And all that you could do was to pen your letter to the Reverend H. B. Gage!

Is it growing at all clear to you what a picture you have drawn of your own heart? I will try yet once again to make it clearer. You had a father: suppose this tale were about him, and some informant brought it to you, proof in hand—I am not making too high an estimate of your emotional nature when I suppose you would regret the circumstance? That you would feel the tale of frailty the more keenly since it shamed the author of your days? And that the last thing you would do would be to publish it in the religious press? Well, the man who tried to do what Damien did is my father, and the father of the man in the Apia bar, and the father of all who love goodness; and he was your father too, if God had given you grace to see it.

Jacob Adler

Claus Spreckels and the Hawaiian Revolution of 1893

Adler, born in 1913 in Chicago, came to Hawaii in World War II as a lieutenant in the United States Air Force. He remained to become a certified public accountant and professor at the University of Hawaii. He holds a doctorate in economics from Columbia University, and has studied especially the economic history of Hawaii. His interest in the Hawaiian sugar industry and in the role played by the "crusty, testy" Claus Spreckels resulted in a book, *Claus Spreckels, the Sugar King in Hawaii* (1966). In the following article from *Journal of the West* for January, 1966, Adler tells how Spreckels tried, after the overthrow of Queen Liliuokalani, to defeat the pro-American annexation party and put the queen back on the throne.

ON January 20, 1891, Hawaiian King David Kalakaua lay dying in his suite at the Palace Hotel in San Francisco. Among the few persons at the deathbed was Claus Spreckels, who had built a sugar empire in California and Hawaii. He may well have reflected on happier days in Hawaii: luaus at King Kalakaua's waterfront boathouse in Honolulu; state dinners at Iolani Palace; poker games and parties, graced by His Majesty's presence, at Spreckels' mansion in the Punahou district of Honolulu.

Partly by loans to the king and kingdom, Spreckels had risen to power in the Hawaiian sugar industry. He had taken full advantage of the reciprocity treaty of 1876 between Hawaii and the United States. In effect the treaty gave Hawaiian planters a price increase of two cents a pound. Spreckels owned the largest sugar plantation in the islands, Hawaiian Commercial and Sugar Company. He was a partner in one of the largest sugar agencies, William G. Irwin and

Co. He controlled the transport of Hawaiian sugar through the Oceanic Steamship Company, and refining through his California Sugar Refinery in San Francisco.

Then in 1886 King Kalakaua and Claus Spreckels had fallen out. Kalakaua wearied of Spreckels' dictation and sought a loan in London to pay him off. When the legislature passed a loan act unacceptable to Spreckels, he returned all his royal decorations to the king and left for San Francisco in a rage. But now, five years later, as King Kalakaua lay dying, old animosities were doubtless forgotten.

The king's body was returned to his beloved Hawaii aboard the U.S.S. *Charleston*. On the day the ship arrived in Honolulu Harbor, January 29, 1891, Princess Liliuokalani, Kalakaua's sister, was sworn in as queen. Liliuokalani was a woman of ability, strong-willed, and critical of foreign interference in Hawaii. She quickly made it clear that she intended to rule in the tradition of the great Hawaiian alii (chiefs), and not merely reign as a passive constitutional monarch. Her brother Kalakaua had in many ways frittered away his power in grandiose schemes intended to return the Hawaiians to what he regarded as their former glory. He had been forced, in 1887, to grant a new constitution which put severe limitations on the monarchy.

The death agony of the monarchy began at the end of a long and bitter legislative session in 1892. Queen Liliuokalani, against the advice of her ministers, tried on January 14, 1893, to proclaim a new constitution which would return power to the throne. Led by Lorrin A. Thurston, a lawyer who had been prominent in politics, persons favoring annexation to the United States quickly took advantage of the queen's "revolutionary" act. With the firing of hardly a shot, they took control of a few government buildings on the afternoon of January 17. They proclaimed the overthrow of the monarchy, and formed a Provisional Government headed by Judge Sanford B. Dole.

Five annexation commissioners, including Thurston, soon left Honolulu by the *Claudine,* arriving at San Francisco on January 27. They conferred with Claus Spreckels, who offered his support. He even offered his private railroad car for the trip to Washington, D. C., but this was declined.

When the annexation commissioners reached Washington, they ran into trouble on some of their proposals. For example, they wanted the United States to allow the contract labor system on the Hawaiian sugar plantations. Under this system there had been a great deal of Chinese and Japanese immigration to Hawaii, beginning in the 1850's. The sugar planters had practically institutionalized the system in quite paternalistic fashion.

Even yielding on all their proposals, the commissioners were unable to lobby an annexation treaty through the United States Congress. Incoming President Cleveland withdrew the treaty from the Senate. On March 11, 1893, he appointed James H. Blount (who had served for eighteen years in the House of Representatives, from Georgia) to make a first-hand report on the overthrow of the monarchy, especially as to charges of complicity by United States Minister John L. Stevens. Blount was to "fully enlighten" the President.

Meanwhile Claus Spreckels began to have some second thoughts about supporting the annexationists. He felt that the Hawaiian sugar industry could not survive without the contract labor system. Suddenly he made up his mind to go to Hawaii and see for himself what was going on.

The *Australia* from San Francisco steamed into Honolulu Harbor on April 18, 1893. This surprised the residents because the ship was docking a full day ahead of schedule. It was a rainy morning. Nevertheless a large crowd gathered expectantly at the wharf. Was Claus Spreckels aboard? (The *Australia* was owned by the Oceanic Steamship Company, commonly known as the Spreckels line.) Was there any startling political news? Had the steamer left San Francisco ahead of time?

These questions were soon answered. Spreckels was aboard with his wife Anna, daughter Emma, and son Rudolph. No, there was no startling political news to report. The steamer had left on time and had made a record run of five days, nineteen hours, and thirty-three minutes. One can easily imagine Spreckels standing next to Captain Houdlette on the bridge and telling him to "pour on the coal!"

On the very day of Spreckels' arrival, according to him, United States Minister John L. Stevens sent a message asking to see him. Spreckels saw him at four o'clock that afternoon. Stevens wanted his help in persuading the queen and her followers to yield to annexation. Within a few days after his arrival Spreckels also saw Queen Liliuokalani and President Sanford B. Dole. According to the *Star*, the queen got little comfort from Spreckels on the question of getting back her throne. But he reportedly assured President Dole he would back the Provisional Government.

Spreckels wanted to leave open the final form of government. He was not opposed to annexation, but he wanted to consider the idea of a republic. "Let me say," he told a reporter from the *Star*, "I am not here to tear down the Provisional Government, but I am here to see justice done to all parties, and when I have determined what I regard as justice I will be heard fast enough."

These statements skirted the question of contract labor, which certainly was much on Spreckels' mind. On April 6 he told a reporter:

"I have come down to investigate. . . . The labor question is the all-important one and constitutes my only objection to annexation. . . . The contract labor system will not be tolerated by the United States, but that system is essential. . . . When Kalakaua was King I practically ran the country. . . . If I could find a man of ability whom I could trust I would favor a republic—the thing to do is to find the man."

Spreckels determined to get the support of the sugar planters for his views. Accordingly, several planters and sugar agents met on April 25 at the office of W. O. Smith, an attorney. They discussed the political outlook, the needs and prospects of the sugar industry, and the contract labor question. A letter from Spreckels was read, and it was expected that the planters would prepare a statement for Commissioner Blount.

In fact, the letter had been drafted by William G. Irwin, Spreckels' partner. Irwin claimed that most of the planters approved the letter, but they thought it best not to present it to Blount because the endorsement was not unanimous. In essence the letter was as follows.

On the question of annexation, one of the main points was the effect on the sugar industry, the most important in the island. The laws of the United States would stop contract labor and Oriental immigration. The contract system assured repayment of advances by the planters for the laborers' transportation. It also protected the planters against strikes, which would be especially serious at harvest time. Not only did the contract protect the planter; it also assured the laborer of regular employment. The Japanese government therefore regarded the contract as a protection for its subjects.

Irwin said he agreed completely with Spreckels that ". . . annexation pure and simple, without regard to our present labor system . . . or [without] protection of the civil rights of Hawaiians against the host of political intriguers who would no doubt invade our shores as soon as the treaty was passed, would prove a disaster instead of a boon to these islands."

Possibly because the planters had failed to endorse his letter, Spreckels stated his views in an interview of May 2, 1893, with Charles Nordhoff of the New York *Herald*.

In the first part of this interview Spreckels repeated and enlarged on much of what he had said in the letter to the planters. Nordhoff asked whether the planters agreed with him on the need for the contract labor system. They did, said Spreckels. But, he added, some planters thought that upon annexation the United States would permit Hawaii to have its own immigration laws and to keep the contract labor system. Spreckels himself did not believe this would be done.

"Is sugar the only possible important crop of the islands?" asked Nordhoff. "Yes," said Spreckels. "If the sugar were destroyed the islands would relapse into a big cow pasture, which they were before sugar was begun."

Nordhoff said that some annexationists thought political stability was not possible without annexation.

Spreckels replied, "I can't see why we should not have stable independent government. I am sure that stable, orderly, and economical government is possible here, and as I am the largest taxpayer on the islands, and have more property at stake and pay more taxes than the whole Provisional Government, you will admit that my interests make me conservative. I need a stable and economical government more than any man on the islands."

Nordhoff asked him what he thought about the future of the islands. Spreckels said that when President Cleveland and the United States Congress knew the truth, they would understand that annexation "would be an act of great injustice, . . . it would also ruin the sugar industry, on which depends the prosperity of all the people of the islands."

As of May 17, 1893, Spreckels was still trying to promote the idea of an independent republic. On that same date Blount formally replaced Stevens as United States Minister to Hawaii. Blount interviewed Spreckels on June 5, about a month after the Nordhoff interview. Spreckels told Blount that President Dole had asked him to discuss the labor question with the cabinet of the Provisional Government. "I went there," said Spreckels, "and I asked President Dole whether he had studied the [U.S.] immigration laws and whether he found that I was correct. He answered that he found I was correct in that way. 'But [said Dole] I have [the] belief that the United States will give us a separate law [so] that we can get laborers here.' "

Between the Nordhoff and Blount interviews mentioned above occurred Spreckels' first act of open hostility to the Provisional Government. This concerned a loan of $95,000 made to the monarchy by the Spreckels Bank. After the revolution the Provisional Government had assumed responsibility for the loan.

Former Queen Liliuokalani had told Blount that "if Mr. Spreckels did not advance [money] to the Government . . . it would go to pieces." In her diary for May 29 she wrote that Sam Parker (one of her former ministers) had told her that Spreckels was going to call the loan and so put her back on the throne. She asked Spreckels to help her form a cabinet. He said he would help and would stay until everything was settled. He also said that when he called the loan the government would fall.

That same afternoon cashier Spaulding of the Spreckels Bank demanded payment of the $95,000. The call for payment was unexpected. The Provisional Government had understood that the bank considered the loan "a perfectly safe investment, was satisfied to draw the interest, and was in no hurry to collect the principal."

Since the government did not have the money to pay, Finance Minister Samuel M. Damon faced a crisis. Failure to pay would cause a loss of confidence in the Provisional Government. No doubt this was what Spreckels intended, though he later denied any such intent. But the government went out on the streets of Honolulu, and in two hours got pledges from Honolulu businessmen for the entire amount due. Newspapers favorable to the government now increased their attacks on Spreckels and the royalists.

"The prophets of the royalist cause," said the *Gazette,* "are experiencing the nausea produced by hope deferred. Since the days of Shakespeare, the calling in of gold has been a typical method of taking revenge on the unsuspicious debtor." The same newspaper said that Hawaii had "refused to be reduced to bankruptcy at the nod of the chief Hawaiian boodler and politician."

Spreckels began freely voicing his opinion that the Provisional Government could not last. The queen would be restored. In reply, the *Star* on June 9, 1893, published an article entitled "Herr Rothschild von Katzenjammer" (meaning Spreckels) containing a threat about what might happen to him if he did not stop his seditious talk. The scene was laid in "Germany":

When the contest between the crown and the people of Germany came to an end, Herr Rothschild von Katzenjammer, who had large holdings of land but had been living abroad, returned to Prussia, and espoused the cause of the ex-Emperor. The government of Germany, then in a transition state and controlled by a committee of the Reichstag, was disposed on many accounts to be lenient with Herr van Katzenjammer, a fact which he mistook for an exhibition of weakness.

The extravagance of Imperial Germany, so said the article, had resulted in debts to Herr von Katzenjammer. These had been assumed by the transitional state.

His next move was to attack his debtors—who were the dominant party—through the courts, and by a quiet word here and useful thaler there, influence the Royalist faction and induce it ... to commit some overt act.

The state brought Katzenjammer before a military court.

It appeared that the inculpated millionaire had carried his sedition on his sleeve. He had run at the mouth about his plans and had entrusted grave secrets to men who could not retain them. It was easy therefore to prove that he was a conspirator against the peace and dignity of the Provisional Government of Germany. The sentence of the court was that his estates and credits should be confiscated and his person banished from the country.

Spreckels, of course, was furious. He filed a suit for libel, which resulted in the arrest of Walter G. Smith, editor of the *Star*. After six months of litigation, the case was thrown out of court in mid-December, 1893, on a technicality.

The Katzenjammer story implied that action might be taken against Spreckels' property in Hawaii. Soon came a threat against his life. As he was about to step into his carriage on the morning of June 22, 1893, he noticed a sign on the gate of his Punahou home: "Gold and silver will not stop lead!" Pictures of a skull and crossbones and of a coffin embellished the sign, which was in blood-red color.

Was the threat really meant to be serious? There is little question that Spreckels so regarded it. He at once applied to Minister Blount for protection because he felt his life was in danger. Blount took the matter up with President Dole. Soon a native policeman was pacing back and forth in front of the Punahou home.

From time to time there were rumors that the person who posted the sign was known and would be arrested. These rumors the government denied. But there is some good later evidence on this point. During an investigation of royalist attempts to restore the queen, Harry A. Juen in December, 1893, made the following sworn statement:

> I ... was [in May, 1893] a police officer serving as a Captain of the Honolulu Police.... I was approached by Klemme, an officer in the mounted police who made a proposition to me to join him in a plot, the object of which should be to blow up with dynamite the residences and persons of the Queen, Colonel Claus Spreckels, and Charles Nordhoff. Klemme made me understand that he belonged to a secret organization which had the aforesaid purpose.... The plot against Spreckels' and Nordhoff's lives was abandoned on my refusal to join Klemme, but after the dynamite episode Klemme told me that he intended to put a placard of a threatening nature on the gate of Claus Spreckels, so as to scare him out of the Islands. This I did in company with him.

Thwarted, ridiculed, threatened, Spreckels in July, 1893, prepared to leave for San Francisco. He would carry on his war against the Provisional Government there and in Washington, D. C. An unnamed friend of Spreckels said that the sugar king "meant to do up the Provisional people, the *Star,* and all concerned in a very small package when he got to California." Shortly before leaving he took possession of the threatening sign, which had been in police custody. He would take it back with him to be reproduced in the San Francisco newspapers. He would "parade it before the horror-stricken eyes of the President and Secretary of State," and begin lobbying in Washington against annexation.

Spreckels called on Queen Liliuokalani on July 15 to tell her he was leaving. He said he would tell President Cleveland that she should be put back on the throne. He made some statements about the types of nobles and ministers who should be appointed. The queen suspected that he was grinding his own ax. She was noncommittal. "I never like to make promises," she wrote in her diary, "and I do not think he ought say who I should appoint for ministers. I will appoint such men who would act with me and not study the interest of any private individual or firm."

Spreckels' departure on July 19 by the *Australia* occasioned somewhat more than the usual fanfare at the wharf. The Hawaiian National Band (the old Royal Hawaiian Band under the monarchy) got permission to play farewell music. By eleven o'clock in the morning, an hour before sailing time, the wharf was swarming with people, mostly royalists.

As Spreckels, his wife Anna, and daughter Emma reached the gangplank, a throng of native women surrounded them and bedecked them with flower garlands. Spreckels was the center of attention. He "paraded the deck absolutely embowered in leis . . . his head rising amid the expanse of roses and posies, like a pumpkin in a big flower patch. Not a sign of his clothing could be seen, so harnessed, sashed, and surcingled was he with flower offerings." He went to Captain Houdlette's cabin about eleven thirty. There a number of royalists, led by Charles Creighton and John E. Bush, joined him.

Creighton presented Spreckels with a gold-headed cane. This was inscribed in passable English, poor German, and worse Latin: *"Ave! Claus! Morituri te Salutans.* In Memoriam from your Fellow Citizens Doomed to Die at the Hands of the Murder Society of the Annexation Club. 'Threatened men live long.' *Leben Sie hundert*

Jahre und niemals sterben [May you live a hundred years and never die.]" Below this salute appeared the names of Liliuokalani, James Blount, Claus Spreckels, and a number of royalists. (United States Minister Blount was furious at the use of his name, and later claimed it was unauthorized.)

Spreckels expressed thanks for the cane. He said he hoped the donors would be decorating his grave rather than he theirs. But before the assassins felled him he "would see right and justice done to the Hawaiians."

John E. Bush, a well-known editor of a Hawaiian newspaper and former cabinet minister under King Kalakaua, then made a speech for the royalist Hawaiian Patriotic League. He claimed the League represented 99 percent of the Hawaiian people:

"On their behalf [I] offer to you their heartfelt appreciation of your conduct toward them . . . in the bold and fearless stand you have taken in opposing the highhanded measures to rob them of their birthright, and as human beings to leave them without a voice in the disposition of its autonomy as an independent state."

After Bush's remarks, Spreckels said that when he came to the islands in 1876 he had found a peaceful and intelligent race. Then he could walk the streets without fear. Now all this was changed. But the native Hawaiians could depend on it, he would see that justice was done. He would go straight to Washington, talk with President Cleveland, and expose the schemes of the Provisional Government. The royalist crowd in the cabin then drank Spreckels' health in fine champagne—at his expense.

Royalists on the wharf, meanwhile, called out again and again, "Where's Spreckels?" He went out on deck to wave and smile at the crowd. Calling on Bush to translate into Hawaiian for him, he started to make a speech. The ship's gong muffled his opening words. He concluded with, "Let me say that I and the whole Spreckels family have the warmest aloha for the natives."

While Spreckels was still speaking, a professor from Oahu College (Punahou School) called for the college yell by some students on the wharf, to drown out the sugar king's remarks. Bush retaliated at the end of the speech by leading a "hip, hip, hurrah!" for Spreckels. The president of Oahu College, who was on the deck above Spreckels, then called for three cheers for the Provisional

Government. These were given while the band played "Aloha Oe" (Farewell to Thee). The bitterness of the Hawaiians at this interruption of "Aloha Oe" can be readily imagined. Queen Liliuokalani herself wrote the words and it is still one of Hawaii's best-loved songs.

Spreckels went back to his cabin in high displeasure. The ship's whistle blew, warning friends of departing passengers to go ashore. When the deck hands had cast off the lines, the passengers threw leis to persons on the wharf. The band played "Hawaii Ponoi" (the Hawaiian national anthem, composed by King Kalakaua) as the *Australia* began her run to the coast. It is not recorded that Spreckels shed any tears. But no one who has witnessed a Hawaiian steamer departure could blame him if he did—and for him this was no ordinary departure.

Spreckels continued to fight against annexation in both California and Washington, D. C. He fought as an individual and also as a member of the United States sugar trust. Although he may have delayed annexation, he could not stop it.

In the islands, annexationists bided their time. The Republic of Hawaii was established in 1894 to replace the Provisional Government. Fruitless efforts were made in the United States Senate in early 1898 to get an annexation treaty ratified. But the forces of anti-imperialism and opposition by United States sugar interests could not be overcome. The Spanish-American War, however, focused attention on Hawaii as a way station to the Philippines, and thus turned the balance in favor of renewed annexation efforts which were already under way. Both houses of the United States Congress passed a resolution which was signed by President McKinley on July 7, 1898. In ceremonies at Iolani Palace on August 12 the Hawaiian flag was struck and the islands became a territory of the United States.

Spreckels returned to Honolulu in 1905, after an absence of twelve years. There was a stirring in commercial circles. The Hawaiian Hotel was up for sale. Was Spreckels going to buy the hotel? No, he soon made it clear that this was not a business trip; he was only looking for health and relaxation. He was seventy-seven years old. A few years earlier he had suffered a stroke.

William G. Irwin's carriage was waiting at the dock. Spreckels stepped into the carriage, and the two men drove to Irwin's home at Waikiki. Spreckels soon went into Honolulu again to walk up and down the streets and say hello to old friends. He could contemplate his vanished Hawaiian empire without bitterness, for his success in California beet sugar had surpassed that of his greatest days in Hawaii. A reporter asked him what he thought of the changes in the city. In the rage of his 1893 departure, Spreckels had sworn he would live to see grass growing in the streets of Honolulu.

"Honolulu is greatly improved since I left," he said. "There have been buildings erected which would do credit to a large city on the mainland. Oh, the city has been tremendously improved."

After staying a few weeks with Irwin at Waikiki Beach, Spreckels unshuttered his Punahou home and brought his family down from San Francisco. There was talk that he would spend the rest of his days in Honolulu. But in a few months he became restless to get back to San Francisco, back to work. He left Honolulu for the last time. Three years later, in 1908, he died.

Of Spreckels' Hawaiian career, what evidence remains? In the Punahou district of Honolulu a street named after Spreckels extends for only a few hundred feet. Here his three-story mansion once stood. In downtown Honolulu, the valuable "Spreckels block" has long since been sold off and the block no longer bears the family name.

On Maui, some of the residents of Spreckelsville have only vague notions about how the small plantation town got its name. From the rise of Puunene, near Spreckelsville, one can see for miles around the fields of waving cane where once lay only a wasteland. Today's green fields on the central plains of Maui endure as the most striking reminder of the sugar king's Hawaiian career.

Jack London

The Sheriff of Kona

One of the best short-story writers ever to use the Hawaiian Islands as a setting was Jack London (1876–1916). After "inconceivable and monstrous" adventures on their forty-three-foot ketch *Snark,* London and his wife Charmian sailed into Pearl Harbor in the spring of 1907 and stayed for four months before setting out on a cruise of the South Seas. They returned to Hawaii for a sojourn of almost a year in 1915, when London was the best-known, highest-paid, and most popular writer in the world. His visits to the Islands provided material for thirteen short stories. These have been collected and reprinted as *Stories of Hawaii by Jack London* (1965), edited by A. Grove Day.

London was sometimes criticized by local friends for writing too often about the afflictions of leprosy, but the subject continued to fascinate him and he used it as the denouement of several of his most effective short stories. The sheriff of Kona is a brave man who is also a lucky man until he, whose duties require him to send others into exile at Molokai, is himself ironically stricken with "the mark of the beast."

"YOU cannot escape liking the climate," Cudworth said, in reply to my panegyric on the Kona coast. "I was a young fellow, just out of college, when I came here eighteen years ago. I never went back, except, of course, to visit. And I warn you, if you have some spot dear to you on earth, not to linger here too long, else you will find this dearer."

We had finished dinner, which had been served on the big lanai, the one with a northerly exposure, though "exposure" is indeed a misnomer in so delectable a climate.

The candles had been put out, and a slim, white-clad Japanese slipped like a ghost through the silvery moonlight, presented us with cigars, and faded away into the darkness of the bungalow. I looked through a screen of banana and lehua trees, and down across the guava scrub to the quiet sea a thousand feet beneath. For a week, ever since I had landed from the tiny coasting steamer, I had been stopping with Cudworth, and during that time no wind had ruffled that unvexed sea. True, there had been breezes, but they were the gentlest zephyrs that ever blew through summer isles. They were not winds; they were sighs—long, balmy sighs of a world at rest.

"A lotus land," I said.

"Where each day is like every day, and every day is a paradise of days," he answered. "Nothing ever happens. It is not too hot. It is not too cold. It is always just right. Have you noticed how the land and the sea breathe turn and turn about?"

Indeed I had noticed that delicious, rhythmic breathing. Each morning I had watched the sea breeze begin at the shore and slowly extend seaward as it blew the mildest, softest whiff of ozone to the land. It played over the sea, just faintly darkening its surface, with here and there and everywhere long lanes of calm—shifting, changing, drifting, according to the capricious kisses of the breeze. And each evening I had watched the sea breath die away to heavenly calm, and heard the land breath softly make its way through the coffee trees and monkeypods.

"It is a land of perpetual calm," I said. "Does it ever blow here? —ever really blow? You know what I mean."

Cudworth shook his head and pointed eastward.

"How can it blow, with a barrier like that to stop it?"

Far above towered the huge bulks of Mauna Kea and Mauna Loa, seeming to blot out half the starry sky. Two miles and a half above our heads they reared their own heads, white with snow that the tropic sun had failed to melt.

"Thirty miles away, right now, I'll wager, it is blowing forty miles an hour."

I smiled incredulously.

Cudworth stepped to the lanai telephone. He called up, in succession, Waimea, Kohala, and Hamakua. Snatches of his conversation told me that the wind was blowing: "Rip-snorting and backjumping, eh? . . . How long? . . . Only a week? . . . Hello, Abe, is that you? . . . Yes, yes. . . . You *will* plant coffee on the Hamakua coast. . . . Hang your windbreaks! You should see *my* trees.

"Blowing a gale," he said to me, turning from hanging up the receiver. "I always have to joke Abe on his coffee. He has five hundred acres, and he's done marvels in windbreaking, but how he keeps the roots in the ground is beyond me. Blow? It always blows on the Hamakua side. Kohala reports a schooner under double reefs beating up the channel between Hawaii and Maui, and making heavy weather of it."

"It is hard to realize," I said lamely. "Doesn't a little whiff of it ever eddy around somehow, and get down here?"

"Not a whiff. Our land breeze is absolutely of no kin, for it begins this side of Mauna Kea and Mauna Loa. You see, the land radiates its heat quicker than the sea, and so, at night, the land breathes over the sea. In the day the land becomes warmer than the sea, and the sea breathes over the land.... Listen! Here comes the land breath now, the mountain wind."

I could hear it coming, rustling softly through the coffee trees, stirring the monkeypods, and sighing through the sugar cane. On the lanai the hush still reigned. Then it came, the first feel of the mountain wind, faintly balmy, fragrant and spicy; and cool, deliciously cool, a silken coolness, a wine like coolness—cool as only the mountain wind of Kona can be cool.

"Do you wonder that I lost my heart to Kona eighteen years ago?" he demanded. "I could never leave it now. I think I should die. It would be terrible. There was another man who loved it, even as I. I think he loved it more, for he was born here on the Kona coast. He was a great man, my best friend, my more than brother. But he left it, and he did not die."

"Love?" I queried. "A woman?"

Cudworth shook his head.

"Nor will he ever come back, though his heart will be here until he dies."

He paused and gazed down upon the beach lights of Kailua. I smoked silently and waited.

"He was already in love ... with his wife. Also, he had three children, and he loved them. They are in Honolulu now. The boy is going to college."

"Some rash act?" I questioned, after a time, impatiently.

The Sheriff of Kona

He shook his head. "Neither guilty of anything criminal, nor charged with anything criminal. He was the sheriff of Kona."

"You choose to be paradoxical," I said.

"I suppose it does sound that way," he admitted, "and that is the perfect hell of it."

He looked at me searchingly for a moment, and then abruptly took up the tale.

"He was a leper. No, he was not born with it—no one is born with it; it came upon him. This man—what does it matter? Lyte Gregory was his name. Every kamaaina knows the story. He was straight American stock, but he was built like the chieftains of old Hawaii. He stood six feet three. His stripped weight was two hundred and twenty pounds, not an ounce of which was not clean muscle or bone. He was the strongest man I have ever seen. He was an athlete and a giant. He was a god. He was my friend. And his heart and his soul were as big and as fine as his body.

"I wonder what you would do if you saw your friend, your brother, on the slippery lip of a precipice, slipping, slipping, and you were able to do nothing. That was just it. I could do nothing. I saw it coming, and I could do nothing. My God, man! what could I do? There it was, malignant and incontestable, the mark of the thing on his brow. No one else saw it. It was because I loved him so, I do believe, that I alone saw it. I could not credit the testimony of my senses. It was too incredibly horrible. Yet there it was, on his brow, on his ears. I had seen it, the slight puff of the earlobes—oh, so imperceptibly slight. I watched it for months. Then, next, hoping against hope, the darkening of the skin above both eyebrows—oh, so faint, just like the dimmest touch of sunburn. I should have thought it sunburn but that there was a shine to it, such an invisible shine, like a little highlight seen for a moment and gone the next. I tried to believe it was sunburn, only I could not. I knew better. No one noticed it but me. No one ever noticed it except Stephen Kaluna, and I did not know that till afterward. But I saw it coming, the whole damnable, unnamable awfulness of it; but I refused to think about the future. I was afraid. I could not. And of nights I cried over it.

"He was my friend. We fished sharks on Niihau together. We hunted wild cattle on Mauna Kea and Mauna Loa. We broke horses and branded steers on the Carter Ranch. We hunted goats through Haleakala. He taught me diving and surfing until I was nearly as clever as he, and he was cleverer than the average Kanaka. I have seen him dive in fifteen fathoms, and he could stay down two minutes. He was an amphibian and a mountaineer. He could climb wherever a goat dared climb. He was afraid of nothing. He was on the wrecked *Luga,* and he swam thirty miles in thirty-six hours in a heavy sea. He could fight his way out through breaking combers that would batter you and me to a jelly. He was a great, glorious man-god. We went through the Revolution together. We were both romantic loyalists. He was shot twice and sentenced to death. But he was too great a man for the republicans to kill. He laughed at them. Later, they gave him honor and made him sheriff of Kona. He was a simple man, a boy that never grew up. His was no intricate brain pattern. He had no twists nor quirks in his mental processes. He went straight to the point, and his points were always simple.

"And he was sanguine. Never have I known so confident a man, nor a man so satisfied and happy. He did not ask anything from life. There was nothing left to be desired. For him life had no arrears. He had been paid in full, cash down, and in advance. What more could he possibly desire than that magnificent body, that iron constitution, that immunity from all ordinary ills, and that lowly wholesomeness of soul? Physically he was perfect. He had never been sick in his life. He did not know what a headache was. When I was so afflicted he used to look at me in wonder, and make me laugh with his clumsy attempts at sympathy. He did not understand such a thing as a headache. He could not understand. Sanguine? No wonder. How could he be otherwise with that tremendous vitality and incredible health?

"Just to show you what faith he had in his glorious star, and, also, what sanction he had for that faith. He was a youngster at the time—I had just met him—when he went into a poker game at Wailuku. There was a big German in it, Schultz his name was, and he played a brutal, domineering game. He had had a run of luck as well, and he was quite insufferable, when Lyte Gregory dropped in and took a hand. The very first hand it was Schultz's blind. Lyte came in, as well as the others, and Schultz raised them out—all except Lyte. He did not like the German's tone, and he raised him back.

Schultz raised in turn, and in turn Lyte raised Schultz. So they went, back and forth. The stakes were big. And do you know what Lyte held? A pair of kings and three little clubs. It wasn't poker. Lyte wasn't playing poker. He was playing his optimism. He didn't know what Schultz held, but he raised and raised until he made Schultz squeal, and Schultz held three aces all the time. Think of it! A man with a pair of kings compelling three aces to see before the draw!

"Well, Schultz called for two cards. Another German was dealing, Schultz's friend at that. Lyte knew then that he was up against three of a kind. Now what did he do? What would you have done? Drawn three cards and held up the kings, of course. Not Lyte, he was playing optimism. He threw the kings away, held up the three little clubs, and drew two cards. He never looked at them. He looked across at Schultz to bet, and Schultz did bet, big. Since he himself held three aces he knew he had Lyte, because he played Lyte for threes, and, necessarily, they would have to be smaller threes. Poor Schultz! He was perfectly correct under the premises. His mistake was that he thought Lyte was playing poker. They bet back and forth for five minutes, until Schultz's certainty began to ooze out. And all the time Lyte had never looked at his two cards, and Schultz knew it. I could see Schultz think, and revive, and splurge with his bets again. But the strain was too much for him.

" 'Hold on, Gregory,' he said at last. 'I've got you beaten from the start. I don't want any of your money. I've got—'

" 'Never mind what you've got,' Lyte interrupted. 'You don't know what I've got. I guess I'll take a look.'

"He looked, and raised the German a hundred dollars. Then they went at it again, back and forth and back and forth, until Schultz weakened and called, and laid down his three aces. Lyte faced his five cards. They were all black. He had drawn two more clubs. Do you know, he just about broke Schultz's nerve as a poker player. He never played in the same form again. He lacked confidence after that, and was a bit wobbly.

" 'But how could you do it?' I asked Lyte afterward. 'You knew he had you beaten when he drew two cards. Besides, you never looked at your own draw.'

" 'I didn't have to look,' was Lyte's answer. 'I knew they were two clubs all the time. They just had to be two clubs. Do you think

I was going to let that big Dutchman beat me? It was impossible that he should beat me. It is not my way to be beaten. I just have to win. Why, I'd have been the most surprised man in this world if they hadn't been all clubs.'

"That was Lyte's way, and maybe it will help you to appreciate his colossal optimism. As he put it, he just had to succeed, to fare well, to prosper. And in that same incident, as in ten thousand others, he found his sanction. The thing was that he did succeed, did prosper. That was why he was afraid of nothing. Nothing could ever happen to him. He knew it, because nothing had ever happened to him. That time the *Luga* was lost and he swam thirty miles, he was in the water two whole nights and a day. And during all that terrible stretch of time he never lost hope once, never once doubted the outcome. He just knew he was going to make the land. He told me so himself, and I know it was the truth.

"Well, that is the kind of a man Lyte Gregory was. He was of a different race from ordinary, ailing mortals. He was a lordly being, untouched by common ills and misfortunes. Whatever he wanted he got. He won his wife—one of the Caruthers, a little beauty—from a dozen rivals. And she settled down and made him the finest wife in the world. He wanted a boy. He got it. He wanted a girl and another boy. He got them. And they were just right, without spot or blemish, with chests like little barrels, and with all the inheritance of his own health and strength.

"And then it happened. The mark of the beast was laid upon him. I watched it for a year. It broke my heart. But he did not know it, nor did anybody else guess it except that cursed hapa-haole, Stephen Kaluna. He knew it, but I did not know that he did. And—yes—Doc Strowbridge knew it. He was the federal physician, and he had developed the leper eye. You see, part of his business was to examine suspects and order them to the receiving station at Honolulu. And Stephen Kaluna had developed the leper eye. The disease ran strong in his family, and four or five of his relatives were already on Molokai.

"The trouble arose over Stephen Kaluna's sister. When she became suspect, and before Doc Strowbridge could get hold of her, her brother spirited her away to some hiding place. Lyte was sheriff of Kona, and it was his business to find her.

"We were all over at Hilo that night, in Ned Austin's. Stephen Kaluna was there when we came in, by himself, in his cups, and quarrelsome. Lyte was laughing over some joke—that huge, happy laugh of a giant boy. Kaluna spat contemptuously on the floor. Lyte noticed, so did everybody; but he ignored the fellow. Kaluna was looking for trouble. He took it as a personal grudge that Lyte was trying to apprehend his sister. In half a dozen ways he advertised his displeasure at Lyte's presence, but Lyte ignored him. I imagined Lyte was a bit sorry for him, for the hardest duty of his office was the apprehension of lepers. It is not a nice thing to go into a man's house and tear away a father, mother, or child, who has done no wrong, and to send such a one to perpetual banishment on Molokai. Of course, it is necessary as a protection to society, and Lyte, I do believe, would have been the first to apprehend his own father did he become suspect.

"Finally, Kaluna blurted out: 'Look here, Gregory, you think you're going to find Kalaniweo, but you're not.'

"Kalaniweo was his sister. Lyte glanced at him when his name was called, but he made no answer. Kaluna was furious. He was working himself up all the time.

"'I'll tell you one thing,' he shouted. 'You'll be on Molokai yourself before ever you get Kalaniweo there. I'll tell you what you are. You've no right to be in the company of honest men. You've made a terrible fuss talking about your duty, haven't you? You've sent many lepers to Molokai, and knowing all the time you belonged there yourself.'

"I'd seen Lyte angry more than once, but never quite so angry as at that moment. Leprosy with us, you know, is not a thing to jest about. He made one leap across the floor, dragging Kaluna out of his chair with a clutch on his neck. He shook him back and forth savagely, till you could hear the half-caste's teeth rattling.

"'What do you mean?' Lyte was demanding. 'Spit it out, man, or I'll choke it out of you!'

"You know, in the West there is a certain phrase that a man must smile while uttering. So with us of the islands, only our phrase is related to leprosy. No matter what Kaluna was, he was no coward. As soon as Lyte eased the grip on his throat he answered:

"'I'll tell you what I mean. You are a leper yourself.'

"Lyte suddenly flung the half-caste sidewise into a chair, letting him down easily enough. Then Lyte broke out into honest, hearty laughter. But he laughed alone, and when he discovered it he looked around at our faces. I had reached his side and was trying to get him to come away, but he took no notice of me. He was gazing, fascinated, at Kaluna, who was brushing at his own throat in a flurried, nervous way, as if to brush off the contamination of the fingers that had clutched him. The action was unreasoned, genuine.

"Lyte looked around at us, slowly passing from face to face.

" 'My God, fellows! My God!' he said.

"He did not speak it. It was more a hoarse whisper of fright and horror. It was fear that fluttered in his throat, and I don't think that ever in his life before he had known fear.

"Then his colossal optimism asserted itself, and he laughed again.

" 'A good joke—whoever put it up,' he said. 'The drinks are on me. I had a scare for a moment. But, fellows, don't do it again, to anybody. It's too serious. I tell you I died a thousand deaths in that moment. I thought of my wife and kids, and—'

"His voice broke, and the half-caste, still throat-brushing, drew his eyes. He was puzzled and worried.

" 'John,' he said, turning toward me.

"His jovial, rotund voice rang in my ears. But I could not answer. I was swallowing hard at that moment, and besides, I knew my face didn't look just right.

" 'John,' he called again, taking a step nearer.

"He called timidly, and of all nightmares of horrors the most frightful was to hear timidity in Lyte Gregory's voice.

" 'John, John, what does it mean?' he went on, still more timidly. 'It's a joke, isn't it? John, here's my hand. If I were a leper, would I offer you my hand? Am I a leper, John?'

"He held out his hand, and what in high heaven or hell did I care? He was my friend. I took his hand, though it cut me to the heart to see the way his face brightened.

" 'It was only a joke, Lyte,' I said. 'We fixed it up on you. But you're right. It's too serious. We won't do it again.'

"He did not laugh this time. He smiled, as a man awakened from a bad dream and still oppressed by the substance of the dream.

" 'All right, then,' he said. 'Don't do it again, and I'll stand for the drinks. But I may as well confess that you fellows had me going south for a moment. Look at the way I've been sweating.'

"He sighed and wiped the sweat from his forehead as he started to step toward the bar.

" 'It is no joke,' Kaluna said abruptly.

"I looked murder at him, and I felt murder, too. But I dared not speak or strike. That would have preciptated the catastrophe which I somehow had a mad hope of still averting.

" 'It is no joke,' Kaluna repeated. 'You are a leper, Lyte Gregory, and you've no right putting your hands on honest men's flesh—on the clean flesh of honest men.'

"Then Gregory flared up.

" 'The joke has gone far enough! Quit it! Quit it, I say, Kaluna, or I'll give you a beating!'

" 'You undergo a bacteriological examination,' Kaluna answered, 'and then you can beat me—to death, if you want to. Why, man, look at yourself there in the glass. You can see it. Anybody can see it. You're developing the lion face. See where the skin is darkened there over your eyes.'

"Lyte peered and peered, and I saw his hands trembling.

" 'I can see nothing,' he said finally, then turned on the hapahaole. 'You have a black heart, Kaluna. And I am not ashamed to say that you have given me a scare that no man has a right to give another. I take you at your word. I am going to settle this thing now. I am going straight to Doc Strowbridge. And when I come back, watch out.'

"He never looked at us, but started for the door.

" 'You wait here, John,' he said, waving me back from accompanying him.

"We stood around like a group of ghosts.

" 'It is the truth,' Kaluna said. 'You could see it for yourselves.'

"They looked at me, and I nodded. Harry Burnley lifted his glass to his lips, but lowered it untasted. He spilled half of it over the bar. His lips were trembling like a child that is about to cry. Ned Austin made a clatter in the ice chest. He wasn't looking for anything. I don't think he knew what he was doing. Nobody spoke. Harry Burnley's lips were trembling harder than ever. Suddenly, with a most horrible, malignant expression he drove his fist into

Kaluna's face. He followed it up. We made no attempt to separate them. We didn't care if he killed the half-caste. It was a terrible beating. We weren't interested. I don't even remember when Burnley ceased and let the poor devil crawl away. We were all too dazed.

"Doc Strowbridge told me about it afterward. He was working late over a report when Lyte came into his office. Lyte had already recovered his optimism, and came swinging in, a trifle angry with Kaluna, to be sure, but very certain of himself. 'What could I do?' Doc asked me. 'I knew he had it. I had seen it coming on for months. I couldn't answer him. I couldn't say Yes. I don't mind telling you I broke down and cried. He pleaded for the bacteriological test. "Snip out a piece, Doc," he said, over and over. "Snip out a piece of skin and make the test." '

"The way Doc Strowbridge cried must have convinced Lyte. The *Claudine* was leaving next morning for Honolulu. We caught him when he was going aboard. You see, he was headed for Honolulu to give himself up to the Board of Health. We could do nothing with him. He had sent too many to Molokai to hang back himself. We argued for Japan. But he wouldn't hear of it. 'I've got to take my medicine, fellows,' was all he would say, and he said it over and over. He was obsessed with the idea.

"He wound up all his affairs from the Receiving Station at Honolulu, and went down to Molokai. He didn't get on well there. The resident physician wrote us that he was a shadow of his old self. You see, he was grieving about his wife and the kids. He knew we were taking care of them, but it hurt him just the same. After six months or so I went down to Molokai. I sat on one side of a plate-glass window, and he on the other. We looked at each other through the glass, and talked through what might be called a speaking tube. But it was hopeless. He had made up his mind to remain. Four mortal hours I argued. I was exhausted at the end. My steamer was whistling for me, too.

"But we couldn't stand for it. Three months later we chartered the schooner *Halcyon*. She was an opium smuggler, and she sailed like a witch. Her master was a squarehead who would do anything for money, and we made a charter to China worth his while. He sailed from San Francisco, and a few days later we took out Landhouse's sloop for a cruise. She was only a five-ton yacht, but we slammed her fifty miles to windward into the northeast trade. Seasick? I never suffered so in my life. Out of sight of land we picked up the *Halcyon,* and Burnley and I went aboard.

"We ran down to Molokai, arriving about eleven at night. The schooner hove to and we landed through the surf in a whaleboat at Kalawao—the place, you know, where Father Damien died. That squarehead was game. With a couple of revolvers strapped on him he came right along. The three of us crossed the peninsula to Kalaupapa, something like two miles. Just imagine hunting in the dead of night for a man in a settlement of over a thousand lepers. You see, if the alarm was given, it was all off with us. It was strange ground, and pitch dark. The lepers' dogs came out and bayed at us, and we stumbled around till we got lost.

"The squarehead solved it. He led the way into the first detached house. We shut the door after us and struck a light. There were six lepers. We routed them up, and I talked in native. What I wanted was a kokua. A kokua is, literally, a helper, a native who is clean that lives in the settlement and is paid by the Board of Health to nurse the lepers, dress their sores, and such things. We stayed in the house to keep track of the inmates, while the squarehead led one of them off to find a kokua. He got him, and he brought him along at the point of his revolver. But the kokua was all right. While the squarehead guarded the house, Burnley and I were guided by the kokua to Lyte's house. He was all alone.

" 'I thought you fellows would come,' Lyte said. 'Don't touch me, John. How's Ned, and Charley, and all the crowd? Never mind, tell me afterward. I am ready to go now. I've had nine months of it. Where's the boat?'

"We started back for the other house to pick up the squarehead. But the alarm had got out. Lights were showing in the houses, and doors were slamming. We had agreed that there was to be no shooting unless absolutely necessary, and when we were halted we went at it with our fists and the butts of our revolvers. I found myself tangled up with a big man. I couldn't keep him off me, though twice I smashed him fairly in the face with my fist. He grappled with me, and we went down, rolling and scrambling and struggling for grips. He was getting away with me when someone came running up with a lantern. Then I saw his face. How shall I describe the horror of it!

It was not a face—only wasted or wasting features—a living ravage, noseless, lipless, with one ear swollen and distorted, hanging down to the shoulder. I was frantic. In a clinch he hugged me close to him until that ear flapped in my face. Then I guess I went insane. It was too terrible. I began striking him with my revolver. How it happened I don't know, but just as I was getting clear he fastened upon me with his teeth. The whole side of my hand was in that lipless mouth. Then I struck him with the revolver butt squarely between the eyes, and his teeth relaxed."

Cudworth held his hand to me in the moonlight, and I could see the scars. It looked as if it had been mangled by a dog.

"Weren't you afraid?" I asked.

"I was. Seven years I waited. You know, it takes that long for the disease to incubate. Here in Kona I waited, and it did not come. But there was never a day of those seven years, and never a night, that I did not look out on . . . on all this. . . ." His voice broke as he swept his eyes from the moonbathed sea beneath to the snowy summits above. "I could not bear to think of losing it, of never again beholding Kona. Seven years! I stayed clean. But that is why I am single. I was engaged. I could not dare to marry while I was in doubt. She did not understand. She went away to the States, and married. I have never seen her since.

"Just at the moment I got free of the leper policeman there was a rush and clatter of hoofs like a cavalry charge. It was the squarehead. He had been afraid of a rumpus and he had improved his time by making those blessed lepers he was guarding saddle up four horses. We were ready for him. Lyte had accounted for three kokuas, and between us we untangled Burnley from a couple more. The whole settlement was in an uproar by that time, and as we dashed away somebody opened up on us with a Winchester. It must have been Jack McVeigh, the superintendent of Molokai.

"That was a ride! Leper horses, leper saddles, leper bridles, pitch-black darkness, whistling bullets, and a road none of the best. And the squarehead's horse was a mule, and he didn't know how to ride, either. But we made the whaleboat, and as we shoved off through the surf we could hear the horses coming down the hill from Kalaupapa.

"You're going to Shanghai. You look Lyte Gregory up. He is

employed in a German firm there. Take him out to dinner. Open up wine. Give him everything of the best, but don't let him pay for anything. Send the bill to me. His wife and the kids are in Honolulu, and he needs the money for them. I know. He sends most of his salary, and lives like an anchorite. And tell him about Kona. There's where his heart is. Tell him all you can about Kona."

Jack London

The House of the Sun

"They don't know what they've got!" Jack London exclaimed about the American people when he and his wife first visited the Islands in 1907. One marvel of nature that they found especially exciting (it may be reached in a few hours by air today) was the gigantic crater of Haleakala, through which London's party traveled wtih pack horses for several days. Emerging at the Kaupo Gap, they took the perilous trail from Hana across the north side of Maui through the torrential Nahiku Ditch country, crossing precipitous gorges on narrow wooden flumes.

Nowadays, the view from the ten-thousand-foot rim of Haleakala is enjoyed by about one hundred thousand tourists every year. Few, however, spend days camping among its cinder cones, and no one has better described this experience than did Jack London some sixty years ago.

THERE are hosts of people who journey like restless spirits round and about this earth in search of seascapes and landscapes and the wonders and beauties of nature. They overrun Europe in armies; they can be met in droves and herds in Florida and the West Indies, at the pyramids, and on the slopes and summits of the Canadian and American Rockies; but in the House of the Sun they are as rare as live and wriggling dinosaurs. Haleakala is the Hawaiian name for "the House of the Sun." It is a noble dwelling situated on the island of Maui; but so few tourists have ever peeped into it, much less entered it, that their number may be practically reckoned as zero. Yet I venture to state that for natural beauty and wonder the nature lover may see dissimilar things as great as Haleakala, but no greater, while he will never see elsewhere anything more beautiful or wonderful. Honolulu is six days' steaming from San Francisco; Maui is a night's run on the steamer from Honolulu, and six hours more, if he is in a hurry, can bring the traveler to Kolikoli, which is ten thousand and thirty-two feet above the sea and which stands hard by the entrance portal to the House of the Sun. Yet the tourist comes not, and Haleakala sleeps on in lonely and unseen grandeur.

Not being tourists, we of the *Snark* went to Haleakala. On the slopes of that monster mountain there is a cattle ranch of some fifty thousand acres, where we spent the night at an altitude of two thousand feet. The next morning it was boots and saddles, and with cowboys and pack horses we climbed to Ukulele, a mountain ranch house, the altitude of which, fifty-five hundred feet, gives a severely temperate climate, compelling blankets at night and a roaring fireplace in the living room. Ukulele, by the way, is the Hawaiian for "jumping flea," as it is also the Hawaiian for a certain musical instrument that may be likened to a young guitar. It is my opinion that the mountain ranch house was named after the young guitar. We were not in a hurry, and we spent the day at Ukulele, learnedly discussing altitudes and barometers and shaking our particular barometer whenever anyone's argument stood in need of demonstration. Our barometer was the most graciously acquiescent instrument I have ever seen. Also, we gathered mountain raspberries, large as hen's eggs and larger, gazed up the pasture-covered lava slopes to the summit of Haleakala, forty-five hundred feet above us, and looked down upon a mighty battle of the clouds that was being fought beneath us, ourselves in the bright sunshine.

Every day and every day this unending battle goes on. Ukiukiu is the name of the trade wind that comes raging down out of the northeast and hurls itself upon Haleakala. Now Haleakala is so bulky and tall that it turns the northeast trade wind aside on either hand, so that in the lee of Haleakala no trade wind blows at all. On the contrary, the wind blows in the counter direction, in the teeth of the northeast trade. This wind is called Naulu. And day and night and always Ukiukiu and Naulu strive with each other, advancing, retreating, flanking, curving, curling, and turning and twisting, the conflict made visible by the cloud masses plucked from the heavens and hurled back and forth in squadrons, battalions, armies, and great mountain ranges. Once in a while, Ukiukiu, in mighty gusts, flings immense cloud masses clear over the summit of Haleakala;

whereupon Naulu craftily captures them, lines them up in new battle formation, and with them smites back at his ancient and eternal antagonist. Then Ukiukiu sends a great cloud army around the eastern side of the mountain. It is a flanking movement, well executed. But Naulu, from his lair on the leeward side, gathers the flanking army in, pulling and twisting and dragging it, hammering it into shape, and sends it charging back against Ukiukiu around the western side of the mountain. And all the while, above and below the main battlefield, high up the slopes toward the sea, Ukiukiu and Naulu are continually sending out little wisps of cloud, in ragged skirmish line, that creep and crawl over the ground, among the trees and through the canyons, and that spring upon and capture one another in sudden ambuscades and sorties. And sometimes Ukiukiu or Naulu, abruptly sending out a heavy charging column, captures the ragged little skirmishers or drives them skyward, turning over and over, in vertical whirls, thousands of feet in the air.

But it is on the western slopes of Haleakala that the main battle goes on. Here Naulu masses his heaviest formation and wins his greatest victories. Ukiukiu grows weak toward late afternoon, which is the way of all trade winds, and is driven backward by Naulu. Naulu's generalship is excellent. All day he has been gathering and packing away immense reserves. As the afternoon draws on, he welds them into a solid column, sharp-pointed, miles in length, a mile in width, and hundreds of feet thick. This column he slowly thrusts forward into the broad battle front of Ukiukiu, and slowly and surely Ukiukiu, weakening fast, is split asunder. But it is not all bloodless. At times Ukiukiu struggles wildly, and with fresh accessions of strength from the limitless northeast smashes away half a mile at a time at Naulu's column and sweeps it off and away toward West Maui. Sometimes, when the two charging armies meet end-on, a tremendous perpendicular whirl results, the cloud masses, locked together, mounting thousands of feet into the air and turning over and over. A favorite device of Ukiukiu is to send a low, squat formation, densely packed, forward along the ground and under Naulu. When Ukiukiu is under, he proceeds to buck. Naulu's mighty middle gives to the blow and bends upward, but usually he turns the attacking column back upon itself and sets it milling. And all the while the ragged little skirmishers, stray and detached, sneak through the trees and canyons, crawl along and through the grass, and surprise one another with unexpected leaps and rushes; while above, far above, serene and lonely in the rays of the setting sun, Haleakala looks down upon the conflict. And so, the night. But in the morning, after the fashion of trade winds, Ukiukiu gathers strength and sends the hosts of Naulu rolling back in confusion and rout. And one day is like another day in the battle of the clouds, where Ukiukiu and Naulu strive eternally on the slopes of Haleakala.

Again in the morning, it was boots and saddles, cowboys and pack horses, and the climb to the top began. One pack horse carried twenty gallons of water, slung in five-gallon bags on either side; for water is precious and rare in the crater itself, in spite of the fact that several miles to the north and east of the crater rim more rain comes down than in any other place in the world. The way led upward across countless lava flows, without regard for trails, and never have I seen horses with such perfect footing as that of the thirteen that composed our outfit. They climbed or dropped down perpendicular places with the sureness and coolness of mountain goats, and never a horse fell or balked.

There is a familiar and strange illusion experienced by all who climb isolated mountains. The higher one climbs, the more of the earth's surface becomes visible, and the effect of this is that the horizon seems uphill from the observer. This illusion is especially notable on Haleakala, for the old volcano rises directly from the sea, without buttresses or connecting ranges. In consequence, as fast as we climbed up the grim slope of Haleakala, still faster did Haleakala, ourselves, and all about us sink down into the center of what appeared a profound abyss. Everywhere, far above us, towered the horizon. The ocean sloped down from the horizon to us. The higher we climbed, the deeper did we seem to sink down, the farther above us shone the horizon, and the steeper pitched the grade up to that horizontal line where sky and ocean met. It was weird and unreal, and vagrant thoughts of Simm's Hole and of the volcano through which Jules Verne journeyed to the center of the earth flitted through one's mind.

And then, when at last we reached the summit of that monster mountain, which summit was like the bottom of an inverted cone situated in the center of an awful cosmic pit, we found that we were at neither top nor bottom. Far above us was the heaven-towering horizon, and far beneath us, where the top of the mountain should have been, was a deeper deep, the great crater, the House of the Sun. Twenty-three miles around stretched the dizzy walls of the crater. We stood on the edge of the nearly vertical western wall, and the floor of the crater lay nearly half a mile beneath. This floor, broken by lava flows and cinder cones, was as red and fresh and uneroded as if it were but yesterday that the fires went out. The cinder cones, the smallest over four hundred feet in height and the largest over nine hundred, seemed no more than puny little sand hills, so mighty was the magnitude of the setting. Two gaps, thousands of feet deep, broke the rim of the crater, and through these Ukiukiu vainly strove to drive his fleecy herds of trade-wind clouds. As fast as they advanced through the gaps, the heat of the crater dissipated them into thin air, and though they advanced always, they got nowhere.

It was a scene of vast bleakness and desolation, stern, forbidding, fascinating. We gazed down upon a place of fire and earthquake. The tie-ribs of earth lay bare before us. It was a workshop of nature still cluttered with the raw beginnings of world-making. Here and there great dikes of primordial rock had thrust themselves up from the bowels of earth, straight through the molten surface ferment that had evidently cooled only the other day. It was all unreal and unbelievable. Looking upward, far above us (in reality beneath us) floated the cloud battle of Ukiukiu and Naulu. And higher up the slope of the seeming abyss, above the cloud battle, in the air and sky, hung the islands of Lanai and Molokai. Across the crater, to the southeast, still apparently looking upward, we saw ascending, first, the turquoise sea, then the white surf line of the shore of Hawaii; above that the belt of trade clouds, and next, eighty miles away, rearing their stupendous bulks out of the azure sky, tipped with snow, wreathed with cloud, trembling like a mirage, the peaks of Mauna Kea and Mauna Loa hung poised on the wall of heaven.

It is told that long ago, one Maui, the son of Hina, lived on what is now known as West Maui. His mother, Hina, employed her time in the making of kapas. She must have made them at night, for her days were occupied in trying to dry the kapas. Each morning, and all morning, she toiled at spreading them out in the sun. But no sooner were they out than she began taking them in, in order to have them all under shelter for the night. For know that the days were shorter then than now. Maui watched his mother's futile toil and felt sorry for her. He decided to do something—oh, no, not to help her hang out and take in the kapas. He was too clever for that. His idea was to make the sun go slower. Perhaps he was the first Hawaiian astronomer. At any rate, he took a series of observations of the sun from various parts of the island. His conclusion was that the sun's path was directly across Haleakala. Unlike Joshua, he stood in no need of divine assistance. He gathered a huge quantity of coconuts, from the fiber of which he braided a stout cord, and in one end of which he made a noose, even as the cowboys of Haleakala do to this day. Next he climbed into the House of the Sun and laid in wait. When the sun came tearing along the path, bent on completing its journey in the shortest time possible, the valiant youth threw his lariat around one of the sun's largest and strongest beams. He made the sun slow down some; also, he broke the beam short off. And he kept on roping and breaking off beams till the sun said it was willing to listen to reason. Maui set forth his terms of peace, which the sun accepted, agreeing to go more slowly thereafter. Wherefore Hina had ample time in which to dry her kapas, and the days are longer than they used to be, which last is quite in accord with the teachings of modern astronomy.

We had a lunch of jerked beef and hard poi in a stone corral, used of old time for the night impounding of cattle being driven across the island. Then we skirted the rim for half a mile and began the descent into the crater. Twenty-five hundred feet beneath lay the floor, and down a steep slope of loose volcanic cinders we dropped, the sure-footed horses slipping and sliding, but always keeping their feet. The black surface of the cinders, when broken by the horses' hoofs, turned to a yellow ocher dust, virulent in appearance and acid of taste, that arose in clouds. There was a gallop across a level stretch to the mouth of a convenient blowhole, and then the descent continued in clouds of volcanic dust, winding in and out among cinder cones, brick-red, old rose, and purplish black of color. Above us, higher and higher, towered the crater walls, while we journeyed on across innumerable lava flows, turning and twisting a devious way among the adamantine billows of a petrified sea.

Saw-toothed waves of lava vexed the surface of this weird ocean, while on either hand rose jagged crests and spiracles of fantastic shape. Our way led on past a bottomless pit and along and over the main stream of the latest lava flow for seven miles.

At the lower end of the crater was our camping spot, in a small grove of olapa and kolea trees, tucked away in a corner of the crater at the base of walls that rose perpendicularly fifteen hundred feet. Here was pasturage for the horses, but no water, and first we turned aside and picked our way across a mile of lava to a known water hole in a crevice in the crater wall. The water hole was empty. But on climbing fifty feet up the crevice, a pool was found containing half a dozen barrels of water. A pail was carried up, and soon a steady stream of the precious liquid was running down the rock and filling the lower pool, while the cowboys below were busy fighting the horses back, for there was room for one only to drink at a time. Then it was on to camp at the foot of the wall, up which herds of wild goats scrambled and blatted, while the tent rose to the sound of rifle firing. Jerked beef, hard poi, and broiled kid was the menu. Over the crest of the crater, just above our heads, rolled a sea of clouds, driven on by Ukiukiu. Though this sea rolled over the crest unceasingly, it never blotted out nor dimmed the moon, for the heat of the crater dissolved the clouds as fast as they rolled in. Through the moonlight, attracted by the camp fire, came the crater cattle to peer and challenge. They were rolling fat, though they rarely drank water, the morning dew on the grass taking its place. It was because of this dew that the tent made a welcome bedchamber, and we fell asleep to the chanting of hulas by the unwearied Hawaiian cowboys, in whose veins, no doubt, ran the blood of Maui, their valiant forebear.

The camera cannot do justice to the House of the Sun. The sublimated chemistry of photography may not lie, but it certainly does not tell all the truth. The Koolau Gap [may be] faithfully reproduced, just as it impinged on the retina of the camera, yet in the resulting picture the gigantic scale of things is missing. Those walls that seem several hundred feet in height are almost as many thousand; that entering wedge of cloud is a mile and a half wide in the gap itself, while beyond the gap it is a veritable ocean; and that foreground of cinder cone and volcanic ash, mushy and colorless in appearance, is in truth gorgeous-hued in brick-red, terra cotta, rose, yellow, ocher, and purplish black. Also, words are a vain thing and drive to despair. To say that a crater wall is two thousand feet high is to say just precisely that it is two thousand feet high; but there is a vast deal more to that crater wall than a mere statistic. The sun is ninety-three million miles distant, but to mortal conception the adjoining county is farther away. This frailty of the human brain is hard on the sun. It is likewise hard on the House of the Sun. Haleakala has a message of beauty and wonder for the human soul that cannot be delivered by proxy. Kolikoli is six hours from Kahului; Kahului is a night's run from Honolulu; Honolulu is six days from San Francisco; and there you are.

We climbed the crater walls, put the horses over impossible places, rolled stones, and shot wild goats. I did not get any goats. I was too busy rolling stones. One spot in particular I remember, where we started a stone the size of a horse. It began the descent easy enough, rolling over, wobbling, and threatening to stop; but in a few minutes it was soaring through the air two hundred feet at a jump. It grew rapidly smaller until it struck a slight slope of volcanic sand, over which it darted like a startled jack rabbit, kicking up behind it a tiny trail of yellow dust. Stone and dust diminished in size, until some of the party said the stone had stopped. That was because they could not see it any longer. It had vanished into the distance beyond their ken. Others saw it rolling farther on—I know I did; and it is my firm conviction that that stone is still rolling.

Our last day in the crater, Ukiukiu gave us a taste of his strength. He smashed Naulu back all along the line, filled the House of the Sun to overflowing with clouds, and drowned us out. Our rain gauge was a pint cup under a tiny hole in the tent. That last night of storm and rain filled the cup, and there was no way of measuring the water that spilled over into the blankets. With the rain gauge out of business there was no longer any reason for remaining; so we broke camp in the wet-gray of dawn and plunged eastward across the lava to the Kaupo Gap. East Maui is nothing more or less than the vast lava stream that flowed long ago through the Kaupo Gap; and down this stream we picked our way from an altitude of six thousand five hundred feet to the sea. This was a day's work in itself for the horses; but never were there such horses. Safe in the bad places, never rushing, never losing their heads, as soon as they found a trail wide and smooth enough to run on, they ran. There was no stopping them until the trail became bad again, and then they stopped of themselves. Continuously, for days, they had performed the hardest kind of work, and fed most of the time on grass foraged by themselves at night while we slept, and yet that day they covered twenty-eight leg-breaking miles and galloped into Hana like a bunch of colts. Also, there were several of them, reared in the dry region on the leeward side of Haleakala, that had never worn shoes in all their lives. Day after day, and all day long, unshod, they had traveled over the sharp lava, with the extra weight of a man on their backs, and their hoofs were in better condition than those of the shod horses.

The scenery between Vieiras's (where the Kaupo Gap empties into the sea) and Hana, which we covered in half a day, is well worth a week or a month; but, wildly beautiful as it is, it becomes pale and small in comparison with the wonderland that lies beyond the rubber plantations between Hana and the Honomanu Gulch. Two days were required to cover this marvelous stretch, which lies on the windward side of Haleakala. The people who dwell there call it "the ditch country," an unprepossessing name, but it has no other. Nobody else ever comes there. Nobody else knows anything about it. With the exception of a handful of men, whom business has brought there, nobody has heard of the ditch country of Maui. Now a ditch is a ditch, assumably muddy, and usually traversing uninteresting and monotonous landscapes. But the Nahiku Ditch is not an ordinary ditch. The windward side of Haleakala is serried by a thousand precipitous gorges, down which rush as many torrents, each torrent of which achieves a score of cascades and waterfalls before it reaches the sea. More rain comes down here than in any other region in the world. In 1904 the year's downpour was four hundred and twenty inches. Water means sugar, and sugar is the backbone of the territory of Hawaii, wherefore the Nahiku Ditch, which is not a ditch, but a chain of tunnels. The water travels underground, appearing only at intervals to leap a gorge, traveling high in the air on a giddy flume and plunging into and through the opposing mountain. This magnificent waterway is called a "ditch," and with equal appropriateness can Cleopatra's barge be called a boxcar.

The House of the Sun

There are no carriage roads through the ditch country, and before the ditch was built, or bored, rather, there was no horse trail. Hundreds of inches of rain annually, on fertile soil, under a tropic sun, means a steaming jungle of vegetation. A man, on foot, cutting his way through, might advance a mile a day, but at the end of a week he would be a wreck, and he would have to crawl hastily back if he wanted to get out before the vegetation overran the passageway he had cut. O'Shaughnessy was the daring engineer who conquered the jungle and the gorges, ran the ditch, and made the horse trail. He built enduringly, in concrete and masonry, and made one of the most remarkable water farms in the world. Every little runlet and dribble is harvested and conveyed by subterranean channels to the main ditch. But so heavily does it rain at times that countless spillways let the surplus escape to the sea.

The horse trail is not very wide. Like the engineer who built it, it dares anything. Where the ditch plunges through the mountain, it climbs over; and where the ditch leaps a gorge on a flume, the horse trail takes advantage of the ditch and crosses on top of the flume. That careless trail thinks nothing of traveling up or down the faces of precipices. It gouges its narrow way out of the wall, dodging around waterfalls or passing under them where they thunder down in white fury; while straight overhead the wall rises hundreds of feet, and straight beneath it sinks a thousand. And those marvelous mountain horses are as unconcerned as the trail. They fox-trot along it as a matter of course, though the footing is slippery with rain, and they will gallop with their hind feet slipping over the edge if you let them. I advise only those with steady nerves and cool heads to tackle the Nahiku Ditch trail. One of our cowboys was noted as the strongest and bravest on the big ranch. He had ridden mountain horses all his life on the rugged western slopes of Haleakala. He was first in the horse breaking; and when the others hung back, as a matter of course, he would go in to meet a wild bull in the cattle pen. He had a reputation. But he had never ridden over the Nahiku Ditch. It was there he lost his reputation. When he faced the first flume, spanning a hair-raising gorge, narrow, without railings, with a bellowing waterfall above, another below, and directly beneath a wild cascade, the air filled with driving spray and rocking to the clamor and rush of sound and motion—well, that cowboy dismounted from his horse, explained briefly that he had a wife and two children, and crossed over on foot, leading the horse behind him.

The only relief from the flumes was the precipices; and the only relief from the precipices was the flumes, except where the ditch was far underground, in which case we crossed one horse and rider at a time, on primitive log bridges that swayed and teetered and threatened to carry away. I confess that at first I rode such places with my feet loose in the stirrups, and that on the sheer walls I saw to it, by a definite, conscious act of will, that the foot in the outside stirrup, overhanging the thousand feet of fall, was exceedingly loose. I say "at first"; for, as in the crater itself we quickly lost our conception of magnitude, so, on the Nahiku Ditch, we quickly lost our apprehension of depth. The ceaseless iteration of height and depth produced a state of consciousness in which height and depth were accepted as the ordinary conditions of existence; and from the horse's back to look sheer down four hundred or five hundred feet became quite commonplace and nonproductive of thrills. And as carelessly as the trail and the horses, we swung along the dizzy heights and ducked around or through the waterfalls.

And such a ride! Falling water was everywhere. We rode above the clouds, under the clouds, and through the clouds! and every now and then a shaft of sunshine penetrated like a searchlight to the depths yawning beneath us, or flashed upon some pinnacle of the crater rim thousands of feet above. At every turn of the trail a waterfall or a dozen waterfalls, leaping hundreds of feet through the air, burst upon our vision. At our first night's camp, in the Keanae Gulch, we counted thirty-two waterfalls from a single viewpoint. The vegetation ran riot over that wild land. There were forests of koa and kolea trees, and candlenut trees; and then there were the trees called ohia-ai, which bore red mountain apples, mellow and juicy and most excellent to eat. Wild bananas grew everywhere, clinging to the sides of the gorges, and, overborne by their great bunches of ripe fruit, falling across the trail and blocking the way. And over the forest surged a sea of green life, the climbers of a thousand varieties, some that floated airily, in lacelike filaments, from the tallest branches; others that coiled and wound about the trees like huge serpents; and one, the ie-ie, that was for all the world like a climbing palm, swinging on a thick stem from branch to branch and tree to tree and throttling the supports whereby it climbed. Through the sea of green, lofty tree ferns thrust their great delicate fronds, and the lehua flaunted its scarlet blossoms. Underneath the climbers, in no less profusion, grew the warm-colored, strangely marked plants that in the United States one is accustomed to seeing preciously conserved in hothouses. In fact, the ditch country of Maui is nothing more nor less than a huge conservatory. Every familiar variety of fern flourishes, and more varieties that are unfamiliar, from the tiniest maidenhair to the gross and voracious staghorn, the latter the terror of the woodsmen, interlacing with itself in tangled masses five or six feet deep and covering acres.

Never was there such a ride. For two days it lasted, when we emerged into rolling country, and, along an actual wagon road, came home to the ranch at a gallop. I know it was cruel to gallop the horses after such a long, hard journey; but we blistered our hands in vain effort to hold them in. That's the sort of horses they grow on Haleakala. At the ranch there was a great festival of cattle driving, branding, and horse breaking. Overhead Ukiukiu and Naulu battled valiantly, and far above, in the sunshine, towered the mighty summit of Haleakala.

Clifford Gessler

Kauai and the "Wettest Spot"

Born in 1893 in Wisconsin, Clifford Gessler earned an M.A. degree at the University of Wisconsin and for a time taught in high school. Entering newspaper work, he came to Hawaii and from 1924 to 1934 was literary editor of the Honolulu *Star-Bulletin*. He accompanied the Mangarevan Expedition of the Bernice P. Bishop Museum in 1934, sailing on the ninety-foot sampan *Islander* throughout southeastern Polynesia, a journey which resulted in his book *Road My Body Goes* (1937). For many years after 1937 he was on the staff of the Oakland, California, *Tribune*. In addition to a number of appearances in magazines, his work includes two collections of verse, *Kanaka Moon* (1927) and *Tropic Earth* (1944) and three volumes of prose about the Pacific region: *Hawaii, Isles of Enchantment* (1937); *Tropic Landfall: The Port of Honolulu* (1942); and *The Leaning Wind* (1943). One of his best pieces of prose is his description of a visit to the "Garden Island" of Kauai.

KAUAI, from the sea, is green and rose, the bright volcanic earth showing through the rich vegetation which has caused its inhabitants to claim for it the name given to an unidentified island somewhere in these seas by an early Spanish navigator: the Garden Island.

At nearer view, it is a maze of worn peaks, striped canyons, and gulches cutting long low fields rippling with cane, and tree-dotted upland pastures sloping to the misty mass of the great central mountain, Waialeale, long thought to be the wettest place on earth. On a slippery trail, high on that spongy dome, stands a government rain gauge, which by official measurement proclaims it second in rainfall only to one spot in the known world.

Yet the whole island does not share without labor the gift of the rain god. Kauai sugar planters, like those of other islands, have built vast irrigation works, as their predecessors the Hawaiians and the still earlier menehune did, on a smaller scale, before them. And a few miles from that boggy mountaintop the Barking Sands lie all but rainless beneath the sun.

Few even of island residents have trodden the upper forests of Waialeale. That great wet roof, only a few miles from motor roads and electric power and the sugar fields that live by its waters, remains virtually unexplored—a legendary place, populated, according to report, by wild swine, equally fierce wild cattle, and survivors of bright birds from whose feathers Hawaiians of old made helmets and mantles for their chiefs.

There, too, is the reputed haunt of the last of the menehune, fabulous dwarfish race said by Hawaiians to have once occupied all the islands. The coasts are dotted with stone fishponds and inland valleys with ditches and trails attributed to their architectural skill.

Science, disentangling the maze of myth, has concluded tentatively that the menehune actually existed, though not as small in size or equipped with such supernatural powers as the legends assert. It identifies them, like the Little People of Ireland and the elves and goblins of the European continent, with an early group of settlers—the first wave of Polynesian migration, overwhelmed by the twelfth-century invasion from the south. Their simpler social organization, lower grade of culture, and slighter physique have been exaggerated by legend to make the myth of the dwarfs.

Kauai seems to have been their last stronghold. From mountain retreats they ventured forth by night and at times were induced to build stoneworks for the conquerors. The tale is that they worked only at night and, if the project was not finished before dawn, left it forever uncompleted.

The last menehune probably perished, or was absorbed into the invading people, long ago, but popular report tells of strange dwarfish beings on these mountain trails, who vanish mysteriously when one seeks a nearer view. A Honolulu scientist tells of a night in one of the precipitous, rarely entered valleys that plunge from Waialeale toward the wild northwestern coast. Seeking land shells, snail-like creatures that cling to leaves and logs and rocks, he had become separated from his companions and was spending the night in a cave. He was awakened by a sound as of hammering on stone. Looking out, he saw a light flickering on the trail. Thinking his companions were seeking him, he called out. The light vanished and a listening silence flowed into the somber valley under the dark looming cliffs.

In the morning, he found new stones laid in an evident attempt to repair the trail. When he overtook his party at the end of the day, they told him they had not been near the place.

"Bootleggers," he explained to himself with a scientist's hard-headedness, "repairing the trail by night to haul contraband okolehao down the mountain from a hidden still."

But the old Hawaiian to whom he told the story smiled a knowing smile. "The menehune work only at night," he said.

There is, too, the story of a Honolulu businessman, hunting wild goats in another of those lost valleys, who awoke at night, in his camp, to hear voices speaking in an archaic Polynesian dialect—though he and his companions, in all their trip through that valley, saw no sign of present habitation nor any human face.

A trail leads, however, up the precipitous ridges into a great spongy plateau near the summit, the Alakai Swamp. Somewhere among those thickly overgrown, miry trails and fog-veiled pools is the sacred lake whither Hawaiians made the long and hazardous journey on foot to present offerings even, it is said, up to the early twentieth century.

Dr. William Alanson Bryan, who spent three weeks on the mountain and four days in the swamp, said afterward that his return to civilization from that watery jungle "has always seemed little short of the miraculous." He and his companions were never out of dense fog during the expedition.

"The thin turf which covered the quagmire," he wrote, "would tremble for yards in all directions at every step and too often would give way, plunging us hip-deep in mire."

Such is Waialeale, where an inch and a third of rain falls daily, three and a quarter feet a month, forty feet a year!

The lowlands of Kauai, like those of most of the other islands, are sealike with cane. Some lands on this rich isle have borne crops of sugar year after year without replanting, for more years than I should venture to quote. Between the fields the road, traversed at apparently reckless speed by hardy planters and laborers, winds over red earth that was the basis for one of the late Bishop Restarick's favorite stories. A Kauai man, he used to say, toured around the world. In San Francisco, on his way home, he entered a Turkish bath where the rubber immediately identified him as from Kauai, by the color of the dirt.

Along that road we crossed the mouths of canyons: Waimea, the most celebrated; Olokele and Hanapepe, less accessible but as wild and beautiful. We turned up between red-banked ditches in which water apparently flowed uphill, to look down from a rocky point into the tremendous chasm of Waimea. Great conical ridges stood like pillars, their sides tinted in blending or contrasting or delicately shaded hues; the winding distances were misty lavender; a bright ribbon of stream coiled half a mile below. Shadows of clouds painted light and dark the various reds and yellows of the cliffs. For twenty-five miles that canyon stretched before us, a vast hall sculptured by the gods. Above its battlements soared long-tailed bos'n birds, floating on air currents against the blue vault of the sky.

Lower down, the Waimea River flowed between bright-green rice fields and groves of palms. In the cliffs behind them, we knew, lay bones of ancient chiefs. Somewhere among those rock tombs, they say, remains an unfound treasure, the green feather mantle of Kauai kings. There were many red and not a few yellow feather robes but, the tale whispers, only one of green. Its value might surpass that of the "million-dollar mamo" of Kamehameha the Great in the Bishop Museum.

History stared back at us from the cliff where an arrow chiseled into the rock preserves the memory of Captain Cook's landing, and from the lichened stones of the fort built by the Russians in 1819. The thick, sloping stone walls still stood in a rough parallelogram; in an inner court was a pyramid where the flags of the czar and of Kamehameha had flown.

I knew well the drowsy country towns of Waimea and Kekaha, with their shabby Chinese stores and *saimin* restaurants, in the summer when the world was waiting for Dick Grace, Hollywood "crash" flyer, to take off from the Barking Sands for an early "trans-Pacific" flight which ended in a keawe tree on the uneven pasture honored by the name of a flying field.

The village of Mana, dozing in the sunshine a few miles away, was our headquarters, having the only telephone in miles. I would sit on the steps of the Japanese store, watching miles of cane rippling in the breeze and the Philippine woman across the way, on the veranda of her cottage, smoking a short pipe as she suckled a plump brown baby. In midafternoon the men would come in from the fields, short, sturdy Ilocanos in blue dungarees and checkered palakas, to buy cheap tobacco or those jars of preserved fish that are their delight. It was a peaceful scene, that village of neat brown cottages among the fields, with its one dusty street in which, through most of the day, the only thing moving was a slow mongrel dog. Sky smiled at earth and earth smiled back as the cane distilled rich juice from earth and sun.

We slept, when a night take-off seemed imminent, upon or rather in the sands themselves, burrowing into them to escape clouds of mosquitoes. The "barking" of the sands, which in our experience was only a faint puppylike squeak, failed to keep the flying nuisances away.

The sands, when very dry, however, produce, in response to stirring, a sound somewhat suggesting the barking of a dog. The early traveler Bates described it, when his horse trampled over the dunes, as "of distant thunder or the starting of heavy machinery." It was loud enough to startle the horse.

The dunes are perhaps a hundred feet high, a desolate stretch of country, yet with a wild charm, pricked with small shrubs and the beginnings of keawe trees. It was a sun-baked land by day, miles from a drink of water, more miles from food. We would sit in the small shade of the car while the aviator, day after day, urged his heavily loaded plane down the bumpy field, only to blow out his tires in the heated air. At last, after weeks of these attempts, the tiny plane soared. We saw it from the road, circling over the lighthouse at Kilauea, then come faltering back, its tail shaking on a cracked longiron, to fold into a tree at the edge of the field, whence the flyer and his puppy mascot emerged unscratched.

A little way beyond the sands none can pass, for the black cliffs of Na Pali rise sheer from the sea, cut by valleys accessible only from narrow beaches reached by boat, or hazardous trails out of the maze of ridges about Waialeale.

The southeast half of the island, however, is a pleasant country, rich with growing things. I watched the peacocks spread lordly tails in the formal Japanese gardens of Kukuiolono Park, and swam in the tall swells that ride into Lawai cove between lava rocks, curling upon a beach beneath lofty palms. Near by, the Spouting Horn, a salt-water geyser similar to the Oahu Blowhole, waved its plume of spray high in the salty air. And in the little harbor of Kukuiula the blue-hulled sampans lay, or chugged out to long voyages under the coppery brilliance of the sun. Picturesque villages clustered under the broad umbrellas of ancient trees. Inland, waterfalls tumbled veil-like over precipices; among them Waipahee, known irreverently to tourists as the Sliding Bathtub, where visitors and natives alike slithered down a natural chute over water-smoothed rock to a deep pool. Around these streams the ohia-ai bore juicy, deep-red, apple-like fruit; wild kalo uncurled tender leaves; guavas ripened on sturdy shrubs. On rolling plains and mountain slopes, ranch cattle roamed among gnarled upland pandanus trees. Farther inland, the cloud-clothed bulk of Waialeale brooded somberly over all.

Beyond Anahola, where a perforation high in a rocky ridge marks where the spear of an ancient warrior pierced the mountain, the country is less luscious. There were pineapples, however, on the uplands and cane along the shores, as I drove in summer mornings past the Oriental rice straw huts that are pointed out to unsuspecting strangers as "Hawaiian grass houses," and past the great grove of candlenut trees whose light-green, star-shaped leaves once shaded gatherings of missionaries and of chiefs. At Kalihiwai, fishermen were drawing a net around a school of akule in the bay, to leave them thus imprisoned in their own element for days while supplies were drawn off gradually as the market demanded.

I spent easeful weeks in a cabin of ohia logs by a quiet bay off the main road. In that secluded region Hawaiians dwelt, as of old, beside the sea, each with his patch of kalo behind his house and the food-giving reef for his front yard. There they would wade, glass-bottom box in hand, at low tide, darting spears at fish clustering below or hunting the lair of the octopus: thrusting a short spear where stones drawn into a hole betrayed his hiding place; drawing out the shaft with tentacles writhing about it; smoothing them down with a broad hand and leaning forward to bite the creature's central nerve ganglion, disabling the prey and freeing the hands for another catch. At night they would stretch nets across narrow channels through the reef and drive fish into them by splashing with hands and feet and beating the water with branches. Everything from odd, stubby Hawaiian lobsters to staring-eyed young hammerhead sharks would come out of the net when it was drawn up on the sand. They would pound fish in a sack and sink it a little way offshore to attract live fish; then cast lines to catch beautiful savory ulua and papio.

It is another country, under the water: the strange, dim, unearthly country of the reef. Vermilion-red sea urchins slowly wave slender spikes in the warm tide; stupid, ugly sea slugs lie sunning themselves in the shallows; strange painted fishes glide and plane through coral caverns—fishes that disdain a hook and can be captured only with the spear. Once, peering over the edge of one of those chasms where fresh water has kept a clear channel through the coral, I saw a dozen baby sharks playing in the transparent water, far below.

Across the shallow bay, horsemen rode in the evening, hoofs splashing softly, cowboys from Princeville ranch, homeward bound, singing of Hanalei.

As their song proclaimed, "Hanalei, beautiful in the great rain!" Rice-green Hanalei, its broad river rolling between paddied fields and misty-green and lavender mountains, and the sea rolling in to meet the stream. Beyond the quiet town at its mouth the valley slopes gently upward to the spurs of Waialeale. Long-horned carabao plow muddy fields, and men and women in broad straw hats, or sometimes in quaint raincoats of rice straw like animated haystacks, wade in irregularly banked pools, planting pregrown young rice. The green of it rising above the water is marvelously fresh and bright, a lasting delight to the eyes. When the milky juice solidifies and swells the tiny husks, long rows of motley rags flutter on cords manipulated from ramshackle watch towers; tin cans rattle and shotguns roar from high platforms, scaring away ricebirds that raid the crop.

There was a silk farm in early days along the river. An uncharitable visitor attributed its failure to the stern New England piety of the missionaries. Silkworms must be tended daily; they keep no

Sabbaths. But the Christian native help, according to report, refused righteously to work on the Lord's Day, and the worms, and with them the industry, became martyrs to the faith.

I should like to explore sometime more deeply the caverns near the Haena shore. Out of a jungle of pandanus and guava one enters the fern-wreathed entrance of the Dry Cave, where a fugitive chief once hid, to sally forth like a ghost from a tomb and slay his enemies after they had thought him dead. Motorcars now profane that dim sanctuary, where crude pictures carved in the rock perhaps record the waiting days of that Hawaiian King Alfred.

Years ago no Hawaiian would enter the first of the two wet caves, sometimes called the Water of Terror. It was believed to be the home of a dragon which had once swallowed an entire party of adventurers. The terror has been forgotten now, and Hawaiian musicians enter without fear to sing against an answering choir of echoes above the cold, clear water that lies deep on the cavern floor.

A little way beyond, a Gothic arch opens upon the Water of Kanaloa. Ferns grow deep within the cave; bodies of swimmers shine strangely green in refracted light. A hundred yards within, another chamber lies darkly beyond a second Gothic portal rising from deep water. It is said the cave goes on, room after vaulted room, deep under the mountain, but I know none who has ventured there to see.

There is no road beyond the caves, where the land lifts jaggedly into the tangled wilderness of the Na Pali coast. But a little of this wild country has been tamed. From the other side of the island we drove up a narrow road climbing out of the sugar fields to the summer camps in the cool upland of Kokee. Kokee does not resemble at all the popular notion of a Hawaiian landscape. It might be a bit of any wooded mountain country. Its meadows lie checkered with sun and shade; air comes clean and cool and bracing; we seemed far, there, from the busy world. Birds from America, Europe, and the Orient, with which bird lovers have stocked the forest, flew in at open doorways to take crumbs and grain from our hands.

Beyond Kokee swirl trout streams, and hunters sometimes venture over headlong trails or seaward by boat to lost valleys that tumble precipitously to the sea. Along these ridges to Kalalau fled

Koolau the leper to defy, from goatlike retreats, the armed expeditions sent from Honolulu. Jack London told that story long ago. But I heard a different story on Kauai. It is whispered there that Koolau was no leper, but victim of a plot—denounced as a leper that a rival might, when Koolau should be banished to Molokai, seize his property and his wife.

A Hawaiian "ladder"—a log with transverse pieces attached—drops down a sheer cliff to a ledge leading into a cave whence another "ladder" slants over a precipice into a still more remote valley. Such is the entrance to the country of the unconquerable. Here lived a tribe apart, admitting no allegiance to the kings of Kauai or to Kamehameha himself. Against armaments of their time the valley was impregnable. A few guards could defend the approach against thousands; withdraw the ladders, and there was no way in by land.

The entrance by sea, at the valley mouth, was and is as precarious. A rope was lowered from an overhanging cliff into a sea cave, accessible only in calm weather. The cliff bulges; one had to grasp the rope on the run and swing out, clambering or being drawn dangerously up the rock. Hence, perhaps, the line of a Hawaiian bard: "Nualolo, swinging in the wind . . ."

Civilization conquered where armies could not. The valley stands empty now, tenanted only by wild swine, wild goats and birds, and the quaint, beautiful land mollusks whose delicately tinted, striated shells collectors prize. For the white man brought trade and industry and the lure of towns. The wild hillmen little by little forsook their lonely fastnesses and trickled down to the populous coast. The terraces of their fields, the crumbling walls of their watercourses remain, a few house platforms overgrown with jungle. The wind cries in the treetops of the lost valley; the long grasses rustle. And at night the rare explorer hears ghostly voices from hollow caverns in the stern cliffs.

From Mana and Kekaha we used to look across the channel to a red, gray, and brown island like the crest of a sea monster, knowing it for a forbidden land. The island barony of Niihau is the most kapu place in a country where that four-letter word for "No Trespassing" is an all too familiar sight. Its isolation is enforced by a

Kauai and the "Wettest Spot"

stern, if paternal, ownership. The story may be sketched briefly here as I heard it on Kauai.

The story goes back to Scotland, in 1840, when Captain Francis Sinclair and his wife left a farm near Stirling Castle to seek wider fortunes in New Zealand. There the quest had only begun. After Captain Sinclair was drowned, the widow and her family, with flocks and herds and piano, embarked on the clipper *Bessie*, owned by her son-in-law. Tahiti failed to please them; British Columbia kept them only a few months, before they put to sea again for California. Blown out of her course, the *Bessie* made port at Honolulu, and in 1864 the Sinclairs bought the island of Niihau from the ever-needy monarchy for ten thousand dollars.

Descriptions of Niihau are mainly from hearsay, for few but the owners, the Australian foreman, and the thirty-odd native families who live there have set foot on its rocky shores. Even government officials have been unable to obtain permission to land.

One version attributes this tabu to desire to keep the natives uncontaminated. A less friendly one suggests that it proceeds from canny maintenance of uncontrolled exploitation. The probable truth is that it is just lairdly exclusiveness.

Kauai residents describe Niihau as a place without movies, liquor, or tobacco; without radio, post office, or school above early grades —and also without police or jail. For infraction of the patriarchal— or matriarchal—law, deportation is the penalty. Since all transportation is by family boat, none may leave without permission. It is said if any do leave, they are not permitted to return. Everybody goes to church; when members of the continuing branch of the family are on the island, services last practically all day.

It is a peaceful, if somewhat dull life the Hawaiians of Niihau live: herding sheep and cattle over the dry pastures, weaving rushes into mats made nowhere else, making wreaths of shells and of peacock feathers to be marketed by the lairds.

Beyond Niihau the islands grow smaller: Lehua, an islanded Diamond Head; Kaula, bleak rock towering from boisterous seas, each of these two with its lighthouse, erected with difficulty and danger. Maui Kaito, aged crippled newsboy whose bent figure was for many years a familiar sight hobbling through the streets of Honolulu, chanting in his native language by way of crying his wares, or clanging a metal rattle, swam with a line to effect landing for the construction when no other would attempt the feat.

Beyond, still more islands lie, a thousand miles and more to the lagoon ring of Kure—bits of coral or of lava rock, each with its own story.

Eugene Burdick

Rest Camp on Maui

Born in Iowa in 1918, Eugene Burdick was taken as a child by his family to live in California. After high school he worked as a clerk, ditchdigger, and truck driver to make enough money to pay for his first quarter's tuition at Stanford University. Earning his way, he was graduated in 1941 and soon thereafter was married, taken into the Navy, and sent to Guadalcanal. He spent twenty-six months in the Pacific as a gunnery officer aboard various ships.

After his discharge Burdick returned to Stanford to take Wallace Stegner's course in creative writing. He then won a Rhodes Scholarship and received a Ph.D. at Oxford. While a professor of political science at the University of California he published his first novel, *The Ninth Wave* (1956). Thereafter he gained fame as coauthor of *The Ugly American* with William Lederer (1958) and *Fail-Safe* with Harvey Wheeler (1962). In *The Blue of Capricorn* (1961) Burdick combined fiction and commentary on life in the Pacific region. He died in 1965 of a heart attack during a tennis match.

"Rest Camp on Maui," one of the most outstanding stories that have come from Wallace Stegner's writing class, dramatizes the clash between battle-worn soldiers and a news hunter who seeks to sensationalize World War II in the Pacific. As Stegner says in his introduction to *Twenty Years of Stanford Short Stories* (1966), " 'Rest Camp on Maui' still rumbles with power like the tank which dominates one of the central episodes."

THE rest camp was as ugly as a place can be in the Hawaiian Islands, which is saying that it was as ugly as slums in New York, mud flats in Georgia, or drought land in Arkansas. Bulldozers had scraped the foliage and trees off several hills and left them red and naked. The hills had been covered with tents and a few Quonset huts. The only tropical thing about the camp was the sun and the heavy, sweet sugar-cane odor which was laced with the sharper odor of flowers when the wind shifted away from the valley.

Lieutenant Terry walked down a row of tents with the correspondent at his side. He stopped in front of a tent and pulled the flap aside to let the correspondent in. Three Marines stood up. A fourth Marine standing in front of a mirror was rubbing Aqua Velva on his face. He rubbed it with short, smooth strokes along his chin and then up his cheeks, splitting his fingers apart to pass on either side of his ears. Terry watched the Marine rub the liquid on his face and said nothing. Then the Marine turned around and, clicking his heels together, said, "Lieutenant Terry." He said it in a mocking, affected way that meant he liked Terry and felt at ease with him.

Terry started to speak rapidly: "Men, this gentleman here is a correspondent who wants to talk to you for a while. Give him whatever information he wants and we'll check it later for security. Mr. Black, this is Sergeant Fellows, Corporal Young, Private Selfensky, and Private Shannon."

By the end of the introduction the Marines all seemed relaxed and their faces went a little blank. They shook hands with the correspondent, squinting over his shoulder as they grasped his hand.

Fellows was round and red, like a beery friar.

"Glad to meet you, Mr. Black. Glad to help you any way we can," he said.

His voice was so flat that the cordiality of the words seemed to be squeezed thin and reluctant. He went back to the mirror and sprinkled some more Aqua Velva in his hands and started to rub his face.

The correspondent picked up his knapsack and opening it slipped out a bottle of whisky and put it on the table, saying, "Something to help pass the afternoon."

The four Marines all heard the bottle come down on the table and turned to stare hard at it. The bottle looked big and new and shiny. Their faces were eager and individual now. Their eyes glistened and Fellows licked a corner of his mouth several times quickly, without looking away from the bottle. They turned and looked at Terry. It was against regulations to drink in camp and they watched to see what Terry would say. Terry looked at Fellows and winked

Rest Camp on Maui

and said, "I'll be back for you in two hours, Mr. Black." He turned and walked out the flap.

Fellows laid out four heavy, metal mess cups and a chipped glass. He picked up the bottle, ripped the cellophane cover off the top, and unscrewed it. He poured out the whisky until the whole bottle was neatly divided into five equal parts.

"I'm not drinking today. Go ahead and use mine," the correspondent said.

Fellows looked up from the bottle and smiled at the correspondent. He picked up the chipped glass and split the whisky in it equally among the four metal cups. The whisky had a heady, rich odor that quickly filled the tent. Selfensky laughed and picking up a cup said, *"Skol."* They rinsed their mouths with the liquor and the heavy fumes flooded up their noses and tickled beautifully. The strength of the whisky brought tears to their eyes and they swallowed it quickly. They all smiled at the correspondent and when he started to talk again the conversation was more relaxed.

The correspondent took off his cap and laid it on the table. It was crumpled like the caps that Army pilots wear. It was cleverly bent and the wire stretcher had been removed from it.

"Men, I'm trying to get the personal angle on some of these shows you've been in," he said.

They felt good now and they grinned when he said "show." Correspondents always said "show," "bloody do," or "rat race," especially in the books they wrote.

"I want to get your attitude on politics and women and how you feel about things back in the States. There weren't any women on Tarawa or Iwo, but how about the women in Sydney and the Hawaiian girls?"

Fellows started to talk loudly about the Australian chicks. The correspondent kept grinning and saying he couldn't print that, but you could see he wanted to hear more of it. Fellows talked about the Sydney girls out at King's Cross and down at Woolloomooloo Dock and how at first they would always shack up with a girl apiece, but later when they got broke, a half dozen of them would all shack up with one girl to save money. The Marines hardly listened to Fellows' talk. They sipped at the whisky and smoked cigarettes.

Lord, Young thought, it's wonderful how good cigarettes taste when you suck in the smoke through the whisky breath of your throat.

Usually Young liked to listen to the older fellows' talk about women. He was only nineteen, the youngest man in his platoon. He'd joined the Corps when he was seventeen and never had a chance to hang around girls much. He had never had a girl, but he picked up the salty talk quickly and felt pretty sure that he sounded like any other Marine talking about women. Today he felt good and mellow, and leaning back in his chair he thought about the time on Okinawa.

He and Fellows had been on a patrol on the northern end of the island and they had come to another one of those little villages that were almost deserted. As they walked past the little houses they saw a few stunted people disappearing around corners or sitting in front of the tiny houses. Even the dogs looked runty and little. In front of one house a woman and her husband were seated on the ground. The husband was puffing on a small clay pipe and looking straight ahead. He looked as if he had been carved and lacquered, and he had a smooth, oily little potbelly that gleamed out of a hole in his shirt. The woman was seated with her back to the wall and she had dark, long hair. It was so black that it looked steel-blue. She must have been forty years old and her skin had an exquisite pattern of wrinkles over it, but somehow it looked soft and well cared for. Perhaps she had powder on her skin. It looked as if it might have a nice odor to it.

Fellows laughed and said, "Look," as he tossed her a small, wax-covered package of K-ration. It landed on her lap and she picked it up and examined it slowly and then looked up at the sergeant. A gift from a man in uniform could mean only one thing to her. She slid down until her shoulders were on the ground, but her head was still angled up against the house. She unfolded her kimono and drew it carefully back from her body until she was naked from the waist down. Young looked at her husband and he was still puffing his pipe slowly and looking straight ahead. The woman looked at the sergeant again and turned her head until the side of her face was flat against the rough material of the house. She closed her eyes. Young thought for a moment it was an odd movement of coquetry, but knew instantly it wasn't. It was artless and completely uninspired, the movement of a tired animal. Lying in the sun on her kimono in the peculiar posture she should have seemed disgusting, but to Young she seemed very lascivious, although she made not the slightest movement and lay inert on the ground.

Young said hoarsely, "Come on, Sarg, let's get going."

"Yeh, yeh," said Fellows, looking at the woman. "She's probably got a lot of screwy Jap diseases we never heard of."

Fellows was no longer smiling and as they went on through the village he said, "You know, kid, they always lay still like that. They're screwy people. I had Asiatic duty once. I know the screwy bastards."

Young stopped in the middle of the street and suddenly vomited. He felt greatly relieved and laughed loudly as Fellows hit him on the shoulder and said, "Take it easy, kid, take it easy."

Later Young had thought of the woman when they'd start to talk about their girls and wives and what they'd do when they got back to the States.

Fellows was still talking about the Aussie women and the correspondent was writing occasionally in a black notebook. Young moved behind him and read what he had written. *"Marines like Aussie girls, but first love still clean-cut American girls."*

The correspondent's pen moved across the notebook again. *"Jews in the Corps. Personal, human angle?"* He looked up.

"How have the Jews in the Corps made out? I'd like to give them a good write-up in my book," he said.

Fellows nodded at Selfensky and said, "Ask Selfensky; he's a Jew."

Selfensky looked straight at the correspondent for a moment and the Marines knew he wanted to talk about Lieutenant Cohen. Usually Selfensky clammed up when someone made a mistake and talked about Jews in front of him, but today he felt loose and oily inside, and talking seemed easy. He chewed at his lip, trying to form words, and then the correspondent said, "Yeah, Selfensky, you probably know more about this than anyone here. You know, some of my best friends are Jews. Damn fine fellows; I really like them."

Selfensky's face went a little hard and he stopped chewing his lip and said, "Ask Fellows. I don't know hardly anyone outside my company."

"Yeah, yeah, I know just about everyone in this damn division," Fellows said. He started telling the correspondent about Horowitz, a Pfc in the quartermaster, who organized an all-Marine show.

Selfensky took a sip of the whisky and he felt a little tight and beautifully lightheaded. He hadn't thought about Lieutenant Cohen for a long time. Selfensky remembered how proud he had felt when he got the word that his company was getting a Jewish officer for a platoon leader replacement. There were only a few Jewish enlisted men and no Jewish officers in his company. He had been disappointed when he first saw Cohen. He was of medium height and had dark eyes and long and very white graceful hands. Selfensky had hoped he would be a big rugged Jewish football player like Sid Luckman or a huge, fast, powerful boxer. Cohen was very quiet and kept to himself, but he was marvelous on weapons. Instead of fieldstripping his platoon's weapons on a clean, canvas-covered table, he made them take them out in the sand in a foxhole. They had to strip them with their eyes bandaged and put the parts in their pockets to keep them from getting sandy or losing them. Cohen could beat anyone by a minute or so. He was always asking questions about new gear and equipment and remembered most of it. Once he took a two-day pass and went to visit a tank outfit. When he came back he could drive a tank. The men started to like him.

One day a big Polack had called Cohen a kike. Loud and clear so that Cohen could hear it, and then looked at Cohen so that he couldn't ignore it. Cohen told him to report to the back of the rifle range and about twenty men drifted along to see what would happen.

Cohen took his shirt off and said, "Corporal, take off your shirt."

The Pole was a little nervous, but he laughed when he saw that Cohen was actually going to fight him with no rank or rate showing. He outweighed Cohen by forty pounds.

Cohen stood very straight and white and said, "Corporal, I can't possibly beat you in an ordinary fist fight. This is going to be a no-holds-barred fight. Do you agree?"

"Yeah, Jew-boy, that's okay with me," the Pole said.

Selfensky felt sick and wondered if he should try and stop the fight, but the Pole had already started after Cohen. The Pole hit Cohen twice—hard blows on the chest. Then Cohen seemed to be all over the Pole, like a mongoose after a dog. He kicked the Pole hard in the shins and as the Pole straightened up Cohen had his finger inside the Pole's lip and ripped it back from the corner of his mouth. The Pole kept hitting Cohen hard, but he was a little scared now. Cohen went after his hands next and when they separated he had broken the little finger of the Pole's right hand. It hung back from his hand at such an impossible angle that it hurt you to look at it.

Cohen drove his knee into the Pole's groin a couple of times and Selfensky could see panic in the Pole's eyes. The Pole tried to kick and knee too and that ended it quickly. Cohen stood back and smashed him time after time in the face. The Pole got weaker and soon his knees buckled and he put his face in his hands and sank to the ground. The broken little finger stuck straight out from the other fingers curled around his face.

The Pole turned into sick bay and said he'd been in a fight with some civilians. Cohen visited him in the hospital and when the Pole got out he transferred to Cohen's platoon. Cohen still worked his men hard and by the time they were ready to stage for Iwo, his platoon was the toughest in the company. The men were lean and hard and they all looked tougher than Cohen, whose hands were still white and graceful-looking.

Their company went into Iwo on D plus 2. Selfensky remembered how much like practice it all had seemed as they went down the nets into the LCVP's and circled around waiting for the rest of their wave. They joked and kidded a bit and a BAR man pretended he was seasick over the side. It didn't seem too bad even when they got up close to the beach and could hear the mortars crumping and could see the F6F's suddenly leave their 500-pound bombs hanging still in the air and then the bombs would start to speed up and go so fast you could hardly see them as they hit into the big mounds of sand and exploded blackly.

As soon as the platoon hit the beach, however, and started to muck through the black volcanic sand, things didn't look so good. The first thing they saw was an aid station that had been hit. There were broken plasma bottles hanging from rifles and a long stream of bandage unrolled neat and white across the black sand. Cots and crates and blankets were all smashed together and big, tarry clots of blood and flesh were plastered over everything. The corpsmen had already set up a few yards down the beach, but you could tell that they didn't expect to stay there long. Funny how corpsmen always looked like kids. Even the middle-aged men looked like kids when they wore the big helmets with red crosses on them and brassards on their arms. Like kids playing soldier.

They moved off the beach fast and alongside the air strip, avoiding the little flags that indicated mines. The mortar fire started to pick up. They hit the line very soon and found the outfit they were supposed to flank. There were a lot of dead Marines around, but no one was bothering about them and Selfensky wondered where the Japs were. He hadn't seen a Jap body or a Jap position yet, although the machine-gun fire was heavy now and occasionally there was some artillery fire. Then a company runner arrived and gave Cohen a field dispatch and he moved the platoon to the right and into a big shell hole.

"We're going to clean out that pillbox on the hill," he said. "We'll have tank support, and everyone except the BAR men keep close to the tank. BAR men keep the pillbox under fire all the time. A couple of grenades ought to do it, but don't pitch one until you're sure you can hit the slit."

Selfensky looked up the low hill and finally saw the long, camouflaged slit. It looked like a crevice between two rocks, but occasionally there would be a stream of smoke-puff from it.

They had to wait a half hour for the tank, so they broke open their K-rations. Selfensky didn't like the candy in the ration and traded it to another man for the little can of cheese.

The tank came early, lumbering down the side of the air strip, with dust thick and black all over it. Wherever there was grease on the tank the dust bulged out in huge mounds, like soft, black cancers growing out of the steel. The tank didn't stop when it came to their shell hole, but the turret swung toward them as if in question and then turned back toward the pillbox. The gun barrel pointed at the pillbox like a long, commanding finger. They threw the paper and tins into the bottom of the hole and started out behind the tank. At once the fire started to increase and mortar shells began to plop around the tank. The pillbox was firing fast now and the smoke puffed steadily out of it. The BAR men lagged a little behind and suddenly they started to fire into the pillbox. You could see the hot, angry tracers powdering the stone around the pillbox and smoke stopped coming out of it.

They were only a hundred yards from the pillbox when they all heard the first screaming ricochet of an antitank shell. Mortar projectiles don't ricochet, they just plop into the ground and explode, but high-velocity antitank projectiles will ricochet off almost anything. The turret of the tank spun around frantically trying to locate the antitank gun. All you could see was dust and mortar shells exploding and ugly little hills held together by dust and great chunks of concrete that you couldn't see. There were two more snarling ricochets and then the fourth round shattered into the tank. It made a terrible ringing sound and Selfensky's ears stopped hearing for a minute and he felt a sharp, cold pain at the base of each tooth. The hatch of the tank was blown off and the tank captain came out behind it. The hatch and the tank captain turned slowly over in the air, the tank captain's clothing shredding away from him in the air. When he hit the ground he lay there white and broken and naked.

The tank was smoking, but the motor was running smoothly. The dust had been shaken from the tank and the green-and-brown camouflage paint looked smooth and new. Selfensky felt fear grip his stomach and suddenly felt very exposed against the sand. He wished he had had a bowel movement back in the shell hole. He heard his name called and looking up saw Cohen lowering himself into the hatch of the tank and motioning him to follow.

Inside, the tank was hot and dusty and the sweat started to stand out on Selfensky's face. He felt secure inside the thick steel walls despite the hole in the side of the tank and the two men who had died, looking over their shoulders into the turret. Cohen boosted the gunner up to him and Selfensky pushed him out the hatch and let him slide to the ground. The driver was harder to get out, and Selfensky was sweating hard. He was feeling better all the time, however, and he was amazed at how safe and snug a tank was. He looked at the hole in the side of the tank and saw that the steel was several fingers thick. Damn it, this was all right! Cohen looked up from the driver's seat and said, "Tell the Pole to take over the platoon and we'll try to get up to the pillbox."

The tank started slowly up the slope and through the periscope the pillbox slit got larger and suddenly smoke started to puff out of it again. Selfensky could feel the bullets hitting the side and bouncing off and he grinned down at Cohen.

Cohen's greens were dark with sweat now and his large white hands were moving over the controls rapidly. They were about fifty feet from the pillbox when a scrawny little Jap started to slide sideways out of the slit and Selfensky saw he had a satchel charge in his right hand. The Jap came hopping bowlegged down the hill, his face all contorted and probably yelling. He had covered about half the distance to the tank when he started to stagger. It looked as if someone were hitting him with an invisible sledge hammer. His forehead dissolved in a red splash and his legs snapped back from under him as the BAR slugs tore into them. Sudden red decorations started to spread over his shirt. He smacked backward into the ground and the satchel charge slipped from his hand. Cohen stopped the tank and crawled over into the gunner's position. He didn't know how to work the sight, but at this range he could fire by eye and not miss. He fired five rounds into the slit and when the pillbox looked like a smoking black eye in the hill he stopped.

Cohen grinned up at Selfensky and started the tank back down the hill. They were about halfway down when they hit one of the 500-pound aerial bombs the Japs had mined the island with. Later, Selfensky was told that the tank flopped over on its back and lay there like a great, helpless turtle. Selfensky only remembered coming to and knowing he didn't hurt anywhere, and almost immediately he knew where he was. Cohen was hanging face down from the driver's compartment and the explosion had clamped the compartment around his legs. He hung from his knees down into the turret. Selfensky was puzzled at Cohen's position for a few minutes and then he started to crawl toward him. At once he heard a rasping sound and a great pain inched up his leg. The bone was sticking almost straight out from his leg and when he moved he had pulled it across the rough surface of the tank. He looked again at Cohen and hoped he was dead because he was sure to lose both his legs.

Cohen's voice sounded low and clear in the hot turret, "Take it easy, Selfensky. Stay where you are and they'll get you out of here."

Cohen's eyes looked big and soft and Selfensky felt embarrassed looking at them upside down. He tried to turn his head so he could see straight into Cohen's face, but Cohen said, "No, no, Ski. Take it easy, boy." Selfensky's whole body ached to have Cohen die or faint before he looked up and saw his legs.

"Two little Jew-boys gone astray, eh, Lieutenant," Selfensky said and wondered if it sounded funny.

Cohen closed his eyes as blood started to bubble out of his nose down into them and Selfensky reached over and wiped them out. The eyes opened and were big and soft again.

Cohen started to sing and Selfensky couldn't place the words for a while. Then he remembered the song. He'd learned it long ago at the synagogue and forgotten it. He started to sing softly with Cohen. Cohen sang beautifully, like a cantor. The words sounded big and glorious in the tank. It sounded like many voices singing. Selfensky felt that his voice was huge and powerful and a queer exultation seized him. He didn't know how long they sang, but gradually Cohen's voice became softer and then it stopped. Selfensky hated to look up because he knew that if Cohen's eyes were open and big and soft he'd go crazy. Finally he looked up and Cohen's eyelids were closed and there was a stream of blood from each nostril that ran out his nose, across the eyelids, and into the dark hair. Selfensky reached out and took Cohen's cold hand and started to say the old Jewish prayer for death: ". . . O, may death be an atonement for all the sins, iniquities, and transgressions of which I have been guilty before thee. . . ."

He was holding Cohen's hand and sitting in the same position when they came and cut the tank open with a welder's torch.

Fellows had just finished telling the correspondent about the show Horowitz had put on. How he'd dressed up a bunch of big Marines like women and brought them out as a chorus line.

"It was really a laugh," Fellows said. "Horowitz had cut coconuts in two and they wore them under the brassieres. They did an awful dance and one big gook fell on his butt twice. Then one of them dropped a coconut out of his brassiere and it bounced on the deck and that really brought down the house. So they all started dropping them out on purpose and pretty soon the whole deck was covered with them. Horowitz was mad about that, but it sure made a good laugh."

Fellows was red-faced now; sweating a little. He had just enough whisky left in his cup to twirl around and he was waiting before he drank that. He kept thinking he wouldn't see any more for a long time. Fellows wished suddenly that he had a whole quart to start in on. He could drink forever and not get sick or sleepy; he'd just keep feeling better and better. The correspondent had an indifferent look on his face and they all knew this wasn't the kind of stuff he wanted to hear, but they didn't care.

The correspondent started to write in his notebook again and Fellows could see the words: *"Jewish boys in the Marines, famed for their entertainment on Broadway and in Hollywood, arrange musicals, shows, and other laugh-fests to keep America's finest fighting men relaxed between battles."*

"Where does this Horowitz come from in the States?" the correspondent asked. "People like to read about where the boys come from."

"Oh, he came from Nebraska. His old man had a peanut farm or something out there," Selfensky answered.

"Not so good, Ski." The correspondent winked at Selfensky. "Jewish boys should come from Brooklyn or Chicago. Gives them more human interest."

The correspondent looked at the empty bottle and Selfensky could see that he was measuring the dope he had got against the whisky and feeling cheated.

"Any of you boys pick up any medals in these shows?" the correspondent asked, changing the subject rapidly. The Marines looked at one another for a second and then, because they were feeling good, they all started to laugh.

"Sure, we all got the Purple Heart," Fellows said.

The correspondent shook his head patiently. "No good. People expect Marines to have Purple Hearts. Any other medals aside from that?" His voice hung somewhere between irritation and patience.

"Yeah, Shannon there has a Silver Star and a Navy Cross. He's got so many medals that they had him go on a bond tour back in the States."

Shannon held back the good, loose feeling in his head and chest and grinned at the correspondent.

"That must have been a pretty fast life after being out here for a couple years. I'll bet you were anxious to get back to your outfit after all those cocktail parties and speeches by politicians," the correspondent said.

"No, I liked it. They sent me back right after Iwo and it was swell. Lots of good food; I gained twenty pounds the first month back. They always fixed me up with a date and I hadn't been out with a girl for three years. Some of the girls still write me. It was a hell of a lot of fun. Everyone was swell to me and the workers at the plants would come up and ask questions about their kids in the Corps and take me out to their homes for dinner. I hated like hell to come back out." Shannon's grin had faded to a serious smile and the other Marines were looking at him oddly.

"I don't know, Shannon," the correspondent said. "What would you say if I wrote you up as being more scared by the speeches and the good-looking girls than you ever were on Iwo? I'll put your name in it and it ought to make a good story. People like that human-interest angle. What do you say?"

The correspondent was mildly excited about the new angle. He didn't notice that the Marines were all quiet and they were watching Shannon.

Shannon was not smiling now and he was trying to understand what the correspondent meant. His mind telescoped the long hot months of training; the nights in combat he had urinated into his pants rather than look for the pit; the grease-packed K-rations; the sleep that was not sleep, but unconsciousness; the Pfc who threw himself on a grenade that had been dropped by accident and whose body jumped two feet into the air and fell back a crumpled sack of khaki; the warm canteen water that turned the dust in his throat into mud. All these his mind telescoped into one experience. He laid it next to the memories of the laughing girls and iced lemonade and the keen exhilaration of three beers and the fragrant pork roasts and blue water in country streams and the yellowing corn.

Shannon smiled uncertainly over his shoulder at Fellows. He felt a sudden relief, for he could tell that Fellows knew what the correspondent meant.

Fellows finished off his whisky and looked in the bottom of the cup and put it on the table. He stood up and walked over in front of the correspondent.

"Get out of here, you son of a bitch," he said.

His voice sounded a little tired, but the words came like cold drops of metal out of his mouth. The correspondent looked up, startled, and started to say something.

"Get out, you lousy bastard," Fellows said again.

His face wasn't red any more and there was even a little white around the nose. He wasn't the slightest bit drunk.

"Look, old man, you don't understand . . ." the correspondent started to say.

"Come on, bum, move on," Fellows said, and walked back to his chair.

Five minutes later the correspondent went into Lieutenant Terry's tent and said he was ready to go back to town. Terry looked at him and started to whistle.

"How did you make out?" he asked.

"So-so, they didn't have a hell of a lot to say. A little too primadonnaish," the correspondent answered.

They went back down the road that overlooks the beautiful valley of Maui. As the sea came into view, sparkling and blue, Terry started to sing:

> There'll be no promotions,
> This side of the ocean,
> So cheer up, my lads,
> Bless 'em all.
> Bless 'em all, bless 'em all,
> The long and the short and the tall . . .

Milton Murayama

I'll Crack Your Head *Kotsun*

A Nisei born in Hawaii, Milton Murayama served in the United States Army as an interpreter in India and China during World War II. He became interested in writing at the University of Hawaii, where he took a bachelor's degree, and later obtained a master's degree from Columbia University. His fresh and appealing story, told from the viewpoint of a fourth-grade boy, son of a Japanese fisherman, gives evidence that young people of Oriental ancestry brought up in Hawaii are becoming aware of their background as a source of unique literary material. "I'll Crack Your Head *Kotsun*" is a subtle evocation of boyhood that has a universal verity.

THERE was something funny about Makot. He always played with guys younger than he and the big guys his own age always made fun of him. His family was the only Japanese family in Filipino Camp and his father didn't seem to do anything but ride around in his brand-new Ford Model T. But Makot always had money to spend and the young kids liked him.

During the summer in Pepelau, Hawaii, the whole town spends the whole day at the beach. We go there early in the morning, then walk home for lunch, often in our trunks, then go back for more spearing fish, surfing, or just plain swimming, depending on the tide, and stay there till sunset. At night there were the movies for those who had the money and the Buddhist Bon dances and dance practices. The only change in dress was that at night we wore Japanese zori and in the day bare feet. Nobody owned shoes in Pepelau.

In August Makot became our gang leader. We were all at the beach and it was on a Wednesday when there was a matinee, and Makot said, "Come on, I'll take you all to the movies," and Mit, Skats, and I became his gang in no time. Mit or Mitsunobu Kato and Skats or Nobuyuki Asakatsu and I were not exactly a gang. There were only three of us and we were all going to be in the fourth grade, so nobody was leader. But we were a kind of a poor gang. None of us were in the Boy Scouts or had bicycles, we played football with tennis balls, and during basketball season we hung around Baldwin Park till some gang showed up with a rubber ball or a real basketball.

After that day we followed Makot at the beach, and in spearing fish Skats and I followed him across the breakers. We didn't want to go at first, since no fourth-grader went across the breakers, but he teased us and called us yellow, so Skats and I followed. Mit didn't care if he was called yellow. Then at lunchtime, instead of all of us going home for lunch, Makot invited us all to his home in Filipino Camp. Nobody was home and he cooked us rice and corned beef and onions. The following day there was the new kind of Campbell soup in cans, which we got at home only when we were sick. So I began to look forward to lunchtime, when we'd go to Makot's home to eat. At home Father was a fisherman and so we ate fish and rice three times a day, and as my older brother Tosh who was a seventh-grader always said, "What! Fish and rice again! No wonder the Japanese get beriberi!" I was sick of fish and rice too.

Mother didn't seem too happy about my eating at Makot's. About the fourth day when I came home at sunset, she said in Japanese, "You must be famished, Kiyo-chan, shall I fix you something?"

"No, I had lunch at Makoto-san's home."

"Oh, again?"

Mother was sitting on a cushion on the floor, her legs hid under her, and she was bending over and sewing a kimono by hand. It was what she always did. I sat down cross-legged. "Uh huh. Makoto-san invited me. I ate a bellyful. Makoto-san is a very good cook. He fixed some corned beef and onions and it was delicious."

"Oh, are you playing with Makoto-san now? He's too old for you, isn't he? He's Toshio's age. What about Mitsunobu-san and Nobuyuki-san?"

"Oh, they still with me. We all play with Makoto-san. He invited all of us."

"Makoto-san's mother or father wasn't home?"

"No, they're usually not home."

"You know, Kiyo-chan, you shouldn't eat at Makoto-san's home too often."

"Why? But he invites us."

"But his parents didn't invite you. Do you understand, Kiyo-chan?"

"But why? Nobuyuki-san and Mitsunobu-san go."

"Kiyo-chan is a good boy so he'll obey what his mother says, won't he?"

"But why, Mother! I eat at Nobuyuki's and Mitsunobu's homes when their parents aren't home. And I always thank their parents when I see them. I haven't thanked Makoto's parents yet, but I will when I see them."

"But don't you see, Kiyoshi, you will bring shame to your father and me if you go there to eat. People will say, 'Ah, look at the Oyamas' No. 2 boy. He's a *hoitobo!* He's a *chorimbo!* That's because his parents are *hoitobo* and *chorimbo!*'"

Hoitobo means beggar in Japanese and *chorimbo* is something like a bum, but they're ten times worse than beggar and bum because you always make your face real ugly when you say them and they sound horrible!

"But Makoto invites us, Mother! Once Mitsunobu didn't want to go and Makoto dragged him. We can always have Makoto-san over to our home and repay him the way we do Mitsunobu-san and Nobuyuki-san."

"But can't you see, Kiyo-chan, people will laugh at you. 'Look at that Kiyoshi Oyama,' they'll say, 'he always eats at the Sasakis'. It's because his parents are poor and he doesn't have enough to eat at home.' You understand, don't you, Kiyo-chan? You're a good filial boy so you'll obey what your parents say, won't you? Your father and I would cry if we had two unfilial sons like Toshio . . ."

"But what about Nobuyuki and Mitsunobu? Won't people talk about them and their parents like that too?"

"But Kiyoshi, you're not a monkey. You don't have to copy others. Whatever Nobuyuki and Mitsunobu do is up to them. Besides, we're poor and poor families have to be more careful."

"But Mitsunobu's home is poor too! They have lots of children and he's always charging things at the stores and his home looks poor like ours!"

She dropped her sewing on her lap and looked straight at me. Her face wasn't kind anymore. "Kiyoshi," she said, "you will obey your parents, won't you?"

I stood up and hitched up my pants. I didn't say yes or no. I just grunted like Father and walked out.

But the next time I went to eat at Makot's I felt guilty and the corned beef and onions didn't taste so good. And when I came home that night the first thing Mother asked was, "Oh, did you have lunch, Kiyo-chan?" Then, "At Makoto-san's home?" and her face looked as if she was going to cry.

But I figured that that was the end of that so I was surprised when Father turned to me at the supper table and said, "Kiyoshi . . ." Whenever he called me by my full name instead of Kiyo or Kiyo-chan, that meant he meant business. He never punched my head once, but I'd seen him slap and punch Tosh's head all over the place till Tosh was black and blue in the head.

"Yes, Father." I was scared.

"Kiyoshi, you're not to eat anymore at Makoto-san's home. You understand?"

"But why, Father? Nobuyuki-san and Mitsunobu-san eat with me too!"

"Nemmind!" he said in English. Then he said in Japanese, "You're not a monkey. You're Kiyoshi Oyama."

"But why?" I said again. I wasn't being smart-alecky like Tosh. I really wanted to know why.

Father grew angry. You could tell by the way his eyes bulged and the way he twisted his mouth. He flew off the handle real easily, like Tosh. He said, "If you keep on asking 'Why? Why?' I'll crack your head *kotsun!*"

Kotsun doesn't mean anything in Japanese. It's just the sound of something hard hitting your head.

"Yeah, slap his head, slap his head!" Tosh said in pidgin Japanese and laughed.

"Shut up! Don't say uncalled-for things!" Father said to Tosh and Tosh shut up and grinned.

Whenever Father talked about this younger generation talking too much and talking out of turn and having no respect for anything, he didn't mean me, he meant Tosh.

"Kiyoshi, you understand, you're not to eat anymore at Makoto's home," Father said evenly, now his anger gone.

I was going to ask "Why?" again but I was afraid. "Yes," I said.

Then Tosh said across the table in pidgin English, which the old folks couldn't understand, "You know why, Kyo?" I never liked the guy, he couldn't even pronounce my name right. "Because his father no work and his mother do all the work, thass why! Ha-ha-ha-ha!"

Father told him to shut up and not to joke at the table and he shut up and grinned.

Then Tosh said again in pidgin English, his mouth full of food; he always talked with his mouth full, "Go tell that *kodomo taisho* to go play with guys his own age, not small shrimps like you. You know why he doan play with us? Because he scared, thass why. He too wahine. We bust um up!"

"Wahine" was the Hawaiian word for woman. When we called anybody wahine it meant she was a girl or he was a sissy. When Father said wahine it meant the old lady or Mother.

Then I made another mistake. I bragged to Tosh about going across the breakers. "You pupule ass! You wanna die or what? You want shark to eat you up? Next time you go outside the breakers I goin slap your head!" he said.

"Not dangerous. Makot been take me go."

"Shaddup! You tell that *kodomo taisho* if I catch um taking you outside the breakers again, I goin bust um up! Tell um that! Tell um I said go play with guys his own age!"

"He never been force me. I asked um to take me."

"Shaddup! The next time you go out there, I goin slap your head!"

Tosh was three years older than me and when he slapped my head, I couldn't slap him back because he would slap me right back, and I couldn't cry like my kid sister because I was too big to cry. All I could do was to walk away mad and think of all the things I was going to do to get even when I grew up. When I slapped my sister's head she would grumble or sometimes cry but she would always talk back, "No slap my head, you! Thass where my brains stay, you know!" Me, I couldn't even talk back. Most big brothers were too cocky anyway and mine was more cocky than most.

Then at supper Tosh brought it up again. He spoke in pidgin

Japanese (we spoke four languages: good English in school, pidgin English among ourselves, good or pidgin Japanese to our parents and the other old folks), "Mama, you better tell Kyo not to go outside the breakers. By-'n'-by he drown. By-'n'-by the shark eat um up."

"Oh, Kiyo-chan, did you go outside the breakers?" she said in Japanese.

"Yeah," Tosh answered for me, "Makoto Sasaki been take him go."

"Not dangerous," I said in pidgin Japanese; "Makoto-san was with me all the time."

"Why shouldn't Makoto-san play with people his own age, *ne?*" Mother said.

"He's a *kodomo taisho,* thass why!"

Kodomo taisho meant general of the kids.

"Well, you're not to go outside the breakers anymore. Do you understand, Kiyo-chan?" Mother said.

I turned to Father, who was eating silently. "Is that right, Father?"

"*So,*" he grunted.

"Boy, your father and mother real strict," Makot said. I couldn't go outside the breakers, I couldn't go eat at his place. But Makot always saved some corned beef and onions and Campbell soup for me. He told me to go home and eat fast and just a little bit and come over to his place and eat with them and I kept on doing that without Mother catching on. And Makot was always buying us pie, ice cream, and chow fun, and he was always giving me the biggest share of the pie, ice cream, or chow fun. He also took us to the movies now and then and when he had money for only one treat or when he wanted to take only me and spend the rest of the money on candies, he would have me meet him in town at night, as he didn't want me to come to his place at night. "No tell Mit and Skats," he told me and I didn't tell them or the folks or Tosh anything about it, and when they asked where I was going on the movie nights, I told them I was going over to Mit's or Skats'.

Then near the end of summer the whole town got tired of going to the beach and we all took up slingshots and it got to be slingshot season. Everybody made slingshots and carried pocketfuls of little rocks and shot linnets and myna birds and doves. We would even go to the old wharf and shoot the black crabs which crawled on the rocks. Makot made each of us a dandy slingshot out of guava branches, as he'd made each of us a big barbed spear out of bedspring coil during spearing-fish season. Nobody our age had slingshots or spears like ours, and of the three he made, mine was always the best. I knew he liked me the best.

Then one day Makot said, "Slingshot waste time. We go buy a rifle. We go buy twenty-two."

"How?" we all said.

Makot said that he could get five dollars from his old folks and all we needed was five dollars more and we could go sell coconuts and mangoes to raise that.

"Sure!" we all said. A rifle was something we saw only in the movies and Sears Roebuck catalogues. Nobody in Pepelau owned a rifle.

So the next morning we got a barley bag, two picks, and a scooter wagon. We were going to try coconuts first because they were easier to sell. There were two bakeries in town and they needed them for coconut pies. The only trouble was that free coconut trees were hard to find. There were trees at the courthouse, the Catholic Church, and in Rev. Hastings' yard, but the only free trees were those deep in the cane fields and they were too tall and dangerous. Makot said, "We go ask Reverend Hastings." Rev. Hastings was a minister of some kind and he lived alone in a big old house in a big weedy yard next to the kindergarten. He had about a dozen trees in his yard and he always let you pick some coconuts if you asked him, but he always said, "Sure, boys, provided you don't sell them." "Aw, what he doan know won't hurt um," Makot said. Makot said he was going to be the brains of the gang and Mit and Skats were going to climb the trees and I was going to ask Rev. Hastings. So we hid the wagon and picks and bags and I went up to the door of the big house and knocked.

Pretty soon there were footsteps and he opened the door. "Yes?" He smiled. He was a short, skinny man who looked very weak and who sort of wobbled when he walked, but he had a nice face and a small voice.

"Reverend Hastings, can we pick some coconuts?" I said.

Makot, Mit and Skats were behind me and he looked at them and said, "Why, sure, boys, provided you don't sell them."

"Thank you, Reverend Hastings," I said, and the others mumbled, "Thank you."

"You're welcome," he said and went back into the house.

Mit and Skats climbed two trees and knocked them down as fast as they could and I stuck my pick in the ground and started peeling them as fast as I could. We were scared. What if he came out again? Maybe it was better if we all climbed and knocked down lots and took them somewhere else to peel them, we said. But Makot sat down on the wagon and laughed, "Naw, he not gonna come out no more. No be chicken!" As soon as he said that the door slammed and we all looked. Mit and Skats stayed on the trees but didn't knock down any more. Rev. Hastings jumped down the steps and came walking across the yard in big angry strides! It was plain we were going to sell the coconuts because we had more than half a bagful and all the husks were piled up like a mountain! He came up, his face red, and he shouted, "I thought you said you weren't going to sell these! Get down from those trees!"

I looked at my feet and Makot put his face in the crook of his arm and began crying, "Wah-wah . . ." though I knew he wasn't crying.

Rev. Hastings grabbed a half-peeled coconut from my hand and grabbing it by a loose husk, threw it with all his might over the fence and nearly fell down and shouted, "Get! Out! At! Once!" Then he turned right around and walked back and slammed the door after him.

"Ha-ha-ha!" Makot said as soon as he disappeared, "we got enough anyway."

We picked up the rest of the coconuts and took them to the kindergarten to peel them. We had three dozen and carted them to the two bakeries on Main Street. But they said that they had enough coconuts and that ours were too green and six cents apiece was too much. We pulled the wagon all over town and tried the fish markets and grocery stores for five cents. Finally we went back to the first bakery and sold them for four cents. It took us the whole day and we made only $1.44. By that time Mit, Skats and I wanted to forget about the rifle, but Makot said, "twenty-two or bust."

The next day we went to the tall trees in the cane fields. We had to crawl through tall cane to get to them and once we climbed the trees and knocked down the coconuts we had to hunt for them in the tall cane again. After the first tree we wanted to quit but Makot wouldn't hear of it and when we didn't move he put on his *habut*. *Habut* is short for *habuteru*, which means to pout the way girls and children do. Makot would blow up his cheeks like a balloon fish and not talk to us. "I not goin' buy you no more chow fun, no more ice cream, no more pie," he'd sort of cry, and then we would do everything to please him and make him come out of his *habut*. When we finally agreed to do what he wanted he would protest and slap with his wrist like a girl, giggle with his hand over his mouth, talk in the kind of Japanese which only girls use, and in general make fun of the girls. And when he came out of his *habut* he usually bought us chow fun, ice cream, or pie.

So we crawled through more cane fields and climbed more coconut trees. I volunteered to climb too because Mit and Skats grumbled that I got all the easy jobs. By three o'clock we had only half a bag, but we brought them to town and again went all over Main Street trying to sell them. The next day we went to pick mangoes, first at the kindergarten, then at Mango Gulch, but they were harder to sell so we spent more time carting them around town.

"You guys think you so hot, eh?" Tosh said one day. "Go sell mangoes and coconuts. He only catching you head. You know why he pick on you guys for a gang? Because you guys the last. That *kodomo taisho* been leader of every shrimp gang and they all quit him one after another. You, Mit, and Skats stick with him because you too stupid!"

I shrugged and walked away. I didn't care. I liked Makot. Besides, all the guys his age were jealous because Makot had so much money to spend.

Then several days later Father called me. He was alone at the outside sink, cleaning some fish. He brought home the best fish for us to eat but it was always fish. He was still in his fisherman's clothes.

"Kiyoshi," he said and he was not angry, "you're not to play with Makoto Sasaki anymore. Do you understand?"

"But why, Father?"

"Because he is bad." He went on cleaning fish.

"But he's not bad. He treats us good! You mean about stealing mangoes from kindergarten? It's not really stealing. Everybody does it."

"But you never sold the mangoes you stole before?"

"No."

"There's a difference between a prank and a crime. Everybody in town is talking about you people. Not about stealing, but about your selling mangoes and coconuts you stole. It's all Makoto's fault. He's older and he should know better but he doesn't. That's why he plays with younger boys. He makes fools out of them. The whole town is talking about what fools he's making out of you and Nobuyuki and Mitsunobu."

"But he's not really making fools out of us, Father. We all agreed to make some money so that we could buy a rifle and own it together. As for the work, he doesn't really force us. He's always buying us things and making things for us and teaching us tricks he learns in Boy Scout, so it's one way we can repay him."

"But he's bad. You're not to play with him. Do you understand?"

"But he's not bad! He treats us real good and me better than Mitsunobu-san or Nobuyuki-san!"

"Kiyoshi, I'm telling you for the last time. Do not play with him."

"But why?"

"Because his home is bad. His father is bad. His mother is bad."

"Why are his father and mother bad?"

"Nemmind!" He was mad now.

"But what about Mitsunobu-san and Nobuyuki-san? I play with them too!"

"Shut up!" He turned to face me. His mouth was twisted. "You're not a monkey! Stop aping others! You are not to play with him! Do you understand! Or do I have to crack your head *kotsun!*"

"Yes," I said and walked away.

Then I went inside the house and asked Mother, "Why are they bad? Because he doesn't work?"

"You're too young to understand, Kiyo-chan. When you grow up you'll know that your parents were right."

"But whom am I going to play with then?"

"Can't you play with Toshi-chan?"

"Yeah, come play with me, Kyo. Any time you want me to bust up that *kodomo taisho* I'll bustum up for you," Tosh said.

That night I said I was going to see Mit and went over to Makot's home. On the way over I kept thinking about what Father and Mother said. There was something funny about Makot's folks. His father was a tall, skinny man and he didn't talk to us kids the way all the other old Japanese men did. He owned a Model T when only the haoles or whites had cars. His mother was funnier yet. She wore lipstick in broad daylight, which no other Japanese mother did.

I went into Filipino Camp and I was scared. It was a spooky place, not like Japanese Camp. The Filipinos were all men and there were no women or children and the same-looking houses were all bare, no curtains in the windows or potted plants on the porch. The only way you could tell them apart was by their numbers. But I knew where Makot's house was in the daytime, so I found it easily. It was the only one with curtains and ferns and flowers. I called from the front porch, "Makot! Makot!" I was scared he was going to give me hell for coming at night.

Pretty soon his mother came out. I had never spoken to her though I'd seen her around and knew who she was. She was a fat woman with a fat face, which made her eyes look very small.

"Oh, is Makoto-san home?" I asked in Japanese.

"Makotooooo!" she turned and yelled into the house. She was all dressed up in kimono. Mother made a lot of kimonos for other people but she never had one like hers. She had a lot of white powder on her face and two round red spots on her cheeks.

"Oh, Sasaki-san," I said, "I've had lunch at your home quite a few times. I wanted to thank you for it but I didn't have a chance to speak to you before. It was most delicious. Thank you very much."

She stared at me with her mouth open wide and suddenly burst out laughing, covering her mouth and shaking all over, her shoulders, her arms, her cheeks.

Makot came out. "Wha-at?" he pouted in Japanese. Then he saw me and his face lit up, "Hiya, Kiyo, old pal, old pal, what's cookin'?" he said in English.

His mother was still laughing and shaking and pointing at me.

"What happened?" Makot said angrily to his mother.

"That boy! That boy!" She still pointed at me. "Such a nice little boy! Do you know what he said? He said, 'Sasaki-san . . .' " And she started to shake and cough again.

"Aw, shut up, Mother!" Makot said. "Please go inside!" and he practically shoved her to the door.

She turned around again, "But you're such a courteous boy, aren't you? 'It was most delicious. Thank you very much.' A-hahahaha. A-hahahaha . . ."

"Shut up, Mother!" Makot shoved her into the doorway. I would never treat my mother like that but then my mother would never act like that. When somebody said, "Thank you for the feast," she always said, "But what was served you was really rubbish."

Makot turned to me, "Well, what you say, old Kiyo, old pal? Wanna go to the movies tonight?"

I shook my head and looked at my feet. "I no can play with you no more."

"Why?"

"My folks said not to."

"But why? We never been do anything bad, eh?"

"No."

"Then why? Because I doan treat you right? I treat you okay?"

"Yeah. I told them you treat me real good."

"Why then?"

"I doan know."

"Aw, hell, you can still play with me. They doan hafta know. What they doan know won't hurt them."

"Naw, I better not. This time it's my father and he means business."

"Aw, doan be chicken, Kiyo. Maybe you doan like to play with me."

"I like to play with you."

"Come, let's go see a movie."

"Naw."

"How about some chow fun. Yum-yum."

"Naw."

"Maybe you doan like me then?"

"I like you."

"You sure?"

"I sure."

"Why then?"

"I doan know. They said something about your father and mother."

"Oh," he said and his face fell and I thought he was going to cry.

"Well, so long, then, Kiyo," he said and went into the house.

"So long," I said and turned and ran out of the spooky camp.

Glossary of Hawaiian Words

ahina, gray
akua, god, divinity
alii, chief, nobility
aloha, greeting, affection, farewell
anana, prayer
aumakua, ancestral spirit
awa, drink of fermented pepper root
hale, house, place
haole, white man, stranger
hapa-haole, part Caucasian
heiau, temple platform
holoku, Mother Hubbard gown
hookupu, gift-giving
hula, Hawaiian dance, drum
ie-ie, strong vine
imu, underground oven
kahili, cylindrical standard of feathers topping a pole
kahuna, sorcerer, priest, wise man
kaimiloa, the explorer
kalo, taro plant
kamaaina, old-timer
Kanaka, man, native, Islander
kani, music
kapa, beaten bark cloth
kapu, forbidden
kapuku, restoration of a corpse to life
kava, see *awa*
kilo, soothsayer
koa, hardwood tree
kokua, helper
konane, game like checkers
kowali, convolvulus vine

GLOSSARY OF HAWAIIAN WORDS

kukini, trained runner
kukui, candlenut tree
kupua, demigod
lanai, veranda
lei, necklace of flowers
lomilomi, massage to relieve pain and fatigue
luau, Hawaiian feast
luna, overseer, foreman
maile, fragrant plant
makahiki, winter festival
mamo, extinct bird whose feathers were used for cloaks
mauna, mountain
mele, song, chant
menehune, legendary dwarf
moa, chicken
morai, see *heiau*
nene, large wild goose
nui, big
ohelo, a berry-bearing shrub
okolehao, liquor distilled from ti root
pahoa, dagger material, dagger
palaka, blue plaid cloth
pali, precipice
pau, finished
pa-u, voluminous skirt
pilikia, trouble
poi, paste of pounded taro root
puoa, tower for exposing corpse
pupule, crazy
rahuiia, prohibited
tabu, see *kapu*
tapa, see *kapa*
ume, enticement
wahine, female, woman

TALES OF THE PACIFIC

JACK LONDON

Stories of Hawaii by Jack London
Thirteen yarns drawn from the famous author's love affair with Hawai'i Nei.
$6.95   ISBN 0-935180-08-7

The Mutiny of the Elsinore by Jack London
Based on a voyage around Cape Horn in a windjammer from New York to Seattle in 1913, this romance between the lone passenger and the captain's daughter reveals London at his most fertile and fluent best. The lovers are forced to outrace a rioting band of seagoing gangsters in the South Pacific.
$5.95   ISBN 0-935180-40-0

South Sea Tales by Jack London
Fiction from the violent days of the early century, set among the atolls of French Oceania and the high islands of Samoa, Fiji, Pitcairn, and "the terrible Solomons."
$5.95   ISBN 0-935180-14-1

HAWAII

Hawaii: Fiftieth Star by A. Grove Day
Told for the junior reader, this brief history of America's fiftieth state should also beguile the concerned adult. "Interesting, enlightening, and timely reading for high school American and World History groups."
$4.95   ISBN 0-935180-44-3

A Hawaiian Reader
Thirty-seven selections from the literature of the past hundred years, including such writers as Mark Twain, Robert Louis Stevenson and James Jones.
$5.95   ISBN 0-935180-07-9

Hawaii and Its People by A. Grove Day
An informal, one-volume narrative of the exotic and fascinating history of the peopling of the archipelago. The periods range from the first arrivals of Polynesian canoe voyagers to attainment of American statehood. A "headline history" brings the story from 1960 to 1990.
$4.95   ISBN 0-935180-50-8

True Tales of Hawaii and the South Seas Edited by A. Grove Day and Carl Stroven
Yarns from the real Pacific by 21 master storytellers, including Mark Twain, W. Somerset Maugham, Robert Louis Stevenson, and James A. Michener. This anthology comprises some of the best nonfiction writing about the South Pacific.
$4.95   ISBN 0-935180-22-2

A Hawaiian Reader, Vol. II
A companion volume to *A Hawaiian Reader*. Twenty-four selections from the exotic literary heritage of the Islands.
$6.95   ISBN 1-56647-207-5

Kona by Marjorie Sinclair
The best woman novelist of post-war Hawai'i dramatizes the conflict between a daughter of Old Hawai'i and her straitlaced Yankee husband. Nor is the drama resolved in their children.
$4.95   ISBN 0-935180-20-6

Claus Spreckels, The Sugar King in Hawaii by Jacob Adler
Sugar was the main economic game in Hawai'i a century ago, and the boldest player was Claus Spreckels, a California tycoon who built a second empire in the Islands by ruthless and often dubious means.
$5.95   ISBN 0-935180-76-1

Russian Flag Over Hawaii: The Mission of Jeffery Tolamy, a novel by Darwin Teilhet
A vigorous adventure novel in which a young American struggles to unshackle the grip held by Russian filibusters on the Kingdom of Kauai. Kamehameha the Great and many other historical figures play their roles in a colorful love story.
$5.95   ISBN 0-935180-28-1

Rape in Paradise by Theon Wright
The sensational "Massie Case" of the 1930's shattered the tranquil image that mainland U.S.A. had of Hawaii. One woman shouted "Rape!" and the island erupted with such turmoil that for 20 years it was deemed unprepared for statehood. A fascinating case study of race relations and military-civilian relations.
$4.95   ISBN 0-935180-88-5

Mark Twain in Hawaii: Roughing It in the Sandwich Islands
The noted humorist's account of his 1866 trip to Hawai'i at a time when the Islands were more for the native than the tourists. The writings first appeared in their present form in Twain's important book, *Roughing It*. Includes an introductory essay from *Mad About Islands* by A. Grove Day.
$4.95   ISBN 0-935180-93-1

Hawaii and Points South by A. Grove Day
Foreword by James A. Michener
A collection of the best of A. Grove Day's many shorter writings over a span of 40 years. The author has appended personal headnotes, revealing his reasons for choosing each particular subject.
$4.95   ISBN 0-935180-01-X

Pearl, a novel by Stirling Silliphant
In a world on the brink of war, the Hawaiian island of Oahu was still the perfect paradise. And in this lush and tranquil Pacific haven everyone clung to the illusion that their spectacular island could never be touched by the death and destruction of Hirohito's military machine.
$5.95   ISBN 0-935180-91-5

Horror in Paradise: Grim and Uncanny Tales from Hawaii and the South Seas, edited by A. Grove Day and Bacil F. Kirtley
Thirty-four writers narrate "true" episodes of sorcery and the supernatural, as well as gory events on sea and atoll.
$6.95   ISBN 0-935180-23-0

HAWAIIAN SOVEREIGNTY

Kalakaua: Renaissance King by Helena G. Allen
The third in a trilogy that also features Queen Liliuokalani and Sanford Ballard Dole, this book brings King Kalakaua, Hawai'i's most controversial king, to the fore as a true renaissance man. The complex facts of Kalakaua's life and personality are presented clearly and accurately along with his contributions to Hawaiian history.
$6.95   ISBN 1-56647-059-5

Nahi'ena'ena: Sacred Daughter of Hawai'i by Marjorie Sinclair
A unique biography of Kamehameha's sacred daughter who in legend was descended from the gods. The growing feelings and actions of Hawaiians for their national identity now place this story of Nahi'ena'ena in a wider perspective of the Hawaiian quest for sovereignty.
$4.95   ISBN 1-56647-080-3

Around the World With a King by William N. Armstrong, Introduction by Glen Grant
An account of King Kalakaua's circling of the globe. From Singapore to Cairo, Vienna to the Spanish frontier, follow Kalakaua as he becomes the first monarch to travel around the world.
$5.95   ISBN 1-56647-017-X

Hawaii's Story by Hawaii's Queen by Lydia Liliuokalani
The Hawaiian kingdom's last monarch wrote her biography in 1897, the year before the annexation of the Hawaiian Islands by the United States. Her story covers six decades of island history told from the viewpoint of a major historical figure.
$7.95   ISBN 0-935180-85-0

The Betrayal of Liliuokalani: Last Queen of Hawaii 1838-1917 by Helena G. Allen
A woman caught in the turbulent maelstrom of cultures in conflict. Treating Liliuokalani's life with authority, accuracy and details, *Betrayal* also is tremendously informative concerning the entire period of missionary activity and foreign encroachment in the Islands.
$6.95   ISBN 0-935180-89-3

HAWAIIAN LEGENDS

Myths and Legends of Hawaii by Dr. W.D. Westervelt
A broadly inclusive, one-volume collection of folklore by a leading authority. Completely edited and reset format for today's readers of the great prehistoric tales of Maui, Hina, Pele and her fiery family, and a dozen other heroic beings, human or ghostly.
$5.95   ISBN 0-935180-43-5

The Legends and Myths of Hawaii by David Kalakaua
Political and historical traditions and stories of the pre-Cook period capture the romance of old Polynesia. A rich collection of Hawaiian lore originally presented in 1888 by Hawai'i's "merrie monarch."
$6.95   ISBN 0-935180-86-9

Teller of Hawaiian Tales by Eric Knudsen
Son of a pioneer family of Kauai, the author spent most of his life on the Garden Island as a rancher, hunter of wild cattle, lawyer, and legislator. Here are 60 campfire yarns of gods and goddesses, ghosts and heroes, cowboy adventures and legendary feats among the valleys and peaks of the island.
$5.95   ISBN 1-56647-119-2

SOUTH SEAS

Best South Sea Stories
Fifteen writers capture all the romance and exotic adventure of the legendary South Pacific, including James A. Michener, James Norman Hall, W. Somerset Maugham, and Herman Melville.
$4.95   ISBN 0-935180-12-5

The Blue of Capricorn by Eugene Burdick
Stories and sketches from Polynesia, Micronesia, and Melanesia by the co-author of *The Ugly American* and *The Ninth Wave*. Burdick's last book explores an ocean world rich in paradox and drama, a modern world of polyglot islanders and primitive savages.
$5.95   ISBN 0-935180-36-2

The Book of Puka Puka by Robert Dean Frisbie
Lone trader on a South Sea atoll, "Ropati" tells charmingly of his first years on Puka-Puka, where he was destined to rear five half-Polynesian children. Special foreword by A. Grove Day.
$5.95   ISBN 0-935180-27-3

Manga Reva by Robert Lee Eskridge
A wandering American painter voyaged to the distant Gambier Group in the South Pacific and, charmed by the life of the people of "The Forgotten Islands" of French Oceania, collected many stories from their past—including the supernatural. Special introduction by Julius Scammon Rodman.
$5.95   ISBN 0-935180-35-4

The Lure of Tahiti selected and edited by A. Grove Day
Fifteen stories and other choice extracts from the rich literature of "the most romantic island in the world." Authors include Jack London, James A. Michener, James Norman Hall, W. Somerset Maugham, Paul Gauguin, Pierre Loti, Herman Melville, William Bligh, and James Cook.
$5.95   ISBN 0-935180-31-1

In Search of Paradise by Paul L. Briand, Jr.
A joint biography of Charles Nordhoff and James Norman Hall, the celebrated collaborators of *Mutiny on the "Bounty"* and a dozen other classics of South Pacific literature. This book, going back to the time when both men flew combat missions on the Western Front in World War I, reveals that the lives of Nordhoff and Hall were almost as fascinating as their fiction.
$5.95   ISBN 0-935180-48-6

The Fatal Impact: Captain Cook in the South Pacific by Alan Moorehead
A superb narrative by an outstanding historian of the exploration of the world's greatest ocean—adventure, courage, endurance, and high purpose with unintended but inevitable results for the original inhabitants of the islands.
$4.95   ISBN 0-935180-77-X

The Forgotten One by James Norman Hall
Six "true tales of the South Seas," some of the best stories by the co-author of *Mutiny on the "Bounty."* Most of these selections portray "forgotten ones"—men who sought refuge on out-of-the-world islands of the Pacific.
$5.95   ISBN 0-935180-45-1

Home from the Sea: Robert Louis Stevenson in Samoa, by Richard Bermann
Impressions of the final years of R.L.S. in his mansion, Vailima, in Western Samoa, still writing books, caring for family and friends, and advising Polynesian chieftains in the local civil wars.
$5.95   ISBN 0-935180-75-3

A Dream of Islands: Voyages of Self-Discovery in the South Seas by A. Gavan Daws
The South Seas... the islands of Tahiti, Hawai'i, Samoa, the Marquesas... the most seductive places on earth, where physically beautiful brown-skinned men and women move through a living dream of great erotic power. *A Dream of Islands* tells the stories of five famous Westerners who found their fate in the islands: John Williams, Herman Melville, Walter Murray Gibson, Robert Louis Stevenson, Paul Gauguin.
$4.95   ISBN 0-935180-71-2

His Majesty O'Keefe by Lawrence Klingman and Gerald Green
The extraordinary true story of an Irish-American sailing captain who for 30 years ruled a private empire in the South Seas, a story as fantastic and colorful as any novelist could invent. Vivid in its picture of Pacific customs, it is also filled with the oddity and drama of O'Keefe's career and a host of other major characters whose adventures are part of the history of the South Pacific. Made into a motion picture starring Errol Flynn.
$4.95   ISBN 0-935180-65-6

How to Order

For book rate (4-6 wekks; in Hawaii, 1-2 weeks) send check or money order with an additional $3.00 for the first book and $1.00 for each additional book. For fiirst class (1-2 weeks) add $4.00 for the first book, $3.00 for each additional book.

1215 Center Street, Suite 210
Honolulu, HI 96816
Tel (808) 732-1709 Fax (808) 734-4094
Email: mutual@lava.net